The American Pragmatists

THE OXFORD HISTORY OF PHILOSOPHY

The Lost Age of Reason: Philosophy in Early Modern India 1450–1700
Jonardon Ganeri

Thinking the Impossible: French Philosophy since 1960
Gary Gutting

The American Pragmatists
Cheryl Misak

The American Pragmatists

Cheryl Misak

OXFORD
UNIVERSITY PRESS

OXFORD
UNIVERSITY PRESS

Great Clarendon Street, Oxford, OX2 6DP,
United Kingdom

Oxford University Press is a department of the University of Oxford.
It furthers the University's objective of excellence in research, scholarship,
and education by publishing worldwide. Oxford is a registered trade mark of
Oxford University Press in the UK and in certain other countries

First Edition published in 2013

Impression: 2

British Library Cataloguing in Publication Data

Data available

ISBN 978–0–19–923120–1

Printed in Great Britain by
CPI Group (UK) Ltd, Croydon, CR0 4YY

Contents

Preface

Pragmatism is America's home-grown philosophy. It originated in Cambridge Massachusetts in the late 1860s and early 1870s in The Metaphysical Club—a reading group whose members included Oliver Wendell Holmes, William James, Charles Sanders Peirce, Nicholas St. John Green, John Fiske, and Chauncey Wright. James, Peirce, and Holmes were sons of New England intelligentsia. James's father was a well-known Swedenborgian theologian with inherited wealth; Peirce's father was an eminent professor of mathematics at Harvard; and Holmes's father professor of anatomy and physiology. Wright, from much humbler circumstances, was the oldest member of the group and was acknowledged by the others as their driving intellectual force.

The members of The Metaphysical Club found themselves at a critical juncture in the history of American thought. They were the first generation of philosophers to put some distance between philosophy and religion. Protestantism, in one variety or another, dominated America when the pragmatists began their careers. The college philosopher tended to be also the college minister or moral tutor and appointments in philosophy were reserved for the religiously orthodox.[1] This was about to change. Two exciting and related ideas about science and philosophy were in the air in Europe and had drifted across the Atlantic. First, the scientific method was being brought to philosophy with a vengeance. In 1740 Hume titled his masterpiece *A Treatise of Human Nature: An Attempt to Introduce the Experimental Method of Reasoning into Moral Subjects* and a century later the kind of naturalism he favored had taken root. When The Metaphysical Club started to meet, the implications of Comte's positivism and Darwin's *On the Origin of Species* were being hotly debated in universities and in drawing rooms. Science seemed to entail the abandonment of the world-view that had God and religious absolutes at its centre.

The other idea was that philosophy should take science as one of its topics for investigation. The three members of The Metaphysical Club who went on to found American pragmatism—Wright, James and Peirce—were all working scientists who wanted not only to have science inform philosophy, but wanted also to develop a philosophy of science. They cut a trail that changed the course of American philosophy for generations to come.

The intellectual world that The Metaphysical Club members exited was very unlike the one they entered as young men. By the time James and Peirce were nearing the end of their lives, the philosopher was no longer the college's moral tutor. He had, rather, a distinctive set of topics to engage and a distinct profession, focused on the training of graduate students and the specialization of the discipline into identifiable sub-fields.

---

[1] See Schneider (1963 [1946]: 208ff.), Campbell (2006: 107) and Wilson (1990: 13ff.).

Professors of philosophy, at least in the elite institutions of Johns Hopkins, Harvard, Michigan, and Chicago, were to be researchers and graduate supervisors, as well as teachers of undergraduates.[2]

The lives of the members of The Metaphysical Club took very different turns. Holmes became one of American's most famous legal theorists and members of the Supreme Court. Wright was a master conversationalist, but suffered from depression, took minimal care of himself, and died in his early forties, leaving a small but impressive body of writing. James was soon one of the most famous academics in the world, in both psychology and philosophy, all the while trying to beat back his own depression, which hit him hard in the 1870s. The brilliant Peirce was by all accounts extraordinarily difficult and never managed to secure a permanent academic position. He was hardly known during his lifetime and died penniless and miserable. One gets the feeling that the great advances in the intellectual world took its toll on those at the frontier, sometimes resulting, in James's evocative phrase, in breakdowns with the head (*CWJ* 1: 177; 1872).

The early pragmatists made major contributions to almost every branch of philosophy and to other fields of investigation—for instance, Peirce in logic and the theory of signs; James in psychology; Dewey in education. But my focus in this book will be on what Bertrand Russell calls "the cardinal point in the pragmatist philosophy"—"its theory of truth" (1992 [1909]: 261). It is the view of truth and knowledge that is most associated with pragmatism and marks it off from other traditions. Indeed, the reader might take this book to have an implicit subtitle: *Truth, Knowledge, Value*. It may be that much that is interesting in some of the pragmatists' work lies elsewhere. But the story I am tracing is the story of pragmatism as a recognizable tradition and I will leave it to others to show in a sophisticated way how, for instance, James forever changed the face of psychology.

The founders of pragmatism took their most significant allied traditions to be empiricism and Kantianism. In 1905, in a letter to F. C. S. Schiller, Peirce puts it perfectly. He says that he learned his pragmatism from Berkeley and Kant. I will not be embarking on a sustained discussion of Berkeley, Kant, or others who influenced the pragmatists, such as Hegel. The mere list of these great philosophers should make it clear that, if I were to try to set out their views, this would be an exceedingly long book. Instead, I try to say just enough to give the reader a sense of their impacts on and contrasts with the pragmatists. In the same vein, some topics have inevitably received short shrift—I could have been more expansive on the American predecessors of pragmatism and on Wilfrid Sellars, to mention only a few.

Pragmatists are empiricists in that they require beliefs to be linked to experience. They want their explanations and ontology down-to-earth (natural as opposed to supernatural) and they require philosophical theories to arise out of our practices. As

---

[2] See Campbell (2006: 107) for an account of this transformation.

Peirce put the pragmatic maxim, we must look to the upshot of our concepts in order to understand them (*CP* 5, 4; 1901). But we shall see that the early pragmatists do not buy wholesale the empiricism and naturalism of their English and Scottish predecessors. They reject the part of empiricism that says that all of our beliefs originate in experience and that our beliefs can be linked in an atomistic way to discrete experiences. We shall see that the nature of the requisite connection between beliefs and experience is a complex matter for the pragmatists. Moreover, they reject any naturalism that gives ontological priority to matter or physicality—they want to consider whether value, generality, chance, etc. might be part of the natural world. They are holists, taking their view to encompass all of science, logic, mathematics, art, religion, ethics, and politics. Unlike most of their empiricist predecessors, they fence off no realm of inquiry from the principles they set out.

Lest it be thought that these empiricist strains in pragmatism are somehow connected with an American disposition to practical, industrial, or entrepreneurial matters, as Russell, Santayana and so many others have suggested, John Dewey slays this idea. It is like saying "that English neo-realism is a reflection of the snobbish aristocracy of the English and the tendency of French thought to dualism an expression of an alleged Gallic disposition to keep a mistress in addition to a wife" (1939: 526).

We shall see that a major Kantian thesis that runs thorough pragmatism is that we need to assume certain things if we are to go on with our practices. I shall argue that the best kind of pragmatism is one that takes seriously Kant's regulative assumptions. Here is Peirce on how important Kant was to him: "I was a passionate devotee of Kant, at least as regarded the Transcendental Analytic in the Critic of Pure Reason. I believed more implicitly in the two tables of the Functions of Judgment and the Categories than if they had been brought down from Sinai" (*CP* 4, 2; 1898). But it will become clear that Peirce wants to naturalize Kant. The "necessity" that Kant vested in the assumptions underlying our practices is brought down to earth—these assumptions are merely required if we are to continue with a practice that we do not contemplate abandoning.

The overarching issue for pragmatism is the problem with which both the empiricists and Kant wrestle. How can we make sense of our standards of rationality, truth, and value as genuinely normative or binding while recognizing that they are profoundly human phenomena? How do normativity and authority arise from within a world of human experience and practice? I shall argue that Peirce was the classical pragmatist who answered this question with the most care and sophistication. In subsequent generations, that care and sophistication resides most strikingly in Lewis and Sellars.

As the reader will surmise, my project straddles the history of ideas and philosophy. One of my aims is to tell what I think is a gripping story in the history of philosophy—a story about how pragmatism came into being, evolved, and branched out. But an equally important aim is to show what is good in pragmatism; where philosophical missteps were taken; and how pragmatists can best go forward. That is, the pages that follow are full of evaluation and argument. This will no doubt irritate those who would rather focus on the history, as stripped as possible from what is acceptable or not in the positions in play. It will also irritate those pragmatists who are not part of what I argue is the most defensible pragmatist lineage. Part of my argument is that it is Richard Rorty who broke with the direction the pragmatist tradition was taking and returned, to pragmatism's misfortune, to some of the excesses of James and Dewey. I trust that those who disagree with my arguments will engage with them seriously and I look forward to the conversation.

Some will think that the lineage I outline privileges an "analytic" reading of the pragmatist tradition and that analytic philosophy is antithetical to pragmatism. But I shall argue that insofar as the distinction between analytic and non-analytic philosophy retains any force, the founders of pragmatism were pioneers of analytic philosophy. The view I outline is rooted very securely in the work of those founders of pragmatism, especially Wright and Peirce, and its tendrils reach into the work of every one of the classical pragmatists. Part of the burden of this book is to show that it is an interesting and defensible view. Others scholars of pragmatism have been and are on the same interpretative page. Indeed, it is impossible to pull apart those commentators who commend this lineage from those pragmatists who are a part of it.

In writing the kind of book that both tells the history of a philosophical position and evaluates living thoughts, even if they were first articulated in 1867, an inevitable problem with tenses arises. I try to solve it by using the past tense to talk about individuals and the evolution of their views and the present tense to talk about the views themselves.

Acknowledgments

This book has benefitted from the insights and comments of Donald Ainslie, Doug Anderson, David Bakhurst, Eric Dayton, Don Howard, Alex Klein, Mark Lance, David Macarthur, Mark Migotti, Trevor Pearce, Huw Price, Alan Richardson, Bob Schwartz, Rob Sinclair, Glenn Tiller, Jennifer Welchman, three readers solicited by Oxford University Press, as well as audiences at many conferences and philosophy departments. Two very special American pragmatists, Richard Bernstein and Morton White, were kind enough to meet with me to discuss periods of the history of American pragmatism in which they were major participants. Their first-person insight into critical moments in that story was enormously helpful and interesting. Thanks also go to Abtin Dezfuli, Ken Boyd, and, most extensively and especially, Diana Heney, excellent research assistants who ran books back and forth from Robarts Library, checked references, and in Diana's case, edited the entire manuscript with great intelligence and care.

As if all this help weren't enough, Robert Talisse organized a workshop on the manuscript at Vanderbilt in the autumn of 2011. He, Scott Aikin, Michael Hodges, Chris Hookway, Henry Jackman and John Lachs spent what were for me two intensely full and fruitful days of interrogation and improvement.

One would think that the book should be mistake-free after all of this, but alas, that will not be the case and I take full responsibility for all remaining errors and gaps. I should also note that I have written on some of these topics before. Parts of this book draw, and I hope improve, upon that earlier work, details of which can be found in the Bibliography.

I have had some demanding jobs at the University of Toronto while writing this book, currently that of Vice President and Provost. These have been challenging times for publicly supported universities and helping my own venerable institution navigate its way through the stormy waters has been no small task. A great group of colleagues—especially the President of the University, David Naylor—have been extraordinarily generous in encouraging me to balance that hard but rewarding work with some philosophical activity. In a corresponding way, my editor at Oxford University Press, Peter Momtchiloff, exhibited grace and patience as each new administrative position stood in the way of a speedy completion.

The reader will correctly infer that my family—David, Alexander, and Sophie Dyzenhaus—had to put up with much more than the usual. But as always, they have done so with immense love and good humor. This book is dedicated to them.

Reference Policy

My reference policy with respect to the work of the classical pragmatists is as follows:

Reference to the works of C. S. Peirce

If a passage occurs in the new *Writings of Charles S. Peirce: Chronological Edition*, I cite that source as "*W* n, m; year," where n is the volume, m the page number, and the year that of the quoted text. If it is not in the *Writings*, but in the older *Collected Papers*, the citation is "*CP* n. m; year," where n is the volume number, m the paragraph number, and the year that of the quoted text. If it appears in print only in *New Elements of Mathematics*, the citation is "*NE* n: m," where n is the volume number and m the page number. If it is available in none of these collections, then I cite the manuscript number in the microfilm edition of Peirce's papers, as "MS n," where n is the manuscript number. Full details of these works can be found in the bibliography.

References to the works of William James

Unless otherwise noted, all citations of William James refer to his *Collected Works*. References to James's correspondence refer to *The Correspondence of William James*, and appear in the following form: "*CWJ*, n: m; year," where n is the volume number, m the page number, and the year that of the quoted text. Full details of these works can be found in the bibliography.

References to the works of John Dewey

Unless otherwise noted, all citations of John Dewey refer to his *Collected Works*. *The Early Works of John Dewey, 1882–1898*, are cited as "*EW* n: m; year," where n is the volume number, m the page number, and the year that of the quoted text. *The Middle Works of John Dewey, 1899–1924*, are likewise cited as "*MW* n: m; year," and *The Later Works of John Dewey, 1925–1953* cited as "*LW* n: m; year." References to Dewey's correspondence refer to *The Correspondence of John Dewey*, and appear in the following form: "*CJD* n: year, i," where n is the volume number, the year that of the quoted letter, and i the item number. Full details of these works can be found in the bibliography.

References to the correspondence of Oliver Wendell Holmes, Jr.

Correspondence between Holmes and Frederick Pollock is cited from the two volumes of *Holmes–Pollock letters: The Correspondence of Mr. Justice Holmes and Sir Frederick Pollock, 1874–1932*, edited by Mark DeWolfe Howe. Citations take the form "Holmes–Pollock Letters (n: m; year)," where n is the volume number, m the page number, and the year that of the quoted letter. Full bibliographical details can be found in the bibliography.

References to the correspondence of George Santayana

Santayana's correspondence is cited from the eight volumes of *The Letters of George Santayana*, edited by William G. Holzberger. Citations take the form "Letters n: m," where n is the volume number and m the page number. Full bibliographical details can be found in the bibliography.

Other authors

I have adopted the following reference policy for works by other authors. Citations of Ralph Waldo Emerson's works are to his *Collected Works,* and take the form "*CW* n: m; year," where n is the volume number, m the page number, and the year that of the quoted text. Wherever possible, citations of Bertrand Russell's works refer to the McMaster edition of *The Collected Papers of Bertrand Russell*, and take the form "*CP* n: m; year," where n is the volume number, m the page number, and the year that of the quoted text. Citations of David Hume's works are to the Nidditch editions, and refer to section number and page number. Citations of Ludwig Wittgenstein's works also refer to section number, and to the translations and editions noted in the bibliography.

Wherever an author has an authoritative collected works published, I try as much as possible to refer to that version of their works.

Introduction: The Trajectory of American Pragmatism

James's *Pragmatism: A New Name for Some Old Ways of Thinking* appeared in 1907, "cometlike on our intellectual horizon" (Carus 2001 [1911]: 44). The received view of pragmatism's fortunes is that it shone brightly right through to John Dewey's death in 1952, then nearly burned out. This view has it that in the 1970s, when Richard Rorty brought into being a renaissance for pragmatism, there were very few pragmatists or students of American philosophy in top-tier American universities and pragmatism was in serious disrepute in Britain. As Dickstein (1998: 1) puts the received view, pragmatism was operating on the margins, driven from philosophy departments by the reigning analytic philosophy. Rorty brought it back, but in a resolutely anti-analytic version, a version despised by the ruling philosophical class. The idea is that pragmatism is set against analytic philosophy and has suffered from challenging this wrong-headed but domineering winner of the philosophical stakes. A sense of persecution has thus hung over certain quarters of American pragmatism since Dewey's demise. We shall see, however, that the story is not as the received view would have it.

"Analytic philosophy" used to have a clear meaning when in the hands of the likes of Bertrand Russell: "logical analysis" was the attempt to clarify a concept by using formal methods to reduce it to its constituent parts. It might have been the case that for some years in the mid to late 1900s, pragmatists had reason to distinguish themselves from that kind of analysis and from a kind of finely wrought philosophy which they took to be irrelevant to the problems we actually face in the world. But logical analysis has come and gone as a way of doing philosophy. Perhaps "analytic philosophy" now suggests to some that the philosophy of language is the foundation of philosophy; perhaps that logic is the foundation of philosophy. But it is more realistic to think that the term has lost any precise meaning it once had.

If "analytic philosophy" is taken in a looser sense, as being a tradition that pays attention to logic and prizes rigorous thinking, we shall see that Wright and Peirce must be seen as the pioneers of analytic philosophy in America. We shall also see that some of the stars of modern analytic philosophy—C. I. Lewis, W. V. Quine, Nelson Goodman, to name a few—were also very much in step with American pragmatism during the years in which it was supposedly driven out of philosophy departments by analytic philosophers. Pragmatism, that is, has a strong and unbroken analytic lineage. Part of the burden of this book is to trace that lineage and argue that it is valuable.

The trajectory of American pragmatism is also not that which is described by Louis Menand in his best-selling and Pulitzer Prize-winning book *The Metaphysical Club*. While Menand is to be thanked for amassing a rich collection of historical detail about the pragmatists and portraying their personalities so well, his story is philosophically misguided. Menand asserts that the early pragmatists "taught a kind of skepticism that helped people cope with life in a heterogeneous, industrialized, mass market society"—a skepticism which helped "free thought from thralldom to official ideologies, of the church or the state or even the academy" (2001: xii). Pragmatism, he says, "belongs to a disestablishmentarian impulse in American culture" (2001: 89). Menand's early pragmatists look a lot like Rorty, arguing that there is no certainty, no truth, and no objectivity to be had, only agreement within a community. His claim is that the American Civil War was, amongst other things, a failure of ideas. It "swept away almost the whole intellectual culture of the North" and "it took nearly half a century for the United States to find a culture to replace it, to find a set of ideas, and a way of thinking, that would help people cope with the conditions of modern life" (Menand 2001: x). That set of ideas, he asserts, was found in pragmatism. After the trauma of the Civil War, in which the lesson was "that certitude leads to violence," people were not in the mood for absolutist philosophies (Menand 2001: 61). Pragmatism thus arose and flourished until its fallibilism and tolerance were thrown into suspicion by the intellectual climate of the Cold War of the 1950s and 1960s. James and Dewey came to be seen as "naïve, and even a little dangerous."[1] With the end of the Cold War, uncertainty was allowable again—hence Rorty's ability to revive pragmatism during the 1980s and 1990s. "For in the post-Cold War world, where there are many competing belief systems, not just two, skepticism about the finality of any particular set of beliefs has begun to seem to some people an important value again" (Menand 2001: 441).

This is a rather breath-taking thesis. In Parts I and II of this book, I will show that it is not the best understanding of pragmatism's reception. The accurate story is less grandiose, but it is actually much more interesting, in terms of the evolution of modern analytic philosophy. There is no doubt that the Civil War was a cauldron of horror that scorched the lives of the early pragmatists. Holmes took part in some of the worst battles and was wounded more than once; one of James's brothers came home shattered. But the Civil War makes no appearance in the stated motivations and in the philosophical writing of the early pragmatists. And while the Cold War had a

---

[1] Menand (2001: 439). He does say that there were also more mundane reasons for the change in status of the reputations of James and Dewey—their disciples were less impressive and other ways of doing philosophy seemed "more obviously suited to academic modes in inquiry" (2001: 438). But his main reason remains one about the "intellectual climate of the Cold War" (2001: 439).

profound effect on Dewey's political views, there is no hint that it influenced his epistemology.

At the heart of my alternative story is the fact that James was the one to unveil pragmatism to the public—in a lecture in California in 1898—and remained its most prominent proponent. Philosophy, James said, "is at once the most sublime and the most trivial of human pursuits. It works in the minutest crannies and it opens out the widest vistas" (1975 [1907]: 6). In his work on psychology, James worked brilliantly in the crannies and on the vistas. But when it came to talking about truth and objectivity, he was less reliable. It was Peirce who worked on both the careful details as well as opening out the panoramic views. Peirce's version of pragmatism, however, hardly saw the light of day, much to pragmatism's misfortune.

In Part I, I shall outline the shape of early American pragmatism. Much of what I discuss will directly or indirectly speak to the debate within pragmatism about its heart and soul. Pragmatism, as Robert Westbrook says, is like a contentious family of thinkers holding distinct but related positions on the "workmanlike" nature of know-ledge, meaning, and truth. Peirce, he says:

quickly denied paternity of the child James had adopted and announced he would henceforth refer to his own position as 'pragmaticism', a word 'ugly enough to be safe from kidnappers'. John Dewey, though deeply indebted to James's thinking, nonetheless took care to distinguish his own 'instrumentalism' from what he took to be James's more tender-minded efforts use pragmatism to secure religious belief. Peirce, in turn, responded to Dewey's praise of his essay on 'What Pragmatism Is' (1905) with a puzzled letter noting that Dewey's instrumental logic 'forbids all such researches as those which I have been absorbed in for the last eighteen years'.

[2005: 1]

The debate within pragmatism continues to this day. There will be plenty of opportunity to make the necessary nuances in the pages that follows. But roughly, it is a debate between those who assert (or whose view entails) that there is no truth and objectivity to be had anywhere and those who take pragmatism to promise an account of truth that preserves our aspiration to getting things right.

On the one side of the divide we have Rorty and his classical predecessors (James and Dewey) holding that there is no truth at which we might aim—only agreement within a community or what works for an individual or what is found to solve a problem. In some moods Rorty goes as far as claiming that truth and objectivity are nothing more than what our peers will let us get away with saying. On the other side of the divide, we have those who think of pragmatism as rejecting an ahistorical, transcendental, or metaphysical theory of truth, but nonetheless being committed to doing justice to the objective dimension of human inquiry—to the fact that those engaged in deliberation and investigation take themselves to be aiming at getting things right, avoiding mistakes, and improving their beliefs and theories. On this more objective kind of pragmatism, which emanates from Wright and Peirce, the fact that our inquiries are historically situated does not entail that they lack objectivity. Neither does the fact that standards of objectivity themselves come into being and evolve. The trail of the human serpent is over everything (to use James's phrase), but (as James himself may or may not have seen) this does not toss us into a sea of arbitrariness, where there is no truth or where truth varies from person to person or culture to culture.

We shall see that Colin Koopman is right to say that Peirce was "more preoccupied with a philosophical conception of truth than he was with a cultural critique of the role that truth plays in our lives."[2] James and Dewey, on the other hand, were concerned with both projects, not always being clear about when they were engaged in one and when they were engaged in the other. These two tendencies in pragmatist thought persist today. But since the pragmatist account of truth links truth with practice, the lines between the tendencies can never be sharply delineated. Koopman is wrong to think that Peircean pragmatism offers us a *"metaphysics* of inquiry" and Deweyan pragmatism offers us a *"hope* regarding progressivism" (2009: 44). For we shall see, for instance, that Peirce was opposed to a metaphysical conception of truth and that he too put tremendous emphasis on the idea of hope.

Westbrook frames the issue thus:

Post-modernist skeptics and their few neopragmatist admirers turn to the old pragmatists because they (correctly) see them as potential partners in a struggle against 'strong', that is, absolutist and 'totalizing', conceptions of truth. But what they neglect is the old pragmatists' conviction (shared by many neopragmatists) that once they had overcome absolutism, they could then resume traveling down the road of inquiry in a more fuel-efficient vehicle than Reason toward a more modest destination than Truth.

[2005: 7]

This is the journey that I shall describe and evaluate.

---

[2] Koopman (2009:43). He is following Joseph Margolis (1998) here.

PART I

The Founders of Pragmatism

1

Pragmatist Themes in Early American Thought

1.1 Introduction: Empiricism and Idealism

The chief antecedent intellectual moments of American pragmatism are the Puritanism of the colonial period, commonsense realism, transcendentalism, and St. Louis Hegelianism. Many of the proponents of these views were preachers or politicians, well-educated and thoroughly enmeshed in the intellectual debates of their time, but not on the whole taken up with the task of setting out what we now would think of as a systematic philosophical theory. George Santayana says of Emerson, for instance, that "[a]t bottom, he had no doctrine at all," only a wonderful inspiration (1957 [1900]: 218). There is thus much in their views that I will leave untouched and I will confine myself to a brief account of those aspects of their thought most relevant to pragmatism. It is grounded largely in an examination of what was on the highly influential Chauncey Wright's mind as he and Peirce and James started to carve out their view.

Some scholars of American philosophy see the seeds of pragmatism growing from these very early views. Insofar as the early American thinkers were working through the issues of realism and idealism imported from Scotland, England, and Germany, this is most definitely the case. But, insofar as more direct causal relationships go, my suggestion shall be that we can identify only two distinct and important pragmatist ideas in early American thought.

The intellectual air that the pragmatists were born into was a heady mix of empiricism and idealism. The empiricism, I shall suggest, was the more important. But the pragmatists took significant steps away from the empiricism of Locke and Hume. One of those advances is taken directly from their American predecessors. It is the persistent attempt of the early American thinkers to try to widen the concept of experience. We shall see this attempt grow in force and magnitude when the pragmatists come on the scene.

Idealism, as Van Leer (1986: 26) argues, manifested itself in four themes in early American thought, emanating from Berkeley, Hegel, and Kant: (i) the spirit is the primary and unifying force in the world; (ii) there is an immutable ideal world behind or above the world of experience; (iii) what we perceive are really ideas and ideas only exist in the mind; (iv) the limits of human knowledge are such that what man can know is limited to what he perceives—he cannot know what might stand behind what he perceives. We might add to this list Jonathan Edward's view that truth consists in the agreement of our ideas with ideas of God. We shall see that the strong theological or (in the parlance of the time) "metaphysical" assumptions of the early American idealists gave the pragmatists something to rebel against.

1.2 Puritanism

As John Ryder (2004) notes, when the American colonists came across the water to their new land, they brought with them a strong Calvinist determinism—the idea that the will of God fully determines everything. They also brought with them the certainty that they were chosen by God to do his will in the New World. Indeed, the Puritans came to America partly so that they could build communities around their religious principles and have social and political authority reside with religious leaders chosen by congregations.

Of the Puritan thinkers, there are a few stand-outs as far as the history of pragmatism goes. One is the colonial governor of New York, scientist, and man of letters, Cadwallader Colden (1688–1776). Colden was a Scot with a good understanding of the empiricism of Locke and Hume. That there is a whiff of pragmatism in the following goes to show just how intimately pragmatism and empiricism are intertwined:

Every thing, that we know, is an agent, or has a power of acting: for as we know nothing of any thing but its action, and the effects of that action, the moment any thing ceases to act it must be annihilated as to us: we can have no kind of idea of its existence.

[Colden 1939 [1751]: 102][1]

Where Colden breaks with his empiricist predecessors is that he thought he could show how we have a perception of immaterial spirit, just as we can have a perception of matter. Spirit also excites action, power, or force (1939 [1751]: 103). He argues that we can acquire a conception of the reality of the divine being from observation or from religious experience. Someone who is "spiritually enlightened" "truly apprehends and sees" the glory and excellence of God. "He don't merely rationally believe that God is glorious," he has a "sense" of it. Just as "[t]here is a difference between having a rational judgment that honey is sweet, and having a sense of its sweetness," there is a difference between having a rational judgment that God is holy and gracious, and having a sense of the holiness and grace.[2] Colden does not elaborate on why we should think of experience so broadly or on how we can perceive something immaterial. But we shall see that his idea that there can be religious experience survives through to William James.

---

[1] As Scott Pratt and John Ryder point out, Colden sounds "remarkably like Peirce" (Pratt and Ryder, 2002: 30).

[2] Colden (1999 [1734]: 415–16). Spelling and grammatical errors are in the original.

Two well-known Puritan preachers, Cotton Mather (1663–1728) and Jonathan Edwards (1703–58), clearly saw that the new science posed a problem for Puritanism. The idea that the world is a machine, governed by mathematics and by empirically discoverable laws of nature, undermined the Puritan belief that God's will is the primary causal force. Similarly, Locke's scientific attitude to the study of man and his belief that all knowledge comes from experience pushes God out of the explanatory story. Mather is perhaps best known as an enthusiastic believer in and prosecutor of witches—he was a major figure in the Salem trials. But in his more philosophical thinking, he argued that there had to be a God who created the machine that Newton described.

Edwards—preacher, theologian, evangelist and short-lived President of Princeton[3]—was intent on squaring his Puritan world-view with the scientific world-view. He argues in favor of Calvinist determinism not on the grounds that Scripture tells us that it is true or that God must have created the machinery of nature, but on the grounds that the new mechanical causation entails that determinism is true. He agrees with Colden that we can perceive the effects of God on the material world and on the spiritual world. He sees that the latter is a challenge. In the midst of a spiritual crisis, he writes in his diary: "The very thing I now want . . . to give me a clear and more immediate view of the perfections and glory of God, is a clear knowledge of the manner of God's exerting himself, with respect to spirits and minds, as I have, of his operations concerning matter and bodies" (Marsden 2003: 104). He never quite manages to show how God makes himself felt on spirits and minds, but, again, we shall see that William James, without referring back to his predecessors, tries to take up the task.

When it comes to the concept of truth, it is Edwards's idealism that shines through, although as Kenneth Winkler (forthcoming) notes, there is an early signal of pragmatism here. Edwards thinks truth is correspondence with how things are, but that this is vague talk. It needs to be made more precise. The way Edwards cashes it out is as follows: "Truth, in the general, may be defined, after the most strict and metaphysical manner, as *The consistency and agreement of our ideas, with the ideas of God*" (1980 [1723]: 341–42). We shall see when we turn to Chauncey Wright that it is this very kind of metaphysics against which the pragmatists reacted. The pragmatists too think that we need to say more about what we mean by "truth is correspondence with how things are." But they want to cash that expression out in experience, not in the ideas of God.

A view allied with Puritan empiricism came to dominance in the small number of departments of philosophy during the mid to late 1700s in America: Scottish Commonsense realism. John Witherspoon, brought from Edinburgh in 1765 to replace Edwards as the President of Princeton, as well as his own successor at Princeton, James McCosh, and Francis Bowen at Harvard, were proponents of this view. They argued that since we so obviously have knowledge of things, events, and other minds, we must have an immediate or intuitive knowledge of the principles that make this knowledge

---

[3] Shortly after taking up the position, he died of an inoculation for smallpox.

possible. The principle of causality, for instance, must be known intuitively, as Hume had shown that it is not given to use through sense experience. We form concepts such as that of causality, which then allow us to interpret experience so that we have a coherent account of the world. While the inferences we might make from experience can be mistaken, the concepts that we get from reason and intuition are certain. We shall see that this combination of rationalism and empiricism was particularly at risk when Darwin's theory of evolution came on the scene.

1.3 Transcendentalism

The transcendentalism that followed Puritanism was a major intellectual force in mid 1800s America. Ralph Waldo Emerson (1803–82) was its leading light. It gave rise to the St. Louis Hegelianism of William Torrey Harris (1835–1909), George Howison (1834–1916), and Henry Conrad Brockmeyer (1828–1906). We shall see that the American idealism that was born with transcendentalism was the view that most engaged the attention of the fledgling pragmatists.

The transcendentalists are sometimes taken to be the forerunners of American pragmatism because of their focus on individuality, independence, and the cultivation of our own resources. But we shall see that these are not the characteristic features of pragmatism and, anyway, the transcendentalists carried the freight of metaphysics that was scorned by the pragmatists. Although there are some important connections between the two views, they do not reside in a purported American attitude of individuality and resourcefulness.

Emerson was very well known and respected amongst The Metaphysical Club members. He was intimate with the families of Peirce and, especially, James. Dewey, casting his eyes back, considered Emerson "the one citizen of the new world fit to have his name uttered in the same breath with that of Plato" (*MW* 3: 191; 1903). But his place in the history of pragmatism is complicated. He too made gestures at an expanded notion of experience and perhaps James took his own talk of philosophical temperaments from him. But while he most certainly formed a part of the intellectual background against which the early pragmatists worked, his style and approach to philosophy has a very different feel than theirs. And we shall see that his view that the natural world is a revelation of God is an antithesis of what the pragmatists stood for.

Peirce does not engage Emerson philosophically and he is pretty clear that the influence, if any, is not strong:

the atmosphere of Cambridge held many an antiseptic against Concord transcendentalism; and I am not conscious of having contracted any of that virus. Nevertheless, it is probable that some cultured bacilli, some benignant form of the disease was implanted in my soul, unawares, and that now, after long incubation, it comes to the surface, modified by mathematical conceptions and by training in physical investigations.

[*CP* 6. 102; 1891]

Transcendentalism was expressly set against the Scottish/English enlightenment and empiricist values that we shall see permeated the members of The Metaphysical Club. Emerson argued, starting with his 1836 *Nature*, that nature was an expression of the divine. A motto of transcendentalism was the anti-empiricist slogan that "the kingdom of man over nature cometh not with observation" (Schneider 1963 [1946]: 242). Nature is the manifestation of God's will—the world is a divine dream. Hence science is not a higher kind of inquiry than we find in theology or in what amounted to the same thing in those days, philosophy.

Emerson says in his 1841 essay "The Transcendentalist," that transcendentalism is the current expression of idealism. These "*new views* here in New England . . . are not really new," but are "the very oldest of thoughts cast into the mould of these new times" (*CW* 1: 201; 1841). He says:

As thinkers, mankind have ever divided into two sects, Materialists and Idealists; the first class founding on experience, the second on consciousness; the first class beginning to think from the data of the senses, the second class perceive that the senses are not final, and say, the senses give us representations of things, but what are the things themselves, they cannot tell. The materialist insists on facts, on history, on the force of circumstances, and the animal wants of man; the idealist on the power of Thought and of Will, on inspiration, on miracle, on individual culture.

[*CW* 1: 201; 1841]

Emerson sides with the idealist. Van Leer (1986: 26) sees all four of idealist theses in Emerson's *Nature*, despite the fact that Van Leer reads *Nature* as being a fundamentally Kantian work.[4] Some of these theses are of course still going concerns in philosophy, others are not. The first thesis—the view that the spirit or the Absolute is primary—is now obsolete. Nonetheless, we need to keep it at the front of our minds as we read the early pragmatists, for we shall see that we can only understand James, for instance, when we see how he sets himself against absolute idealism. The pragmatists grew up, intellectually, amongst idealist Hegelians, William Torrey Harris, one of the St. Louis Hegelians and founder of *The Journal of Speculative Philosophy*, being the most prominent. They took seriously, even if their aim was one of refutation, the idea that there is one overarching and unifying consciousness which encompasses everything else—an Absolute which is in the world, not in some way independent of it.

The fledgling pragmatists had very diverse attitudes towards Hegelian idealism. Wright hardly mentions it, James sets his view in opposition to it, and Peirce sees the affinities between his brand of pragmatism and Hegelianism (Dewey was later to be the most Hegelian of all the pragmatists). But one thing is clear—the early pragmatists, one way or another, were heavily engaged with idealism. Indeed, Josiah Royce—the most famous idealist of his generation—was the primary interlocutor of Peirce and James.

The part of New England that the founders of pragmatism wanted to preserve was the idea that experience is broad. In Edwards's hands, this thought played out so that experience is central to religion—we perceive the divine. Emerson followed up and

---

[4] See Winkler (forthcoming) for the argument that Emerson's idealism is more like Berkeley's than Kant's.

amplified. "Life," he wrote in the 1844 essay "Experience," is a train of "temperaments" or "moods like a string of beads, and, as we pass through them, they prove to be
many-colored lenses which paint the world their own hue, and each shows only what
lies in its focus" (CW 3: 30; 1844). "Thus inevitably does the universe wear our color"
(CW 3: 45; 1844). This is the Kantian idea that human thought structures the world.
Emerson's novel contribution is to introduce temperaments or moods. Feelings or
emotions are a part of that structuring apparatus.

Emerson, with Kant, wanted to humanize the world. The world is not the inani-
mate and unknowable world the empiricists would have us living in. He brought to
this view a particular focus, one which, as Russell Goodman has shown, is the focus of
the European Romantics Wordsworth and Coleridge. The problem is not with
empiricism, but with "paltry empiricism."[5] There's nothing wrong with focusing on
experience, as long as experience is conceived broadly—as long as experience includes
more than what our five senses deliver. Feeling or emotion is a kind of experience.
This, I submit, is one of the two primary links between Emerson and the pragmatists.[6]
They were joined together by their concern to thoroughly reconstruct the notion of
experience so that feeling, passion, and emotion were included.

When Emerson first invokes moods, he seems to do so in order to suggest that all
experience is illusory. But as Van Leer (1986: 165f.) argues, he curbs the excesses of this
thought in the essay "Experience" with the idea that experience surprises us—with the
idea that life is a "series of surprises."[7] And surprise is the stuff of discovery: "In the
thought of genius, there is always a surprise" (CW 3: 40; 1844). The fact that we can be
surprised suggests that experience is not illusory and the world is not structured entirely
by us. Although we may color the universe, there is something real that we are
coloring.[8] This idea of experience coming to us in surprises is the second primary
connection between Emerson and the founders of pragmatism. We shall see that it is
precisely the notion of experience Peirce puts forward and that it forms a critical part of
his epistemology. He had to have picked it up from Emerson. Experience is, in
Emerson's words, "an unlooked for result" or something "somewhat new, and very
unlike what he promised himself" (CW 3: 40; 1844). We shall see that these words
could just as well have come from Peirce's pen.

In 1837, Emerson argued that it was time for an "American scholar" to free
American thought from the dominance of the Europeans. He looked forward to a
time "when the sluggard intellect of this continent will look up from under its iron lids
and fill the postponed expectation of the world with something better than the

---

[5] Emerson CW 3: 48; 1844, see Goodman (1990: 13f., 19).
[6] See also Clebsch (1973: 113), and Goodman (2008).
[7] CW 3: 39; 1844. See also CW 2: 189–90; 1841 and CW 2: 195; 1841.
[8] Van Leer (1986: 25) also points out that the notion of experience as surprise can be found in the early
(1836) Nature.

exertions of mechanical skill" (1940: 45). Douglas Anderson (2008) argues very persuasively that C. S. Peirce was that American scholar.

Santayana bemoaned the "genteel tradition" of the Calvinism and transcendentalism in early American thought. He thought it originated in the agonized conscience of the Puritans coming to America. These colonists "were occupied, as they expressed it, in wrestling with the Lord" (1967: 38). Santayana thought the imported Puritan ideal was "an old wine in new bottles," and had the unfortunate consequence of rendering America "a young country with an old mentality" (1967: 38–39).[9] It was only when the likes of Charles Peirce and William James arrived on the intellectual scene that America moved away from its being an apprentice of Europe and came into its own. James "has given a rude shock to the genteel tradition. What! The world a gradual improvisation? Creation unpremeditated? God a sort of young poet or struggling artist?" (Santayana 1967: 59). Santayana was right. Pragmatism was rude and shocking to the America of the mid and late 1880s.

[9] In his biography of Emerson, Oliver Wendell Holmes makes the same point (Holmes 1886: 146).

2

Chauncey Wright (1830–75)

2.1 Introduction

Now that we have a sketch of the intellectual world the early pragmatists were born into, we can turn properly to the founders of pragmatism—Chauncey Wright, Charles Peirce, and William James. Wright, obscure to all but aficionados of American philosophy, is a much underrated figure in American thought. He was not born into wealth or academia. His father was a deputy sheriff and merchant in Northampton Massachusetts and his way to Harvard was paid through the generosity of a local woman. While there, he exhibited a distinct loathing for the rote learning of classical languages and seemed not to be doing much of the reading for his courses. Nonetheless, he made a great impression on many of his contemporaries and on Benjamin Peirce, the Professor of Mathematics and father of Charles. Once graduated, the job he found was outside the college system—he was a "computer" for the American Nautical Almanac. His heart was not in it. As Simon Newcomb, the eminent mathematician and astronomer who was a colleague at the Almanac put it, he had:

an abominable habit of doing his whole year's work in three or four months, during which period he would work during the greater part of the night as well as of the day, eat little, and keep up his strength by smoking. The rest of the year he was a typical philosopher of the ancient world, talking, but, so far as I know, at this period, seldom or never writing.[1]

After devising calculating shortcuts that enabled him to dispense quickly with his Almanac work, Wright would get on with what really seized him—philosophical talk, correspondence, and, when pressured, a bit of reviewing for *The Nation* and *The North American Review*.

At these things he was very good indeed. His correspondence with Darwin impressed the great evolutionist.[2] He was generally held in very high regard and was admitted to the American Academy of Arts and Sciences, where he became its recording secretary. But it is clear that Wright's real genius came out in his talk. He was a wonderful friend and a brilliant interlocutor. He died in 1875, when he was only

---

[1] Thayer (1971 [1878]: 70). Newcomb's reminiscences of Wright make it clear that he was very fond of his unusual colleague. But he did not feel the same about Peirce, intervening to prevent him from getting appointments and grants. See Brent (1993: 128, 150–53, 287) and Houser (1986: xl–xli).

[2] See Wiener (1945) and Madden (1963: 23).

forty-five, after suffering from general poor health, abuse of "stimulants," terrible sleep habits, and intermittent spells of serious depression (Thayer 1971 [1878]: 137).

His thought had a significant impact on the other early pragmatists. Perry notes that James frequently prefaced remarks with "as Chauncey Wright used to say" (1976 [1935]: 127). Here is Peirce's description of the members of The Metaphysical Club and of Wright's superiority:

It was in the earliest seventies that a knot of us young men in Old Cambridge, calling ourselves, half-ironically, half-defiantly, "The Metaphysical Club,"—for agnosticism was then riding its high horse, and was frowning superbly upon all metaphysics—used to meet, sometimes in my study, sometimes in that of William James. It may be that some of our old-time confederates would today not care to have such wild-oats-sowings made public, though there was nothing but boiled oats, milk, and sugar in the mess. Mr. Justice Holmes, however, will not, I believe, take it ill that we are proud to remember his membership . . . Nicholas St. John Green was one of the most interested fellows, a skillful lawyer and a learned one, . . . Chauncey Wright, something of a philosophical celebrity in those days, was never absent from our meetings. I was about to call him our corypheus; but he will better be described as our boxing-master whom we—I particularly—used to face to be severely pummelled . . . . Wright, James, and I were men of science, rather scrutinizing the doctrines of the metaphysicians on their scientific side than regarding them as very momentous spiritually. The type of our thought was decidedly British. I, alone of our number, had come upon the threshing-floor of philosophy through the doorway of Kant, and even my ideas were acquiring the English accent.

[CP 5. 12; 1907]

For his part, Wright "thought more of [Peirce's] ability than of that of any one he knew" (*CWJ* 4: 525; 1875). Indeed, as one reads Wright, one hears the echo of Peirce, who was thinking about many of the same topics at the same time.[3] Wright, more than anyone else, seems to have been on the same intellectual track as Peirce.

The three founding pragmatists clearly had a great deal of intellectual engagement with each other. In 1857 Peirce said that he talked philosophy almost every day with Wright (Menand 2001: 221, 477 n. 42). After Wright's death, Peirce penned the following to James:

As to [Wright] being *obscure* & all that, he was as well known as a philosopher need desire. It is only when a philosopher has something very elementary to say that he seeks the great public or the great public him . . . I wish I was in Cambridge for one thing. I should like to have some talks about Wright & about his ideas and see if we couldn't get up a memorial of him. His memory deserves it for he did a great deal for every one of us.

[*CWJ* 4: 523–24; 1875]

Like both Peirce and James, Wright was trained as a scientist: his was a mind "bred in physical studies" (Wright 1871: 131). Charles Eliot Norton, Professor of the History of

---

[3] Here is but one instance: Peirce, we shall see, thought that science could afford to wait for the real truths of nature, whereas, in matters of ethics or law, a decision has to be made here and now about what to do. Wright makes the very same assertion (1872: 170).

Art at Harvard and co-editor of The *North American Review* noted in 1877 that these three early titans of American philosophy were fixed not so much on "the side of abstract truth, but much more on the application of truth to the life and conduct of man" (1971 [1877]: xxi). Perhaps this is because, in Peirce's words, they were all "laboratory men" (*CP* 5. 412; 1905).

   The upheaval in American thought that was beginning to take hold in the mid 1880s might have been traumatic for the older generation of scholars already well-ensconced in American universities. But it was not difficult for Chauncey Wright, Charles Peirce, and William James. They were champing at the bit for the new scientific way of thinking to take hold.

2.2 The English and Scottish Influence

British empiricism lingers everywhere in the history of early American pragmatism. James is the most explicit about pragmatism's links to its empiricist predecessors, asserting that "the chief glory of English and Scottish thinkers" is to have brought to philosophy the thought that every difference in theory must make a difference in practice (1985 [1902]: 350). We shall see that early American pragmatism is far from being identical to British empiricism, but the relationship between the two is strong. It is important to see how one of the early founders of pragmatism—Wright—was marked by the English and the Scots. Wright was interested in the work of the psychologist Alexander Bain, the philosophers William Hamilton, David Hume, and John Stuart Mill, and the great evolutionist Charles Darwin. Mill and Darwin were his contemporaries and he was fully engaged with their views. *The Origin of Species* was published in 1859 and immediately stirred the intellects of some young bright thinkers in America— Chauncey Wright being one of the very brightest.[4] Wright was a participant in debates about how to interpret Darwin and he caught the attention of the great man himself. His thoughts on phyllotaxis (the pattern of clockwise and anti-clockwise spirals exhibited by plants) were of real interest to Darwin, despite the fact that the mathematics was beyond him (Thayer 1971 [1878]: 235–36). Wright had argued that this kind of arrangement, as in the petals on a flower, gives each part of the petal maximum exposure to light and hence it is a selected-for trait. Darwin arranged for Wright's "The Genesis of Species" to be published as a pamphlet in England and said "I have hardly ever in my life received an article which has given me so much satisfaction" (Thayer 1971 [1878]: 230). He also persuaded Wright to write a book on how consciousness might have evolved— the book was unfinished at the time of Wright's death.[5]

---

[4] Peirce was occasionally wary of Wright's involvement with Darwinian ideas. He thought, for instance, that Wright tried to link the concepts of utility and natural selection in an unwarranted or "incongruous" way (*CP* 5. 12; 1907; 5, 64; 1903) and he thought that the theory of evolution must reject Wright's nominalism and adopt something like his own scholastic realism and synechism. Nonetheless, Peirce joins with all the early pragmatists in taking Darwin and his ideas to be of the utmost importance.

[5] See Fisch (1947: 367f.).

One thing Wright's heroes have in common is, in the words of Norton, that they are "models of scientific investigation and philosophic inquiry" (1971 [1877]: xvi). They are scientist-philosophers. Wright takes "science" to be very broad—it is not just the physical and biological sciences he is interested in, but also sciences such as "political economy," "economics," and "political science" (1873b: 415, 417). He respected those who treated their subject matters, whatever they may be, "in the manner and by the method of physical philosophy, or as a science of causes and effects" (1873b: 417). He rails against the "a priori school" of philosophy, aligning himself firmly with the "positive mode of thought," which investigates the world by observation, experiment, and verification (1865b: 44). He is set against intuitions, innate ideas, laws of the faculty of mind, or primitive convictions—those supposed truths that have the mark of self-evidence, necessity, and universality (1865c: 330). He thinks that "a priori too often means no more than *ab ignorantia et indolentia*"—an expression understandable even for those without any Latin at all (1875b: 393).

It was Darwin's ideas that imperiled the a priori school. Intuition and reason were now to be seen as products of evolution, not as sources of certainly true principles. The faculties of our mind evolve in response to pressures of survivability. They are not given to us as principles that allow us to get reality right. We shall see that this was one of James's central insights in *Principles of Psychology*. We shall also see that the pragmatists' varying responses to Darwin were in part responsible for the evolution of two distinct kinds of pragmatism.

Wright was critical of suggestions, such as Hamilton's, that we hold some beliefs on faith—for example, that space, time, and the Deity are infinite. His view is that these "presuppositions" must be always and everywhere open to criticism (1865c: 340). "The principal question of philosophy is, whether any general truth is known by any mind except in consequence—the evidential consequence—of particular experiences, or else inductively" (1866: 346). He was similarly also critical of Trancendentalism's assertion that "certain so-called a priori elements of knowledge or general truths *could not* be vouched for by any amount of particular experience" (1866: 347).

This does not mean that Wright wanted to align himself with the idea, prominent in British empiricism, that all knowledge must come via the senses. He is very clear that the sources of our beliefs are varied and the primary pragmatist thought is that, once we have them, they need to be verifiable or linked to experience. He says:

But whatever be the origin of the theories of science, whether from a systematic examination of empirical facts by conscious induction, or from the natural biases of the mind, the so-called intuitions of reason, what seems probable without a distinct survey of our experiences— whatever the origin, real or ideal, the *value* of these theories can only be tested . . . by an appeal to sensible experience, by deductions from them of consequences which we can confirm by the undoubted testimony of the senses.

[1865b: 46]

This is a signal difference between pragmatism and British empiricism. Pragmatism is not primarily a view about the sources or origins of belief, but a view of what tests a belief must pass once we have it. It is a view about what it is for a belief to count as non-spurious, genuine, or legitimate.

2.3 Science, Metaphysics, and Religion

In Wright's day, "metaphysics" meant the kind of metaphysics that is infused with religion: the kind that speaks of the infinite and the absolute. There seems to be no room for such talk in the new scientific world view. Darwin's explanation of the natural world makes no reference to a divine will and appears to be in bald contradiction with the Bible's story of creation. Indeed, empiricism seems in a more general way to eliminate metaphysics, never mind a metaphysics that appeals to God. Empiricism, Wright says, leaves no room for "unknown inscrutable powers"; powers which "are known only to a higher form of intuition through the faculty of 'Reason'"; and "mystery" (1873a: 246). These kinds of phenomena are not verifiable. They cannot be the objects of scientific study. Wright adds to this well-known empiricist anti-metaphysical thought another idea, which we shall see surface in Peirce's work as well: metaphysics impedes inquiry. It fosters devotion and obedience, two attitudes that can only hobble science (1873a: 239, 248). Science "does not stand in awe before the unknown" (1873a: 239, 249).

Religious hypotheses caused a fair bit of consternation for the early pragmatists. Calling into question the very place of God within the natural order could have unwanted personal consequences. John Fiske, one of the members of The Metaphysical Club who was seized by the new evolutionary biology, was caught reading Comte in church while a student at Harvard. Comte's verificationist questioning of religion was a source of much discussion in educated America in the 1860–70s. Fiske was docked merit points and had a letter from the President sent to his parents, threatening expulsion if he tried to spread his "infidel" views.[6] The President was right to see that Fiske was part of a new wave of thinkers who would not begin with religious principles, but rather, with scientific ones.

Of the early pragmatists, Wright was clearest about the implications of science on religion. He argued that religion must make itself part of science and held no truck with the view that science is subject to criticism as the enemy of religion (1865a). Indeed, he was infamous in Cambridge for his agnosticism and his good-natured but devastating challenges to arguments for the existence of God. Here is what he says to Professor Lesley—friend, Professor of Geology at the University of Pennsylvania, official geologist of the state of Pennsylvania, and minister in the Orthodox Congregational Church:

Thank you very much for your objection to one of my theological arguments ... The theological arena is a new one for me, and I am painfully conscious of being poorly armed for its contests. The study of the exact sciences, where one cannot go astray without falling into

---

[6] See Richardson (2006: 42).

absurdity and incomprehensibility, is not so good a discipline as is commonly supposed, for preparing the mind against inaccuracies of thought and expression in matters full of darkness and pitfalls . . . . In mathematics we attend principally to the reasons, and let the conclusions follow if they will; but in theology the conclusions are of the first importance, and the reasons are dragged after them.

[Thayer 1971 [1878]: 67–68]

If this were not damning enough, he then delivers his blow to the argument from design. It only seems plausible if you grant the conclusion before you start your argument: "It is doubtless true, granting the conclusion,—the existence of a law-giver and designer,—that the laws and apparent designs which are discovered by science are the signs or symbols of final cause or purpose; but how, then, can we use them as proofs of what we have assumed in thus interpreting them?" (Thayer 1971 [1878]: 68).

Wright was able to be heretical while maintaining respect. This is in large part due to his shy and honest character—he seems to have been loved by everyone. We find people like Lesley being effusive about Wright after his death, despite the fact that "[h]is tendencies were all towards that New City which men are building on the fens of Mattershire, and I found him speculating on its water lots . . . He traversed my opinion that phyllotaxis is merely a well-bred habit of the *soul of the plant* . . . He called for a proof of the invisible, and would accept of no half proof" (Thayer 1971 [1878]: 66–67).

Wright's "verdict" on the existence of God and the immortality of the soul is: "not proven" (Thayer 1971 [1878]: 133). "Not proven," for him, is a serious judgment. He means by it that there is no evidence in its favor. But he is careful to say that atheism has as little evidence going for it as does theism. Wright sees that the participants in the debate about theological metaphysics feel that they are talking at cross-purposes. But the way he sets out the cross-purposes make it clear who he thinks is being unreasonable:

the main summary objection which the metaphysical spirit makes to the theories of the sceptical school is, that they fail to answer the questions which the metaphysical school has started. And the main objection of the sceptical spirit to metaphysics is, that these questions are gratuitous, idle, and foolish.

[1867: 350]

He argues that Pyrrhonian is mistaken in thinking that the best course of action is to abstain from such debates. For theological metaphysics wants to have an impact on how people think about religion and morals. Wright thinks the impact it in fact has is pretty much to encourage "false judgments" (1971 [1877]: 355). So one must take the debate seriously.

We shall see that the way Wright frames the debate about metaphysics turns out to be one of the core features of pragmatism—from its inception to the current day. Metaphysics' "arrant nonsense" (1867: 355) must be exposed, but this does not mean that skepticism reigns supreme. It does not mean that all metaphysics must be tossed into the rubbish bin. We need to find a way of discriminating between good metaphysics and bad. Wright's friends James and Peirce tried mightily to follow through on this thought after the death of their mentor.

In almost every review and philosophical letter Wright penned, he speaks of the problematic nature of metaphysics. It is the cord that runs through all the aspects of his thought. We shall see that he is not alone. When Peirce, for instance, was at Hopkins in the early 1880s, he reignited The Metaphysical Club, with the same sense of irony in the naming of the first Metaphysical Club. Christine Ladd-Franklin, Peirce's student, says: "In fact, so devious and unpredictable was his [Peirce's] course that he once, to the delight of his students, proposed at the end of his lecture, that we should form (for greater freedom of discussion) a Metaphysical Club, though he had begun the lecture by defining metaphysics to be the 'science of unclear thinking'."[7]

Science, Wright asserted, is mostly about induction. We shall see that one of Peirce's great innovations was to envision a new kind of inference for the scientific method—hypothesis or abductive inference, which is concerned with the development of hypotheses for subsequent testing by induction. It is very similar to what is today called inference to the best explanation.[8] Perhaps he was already worrying about the following kind of statement of Wright's, when it was made in 1865: "But when and however ideas are developed science cares nothing, for it is only by subsequent tests of sensible experience that ideas are admitted into the pandects of science" (1865b: 47). Peirce thought that science had better care about how ideas are developed.

One wonders, however, whether Wright was toying with the idea of abduction himself. He argues that a great thinker, like Pythagoras or Darwin, would not have advanced his groundbreaking hypothesis, "if he had not had some ground of believing it beforehand" (1870: 98). Similarly, he thinks:

[the] very hope of experimental philosophy . . . is based on the induction, or, if you please, the *a priori* assumption, that physical causation is universal; that the constitution of nature is written in its actual manifestations, and needs only to be deciphered by experimental and inductive research; that it is not a latent invisible writing, to be brought out by the magic of mental anticipation or metaphysical meditation.

[1871: 131]

We will see that these kinds of assumptions, or hopes—as Peirce often called them—were what Peirce meant by "abductive" hypotheses. What is required for inquiry is engaging in "researches for unknown causes by the skillful use of hypothesis and experiment" (1871: 141). This idea remains underdeveloped in Wright's work and we shall have to wait until we come to Peirce before we get a sense of its power.

Both Wright and Peirce, however, were loathe to allow metaphysical or "*transcendental hypotheses*" into experimental philosophy (Wright 1871: 136, emphasis in

---

[7] See Christine Ladd-Franklin (1916: 716–17).
[8] The difference is that Peirce did not think that the conclusions of such inferences could be taken as true—they are hypotheses to be tested.

original). These "metaphysical, occult" hypotheses, such as the vitalist hypothesis, have no place in a scientific philosophy (1871: 138).

2.4 Pragmatism, Positivism, Verificationism

It is clear that the positivist idea of verification was swirling around the members of The Metaphysical Club in the 1860s and 1870s. It is also clear that verificationism is inextricably linked to the very idea of pragmatism—of keeping our hypotheses and theories connected to experience and practice. Some of the pragmatists' predecessor empiricists were constructing an atomistic verificationism that focused on a simple equation between ideas and things (or the visible effects of things). The pragmatists, we shall see, were after a different kind of verificationism.

"Verificationism" is now taken to refer to the core doctrine of logical empiricism or logical positivism, the position that arose in the mid 1920s in Vienna and Berlin and that was imported to America and England at the outset of the Second World War. The aim of logical empiricism was to unify all inquiry under the umbrella of science. The verifiability principle did most of the work: it required all legitimate beliefs and theories to be reducible, via formal deductive logic, to statements that are empirically verifiable. Since metaphysics does not meet this test, aspersion is cast upon it—it is meaningless nonsense. But the verificationist idea has its roots in the British empiricists and in Comte and, of course, it is these thinkers to whom we must look if we are going to arrive at a view of the early pragmatists that is not misleadingly anachronistic.

Wright saw the subtleties of and the difficulties for the verificationist idea straight away. Comte was at the time the standard-bearer for what he had just started to call "positivism." In his six-volume *Cours de Philosophie Positive*, he argues that legitimate disciplines must be based on observation; that they all must measure up to the standards of science; and hence they must aim to predict and control sensory phenomena. Domains of inquiry start off in a theological, fictitious, or mythological stage, where we try to explain nature by appeal to the rule of gods. This kind of explanation is rejected as people discover that nature is ruled by laws. The gods are then depersonalized and become abstract metaphysical entities—essences or causes. Rather than invoke the will of the gods as an explanation for phenomena, powers or essences are said to do the job. But Comte argued that these too are beyond our reach. Metaphysics simply substitutes mysterious entities for mysterious gods. Metaphysics is a primitive precursor of science and will disappear as science restricts itself to dealing with appearances.

Wright sees a problem with positivism. As Edward Madden (1963: 108ff.) notes, he anticipates a major correction made in verificationist thought in the late 1940s and early 1950s. Instead of suggesting that every concept must be itself verifiable by experience, Wright has it that hypotheses must "show credentials from the senses, either by affording from themselves consequences capable of sensuous verification or by yielding such consequences in conjunction with ideas which by themselves are verifiable"

(1865b: 46). We shall see in Part III that the logical empiricists eventually conceded that a concept can "receive some or all of its meaning from the *system* of concepts in which it occurs ... and thus the only requirement for the legitimate use of a concept is that *some* of the hypotheses that utilize a system of concepts must be empirically testable" (Madden 1963: 110; Carnap 1937: 318). We need to look to a whole system of interconnected concepts and hypotheses—a theory—and then require that theory to be verifiable.

Wright is of the same view. In the paper in which he expresses it, he also presages another excellent objection to logical empiricist forms of verificationism that was to come almost a hundred years after his death:

It is indisputable that verification is essential to the completeness of scientific method; but there is still room for debate as to what constitutes verification in the various departments of philosophical inquiry. So long as the philosophy of method fails to give a complete inventory of our primary sources of knowledge, and cannot decide authoritatively what are the origins of first truths, or the truths of observation, so long will it remain uncertain what is a legitimate appeal to observation, or what is a real verification.

[1865b: 45]

To take for granted that direct reports from our five senses are the sum total of what counts as legitimate verification is to blithely assume the answer to some very hard questions.

Wright notes that Comte himself got the nature of verification wrong—for instance, he "resisted the undulatory theory of light" because he thought it involved unverifiable hypotheses (1875a: 383). We can now add that Ernst Mach got it wrong too. His requirement that scientists must not venture beyond the boundaries of experience led him to reject the atomic hypothesis. Since atoms and molecules cannot be perceived by the unaided senses, they are, Mach said, "merely a product of thought" and cannot refer to reality (Mach 1911 [1872]: 51). Legitimate scientific hypotheses like these can be imperiled if the philosopher thinks he knows exactly what kind of experience is required of a hypothesis in order for it to meet the test of legitimacy. Wright's point is that we must not assume that all legitimate belief requires a touchstone in the sensory. In doing so, we assume the answer to what Wright thinks are some deeply interesting questions. What, for instance, should we think about "appeals to the tests of internal evidence, tests of reason, and the data of self-consciousness" (1865b: 46)?

Appeals to these kinds of evidence are part of the "subjective method" of inquiry, in which "natural universal human interests and emotions" are the testing ground of hypotheses. This method is characteristic of metaphysical and theological speculation. The "objective method," on the other hand, is empirical and is not interested in "what we have always felt" (1865b: 49). But what gives us confidence in thinking that the subjective method has no value at all? Unlike Comte, Wright does not think that philosophy and theology are superseded by science. Science and philosophy, for instance, have always coexisted in first-rate inquiry. It is just that science is only now coming to maturity and it promises "to throw a flood of light" on subjects such as history, society, laws, and morality (1865b: 54). In order to get this illumination, we must not start off with a set of prejudices about what science is.

We thus find in Wright the first careful articulation of the idea we have seen nascent in the very early American thinkers. It is the idea that experience might go beyond what our five senses deliver; that we might experience value; that inquiry must be thought of as a seamless whole. It is what I will call, from here on, holism. It will become a defining feature of pragmatism.

Here is how holism plays itself out in Wright's thought. In 1875, he asserts that mathematical laws or axioms "have their truest proof in the broadest possible tests of experience, through the experimental and observational verifications of their mathematical consequences" (1875b: 393). Moral philosophy can also be conducted in this observational or scientific spirit. In his view, this way of thinking about morals amounts to being a utilitarian.

It will be no surprise that Wright considers himself a follower of Mill. Mill thought that $2 + 1 = 3$ is an empirical truth about collections—we observe that the collections oo and o can be rearranged as the collection ooo (1973 [1872]: 257). This thought did not go over very well—Frege pointed out that it is a good thing that all objects are not bolted to the ground. For if we couldn't move collections around then, on Mill's view, $2 + 1$ would not equal 3 (Frege 1950 [1884]: 9e). Wright does not tell us what kind of experience he has in mind for mathematics. We shall see that when Peirce grabs hold of the idea that mathematics is an observational science, the result is something much more interesting than Mill offers.

Nonetheless, Wright thought that Mill was an excellent example of someone who engaged in inquiry in the right way:

[Mill] sincerely welcomed intelligent and earnest opposition with a deference due to truth itself, and to a just regard to the diversities in men's minds from differences of education and natural dispositions. These diversities even appeared to him essential to the completeness of the examination which the evidences of truth demand. Opinions positively erroneous, if intelligent and honest, are not without their value, since the progress of truth is a succession of mistakes and corrections. Truth itself, unassailed by erroneous opinion, would soon degenerate into narrowness and error . . . The human mind cannot afford to forget its past aberrations. These, as well as its true discoveries, are indispensable guides; nor can it ever afford to begin from the starting-point in its search for truth, in accordance with the too confident method of more ambitious philosophers.
[1873b: 417–18]

There is a lot packed into this passage. Indeed, some of the core themes of the pragmatist epistemology are present here. There is the anti-foundationalist, inquiry-centered idea. We cannot start from scratch—from indubitable or certain foundations. Rather, we must start from where we find ourselves, laden with the beliefs our inquiries may have put in place. There is also the idea that we need to take into account as much evidence and diverse perspective as we can if we want to discover the truth about some matter. One must prize the differences in the way people think "for the sake of truth," just as you would prize "the addition of a new sense to the means of extending and testing knowledge" (1873b: 419).

I have argued (Misak 2000), employing Peirce's view as a basis, that the best pragmatist view of morals and politics follows these very lines. In other words, what Wright says about the need to take different perspectives seriously is especially appropriate in the case of ethical inquiry. In ethical inquiry the diverse experiences of others are of special importance. Had Wright expanded on these cursory remarks, perhaps he would have been considered the originator of the pragmatist democratic account of moral and political inquiry, rather than Peirce or Dewey.

Wright also makes a distinction that will prove to be a central issue for pragmatism—the distinction between what people in fact desire and what people ought to desire. He thinks that Mill:

> redeemed the word 'utility' from the ill-repute into which it had fallen . . . it is no longer . . . the name of . . . anything which conduces to the satisfaction of desires common to all men. He made it mean clearly the quality in human customs and rules of conduct which conduces to realize conditions and dispositions which for men (though not for swine) are practicable, and are the most desirable; their desirableness being tested by the actual preference which those who possess them have for them as elements in their own happiness.
>
> [1873b: 418]

This may not be getting exactly right the relationship between "is" and "ought," but it is certainly a step in the right direction. There is a distinction between what we do desire and what is most desirable. A serious question for pragmatism arises because, on that view, the only way of testing what is most desirable or what we ought to desire is by seeing what human beings do desire. Wright sees that the connection between the two is complex—that desiring x does not entail that x ought to be desired. But he also sees that the connection cannot be ignored. In our quest for the normative—in our quest to say something about what we ought to desire—we need to look at what desires work for human beings in practice and what desires would in fact contribute to happiness and thriving. Normativity must be built up in a naturalistic way.

Wright's point applies in an equally important way to belief. There is a distinction between what we do believe and what we ought to believe. The only way of getting at what we ought to believe is by seeing what human beings do believe, what beliefs work for them and what beliefs in fact contribute to successful action in the world. This point will go through changes—some forward and some backward—as we look to how the pragmatist account of truth and normativity shifts over the decades since Wright first saw its significance. For instance, a central debate within pragmatism concerns what sorts of consequences a belief needs to have if it is to pass the pragmatic test. Wright's kind of empiricism is such that "it discriminates between the desirableness of a belief and the evidence thereof" (Thayer 1971 [1878]: 103). A belief can have consequences for the believer—it can make me feel better, it can influence my train of thought, I can desire it to be true, etc. But that is not the kind of consequence Wright thinks salient. A belief must have consequences not only for the believer, but for the world. The importance of this distinction will amplify as we march through the history of pragmatism.

It is clear already that Wright was a strong thinker and deserves, as much as Peirce and James, to be called a founder of pragmatism. He takes his cue from Darwin and the theory of evolution and sows the seeds for the pragmatist account of truth: "our knowledges and rational beliefs result, *truly and literally*, from the survival of the fittest among our original and spontaneous beliefs" (1870: 116). Certainty is not to be had: the inquirer must be "contented with the beliefs that are only the most probable, or the most authentic on strictly inductive grounds" (1875c: 396). What we have are "working ideas—finders, not merely summaries of truth" (1971 [1877]: 56). "A theory which is utilized receives the highest possible certificate of truth" (1971 [1877]: 51). We shall see that Peirce's great addition to these thoughts is that, were a belief to show itself to be forever fit, that belief is true.

3

Charles Sanders Peirce (1839–1914)

3.1 Introduction

Everyone seems to have been fond of Wright and James. Peirce, on the other hand, was clearly a difficult and not very modest man. William James advises his brother Henry, who was dining with Peirce in Paris in 1875: "I am bemused that you should have fallen into the arms of C. S. Peirce, whom I imagine you find a rather uncomfortable bedfellow, thorny and spinous, but the way to treat him is after the fabled 'nettle' receipt: grasp firmly, contradict, push hard, make fun of him, and he is as pleasant as anyone ... " (*CWJ* 1: 246; 1875). Henry ended up not seeing much more of Peirce, saying that although "one must appreciate his mental ability," "he has too little social talent, too little art of making himself agreeable" (*CWJ* 1: 255; 1876). In William's view, Peirce "hates to *make connexion* with anyone he is with. With all this curious misanthropy, he has a genuine vein of sentiment and softness running through him, but so narrow a vein that it always surprises me when I meet it. Anyhow, he's a genius, and I look forward with avidity to his work" (*CWJ* 7: 498; 1874; emphasis in original). James may well have Peirce in mind when he says in *The Varieties of Religious Experience* that crankiness and loss of mental balance, when combined with a superior intellect, is often a mark of genius (1985 [1902]: 27).

Peirce's brother, James Mills Peirce, thus strikes a common and compelling note when he writes to William James during a dangerously low point in Peirce's fortunes:

It is certainly amazing that with all Charlie's power of doing work of high ability, scientific, literary, philosophic, & his devotion to work, he commands no public & offers his wares in vain. Admitting all that is erratic in his judgment & temperament, all that is rebellious against the commonplace in his personality, I must think it a glaring proof of the want in our country of the sincere love of intellectual truth, & even of the ordinarily current respect for intellectual standards that we see in Europe, that nobody cares even to render a formal encouragement to one who shows intellectual originality without popular gifts.

[*CWJ* 8:17; 1895]

Peirce was not self-deceived about the state of his "popular gifts." He knows that he and his dear friend William have completely different natures: "He so concrete, so living; I a mere table of contents, so abstract, a very snarl of twine" (*CP* 6. 184; 1911).

With these unhappy traits at the fore, Peirce's career was stunted. He behaved badly in his marriage to Melusina Fay, who was from a prominent Cambridge family. The scandal over his infidelity, divorce in 1883, and quick remarriage (six days later) seems to have damned him. He was not the kind of pious man upon which universities in America were at that time insistent. Even in 1869, well before any scandalous behavior, James sees trouble on the rise:

The poor cuss sees no chance of getting a professorship anywhere . . . It seems a great pity that as original a man as he is, who is willing and able to devote the powers of his life to logic and metaphysics, should be starved out of a career, when there are lots of professorships . . . to be given . . . to "safe", orthodox men.

[1920, v.1: 149; 1869]

The concern expressed did not dissipate. James, in his characteristically generous way, never abandoned Peirce or gave up his intense but fruitless efforts to secure him a position, a set of lectures, or any academic crumb. It appears that this is why Peirce sometimes uses his initial to refer to "Santiago" rather than "Sanders"—the former means "Saint James" in Spanish.[1]

Peirce did manage to get a part-time post at Johns Hopkins, where he taught logic and had a great impact on a select number of excellent students. But in 1884, after four years there, he lost his job and was never able to return to a paid position in a university, despite his desperation to do so and his manifest talent. The president of Johns Hopkins was generally not enthusiastic about philosophy[2] and especially not enthusiastic about this particular problematic philosopher.

What money he had, from here on, was earned at his day job for the U.S. Coast and Geodetic Survey. Like Chauncey Wright, he worked full-time for a prestigious scientific agency and worked on his philosophical contributions after hours. His thirty-one years at the Survey, while certainly a second-best as far as his own ambitions went, were very productive. He made significant advances in pendulum studies to determine the shape of the earth, in photometric research on stars, and in chromatics. But he was let go in 1891. He was not the most punctual deliverer of reports. His father was no longer alive to protect him from the fallout of his behavior and his health had diminished from working intensely at two full-time vocations, one of which involved considerable fieldwork. From then until his pauper's death in 1914, he lived off of charity, much of it organized by James, and sometimes not enough to heat his house and put sufficient food on his plate.

James, Dewey (who was a student at Johns Hopkins while Peirce was there), and Royce were all very open about their debts to Peirce. Today he is often regarded as the most original and outstanding philosopher America has produced. But at the height of his powers, his name was frequently misspelled—even on proofs of his own essays and in the American Philosophical Association's minutes recording his death.

As a result of Peirce's troubled life and frustrated career in philosophy, we do not have a sustained body of published work from which to garner his settled view on

---

[1] See Brent (1998 [1993]: 315–16, 374), as well as (CP 5. 614; 1906).

[2] See Dykhuizen (1973: 29) and Green (2007).

matters. As Peirce himself says: "In the little I have published (in default of a publisher) I have been grievously hampered by having to address a public of magazine-readers."[3] In order to get a good sense of what Peirce thought, one needs to immerse oneself in thousands of handwritten manuscript pages, still available in its entirety only on microfilm. *The Writings of Charles Sanders Peirce*, a careful, beautifully produced, chronological collection, complete with the many drafts Peirce penned, is currently in the midst of what seems destined to be an astonishingly long publication period. The first volume appeared in 1982. The most recent appeared in 2009, with a projected twenty-three more to come.

Peirce conceived of his philosophy as an architectonic system, the footings consisting of a grand scheme of categories—Firstness, Secondness, and Thirdness—with his theory of logic and theory of signs providing much of the load-bearing walls. I will not try to describe in any detail how he tried to construct his edifice. He never really managed to get it properly built. Rather, I will draw on elements of the structure relevant to understanding the core of pragmatism: meaning, truth, and the growth of knowledge.

3.2 Influences

Peirce was thoroughly immersed in the work of Kant and Hegel, as well as that of the British and German logicians. His allegiance to Kant, however, waxed and then waned. We find him saying in 1902 that when he "was a babe in philosophy my bottle was filled from the udders of Kant" but he now wants "something more substantial" (*CP* 2. 113; 1902). He tries to take what he saw as spurious metaphysics out of transcendental idealism. He thinks that there are indeed preconditions for some of our central capacities. But these preconditions are not necessary, as Kant thought they were. They are simply regulative assumptions of our practices—things that we have to assume are true if we are to carry on in the way it seems that we must carry on.

In much of his thinking, Peirce is aligned with the British empiricists. We will see in the next section that he, like Wright, advanced a kind of verificationism. He also put forward a sustained and careful argument against the rationalist view that we have innate ideas, or intuitions, or ideas that are not inferred from other ideas (*CP* 5. 264ff.; 1868). But he hardly mentions the empiricists and when Paul Carus associated him with Hume in an article published in *The Monist* titled "Mr. Charles S. Peirce's Onslaught on the Doctrine of Necessity," Peirce resisted the comparison (*CP* 6. 605; 1891). It is interesting, though, that it was not the empiricism he objected to. It was the nominalist metaphysical underpinnings of it.

He is also not tempted by what were taken to be the most central tenets of British empiricism. With Wright, he rejects the idea that the *sources* of all knowledge are the senses. And Peirce sees experience as the means of getting in touch with the world,

---

[3] Letter reprinted in Scott (1973: 376).

rather than a veil between inquirers and the world. This was more than enough to warrant, in his view, a distancing from the British empiricists. One of the guiding thoughts of Peirce's (and any pragmatist's) position is the idea that "all our knowledge is, and forever must be, relative to human experience and to the nature of the human mind" (*CP* 6. 95; 1903). Whether he got this from the British empiricists or from Kant, we shall see that he did not think that it means that we are trapped within the walls of our experience—that we can't have access to the world as it is independent of human purpose.

3.3 The Pragmatic Maxim

Peirce published a famous set of six papers in 1877–78 in the *Popular Science Monthly* with the general title *Illustrations of the Logic of Science*. One of those papers, "The Fixation of Belief" will be the subject of the next section and another, "Deduction, Induction, and Hypothesis," will figure prominently in section 3.8. Here we will be concerned with "How to Make our Ideas Clear," which contains the best-known statement of the pragmatic maxim. That maxim has it that our theories and concepts must be linked to experience, expectations, or consequences.

In "How to Make our Ideas Clear," Peirce is interested in clarifying our ideas so that they are not subject to metaphysical "deceptions." His notorious statement is as follows: "Consider what effects, which might conceivably have practical bearings, we conceive the object of our conception to have. Then, our conception of these is the whole of our conception of the object" (*W* 3: 266; 1878). His aim is to "come down to what is tangible and practical, as the root of every real distinction of thought, no matter how subtle it may be; and there is no distinction of meaning so fine as to consist in anything but a possible difference in practice" (*W* 3: 265; 1878).

In this essay, the effects Peirce identifies as being at the root of our distinctions are characterized as "effects, direct or indirect, upon our senses" (*W* 3: 266; 1878). As an example, he asks about the meaning of "this diamond is hard" and finds that it amounts to "it will not be scratched by many other substances" (*W* 3: 266; 1878). He says, setting pragmatism up for trouble for the rest of its life: "There is absolutely no difference between a hard thing and a soft thing so long as they are not brought to the test. Suppose, then, that a diamond could be crystallized in the midst of a cushion of soft cotton, and should remain there until it was finally burned up" (*W* 3: 267; 1878). His view is that it is meaningless to speak of such a diamond as being hard.

Peirce tinkered with and improved this early published account of the pragmatic maxim for decades afterwards. He sees, for instance, that the use of the indicative conditional—it *will* not be scratched—is highly problematic and he retracts it. In 1905, he is adamant that the "will-be" in that formulation be replaced by a "would-be."[4] He

---

[4] *CP* 5. 453; 5, 457 (1905), 8, 380 n. 4 (undated); 6, 485 (1906); MS 841, pp. 15, 16 of "variants" (1908); MS 318, p. 11 (1907).

has already by then turned his back on all things nominalist and is a realist about universals and subjunctive conditionals. In correspondence with the Italian pragmatist Calderoni, Peirce says of the unscratched diamond that "it is a real fact that it *would* resist pressure" (*CP* 8. 208; 1905).

Given that Peirce published so few articles, it is no wonder that the "How to Make our Ideas Clear" version of the maxim has stuck in people's minds as the official one. But it is far from his considered view and it is unfortunate that the above account ("consider what effects . . . ") gets repeated so frequently. For even in "How to Make our Ideas Clear," it was not obvious that the principle Peirce was articulating was designed to be a semantic principle about the very meaning of our concepts.

As the title of the paper suggests, Peirce took the maxim to be about achieving clarity. He took his contribution to be an addition to a well-worn set of assumptions. Here is the first sentence of "How to Make our Ideas Clear":

Whoever has looked into a modern treatise on logic of the common sort, will doubtless remember the two distinctions between *clear* and *obscure* conceptions, and between *distinct* and *confused* conceptions. They have lain in the books now for nigh two centuries, unimproved and unmodified, and are generally reckoned by logicians as among the gems of their doctrine.
[*W* 3: 257–58; 1878]

"The books," he says, "are right in making familiarity with a notion the first step toward clearness of apprehension, and the defining of it the second" (*W* 3, 260; 1878). He wants to add an important third "grade of clearness" or grade of "apprehensions of the meanings of words." His contribution to the debate is to add "a far higher grade" of clarity to the standard two: knowing what to expect if hypotheses containing the concept are true.

We need to see, that is, that Peirce's empiricist criterion is designed to capture just one, albeit very important, aspect of what it is to understand something. Not only does an interpreter have to know how to give an analytic definition of a concept and how to pick out instances of it, but he has to know what to expect if propositions or beliefs containing the concept are true or false. If a belief has no consequences then it lacks a dimension we would have had to get right were we to fully understand it. Peirce thought that the pragmatic grade of clarity is a higher grade than the other two because it plays a special role in inquiry. If a belief has no consequences—if there is nothing we would expect would be different if it were true or false—then it is empty or useless for inquiry and deliberation. We have no way of inquiring into it. The maxim thus determines "the admissibility of hypotheses to rank as hypotheses" (MS 318, p. 8; 1907).

Peirce bemoaned the fact that people had misunderstood his slogan in "How to Make Our Ideas Clear." He says in 1910 of that essay:

I believe I made my own opinion quite clear to any attentive Reader, that the pragmaticistic grade of clearness could no more supersede the Definitiary or Analytic grade than this latter grade could supersede the first. That is to say, if the Maxim of Pragmaticism be acknowledged, although Definition can no longer be regarded as the supreme mode of clear Apprehension;

yet it retains all the *absolute* importance it ever had, still remaining indispensable to all Exact Reasoning.

[MS 647, p. 2.]

This appears in an unpublished manuscript, yet to see the light of day in Peirce's *Writings*. Nonetheless, C. I. Lewis reports that Josiah Royce "used to speak to his classes of the three grades of clearness about the meanings of terms" and attribute them to Peirce (Lewis 1956 [1929]: 86). What is most important about Peirce's theory of meaning (the 'three aspects' thought) was what was seen to be most important by his contemporary, Royce. It's a shame that generations then went by without it being front and center.

So rather than take that snappy summary provided in "How to Make Our Ideas Clear" as capturing Peirce's intentions, I suggest that we focus rather on the following kinds of expressions of the pragmatic maxim. We "must look to the upshot of our concepts in order to rightly apprehend them" (*CP* 5. 4; 1901). In order to get a complete grasp of a concept, we must connect it to that with which we have "dealings" (*CP* 5. 416; 1906). And my favourite: "we must not begin by talking of pure ideas,—vagabond thoughts that tramp the public roads without any human habitation,—but must begin with men and their conversation" (*CP* 8. 112; 1900). This less severe principle of course is less precise. But it is also less wrong and much more helpful, as we shall soon see. Peirce's idea is put nicely by David Wiggins (2002: 316). When a concept is "already fundamental to human thought and long since possessed of an autonomous interest," it is pointless to try to define it. Rather, we ought to attempt to get leverage on the concept, or a fix on it, by exploring its connections with practice.

That Peirce's pragmatic maxim is not designed to capture a full account of meaning can be seen through a different lens—by taking an excursion into his theory of signs. For in his theory of signs, the pragmatic maxim figures in one, again important but not stand-alone, "interpretant" of signs. Peirce is a major contributor to the theory of signs or, as he called it, semeiotic. He wants to develop an account of what it is to understand all of the very many kinds of signs human beings use. The idea of interpretation, or the effect that a sign has on its interpreter, is central to his thought. Representation is, he argues, triadic: it involves a sign, an object, and an interpreter. Each aspect of this representation relation corresponds to one of the elements in Peirce's primary division of signs into icons, indices, and symbols.

Icons are signs that represent their objects by virtue of a similarity or resemblance—a portrait is an icon of the person it portrays and a map is an icon of a certain geographic area. Indices are signs that point to their object by "being really connected with it" (*W* 2: 56, 1867)—a pointing finger, a demonstrative pronoun such as "this" or "that" draws the interpreter's attention to the object. Smoke, for instance, is an index of fire. A symbol is a word, proposition, or argument that depends on conventional or habitual rules; a symbol is a sign "because it is used and understood as such" (*CP* 2. 307; 1901). It has the same effect from interpreter to interpreter.

Meaning, for Peirce, resides in the effects a sign has on interpreters—on what Peirce calls its interpretant. He catalogues many varieties of interpretants—from the simple reaction of one who turns his head at the indexical shout of "look!" to sophisticated responses to propositions.[5] The highest kind of meaning, Peirce thinks, is the effects of the acceptance of a proposition on the interpreter's train of thought and action. This distinguishes pragmatism from cruder behaviorisms, on which meaning and mental states are reducible to behavior. For Peirce and for most of the pragmatists who followed him, meaning is partially a matter of effects on the interpreter. And these effects can be effects on the interpreter's physical behavior or on the interpreter's cognitive behavior. We shall see that how this latter thought is cashed out will differentiate one kind of pragmatist from the other.

3.4 Inquiry: The Fixation of Belief

In "The Fixation of Belief," Peirce sets out a conception of inquiry that leads to his account of truth. He does so in a very provocative way. Inquiry, he says, is the struggle to rid ourselves of doubt and achieve a state of belief. He tells us that "the sole aim of inquiry" is to settle belief and that a belief that is permanently settled is a true belief. Much of the rest of the paper is taken up with addressing the objection that wants to leap off the page: what if a belief was settled by "the fagot and the rack" or by a totalitarian regime? Would such a belief be true? His first answer is as follows: "We may fancy that this is not enough for us, and that we seek, not merely an opinion, but a true opinion. But put this fancy to the test, and it proves groundless; for as soon as a firm belief is reached we are entirely satisfied, whether the belief be true or false" (W3: 248; 1877). What the inquirer wants "is to see questions put to rest. And if a general belief, which is perfectly stable and immovable, can in any way be produced, though it be by the fagot and the rack, to talk of any error in such belief is utterly absurd" (*W* 2: 471; 1871).

Peirce is setting out the core pragmatist thought that our concepts—truth in this instance—must be connected with actual experience and practice. The problem for this naturalism,[6] is that it is very hard to see how we can get a normative concept from a mere description of our practices. In fact, it looks like Peirce has presented us with an excellent illustration of why naturalism won't work. But the argumentative structure of the paper suggests that he knows just what he needs to do. Despite the apparently unpromising start, he is of the view even in this early paper that we can get a truly

---

[5] See *CP* 5. 13; 8, 191; 5, 438. Tom Short (2007, ch. 2) also connects Peirce's semiotic to the pragmatic maxim in his discussion of how Peirce's semiotic evolved.

[6] See De Caro and Macarthur (2004, 2010) for an exploration of liberal naturalism. Macarthur (2012) distinguishes the epistemological from ontological claim of naturalism. The former holds that knowledge obtained by scientific inquiry is all the knowledge there is. The second holds that only the entities of science are real. My argument is that the pragmatists make both claims, as long as science is construed broadly so that it includes mathematics and ethics.

normative concept of truth out of facts about our practices of inquiry. I will augment the argument in "The Fixation of Belief" with some of his later expansions on it.[7]

An inquirer has a body of settled beliefs, which are in fact not doubted. Such beliefs take a variety of forms: they may be ordinary empirically confirmed beliefs; regulative assumptions that act as working hypotheses in the business of life; or even deeply engrained beliefs whose origins are intangible—the latter being those that we shall see Royce call "leading ideas." When something happens to throw a belief into doubt, the inquirer struggles to escape that unhappy state. Inquiry is the struggle to regain belief. It is ignited by a doubt and ceases only when a new belief or habit of expectation is re-established.

In Peirce's view, what is wrong with the state of doubt is not that it is uncomfortable, although it is in fact uncomfortable. What is wrong with doubt is that it leads to a paralysis of action. If an inquirer has an end in view and two different lines of action present themselves, action is brought to a halt: "he waits at the fork for an indication, and kicks his heels ... a true doubt is accordingly a doubt which really interferes with the smooth working of the belief-habit" (CP 5. 510; 1905). Doubt is problematic because we don't know what to do.

Peirce's "critical commonsensism" is the position that our background beliefs are not subject to Cartesian "paper" or "tin" doubts. Such doubts are not genuine and cannot motivate inquiry. An inquirer has a body of settled belief that is not in fact in doubt, against which to assess new evidence and hypotheses, and on which to act. Peirce's "fallibilism" is that any belief is in principle susceptible to real doubt. But the mere possibility of being mistaken about what one believes is not a reason to express a living doubt. He says:

there is but one state of mind from which you can 'set out', namely, the very state of mind in which you actually find yourself at the time you do 'set out' - a state in which you are laden with an immense mass of cognition already formed, of which you cannot divest yourself if you would ... Do you call it doubting to write down on a piece of paper that you doubt? If so, doubt has nothing to do with any serious business ...

[CP 5. 416; 1905]

Our body of background belief is susceptible to doubt on a piecemeal basis, so long as that doubt is prompted by "some positive reason" (CP 5. 51; 1903)—a surprising or recalcitrant experience. We must regard our background beliefs as true, until experience throws one or some group of them into doubt. The inquirer "is under a compulsion to believe just what he does believe ... as time goes on, the man's belief usually changes in a manner which he cannot resist ... this force which changes a man's belief in spite of any effort of his may be, in all cases, called a *gain of experience*" (MS 1342, p. 2, undated). Peirce links the scientific method to this epistemology. It is the method that pays close attention to the fact that beliefs fall to the surprise of recalcitrant experience.

---

[7] See Misak (2004 [1991]), ch. 2 for a full account.

So on the Peircean epistemology, an inquirer has a fallible background of "commonsense" belief that is not in fact in doubt. Only against such a background can a belief be put into doubt and a new, better, belief be adopted. All our beliefs are fallible but they do not come into doubt all at once. Those which inquiry has not thrown into doubt are stable and we should retain them until a reason to doubt arises. "Practically speaking," many things are "substantially certain" (*CP* 1. 152; 1897). Practical certainty must be distinguished from absolute certainty. The former can be had, while the latter cannot. Inquiry "is not standing upon the bedrock of fact. It is walking upon a bog, and can only say, this ground seems to hold for the present. Here I will stay till it begins to give way" (*CP* 5. 589; 1898). When it gives way, the ground merely shifts, rather than opens up underneath us. We can doubt one belief and inquire, but we cannot doubt all of our beliefs and inquire. Some things have to be held constant. For Peirce, the cardinal sin in philosophy is to adopt a view that blocks the path of inquiry, and the Cartesian view would stop inquiry in its tracks.

With these Peircean essentials in hand, we can now turn to that provocative argument in "The Fixation of Belief." Peirce discusses methods of belief fixation that we want to call defective: the method of tenacity (holding on to our beliefs come what may); the method of authority (letting a powerful regime or religion determine what you believe); the a priori method (believing that which is agreeable to reason without experiential input). His provocative claim is that if these methods were to permanently fix belief, then that belief would be true.

His strategy with respect to these specious methods is to articulate a number of reasons why the beliefs they fix won't stick or why they will eventually be assailed by doubt. Some of those reasons turn on a purported fact about inquirers—for example, when they see that others don't share their belief, they will be thrown into doubt. But here is the key passage in "The Fixation of Belief," hinting at his most compelling answer and at how his view will unfold in the future. The a priori method is a "failure," for:

> [it] makes of inquiry something similar to the development of taste; but taste, unfortunately, is always more or less a matter of fashion . . . [And] I cannot help seeing that . . . sentiments in their development will be very greatly determined by accidental causes. Now, there are some people, among whom I must suppose that my reader is to be found, who, *when they see that any belief of theirs is determined by any circumstance extraneous to the facts, will from that moment not merely admit in words that that belief is doubtful, but will experience a real doubt of it, so that it ceases to be a belief.*
> [*W* 3: 253; 1877 emphasis added]

Peirce's argument is that a belief that would be permanently settled is indeed entirely satisfactory and true. But it is very hard *really* to settle beliefs. If they are genuine beliefs, they resign in the face of recalcitrant experience or in the knowledge that they were put in place by a method that ignored experience. We will see in what follows that Peirce argues that recalcitrant experience can take many forms—it can be had in diagrammatic contexts; it can be a confrontation with the beliefs of others; and so on.

In 1911, he tries to correct the "illogical obstinacy" that he seemed at first to exhibit in "The Fixation of Belief." He wants to make it clear that those who settle belief by a method that fails to take account of the evidence for or against it can be criticized: "it is one of the essentials of belief, without which it would not *be* belief . . . that a man could hardly be considered sane who should wish that though the facts should remain lamentable, he should believe them to be such as he would wish them to be."[8] It is a constitutive norm of belief that a belief is responsive to the evidence and argument for or against it.

Hence, for Peirce, the inquirer is not merely after any old settled belief. He is after beliefs that are settled in a way that is connected with reasons and evidence. The inquirer is after beliefs that will serve him well in the future—beliefs that will not disappoint; that will guide action on a safe course; that will continue to fit with experience, evidence and argument. It is not so easy to end the irritation of doubt. It is not so easy to really fix belief.

3.5 Truth as Indefeasibility

When Peirce turns his pragmatic maxim on the concept of truth, the upshot is an aversion to "transcendental" accounts of truth, such as the correspondence theory, on which a true belief is one that corresponds to, or gets right, or mirrors the believer-independent world (*CP* 5. 572; 1901). Such accounts of truth are examples of those "vagabond thoughts" that tramp the public roads without any human habitation. They make truth the subject of empty metaphysics. For the very idea of the believer-independent world, and the items within it to which beliefs or sentences might correspond, seems graspable only if we could somehow step outside our corpus of belief, our practices, or that with which we have dealings.

That is, the correspondence concept of truth is missing the dimension that makes it suitable for inquiry. It fails to make "readily comprehensible" the fact that we aim at the truth or at getting things right (*CP* 1. 578; 1902). How could anyone aim for a truth that goes beyond what we can experience or beyond the best that inquiry could do? How could an inquirer adopt a methodology that might achieve that aim? The correspondence theory makes truth "a useless word" and "having no use for this meaning of the word 'truth', we had better use the word in another sense" (*CP* 5. 553; 1905).

Peirce, that is, is set against representationalist theories of truth—theories that take truth to be a matter of words representing, mirroring, or copying reality. We shall see that this is a persistent theme throughout the pragmatist tradition. Also persistent is the "meliorism" at the heart of Peirce's theory of truth and inquiry—the idea that we are always trying to improve the situation in which we find ourselves by replacing doubt with the settlement of a better belief.

---

[8] MS 673, p.11, 1911, see also MS 675, sheets marked "8."

Peirce is perfectly happy with the correspondence theory as a "nominal" definition, useful only to those who have never encountered the word before (*CP* 8. 100; 1910). But we want a more robust or a full account of truth—one that is useful in inquiry and to those who already are familiar with the concept. Hence, we need to provide a pragmatic elucidation—an account of the role the concept plays in practical endeavors. We need to illuminate the concept of truth by considering its linkages with inquiry, assertion, and acquisition of belief. For those are the human dealings relevant to truth.

Peirce's account of truth is the first developed pragmatist account of truth. It is resolutely and expressly naturalist. We have to extract the concept of truth from our practices of inquiry, reason-giving, and assertion. When we inquire, give reasons, or believe, we take ourselves to be aiming at truth. We want to know, for instance, what methods might get us true belief; whether it is worth our time and energy to inquire into certain kinds of questions; whether a discourse such as ethics aims at truth or whether it is a radically subjective matter, not at all suited for truth-value. We must make sense of and answer these questions without engaging in spurious metaphysics.

Once we see, for instance, that truth and assertion are intimately connected—once we see that to assert that *p* is true is to assert *p*—we can look to our practices of assertion to see what commitments they entail. As Wiggins (2004) puts it, hard on the heels of the thought that truth is internally related to assertion comes the thought that truth is also internally related to inquiry, reasons, evidence, and standards of good belief. If we unpack the commitments we incur when we assert, we find that we have imported all these notions. Peirce argues that an assertion is something speakers take responsibility for: "Nobody takes any positive stock in those conventional utterances, such as 'I am perfectly delighted to see you,' upon whose falsehood no punishment at all is visited" (*CP* 5. 546). An assertion must be such that the speaker is held to account if what she says is false.[9] Norms, standards, and aiming at truth are built into assertion.

Peirce argues that a belief is true if it would be "indefeasible"; or would not be improved upon; or would never lead to disappointment; or would forever meet the challenges of reasons, argument, and evidence. A true belief is the belief we would come to, were we to inquire as far as we could on a matter. He was very careful not to make this a reductive definition of truth. He did not want to *define* truth as that which satisfies our aims in inquiry. A dispute about definition, he says, is usually a "profitless discussion" (*CP* 8. 100; 1910). David Wiggins sees his point clearly:[10] "To elucidate truth in its relations with the notion of inquiry, for instance, as the pragmatist does, need not . . . represent any concession at all to the idea that truth is *itself* an 'epistemic notion'" (2002: 318). The pragmatist is merely getting one fix on the idea of truth.

Peirce sometimes expresses his account of truth in the following unhelpful way: a true belief is one which would be agreed upon at the hypothetical or "fated" end of inquiry (See *W* 3: 273; 1878). But on the whole, he tries to stay away from ideas such as

---

[9] For a concise and good account of Peirce on assertion see Atkins (forthcoming).
[10] See also Sellars (1962: 29) and Migotti (2011).

the final end of inquiry. We cannot make good sense of this idea and it has caused much mischief for pragmatism. How would we know when we reached the end of inquiry? Are we to characterize it as perfect or ideal in some question-begging manner? His considered and much better formulation is this: a true belief is such that it would withstand doubt, were we to inquire as far as we fruitfully could into the matter. A true belief is such that, no matter how much further we were to investigate and debate, it would not be overturned by recalcitrant experience and argument. Peirce says: "if Truth consists in satisfaction, it cannot be any *actual* satisfaction, but must be the satisfaction which *would* ultimately be found if the inquiry were pushed to its ultimate and indefeasible issue" (CP 5. 569; 1901; CP 6. 485; 1908). On Peirce's view, we aim at beliefs that would be forever stable—we aim at getting the best beliefs we can.

Notice the "we" in Peirce's account of truth. He thought that truth was a matter for the community of inquirers—not for this or that individual inquirer. Since individuals have finite lives, "logicality inexorably requires that our interests shall *not* be limited. They must not stop at our own fate, but must embrace the whole community" (W 3: 284; 1878). Science, inquiry, and rationality are matters of getting your beliefs in line with experience, evidence, and reasons in an ongoing community project. In our efforts to understand reality "each of us is an insurance company" (CP 5. 354; 1868). Logic is rooted in a "social principle," for investigation into what is true is not a private interest but an interest "as wide as the community can turn out to be" (CP 5. 357; 1868). With Wright, Peirce thinks that inquiry must be a democratic, community project, with no prior ring-fencing of what counts as the community.

As Christopher Hookway (2000: 57) has helpfully added, Peirce's argument is that when we assert *p*, we commit ourselves to believing that experience will fall in line with *p or with some successor of it*. We expect that *p, in some form*, will survive the rigors of inquiry. We hope that *p* will prove indefeasible, but what would be undefeated is some refined version of *p*. In this way, an inquirer can assert something she thinks is probably not precisely true.[11]

We have in our various inquiries and deliberations a multiplicity of local aims—empirical adequacy, coherence with other beliefs, simplicity, explanatory power, getting a reliable guide to action, fruitfulness for other research, greater understanding of others, increased maturity, and the like. When we say that we aim at the truth, what we mean is that, were a belief really to satisfy all of our local aims in inquiry, then that belief would be true. There is nothing over and above the fulfillment of those aims, nothing metaphysical, to which we aspire. Truth is not some transcendental, mystical thing and we do not aim at it for its own sake.

---

[11] Meaning, on this view, is preserved over time. The concept of mass, for instance, has undergone significant revision, but we can still think of Newton and today's physicists as referring to the same thing.

3.6 Experience and Reality

In the early 1900s Peirce tries to divert attention from sensory experience and direct it to a broader notion of experience. Experience is that which is compelling, surprising, unchosen, brute, involuntary, or forceful: "anything is...to be classed under the species of perception wherein a positive qualitative content is forced upon one's acknowledgement without any reason or pretension to reason. There will be a wider genus of things *partaking* of the character of perception, if there be any matter of cognition which exerts a force upon us..." (*CP* 7. 623; 1903). This broad conception of experience is clearly going to allow for a criterion of legitimacy that encompasses more than beliefs directly verifiable by the senses.

Peirce's focus on the force of experience arises from his rich theory of categories. He had a number of ways of deriving his categories of Firstness, Secondness, and Thirdness,[12] each of which, he argued, is present in everything that comes before the mind or is experienced. Each category is distinguishable by the Aristotelian/Scholastic method of abstraction or prescission, in which we can distinguish different elements of a concept by attending to those elements, but we cannot actually pull them apart or imagine a situation in which they are isolated. A condensed summary of the clearest derivation of the categories is as follows.

A First is a simple, monadic element—a quality of feeling, an image, or a mere possibility. It is indescribable: "It cannot be articulately thought: assert it, and it has already lost its characteristic innocence...Stop to think of it, and it has flown!" (*CP* 1. 357; 1890). The difficulty of pinning down as an ontological category something that is "a special suchness with some degree of determination" is not lost on Peirce (*CP* 1. 303; 1894). It is perhaps helpful to focus on the idea that Firstness comes first: it is "predominant" in being, in feeling, and in the ideas of life and freedom (*CP* 1. 302; 1894). Even more importantly, given the continuity of Peirce's metaphysics with his logic of relations, a First is singular: "a pure nature...in itself without parts or features, and without embodiment" (*CP* 1. 303; 1894). The First is a relatum prior to any relation, providing the metaphysical stuff to make relations possible. Our experience of the relations between things is a more complex matter.

A Second is a dyadic element: the duality of action and reaction, or brute force. It is the category that "the rough and tumble of life renders most familiarly prominent. We are continually bumping up against hard fact" (*CP* 1. 324; 1903). This bumping up against fact reveals "something within and another something without" (*CP* 2. 84; 1902). But, as with the first category, this is all we can say of our encounters with hard fact. Any interpretation of what we experience takes us into the third category—the triadic realm of experience proper, which involves interpretation, signification, intention, endeavor, and purpose. We cannot say anything about our bumping up against

---

[12] Some of his derivations draw heavily on Kant and others on Aristotle. For a more sustained exposition and explanation of the categories, see Misak (2004 [1991]: 70ff.).

the world without bringing interpretation into play. For as soon as we try to describe our encounters with the world, thought and signs are involved. Any perception that we can think of ourselves as *having* is a perceptual judgment, something that requires, in Peirce's terms, a "theory of interpretation."[13]

He describes what he sees in his study:

> But hold: what I have written down is only an imperfect description of the percept that is forced upon me. I have endeavored to state it in words. In this there has been an endeavor, purpose— something not forced upon me but rather the product of reflection . . . I recognize that there is a percept or flow of percepts very different from anything I can describe or think. What precisely that is, I cannot even tell myself . . . I am forced to content myself not with the fleeting percepts, but with the crude and possibly erroneous thoughts or self-informations, of what the percepts were.
>
> [*CP* 2. 141; 1902]

Everything we experience, Peirce argues, is interpreted and is hence fallible. He is adamant that "going back to the first impressions of sense" "would be the most chimerical of undertakings" (*CP* 2. 141; 1902). "Practically, the knowledge with which I have to content myself, and have to call "the evidence of my senses" instead of being in truth the evidence of the senses, is only a sort of stenographic report of that evidence, possibly erroneous" (*CP* 2. 141; 1902). That is, Peirce does not think that experience gives us something pure or unadulterated. He is clear about this even in 1868, in another of those rare published papers, "Questions Concerning Faculties Claimed for Man," in which he argues that there is no cognition "not determined by a previous cognition" or "by something outside of consciousness" (*CP* 5. 213; 1868). All knowledge is inferential and hence open to error.

As Dorothy Emmet so nicely put it: there is a difference between being brute and stubborn and being bare and naked (1994: 186). Experience can bring our beliefs up short, but it does not give us access to a truth unclothed by human perceptual and cognitive capacities. But neither does "compelling" mean "compelling to me." Peirce tries to make it clear that he is not talking about mere psychological or emotional compulsion when he talks about the force of experience. The emotion of surprise "is merely the instinctive indication of the logical situation. It is evolution . . . that has provided us with the emotion" (*CP* 7. 190; 1901). He wants to distinguish the bruteness of experience from other kinds of compulsions. He asks us to imagine that "the human race like moths had an unconquerable disposition to get into the fire (and some of the dispositions of young men are much like that)." Peirce argues that such a compulsion is merely psychological and would soon bump up against the world. We would find that: "on trying the experiment we should meet with a surprise. Now I think that sound reasoning is constituted by its leading us to believe what will reduce our surprises to a minimum. For sound reasoning seems to me to be reasoning that tends towards the truth as much as possible" (MS 693, p. 162). Clearly, he is trying to

---

[13] *CP* 1. 145; 1897; *CP* 2. 141; 1902; *CP* 5. 54; 1903; *CP* 7. 643; 1903; *CP* 5. 116; 1903; *CP* 5. 568; 1901.

invest the shock of experience with something that is objective. But he sees that you cannot say much more without getting yourself into philosophical trouble.

What we can say, he thinks, is that the fact that we have only our interpretations of what we experience does not throw us into a sea of arbitrary interpretations, where there is no connection to what is real. Our perceptual judgments, Peirce argues, are indices of our percepts—of the actual clash between us and the world. The external world, Peirce says, cannot be described as it "really" is. It can only be denoted by indices (*CP* 4. 530; 1905). These indices "provide positive assurance of reality and of the nearness of their objects" without giving "any insight into the nature of those objects" (*CP* 4. 530; 1905). An interpreter connects the index and its objects by a belief in a causal law. Although the judgment is "unlike" the reality, "it must be accepted as true to that reality" (*CP* 5. 568; 1901).

It is interesting that Peirce thought that Hegel had things right, but for the fact that the Absolute whitewashed out the category of immediacy or Secondness:[14]

The truth is that pragmaticism is closely allied to the Hegelian absolute idealism, from which, however, it is sundered by its vigorous denial that the third category . . . suffices to make the world, or is even so much as self-sufficient. Had Hegel, instead of regarding the first two stages with his smile of contempt, held on to them as independent or distinct elements of the triune Reality, pragmatists might have looked up to him as the great vindicator of their truth.

[*CP* 5. 436; 1904]

Hegel, that is, failed to take seriously the brute clash between perceivers and the world. He needed to be "educated in a physical laboratory instead of in a theological seminary" (*CP* 8. Bibliography; 1893).

Peirce, unlike Hegel (at least, unlike his interpretation of Hegel) thinks that we can know something of the world as it exists independently of us—we can know that it is there and that it constrains us. Peirce turns to the idea that we can be mistaken in order to show that there is an objective truth and that reality that goes beyond what you or I or any collection of people happen to think: "The experience of ignorance, or of error, which we have, and which we gain by means of correcting our errors, or enlarging our knowledge, does enable us to experience and conceive something which is independent of our own limited views" (*CP* 7. 345; 1873).

It may seem that Peirce's assumption that there is a reality independent of beliefs invites the claim that he really holds some kind of correspondence theory of truth. But this would be a mistake, for we shall see that the assumption that there is a reality is one made for the sake of inquiry. If we do not assume that there is a reality, we shall be unable to believe, know, or act. While all of our experiential judgments are fallible and laden with interpretation, they must, in the first instance, be accepted as they come. They are authoritative in that they force themselves upon us without "reason or

---

[14] See Stern (2007) for the argument that Peirce has Hegel wrong and that their views are in fact very similar.

pretension to reason" (*CP* 7. 623; 1903). This forceful element is our link with a reality, with something that goes beyond us: "Now the 'hardness' of fact lies in the insistency of the percept, its entirely irrational insistency, the element of Secondness in it. That is a very important factor of reality" (*CP* 7. 659; 1903).

One thing that we can say about the authority of perceptual judgments is that they are brute and compelling. Another thing we can say is that our perceptual judgments tend not to lead us astray or, when they do lead us astray, we can find explanations for why this is the case. That is, our experiential judgments are authoritative first in that we have no choice but to pay attention to them. They arrive uncritically and uninvited, and then we subject them to reason and scrutiny. When we are careful in evaluating our experiential judgments, they tend not to lead us astray and hence our taking them seriously seems wise as well as necessary.[15]

With this view of experience in hand, we can now turn to how Peirce broadens the range of the experiential. He is not interested in giving us a causal account of knowledge, on which the external world causes us to have perceptions, which then justify our beliefs about the external world. Peirce made a careful change in his terminology in 1907: from the idea that we seek a method of inquiry on which our beliefs are "caused" by nothing human, to the idea that we seek a method of inquiry on which our beliefs are "determined" by nothing human.[16] That subtle shift makes explicit room for a broad account of experience and knowledge that merely gestures at something "on which our thinking has no effect"—something *real* that restricts what can count as knowledge.[17]

3.7 Mathematics, Metaphysics, Religion, and Morals

Peirce was concerned to put forward a broad version of the pragmatic maxim and of experience-driven inquiry. Unlike the logical empiricists who would appear on the American scene in the 1940s, he was not interested in narrowing the scope of the legitimate to the empirical sciences. But like the logical empiricists, he wanted to set out some principles that would allow one to distinguish the empirically legitimate from the illegitimate.

---

[15] For a sustained discussion of this view of experience and its role in critical inquiry, see Misak (2000) and (2004a). See Hookway's "Common Sense, Pragmatism, and Rationality" in Hookway (2000) for an excellent account of how we subject our experiential judgments to rational scrutiny after they arrive uncritically.

[16] See Short (2000), n. 9.

[17] *CP* 5. 384; 1877. This move marks Peirce off from what we shall see is the central idea in Dewey and his followers. Dewey takes the theory of evolution to teach us that our capacities have been selected for survival and hence all our inquiry and all our beliefs are aimed at the organism surviving. Peirce thinks that the theory of evolution tells us, indeed, that our capacities have been selected for survival, but that, nonetheless, we aim at getting beliefs not merely with survival benefits, but beliefs that are independent of human capacities and contexts of inquiry.

His treatment of mathematical and logical beliefs is the most interesting example of how he distinguishes himself from other empiricists. The history of empiricism is littered with attempts to show how mathematical and logical statements need not be made to pass the empiricist test. Hume, for instance argued that the legitimate contents of the mind were either impressions of sense or demonstrative truths. The former are subject to the empiricist criterion but the latter—the truths, for instance, of geometry, algebra, and arithmetic—are not (1975 [1777]: 19–25). We shall see that the logical empiricists follow a similar line of thought: analytically true statements, such as mathematical and logical statements, are meaningful despite their lack of connection to experience. They are true by definition, whereas synthetically true statements are made true by the world.[18] John Stuart Mill was a rare empiricist. He made a serious attempt to have logic and mathematics pass the empiricist test. He was scorned for doing so.

Peirce, with Mill (and we will see, Quine) treats mathematics and logic as one with the rest of genuine inquiry. That is, he was a resolute holist who argued that mathematics and logic are indeed connected to experience in the requisite way. We expect certain things to be the case if they are true. Not only might we have practical bridge-building kinds of expectations using applied mathematics, but even hypotheses in pure mathematics have consequences. They have consequences in diagrammatic contexts. When we manipulate diagrams, we can find ourselves surprised.

Peirce puts considerable effort into trying to get this thought right. In 1905, he suggests that there are two kinds of experience: ideal and real. The latter is sensory experience and the former is experience in which "operations on diagrams, whether external or imaginary, take the place of the experiments upon real things that one performs in chemical and physical research" (*CP* 4. 530; 1905). As early as 1872, this idea already had a central place in his thought. Mathematical and logical inquiry:

involves an element of observation; namely, [it] consists in constructing an icon or diagram the relation of whose parts shall present a complete analogy with those of the parts of the object of reasoning, of experimenting upon this image in the imagination, and of observing the result so as to discover unnoticed and hidden relations among the parts.

(*W* 3: 41; 1872)

The mathematician's "hypotheses are creatures of his own imagination; but he discovers in them relations which surprise him sometimes" (*CP* 5. 567; 1901). This surprise is the force of experience.

Sometimes Peirce distinguishes the two kinds of experience by saying that everyone inhabits two worlds: the inner (or the ideal) and the outer (or the real). We react with the outer world through a clash between it and our senses. We react with the inner world by performing thought experiments. Inquiry, he says, has "two branches; one is inquiry into Outward Fact by experimentation and observation, and is called *Inductive Investigation*; the other is inquiry into Inner Truth by inward experimentation

---

[18] See e.g. Hempel (1964 [1945]: 368).

and observation and is called *Mathematical* or *Deductive* Reasoning" (MS 408, p. 150; 1893–95).

The distinction between these two kinds of experience and two kinds of inquiry is not, however, hard and fast. External facts are simply those that are "ordinarily regarded as external while others are regarded as internal" (*W* 2: 205; 1868). The inner world may exert a comparatively slight compulsion upon us, whereas the outer world is full of irresistible compulsions. Nonetheless, the inner world can also be "unreasonably compulsory" and have "its surprises for us" (*CP* 7. 438; 1893). Peirce intends to leave the difference between these two kinds of experience vague: "We naturally make all our distinctions too absolute. We are accustomed to speak of an external universe and an inner world of thought. But they are merely vicinities, with no real boundary between them" (*CP* 7. 438; 1893). Of course, the trouble with leaving this distinction vague is that vagueness takes the precision out of the criterion. If Peirce is to arrive at a useful maxim or demarcating principle, he will have to say something more about what counts as legitimate internal experience. We shall see in the next chapter that he thought that James got this whole matter wrong. Here we shall see how he tries to manage the issue himself.

Peirce was as keen as Wright to bring philosophy away from spurious metaphysics and into the world of science. He thinks "philosophy is either a science or it is balderdash" and "if philosophy is ever to stand in the ranks of the sciences, literary elegance must be sacrificed—like the soldier's old brilliant uniforms—to the stern requirements of efficiency."[19] If philosophy has consequences for experience, then it is a science.

Peirce worried over what kinds of consequences counted—he worried about what kinds of things we must expect from our beliefs if they are to be legitimate. He amended the pragmatic maxim over the whole of his writing life. We have seen that one significant amendment is that the maxim must be expressed with a subjunctive, not an indicative conditional. Hence the pragmatic meaning of "this diamond is hard" is not "if you scratch it, it will resist," but rather "if you were to scratch it, it would resist." Otherwise, diamonds stuck forever on the ocean floor would not be hard (*CP* 8. 208; 1905). The practical effects that pragmatism is concerned with are those that *would* occur under certain circumstances, not those that *will* actually occur.

As his thoughts settled, he also made amendments regarding the nature of the required practical consequences. In "How to Make Our Ideas Clear" he suggests that they must be consequences for the senses—directly observable effects. But when he reflects on the matter, he is clear that he is not interested in narrowing the scope of the legitimate so severely. We have already seen that his broad conception of experience allows mathematics and logic to be connected to experience. He also thought that some metaphysical inquiry was perfectly acceptable. In metaphysics, "one finds those

---

[19] *CWJ* 12: 172; 1909; *CP* 5. 13; 1907.

questions that at first seem to offer no handle for reason's clutch, but which readily yield to logical analysis" (*CP* 6. 463; 1908). Metaphysics, "in its present condition" is a "puny, rickety, and scrofulous science," but it need not remain so. The pragmatic maxim will sweep "all metaphysical rubbish out of one's house. Each abstraction is either pronounced gibberish or is provided with a plain, practical definition" (*CP* 8. 191; 1904). Peirce was himself something of a metaphysician, putting forward at least two metaphysical doctrines he thought scientifically respectable: tychism and synechism. The former is the view that there is an element of chance in the universe. The latter is that reality is continuous. It is no accident that both these ideas are bound up with probability theory and infinitesimals, for Peirce was deeply engaged in the exact sciences.[20]

Peirce also examined the question whether religious claims meet the test. His answer, though deeply unsatisfactory in the end, tells us much about how his pragmatic maxim is designed to operate. He wants to explore whether there is a place for religion within the scientific world-view. We shall see that the way he tries to reconcile religion and the scientific method speaks loudly to the similarity between Peirce and Wright and to the difference between Peirce and James.

Peirce's attempt is found in his "A Neglected Argument for the Reality of God." Between 1905 and 1908, he struggled mightily with drafts of this essay. He notes that the belief in God has "a commanding influence over the whole conduct of life of its believers" (*CP* 6. 490; 1910). But Peirce does not take what we shall see is James's path. He does not argue that these commanding influences—these conse-quences for the lives of believers—are the sorts of consequences that can support the belief.

We have seen that for Peirce, mathematical and logical statements are about the "ideal" or the "internal" world and hence they require verification in diagrammatic contexts. He sees, though, that the belief that God is real, as it is usually conceived, is a belief about the external or the outer world—God is an existing entity or he is not; Jesus walked the earth or he did not. Hence the belief needs empirical verification of the non-diagrammatic sort. Peirce sets himself the task of showing how the hypothesis asserting the reality of God has consequences and he is resolute that these consequences must be something that can be tested by induction. His idea is that if "God is real" were true, then we would expect a tendency towards "growth" and "habit-taking" in the universe, and we would expect that the universe would be "harmonious." He says that the hypothesis of God's reality is a good explanation of the growth of "motion into displacement" and the growth of "force into motion." This is his neglected argument: the hypothesis of God's reality is a good explanation of some existing phenomenon. It's what Peirce called an abductive inference, or what today gets called an inference to the best explanation.

---

[20] For good accounts of these metaphysical positions, see Reynolds (2002) and Putnam (1995).

The reader may well think that this is a *rightly* neglected argument for God's reality. It is not at all clear *what* we would expect if God were real and it is not at all clear that we would expect what Peirce suggests. Indeed, many have thought that we would expect there to be less gratuitous pain and suffering in the world. Peirce seems to be aware of the difficulties, for each time he begins to talk about "tracing out a few consequences of the hypothesis" he quickly breaks off and changes the subject.[21] But in his 1910 "Additament" to the paper, he simply states: "the doctrine of the *Ens necessarium* has a pragmatist meaning, although I will not here attempt to sum up the whole of its meaning. So far as it has such a meaning, it is verifiable."[22] That is, he boldly asserts that he has shown that the belief has testable empirical consequences, when he has done no such thing. Nonetheless, we shall see that his attempt to find empirical consequences is a mark that distinguishes Peirce from some of his fellow pragmatists.

Peirce thought far less about the role of ethics and politics, but I have argued that he was in principle willing to consider that they might be legitimate domains of deliberation and inquiry.[23] When politicians disagree, he thought, the dispute usually has "some other object than the ascertainment of scientific truth" (*CP* 4. 34; 1893). And sometimes politicians and ethical deliberators might be justifiably hesitant to revise their beliefs. But sometimes truth is at stake and change of belief is justified: "Like any other field, more than any other [morality] needs improvement, advance . . . But morality, doctrinaire conservatist that it is, destroys its own vitality by resisting change, and positively insisting, This is eternally right: That is eternally wrong" (*CP* 2. 198; 1902). Ethical judgments, Peirce thinks, should be brought into the field of inquiry. They are revisable in light of experience: "just as reasoning springs from experience, so the development of sentiment arises from the soul's Inward and Outward Experiences" (*CP* 1. 648; 1898). As with every other kind of experience, "[t]hat it is abstractly and absolutely infallible we do not pretend; but that it is practically infallible for the individual—which is the only clear sense the word "infallibility" will bear . . . *that* we do maintain" (*CP* 1. 633; 1898).

My interpretation of Peirce on this matter has its detractors. Peirce sometimes stated that "vital" or ethical matters are not amenable to reason and experiences. Unlike the scientist, who can wait generations for an answer, in ethics we need to act immediately. Hence we do and should go on instinct. I have argued that we should not take these assertions that ethics must be exiled from inquiry too seriously. For one thing, "instinct" is for Peirce simply a way of paying attention to the experience that impinges upon us.[24] Ethical deliberation is a legitimate kind of inquiry, aimed at getting things right, and part of ethical inquiry is going on one's internal experience, feeling or instinct that *A* is right or *B* is wrong.

There is a telling background to which we must also pay heed. The paper in which Peirce most clearly asserts that reasoning and experience are out of place in ethics is his

---

[21] See for instance MS 842, p. 127.   [22] MS 844, last page. See also *CP* 6. 491; 1910.
[23] See Misak (2004b).   [24] See Misak (2004b: 158–60).

"Vitally Important Topics" (*CP* 5. 616–61; 1898). In 1897, James's strenuous efforts to secure Peirce some kind of job at Harvard were coming to grief, President Eliot being adamantly against it. James wrote to Peirce: "I regret to say that there is *no* chance whatever of *any* University appointment for you here. I have been active in your behalf lately, and have come to that permanent conclusion. You must divert your attention from this institution" (*CWJ* 8: 323; 1897). But James had "another scheme on the tapis which may bear fruit"—a course of lectures for Peirce to give in Cambridge (*CWJ* 8: 324; 1897). James had gone begging for subscriptions, noting to potential subscribers that it would be a shame if Peirce died without getting his thoughts down on paper (*CWJ* 8: 606, 607; 1897). The one thing he asks of Peirce in these lectures is for "not too much logical or mathematical technics" (*CWJ* 8: 324; 1897).

Peirce, no doubt bitterly disappointed at the Harvard door shutting with such finality, is nonetheless grateful to James, saying that arranging for these lectures is "an achievement more amazing than the Principles of Psychology" (*CWJ* 8: 325; 1897). Nonetheless, he puts together a plan for a highly technical set of lectures on logic. James, his patience and goodwill being taxed, writes back sharply:

I am sorry you are sticking so to formal logic. I know our graduate school here, and so does Royce, and we both agree that there are only 3 men who could possibly follow your graphs and relatives. . . . Now be a good boy and think a more popular plan out . . . . You are teeming with ideas—and the lectures need not by any means form a continuous whole. Separate topics of a vitally important character would do perfectly well.

[*CWJ* 8: 326; 1897]

He also writes that the subscribers to this lecture series "*cannot be known*" and that half of the subscription revenues must be paid to Peirce's wife, "*ten dollars a week*," until $450 is exhausted (emphases James). Clearly, things were not going well for Peirce. He was irresponsible with whatever money he managed to get his hands on; he was on the verge of losing his house; he could no longer afford to heat it. James had clearly got some charity subscribers to contribute to his lecture series and was going to eek out the subscription money to Peirce's wife so that bills would be paid.

Peirce was hurt and furious. He had already put together the lectures he thought interesting and important and in a fit of ill temper he agreed to James's demand that he rewrite the lectures so that they are on "vital" matters:

I will begin again, and will endeavor to write out some of the "ideas" with which I am supposed to be "teeming" on "separate topics of vital importance." I feel I shall not do it well; because in spite of myself I shall betray my sentiments about such "ideas"; but being paid to do it, I will do it as well as I possibly can. After all, I have no reason to distress myself that my philosophy does not get expounded. Your Harvard students of philosophy find it too arduous a matter to reason exactly. Soon your engineers will find it better to leave great works unbuilt rather than go through the necessary calculations.

[*CWJ* 8: 330; 1897]

The last line of the letter is "The audience had better go home and say their prayers I am thinking" (*CWJ* 8: 331; 1897). Peirce was in a volatile mood. These lectures and the account of vital matters he gives in them must be taken with a grain of salt. Peirce was giving the audience what he was ordered to give them.

3.8 Abduction, Deduction, Induction

Peirce conceived of himself first and foremost as a logician. He says that the English logician and economist Jevons (along with Boole, Whewell, Berkeley, Glanville, Ockham, and Duns Scotus) would capture "the purpose of my memoirs." That purpose is "to lay a solid foundation upon which may be erected a new logic fit for the life of twentieth century science" (*CP* 7. 161; 1902). It is hard to overestimate the place that logic had in Peirce's philosophy. One of his major criticisms of the work others is that it suffers from a lack of logical acumen. Kant manifests "a most astounding ignorance of the traditional logic" (*CP* 1. 560; 1907); Hegel is "decidedly weak" in logic (*CP* 1. 453; 1896); and James has an "almost unexampled incapacity for mathematical thought" (*CP* 6. 182; 1911).

"Logic," for Peirce, is very broad. Sometimes he described it as "the doctrine of truth, its nature and the manner in which it is to be discovered" (*W* 3: 14; 1872). He was forever outlining proposals for a grand book of logic that had at its center the study of inquiry aimed at the truth. This is not how logic is understood today. But Peirce was also a brilliant logician in the current meaning of that word. He invented a quantified first-order logic with a diagrammatic proof system independently of and at the same time as Frege and he discovered the Sheffer stroke decades before Sheffer. He also made lasting advances in the logic of statistical reasoning. As Alan Richardson says, Peirce "serves notice that the central topic of logic or scientific method for him and his successors will be the logic of statistical reasoning, a logic that stands in complicated relations to concepts like individual causation" (2008: 346).

Those who knew of his work in logic, both deductive and statistical, were suitably impressed. The mathematician and logician W. K. Clifford thought him to be "the greatest living logician, and the second man since Aristotle who has added to the subject something material." John Venn says: "Mr. C. S. Peirce's name is so well known to those who take an interest in the development of Boolean or symbolic treatment of Logic that the knowledge that he was engaged in lecturing upon the subject to advance classes at the Johns Hopkins University will have been an assurance that some interesting contributions to the subject might soon be looked for" (1883: 594).

One of Peirce's great contributions to logic, however, is not the formal kind. He identifies a third mode of reasoning, in addition to deduction and induction, along the way coming to a deeply interesting answer to the problem of induction so famously set by Hume. Peirce calls his third kind of reasoning "abductive inference" (he sometimes calls it "retroductive inference" or "hypothesis"). It is fundamentally *creative.*[25] It goes beyond what the positivist tradition, even in Peirce's time, restricted itself to: it sees beyond the reports of sensations and what can be built upon them via formal deductive reasoning.

Abduction, like induction (which includes for Peirce both inference from observed instances to unobserved instances and statistical inference) is ampliative. It amplifies what is in the premises, unlike deduction, which explicates what is in the premises. But only abduction can potentially import new ideas into our body of belief. It takes the form:

The surprising fact, C, is observed;
But if A were true, C would be a matter of course.
Hence, there is reason to suspect that A is true.

[*CP* 5. 189; 1903]

Something very like this now gets called inference to the best explanation. It is "the process of forming an explanatory hypothesis." Such a hypothesis is not one that we can assert as true. The conclusions of abductive inferences are mere conjectures—we must "hold ourselves ready to throw them overboard at a moment's notice from experience" (*CP* 1. 634; 1898). "Abduction commits us to nothing. It merely causes a hypothesis to be set down upon our docket of cases to be tried" (*CP* 5. 602; 1903).

Peirce debated with Paul Carus, the editor of *The Open Court* and *The Monist*, about when an explanation is called for. Carus was of the view that an irregularity demands an explanation, but Peirce's retort was that no one "is surprised that the trees in a forest do not form a regular pattern, or asks for any explanation of such a fact" (*CP* 7. 189; 1901). On Peirce's view, irregularity is "the overwhelming preponderant rule of experience, and regularity only the strange exception." Only an unexpected regularity or the breach of an expected regularity calls for an explanation.

Peirce takes the first step in the scientific method to be an abductive inference. A hypothesis or a conjecture is identified that explains some surprising experience— some strange exception. Consequences are then deduced from this hypothesis and are tested by induction. If the hypothesis passes the test of experience, then it is accepted— it is stable and believed until upset by a new surprising experience. The scientific method thus proceeds by abduction-deduction-induction. Peirce thinks that because abduction and induction both add to our knowledge, "some logicians have confounded them." But he is clear that he means to describe the two types of inference as separate stages of scientific inquiry (*W* 3: 330; 1878). Peirce's account of scientific method—the method that puts in place a settled belief—is tripartite.

Peirce is silent about Hume's problem of induction. His philosophical sparring partner, Chauncey Wright, was certainly very interested in both Hume and Mill on induction, taking Mill's account of induction to be his most important contribution, amongst many, to logic.[26] And Peirce certainly thought about Hume on the related

---

[25] Richardson (2008: 346) uses this term. It is exactly right.
[26] See Wright (1873b).

topic of the uniformity of nature, arguing in support of Hume that we have no evidence for the principle that nature is uniform. We have seen that he thinks that "Nature," "is not regular . . . It is true that the special laws and regularities are innumerable; but nobody thinks of the irregularities, which are infinitely more frequent" (*W* 2: 264; 1869). Even if nature were uniform, adding a major premise stating that fact would not be the right way to attempt to justify inductive inference. Inductive inference "needs no such dubious support" (*CP* 6. 100; 1901). For Peirce, it is their ampliative power that makes both induction and abduction justified. They are irreplaceable and essential kinds of reasoning.

There is, however, much that we can extract from Peirce about the problem Hume posed for induction. Hume had delivered a devastating argument to show that the move from "all observed *A*'s are *B*'s" to "All *A*'s are *B*'s" is not valid. Peirce will have thought that his fallibilism and critical commonsensism skirted Hume's problem. There is only a problem there if you are looking for certainty. He argues that this kind of inductive inference (what he called a "crude induction") is a weak form of inference that can be overturned by a single experience. We do, and should, believe that the sun will rise tomorrow, yet it might not. Peirce has no interest in showing that induction delivers us certainty. He tells Lady Welby (unfairly to Hume) that Hume's mistake is that he is a deductivist trying to get too much out of induction.[27] Peirce is interested in whether induction is a reliable part of inquiry. While deduction merely allows us to apply known rules, induction allows us to discover what is unknown, and it is this possibility of discovery that causes Peirce—a practising scientist—to view induction as an indispensible form of inference. His attention turns to the reliability of statistical inference, as opposed to whether induction is a form of inference that blesses its conclusion with guarantees.

I will not go into his many significant contributions to the topic of statistical inference here, but will instead flag that when in Part III we turn to Nelson Goodman's brilliant reshaping of Hume's problem, we shall see how Peirce's account of abductive inference allows us to see our way through the problem of induction. The seemingly unsolvable problem of induction disintegrates once we acknowledge that regularities abound, but only some of them want explanations. Only unexpected or surprising regularities make a demand on us to make an inference to the best explanation. Once that work is done by abductive reasoning, then the job of induction is to test those abductive hypotheses. Peirce, that is, reframed the problem of induction as the problem of when abductively arrived-at hypotheses should be the ones selected for inductive testing. He reframed the problem as the problem of deciding which abductive inferences are good. His own suggestions were along the lines that we should choose hypotheses that bring "the most facts under a single formula" (*CP* 7. 410); that

---

[27] In a letter dated 1911 May 20, p. 43 Peirce tells her that "all the old metaphysicians such as Hume support their skepticism by virtually assuming . . . that the only kind of valid inference is deductive" (1953 [1911]: 43). See Misak (2004 [1991]: 111ff.) for a more complete account of Peirce on induction.

we should choose simple hypotheses (*CP* 5. 60); and that we should construct our hypotheses so that they actually explain the surprising observations we have before us (*CP* 7. 202).[28]

3.9 Regulative Assumptions

Abductive inference rests on what Peirce calls a regulative assumption of inquiry. We assume that whenever we observe *C*, there will be some hypothesis *A* that entails *C* or makes *C* probable—we assume that there is an explanation for our surprising observations. This is but one place in Peirce's thought where we find the idea of a regulative assumption of inquiry doing some heavy lifting. While many of our regulative assumptions will be experimental, temporary hypotheses, and likely to be modified or rejected, some regulative assumptions are more stable or more essential to the very activity of inquiry and knowing.

In order to understand just how important the idea of a regulative assumption is in Peirce's thought, we need to turn to the assumption about which he is most expansive. Peirce understands that he needs to answer a question that every pragmatist must face. He puts it thus:

> But I may be asked what I have to say to all the minute facts of history, forgotten never to be recovered, to the lost books of the ancients, to the buried secrets . . . Do these things not really exist because they are hopelessly beyond the reach of our knowledge?
>
> [*W* 3: 274, 1878]

His answer is that it is a regulative assumption of inquiry that, for any matter into which we are inquiring, we would find an answer to the question that is pressing in on us. Otherwise, it would be pointless to inquire into the issue: "the only assumption upon which [we] can act rationally is the hope of success" (*W* 2: 272; 1869). Thus the principle of bivalence—for any *p*, *p* is either true or false—rather than being a law of logic, is a regulative assumption of inquiry. It is something that we have to assume if we are to inquire into a matter.

Peirce is clear and explicit on this point. To say that bivalence is a regulative assumption of inquiry is not a claim about special logical status (that it is a logical truth); nor is it a claim that it is true in some plainer sense; nor is it a claim about the nature of the world (that the world is such that the principle of bivalence holds). The principle of bivalence, he says, is taken by logicians to be a law of logic by a "saltus"—by an unjustified leap (*NE* 4: xiii). He distinguishes his approach from that of the transcendentalist:

> when we discuss a vexed question, we *hope* that there is some ascertainable truth about it, and that the discussion is not to go on forever and to no purpose. A transcendentalist would claim that it is an indispensible "presupposition" that there is an ascertainable true answer to every intelligible

---

[28] See Misak (1991 [2004]: 98ff.) for a summary of this work.

question. I used to talk like that, myself; for when I was a babe in philosophy my bottle was filled from the udders of Kant. But by this time I have come to want something more substantial.

[CP 2. 113; 1902]

Indispensability arguments of the Kantian kind were frequently employed in the late nineteenth century. Royce, for instance, is very fond of them. But Peirce was clear that not only should the fact that an assumption is indispensable to our practice of inquiry not convince us of its necessary truth, it should not even convince us of its truth. He says: "I do not admit that indispensability is any ground of belief. It may be indispensible that I should have $500 in the bank—because I have given checks to that amount. But I have never found that the indispensability directly affected my balance, in the least" (CP 2. 113; 1902, see also CP 3. 432; 1896). We must make these assumptions "for the same reason that a general who has to capture a position or see his country ruined, must go on the hypothesis that there is some way in which he can and shall capture it" (CP 7. 219; 1901).

Peirce's view is that "we are obliged to suppose, but we need not assert," that there are determinate answers to our questions. A regulative assumption is a claim about inquiry and what those engaged in inquiry must assume. To make a regulative assumption is to make a statement about a practice and what that practice requires in order to be comprehensible and in order to be sensibly carried out. His argument is that if we are to inquire rationally about some particular issue, then we must assume that there is at least a chance of there being an upshot to our inquiry. And we need also to assume that there is a truth in matters that currently, for one reason or another, are beyond the reach of our investigations.

We have seen that Peirce also thinks that we must assume that there is a reality independent of our beliefs about it and that there is an explanation for what we observe. In "The Fixation of Belief," he states that a "fundamental hypothesis" is taken for granted in inquiry or in the method of science. That hypothesis is that "there are real things whose characters are both independent of our beliefs about them," and can be discovered through empirical investigation (W 3: 254; 1877).

Refusing to make such essential assumptions is to block the path of inquiry and, in Peirce's books, that is the cardinal philosophical sin. Our reason for making the assumptions is driven, Peirce says, by "desperation." If we do not make them, we will "be quite unable to know anything of positive fact" (CP 5. 603; 1903). Faced with an assumption without which we cannot continue in a practice of utmost importance, we must embrace it, "however destitute of evidentiary support it may be" (CP 7. 219; 1901). He says:

The sole immediate purpose of thinking is to render things intelligible; and to think and yet in that very act to think a thing unintelligible is a self-stultification. It is as though a man furnished with a pistol to defend himself against an enemy were, on finding that enemy very redoubtable, to use his pistol to blow his own brains out to escape being killed by his enemy. Despair is insanity.... We must therefore be guided by the rule of hope...

[CP 1. 405]

The fact that Peirce thinks of indispensability arguments in such a modest,[29] low profile way distinguishes him from some of his pragmatist successors.[30] He has no grandiose plans for this mode of argument: "I am not one of those transcendental apothecaries, as I call them—they are so skilful in making up a bill—who call for a quantity of big admissions, as indispensible *Voraussetzungen* of logic" (*CP* 2. 113; 1902). As Hookway puts Peirce's point, "to show that a belief is unavoidable for us gives us no reason to believe that it is true" but it provides a strong reason for hoping that it is true and for regarding it as legitimate in our search for knowledge (1999: 181). We shall see, in what immediately follows, that the treatment of indispensability, or human need, is also part what distinguishes Peirce's work from that of his friend William James.

---

[29] I somehow came to Chris Hookway's "Modest Transcendental Arguments" (Hookway 1999) after I wrote this chapter and after I wrote "American Pragmatism and Indispensability Arguments" (Misak 2012). I am sure that his views nonetheless shaped mine, since I have been learning from him for almost thirty years.

[30] See Habermas (1990a) and Apel (1990).

4

William James (1842–1910)

4.1 Introduction

After giving up early thoughts of being a painter, William James trained as a scientist—in chemistry, anatomy, and physiology—and then went to medical school. He had difficulty settling down and deciding on the shape of his life. When all was said and done, he was the father of modern psychology and the face of American pragmatism for both philosophers and the wider public. While Peirce and Wright died without leaving a major mark on journals or having a significant impact on the next generation of students, James registered on every part of American intellectual life. He had a tremendous influence on his students and colleagues—he was supportive, full of good advice, open, warm, generous, and engaging. He wrote beautifully and many of his expressions are still ingrained in our philosophical consciousness. He was widely published, widely translated, and in his time, he was America's most famous academic. He is still revered in psychology.

James thought that Peirce was the archetype of a "technical" philosopher taken with mathematical logic, and he makes it clear that he is not interested in being such a thinker. At the beginning of his famous *Pragmatism*, James says: "the philosophy which is so important to each of us is not a technical matter; it is our more or less dumb sense of what life honestly and deeply means" (1975 [1907]: 9). James wanted to get his views across to the educated public. He was hugely successful—his ideas were discussed extensively in the magazines and literature of the day. He wrote crisply and was a pleasure to read. The less successful aspect of this way of proceeding was that it tended to blur the subtleties of the point he was trying to make. Indeed, some of his contemporaries objected to the very project of trying to reach a popular audience. In his rather bad-tempered (and generally bad) *Anti-Pragmatism*,[1] Albert Schinz rants: "Popular science, popular art, popular theology—only one thing was lacking—popular philosophy. And now they give that to us. What a triumph for a weak cause!" (Schinz 1909: xvi).

To further complicate the interpretation of James's philosophy, he moves frequently, if not altogether easily, from one version of pragmatism to the other. He sometimes puts forward the Peircean position that truth is what is really indefeasible

---

[1] Dewey quite rightly savages the book in a review. See *MW* 4: 245–49; 1909.

and that the world constrains our beliefs. But he can also frequently be found suggesting that widely variable and local human experience is all we have to go on when it comes to belief and truth. We shall see that it is this latter version of James that influenced the trajectory of American pragmatism and came under fire from Peirce and other contemporaries.

James's allies tried to modify his tendency toward popular expression and what they viewed as his excess. His friend Howison chides him: "How *could* you put down in cold and permanent print the bagatelle diatribes about 'Hegelisms' and what not?"[2] Santayana recalls his teacher as being "short-winded in argument" (1944: 242). Chauncey Wright captures his "interest" in James as follows: "He rather attracts me by the Jamesian traits; crude and extravagant as are many of his opinions, and more especially his language. Perhaps the attraction is at bottom the opportunities afforded by such a temperament to display the greater effectiveness of a more even one . . . "[3] His friend and colleague Royce uses the same term: "A man's personal tone is his own. Yours is a most effective one."[4] The trouble is such popular efficacy, we shall see, was not always good for the fortunes of pragmatism.

Since I am tracing the trajectory of American pragmatism in this book, it will be my duty to get James's cruder and extravagant account of truth on the page along with nods to his more careful view. Henry Jackman (1999, 2008) and Robert Schwartz (2012) are two of many who put James in his best light and the reader should turn to them, as well as to James's own "The Moral Philosopher and the Moral Life," to see the more sophisticated James.

4.2 Psychology and Radical Empiricism

James's 1890 *Principles of Psychology* remains a classic. It may be the most important book in the whole of the history of psychology, not only demarcating psychology off from philosophy[5] but making points that are still fruitful and important today. James puts forward an empiricist position on which states of consciousness must be explained by psychological laws that are verifiable (1981 [1890] 1: 182). Psychology must be empirical if it is "to be clear, and to avoid unsafe hypotheses" (1981 [1890] 1: 182). But James manages to make this empiricism a non-atomistic, non-reductive account of mental states. The chapter on Conceptions in *The Principles of Psychology* is especially important, in that it destroyed the Scottish Critical Commonsense position that the principles of the mind are infallibly drawn from intuition. James suggests that we replace vague talk of "concepts" with talk of "conceptions," which are "neither the mental state nor what the mental state signifies, but the relation[s] between the two"

---

[2] For a discussion of James versus the Hegelians, see Perry (1976 [1935]): 714, 715, 773. The original letters cited by Perry can be found at *CWJ* 5: 181–82; 1881, *CWJ* 5: 226; 1882, *CWJ* 7: 133; 1871.

[3] Quoted in Madden (1963: 45).

[4] Quoted in Perry (1976 [1935]: 820–1).   [5] See Klein (2008).

(1981 [1890] 1: 436). Notice the similarity between this thought and Peirce's categories—the founders of pragmatism were all trying to show how we cannot pull apart what is signified from the signification of it. James also joins Peirce in arguing that the nature of the relations established by the faculties of the mind is to be inquired into in the same way as any other hypothesis about the human body or any other natural phenomenon. We have no infallible introspective analysis of them (1981 [1890] 1: 191).

On James's view, the way we discover psychological laws is through observation of our own mental states—"the looking into our own minds and reporting what we there discover" (1981 [1890] 1: 185).[6] He thinks that Locke and Hume have taken the study of personal identity "out of the clouds" and turned it into an empirical, verifiable science (1981 [1890] 1: 186, 319). We can *study* feelings and thoughts (1981 [1890] 1: 185–86). Like his empiricist predecessors, James has an unwavering commitment to the method of observation. All inquiry must begin with and then stick to experience. James calls himself a "radical empiricist" and we shall see that the term "radical" is apt. But the less radical "postulate" of the position is this: "the only things that shall be debatable among philosophers shall be things definable in terms drawn from experience" (1975 [1909]: 6).

But while the empiricists might have got the methodology right, James thinks they were mistaken about the very nature of consciousness. Ideas are not discrete and divisible entities, as Hume would have us believe and "[c]omplex mental states" are not "resultants of the self-compounding of simpler ones," as Mill and Wundt would have us believe.[7] Consciousness, rather, is a stream of thought, which cannot be broken up into individual parts. James's theory of consciousness foreshadows some of the most important insights of contemporary neuropsychology and current thoughts about the plasticity of the brain.[8] "Experience," James says, "is remoulding us every moment"; "the brain redistributions are in infinite variety" (1981 [1890] 1: 228–29).

James's empiricism can be fully understood only against the position he wants to discredit—the metaphysics of idealism, or monism, or absolutism that was popular not just in America, but in England as well. James takes himself to be arguing against the absolute idealism of Bradley in Oxford and Royce at Harvard—the view that there is one overarching or all-absorbing mind or unitary consciousness which includes everything else that exists.[9] As Arthur Lovejoy puts it in 1920, James's pragmatism is

---

[6] See Klein (2009), though, for the argument that James does not rely exclusively on simple observation as the empirical methodology for studying the mind.

[7] 1981 [1890]: xlviii; 1977 [1909]: 85. See Roth (1993) for an extended discussion of British empiricism and American pragmatism. See Klein (2009) for the additional point that that although James's insistence on seeing experience as indivisible is aimed at denying a view that is central to British empiricism, it is also aimed at Helmholtz's view that there are atom-like entities called "sensations" that are intermediaries between brain states and full-blown experience.

[8] For the currency of James's views, see Taylor (1996).

[9] Peirce was less concerned with contrasting his position with idealism—indeed, he at times asserted that his view of truth and knowledge was a kind of idealism with the external world added in.

set against the view that the world is pre-determined (Lovejoy 1920a: 192). James characterizes his opponent as follows:

For monism the world is no collection, but one great all-inclusive fact outside of which is nothing ... When the monism is idealistic, this all-enveloping fact is represented as an absolute mind that makes the partial facts by thinking them, just as we make objects in a dream by dreaming them ... To *be*, on this scheme, is, on the part of a finite thing, to be an object for the absolute; and on the part of the absolute, it is to be the thinker of that assemblage of objects.

[1977 [1909]: 21]

This passage is from the 1909 Hibbert Lectures, delivered in Oxford. The lectures are an attack on what James took to be the "vicious intellectualism" or absolute idealism rampant there. Radical empiricism is offered as the alternative and James expressly aligns that alternative with the humanism being promoted, with not much success, at Oxford by his follower F. C. S. Schiller. "Reduced to their most pregnant difference," empiricism, he says, is the habit of explaining wholes by parts, and idealism is the habit of explaining parts by wholes (1977 [1909]: 9). His general complaint about idealists is as follows:

[P]hilosophers have always aimed at cleaning up the litter with which the world is apparently filled. They have substituted economical and orderly conceptions for the first sensible tangle; and whether these were morally elevated or only intellectually neat, they were at any rate always aesthetically pure and definite, and aimed at ascribing to the world something clean and intellectual in the way of an inner structure.

[1977 [1909]: 26]

This quest for tidiness leads one astray. It encourages misguided dichotomies: we either have to "choose the complete disunion of all things or their complete union in the Absolute One"; "the whole complete block-universe through-and-through ... or no universe at all"; complete inter-connectedness of experience or reality unrelated and unconnected monads—"absolute chaos" (1977 [1909]: 30, 33). This breaking down of false dichotomies will remain one of the marks of pragmatism as it moves through subsequent generations of philosophers.

James's radical empiricism does more than merely assert that idealism rests on a false distinction. It also tries to answer idealism's charge. Despite the fact he is convinced that idealism is on the wrong path, James thinks that it does present a real challenge for traditional British empiricism. If, as the traditional empiricist would have us believe, perceptions are discrete and separable, if there are no connections between them, then it is hard to see how we bring them together as coherent experiences. It is also hard to see how we represent what is outside the mind.

James's aim is to make sense of the world and the way we experience and represent it without exerting a viselike grip. He wants to leave room for freedom and creativity on our part, as we partly make the world. Part of his argument is to reject the "mental atoms" brand of empiricism and appeal to the idea that experience is continuous.

Sensations, he argues, contain a "relational element" (1977 [1909]: 125). These relations between sensations are "just as immediately given" as are the individual sensations themselves. Sensations are not isolated atoms, but are part of the "sensational flux" (1977 [1909]: 126). "Inwardly they [experiences of sensations] are one with their parts, and outwardly they pass continuously into their next neighbors... Their *names* to be sure, cut them into separate conceptual entities, but no cuts existed in the continuum in which they originally came" (1977 [1909]: 129).

It is an allied point, made in 1904,[10] that does most of the work for James. On his account of experience, there is no hard-and-fast distinction between the unknown reality and the knowing consciousness; between objective matter and subjective mind. There is only "pure experience" which functions both as reality and as consciousness. He explains: "This very desk which I strike with my hand strikes in turn your eyes. It functions at once as a physical object in the outer world and as a mental object in our sundry mental worlds" (1977 [1909]: 120). Reality and experience, like consciousness, are continuous.

The "intellectualist" position that our only access to the world is through our concepts is misguided. Bergson, with his account of continuity, is on the right path in "remanding us to the sensation life" and the "attempt to limit the divine right of concepts to rule our mind absolutely" (1977 [1909]: 118, 125). Peirce, we have seen, also remands us to the sensation life. Brute experience gives us indexical access to the world. James calls such brute experience "the real units of our immediately felt life" (1977 [1909]: 129). On James's view, just as in Peirce's, sensation, experience, or the immediately felt life provides us with a connection to that which exists apart from us. Then what we do is "*harness up* reality in our conceptual systems in order to drive it the better" (1977 [1909]: 111). We cannot, however, harness up reality in a way that accurately represents it.

4.3 The Pragmatic Maxim and Truth as Usefulness

Although James occasionally speaks to a theory of meaning that underpins his pragmatic maxim,[11] nowhere does he work out the details in the sustained way Peirce did. But like Wright and Peirce, James thinks that the pragmatic maxim will make short work of many long-standing and seemingly intractable philosophical problems. Here is one way he puts it in *Pragmatism*: "If no practical difference whatever can be traced, then the alternatives mean practically the same thing, and all dispute is idle" (1975 [1907]: 28). The best-known of his snapshots is as follows:

---

[10] See his "Does 'Consciousness' Exist?" (1976 [1904a]: 3–20) and "A World of Pure Experience" (1976 [1904b]: 21–44).

[11] See his 1975 [1909]: 284.

There can *be* no difference anywhere that doesn't *make* a difference elsewhere—no difference in abstract truth that doesn't express itself in a difference in concrete fact and in conduct consequent upon that fact, imposed on somebody, somehow, somewhere, and somewhen.

[1975 [1907]: 30]

Lingering in the background is Peirce's "How to Make our Ideas Clear"—James's idea that there can be no difference in abstract thought that fails to make a concrete difference mirrors Peirce's idea that something "tangible and practical" must be at "the root of every real distinction of thought."

But James's next sentence is regrettable and compounds the infelicity of Peirce's notorious slogan. "The whole function of philosophy," James says, "ought to be to find out what definite difference it will make to you and me, at definite instants of our life, if this world-formula or that world-formula be the true one" (1975 [1907]: 30). Not only does James put the maxim in the indicative rather than the subjunctive mood, but his reference to "you and me" proves disastrous.

In his view, the pragmatic maxim ought to "be expressed more broadly than Mr. Peirce expresses it" (1975 [1907]: 258–59). The "ultimate test for us of what a truth means is indeed the conduct it dictates or inspires . . . . I should prefer to express Peirce's principle by saying that the effective meaning of any philosophic proposition can always be brought down to some particular consequence, in our future practical experience" (James 1975 [1898]: 124). His way of distinguishing himself from Peirce is to highlight the consequence a belief might make to a *particular* individual. The difference a concept might make to "you and me, at definite instants of our life" is highly variable.

When James applies this more broadly expressed pragmatic maxim to the concept of truth, it is not surprising that he arrives at a more expansive account of truth. We shall see that at times James comes close to articulating a view very similar to Peirce's. At times, that is, he clearly distinguishes between a stable truth and the temporary "truths" that we live with here and now. But he certainly was inclined more often than not to blur this distinction.

James sets out his view on truth and objectivity thus: "Any idea upon which we can ride . . . any idea that will carry us prosperously from any one part of our experience to any other part, linking things satisfactorily, working securely, simplifying, saving labor, is . . . true *instrumentally*" (1975 [1907]: 34). "Satisfactorily," for James, "means more satisfactorily to ourselves, and individuals will emphasize their points of satisfaction differently. To a certain degree, therefore, everything here is plastic" (1975 [1907]: 35). Here we see the individuality or subjectivity built into James's version of the pragmatic maxim manifest itself in his account of truth. Sometimes he puts his position as follows: "True ideas are those that we can assimilate, validate, corroborate and verify";[12] "truth *happens* to an idea" (1975 [1907]: 97).

---

[12] Emphasis in original omitted.

We shall see that it is this kind of statement of pragmatism that inspired so much vitriol. George Bernard Shaw, for instance, said of it: "the weakness of Pragmatism is that most theories will work if you put your back into making them work" (1921: lxxxvii). There is an important point underneath the humor here. The pragmatist needs to distinguish a belief's working from our thinking that it works. Peirce was so disconcerted by how some versions of pragmatism failed in this regard that, in 1905, he made the following radical move. The term "pragmatism":

gets abused in the merciless way that words have to expect when they fall into literary clutches.... So then, the writer, finding his bantling "pragmatism" so promoted, feels that it is time to kiss his child good-by and relinquish it to its higher destiny; while to serve the precise purpose of expressing the original definition, he begs to announce the birth of the word "pragmaticism", which is ugly enough to be safe from kidnappers.

[*CP* 5. 414; 1905]

"Pragmaticism" should be used in a narrow sense—for his position only—and "'prag-matism' should hereafter be used somewhat loosely to signify affiliation with Schiller, James, Dewey, Royce, and the rest of us" (*CP* 8. 205; 1905). But of course, the term is indeed so ugly that it never caught on.

A few words of caution are required. First, a careful reading of James shows that sometimes when he asserts that truth is "plastic," what he is quite clearly talking about is not truth, but what we *take* to be true. In *Pragmatism* he says "the great assumption of the intellectualists is that truth means essentially an inert static relation. When you've got your true idea of anything, there's an end of the matter. You're in possession; you *know*; you have fulfilled your thinking destiny" (1975 [1907]: 96). James, with Peirce, wants to correct this mistaken assumption. When you have a settled, well-grounded belief, you don't *know*; you don't have an end to the matter. Inquiry might well overturn your belief. Despite his sometimes infelicitous wording, James is at times simply making the fallibilist point that any of our beliefs could be shown to be false.

Second, James at his best makes it clear that he was concerned to characterize truth as something that was of human value, without making a true belief what this or that human finds valuable at this or that time. He sometimes tries to correct what he takes to be a misunderstanding of his position by arguing that, contrary to his critics, he holds that the true is "the expedient," but the expedient "in the long run and on the whole, of course" (1975 [1909]: 4). That is, when James is being most careful, he too wants to argue that true beliefs are beliefs that survive because they deserve to survive, not because they happen to survive for this or that person.[13] At his best, he wants to argue that we need to start with inquiry and extract an account of stable truth from it. Like Peirce, he thinks that any account of truth that would ignore the role that truth plays in inquiry would be an empty view. For instance, to those absolutists who throw objections at James, he lands the following blow: "Well, my dear antagonist, I hardly

[13] See Kappy Suckiel (1982: 105–15).

hoped to convert an eminent intellectualist and logician like you; so enjoy, as long as you live, your own ineffable conception" (1975 [1909]: 159).

In *Pragmatism*, he offers us a clutch of metaphors for this naturalist account of inquiry and growth of knowledge. One of them likens the change in belief to house renovations: "You may alter your house *ad libitum*, but the ground plan of the first architect persists—you can make great changes, but you cannot change a Gothic church into a Doric temple" (1975 [1907]: 83). Another ties the growth of knowledge to a different kind of human contingency: "You may rinse and rinse the bottle, but you can't get the taste of the medicine or whisky that first filled it wholly out" (1975 [1907]: 83). All of his metaphors have the pragmatist theme that "we patch and tinker"— "knowledge grows in *spots*" or in a piecemeal fashion (1975 [1907]: 82–83). All of his metaphors cohere with Peirce's: the inquirer is standing on a bog and only moves forward when the ground underneath him begins to give way. We start from where we find ourselves in inquiry and move forward from there, laden with beliefs and frameworks that were put in place by previous generations of inquirers.

In one of James's *Talks to Students*, titled "On a Certain Blindness in Human Beings," he remarks: "We are practical beings, each of us with limited functions and duties to perform" (1983 [1899]: 132). The emphasis on individual human fallibility is a hallmark of pragmatism—we have seen the role it plays in Peirce's account of inquiry, and how it motivates him to conceive of truth as the product of human inquiry in the long run. But again, James adds to Peirce that we must pay attention to the significance that each of us places upon our own particular actions (1983 [1899]: 132). The emphasis on the individual, whose limits constrain his own pursuit of knowledge, paves the way for a kind of radical subjectivism. This difference between the "truth" as a product of the individual as opposed to truth as a product of the community over time is at the heart of the dispute between James and Peirce. The dispute manifests itself most strikingly with respect to James's voluntarism, to which we now turn.

4.4 The Will to Believe

James is perhaps best known for his essay "The Will to Believe." Interest in it has been remarkably sustained, beginning immediately upon publication in 1896 and continuing to the present. In this essay, James argues that that it is reasonable to believe a hypothesis before one is presented with evidence for it. In particular, it is reasonable to believe the hypothesis of God's existence in advance of evidence for or against it. That is about as far as one can go before entering into interpretatively murky waters.

One might read James as claiming that there is a certain class of beliefs—religious beliefs—in regard to which "faith," rather than scientific evidence, is appropriate. He at times seems to identify those beliefs whose decision is "forced" for this special treatment.[14] Whether to believe in God is one of those forced beliefs—it is so

---

[14] See also the 1879 "The Sentiment of Rationality", where his point holds only for "a certain class of truths of whose reality belief is a factor" (1979 [1879]: 80).

important that we cannot wait around for the evidence to come. We can't "put a stopper on our heart, instincts and courage, and *wait*—acting of course meanwhile more or less as if religion were *not* true" (1979 [1896]: 32). Given how important religion is in life, we are justified in believing in God before we have evidence.[15] On this reading of James, believing ahead of the evidence or independently of the evidence is exactly what is required for religious belief, but not for all beliefs.

This interpretation makes James seem very much like Wittgenstein: reasons and evidence are not appropriate in matters of faith, where the evidence runs out. The interpretation is perhaps made stronger when we note that Wittgenstein was deeply interested in what James had to say about religion.[16] There is no doubt that James at many points expressed these interesting thoughts. But however tempted he may have been by this moderate view, this reading is not, I think, supported in the end by the text. For one thing, in James's very insistence that the evidence for religious beliefs is inconclusive, he shows himself to be committed to the idea that evidence is appropriate for religious belief. Religious belief falls within the sphere of the rational—within the sphere of that which might rise or fall according to the evidence for or against it.[17]

Just as importantly, the category of "forced" belief encompasses much more than religious belief. He does not only discuss religious belief in "The Will to Believe," but offers us some more mundane illustrations of his argument for believing ahead of the evidence, such as the following. Let's say that I have no evidence for whether Mary likes me or thinks of me as a friend. If I believe that she does like me, then that belief will lead to actions that support friend-making. It is then more likely that Mary will end up my friend and I will reap benefits. If I fail to believe, that will lead to actions that undercut friend-making. It will make it less likely that Mary will become my friend and I will forgo the potential benefits. Similarly, an alpine climber who needs to jump across a chasm should believe he can make it, for the belief increases the likelihood of a successful jump. James takes it as unreasonable to be committed to self-fulfilling defeatist prophecies—where the belief that one will fail ensures or encourages the failure. Positive believing, in these and many other instances that have nothing to do with religion, yields results that are desirable and negative believing yields results that are not desirable.

Hence the more usual interpretation[18] takes James's point to be a straightforward point against the evidentialism of Huxley and Clifford—against the view that one should believe only in proportion to the evidence. Clifford had argued in a provocative

[15] James also makes a different but related point—one that Peirce and Wright were fond of. If a matter isn't "vital," as Peirce says, or "momentous" as James says, we can wait and make up our mind when "objective evidence has come." "In scientific questions, this is almost always the case" because action does not require an immediate answer. But in matters of law, ethics and religion, we cannot wait until inquiry takes its full course. We have no choice but to act and so we need to go on the best evidence available (Peirce) or our passions (James) (1979 [1896]: 26–27).

[16] See Wittgenstein (1938) and Goodman (2002).

[17] See Madden (1979: xx) for this point.

[18] See e.g. Adler (2002: 16) and Madden (1979).

essay titled "The Ethics of Belief" that if evidence underdetermines a matter, one must suspend judgment: "it is wrong always, everywhere, and for anyone, to believe anything upon insufficient evidence" (1886 [1877]: 346). James takes on this view of the "logicians" and "scientists," responding that, in religious matters, agnosticism is also a decision. It is a decision, moreover, that is based as much on passion as the theist's decision. The agnostic is also not waiting for the evidence to come around. He is passionate about not being wrong. He is unwilling to risk error and hence suspends his belief.

On this anti-evidentialist interpretation, James's point is that one must either act as if God exists or act as if he does not exist—there is no acting as if you do not know which is true. Then, on this reading, James argues that once one takes the benefits of believing into account, the belief is God is perfectly rational, despite the absence of evidence. He says:

The thesis I defend is, briefly stated, this: Our passional nature not only lawfully may, but must, decide an option between propositions, whenever it is a genuine option that cannot by its nature be decided on intellectual grounds; for to say, under such circumstances, 'Do not decide, but leave the question open' is itself a passional decision—just like deciding yes or no—and is attended with the same risk of losing the truth.[19]

That is, if the available evidence underdetermines *p*, and if there are non-epistemic reasons for believing *p* (my people have always believed *p*, believing *p* would make me happier, and so on), then it is rational to believe *p*. A particular outcome is desirable and in order to get the desirable outcome we are entitled to believe ahead of the evidence. If the belief in God would have a positive impact on someone's life, then it is a reasonable belief for that person.

But the story is more complex than the standard reading suggests. For one thing, we have seen that James is happy for the alpine climber, who will be in possession of some evidence, to have his need to believe legitimize the belief. For another, we see his original intent in some remarks in a review in the *Nation* (1987 [1875]: 293) and in the penultimate draft of "The Will to Believe." He argues in these earlier pieces that, given the dearth of evidence for or against the existence of God, if believing in God makes me happier, then I have a *duty* to believe in God. James makes a shockingly strong point: "any one *to whom it makes a practical difference* (whether of motive to action or mental peace) is in duty bound to . . . it" (1987 [1875]: 293).

Chauncey Wright, in the last year of his short life, was appalled by this idea and lay in wait for an opportunity to have what he thought was a much-needed "duel" with his friend over the matter. It is worth quoting extensively from Wright's sharp account of that duel, for it shows just how much James's thesis was bandied about by the pragmatists before it became "The Will to Believe":

[19] 1979 [1896]: 20. Emphasis in original omitted.

I have carried out my purpose of giving Dr. James the two lectures I had in store for him. I found him just returned home on Wednesday evening. His father remarked in the course of talk, that he had not found any typographical errors in William's article.... I said that I had read it with interest and had not noticed any *typographical* errors. The emphasis attracted the youth's attention, and made him demand an explanation, which was my premeditated discourse.... He fought vigorously, not to say manfully; but confessed to having written under irritation ... On Friday evening I saw him again and introduced the subject of the 'duty of belief' as advocated by him in the *Nation*. He retracted the word 'duty'. All that he meant to say was that it is foolish not to believe, or try to believe, if one is happier for believing. But even so he seemed to me to be more epicurean (though he hates the sect) than even the utilitarians would allow to be wise ... He quite agrees that evidence is all that enforces the obligation of belief, and that it does this only in virtue of its own force as evidence. Belief is only a matter of choice, and therefore of moral duty, so far as attending to evidence is a volitional act; and he agreed that attention to all accessible evidence was the only duty involved in belief'.[20]

Although James was not keen on Wright's "anti-religious teaching,"[21] he altered his position in light of this onslaught. When "The Will to Believe" was finally published twenty years later, he argued that one has a *right* to believe ahead of the evidence, not a duty.

It is significant, though, that James had to be argued (one might even say bullied) into making this alteration. The fact that he was tempted to think that we *must* believe when there is a positive benefit to believing puts the anti-evidentialist interpretation into question. It puts into question the reading on which James thinks that only when a question is under-determined by the evidence do non-epistemic factors come into play. My suggestion is that James was already in the 1870s radically rethinking the concept of truth and that "The Will to Believe" can be best understood in light of that new view of truth. On this reading, what James was trying to do was not to refute evidentialism but, rather, to expand the concept of what can count as evidence for the truth of a belief. We have seen that Peirce also wants to expand the concept of evidence—it can be had, for instance, when we manipulate diagrams, engage in thought experiments, etc. The evidentialist can accept these different kinds of evidence unless he is a restrictive sort of empiricist. However, one of the ways in which James wants to expand the concept of evidence is to include as evidence the satisfaction of the believer. This is something any evidentialist will be loathe to accept. He will argue that the evidence for the truth of a belief cannot come in the form of the belief making me happy, or you comfortable.

The best way to see this point is to contrast Peirce and James on the idea of willing to believe. The collection *The Will to Believe* is dedicated:

[20] Part of this letter can be found in Thayer (1971 [1878]: 341–43). But one must turn to the excellent Madden (1963: 45) to find the longer, more interesting excerpt quoted here.
[21] 1987 [1909]: 190. This piece originally appeared as a letter to the editor of *The Monist*, under the title "James on Tausch" (*The Monist* XIX, 1909: 156).

To My Old Friend, Charles Sanders Peirce, To whose philosophic comradeship in old times and to whose writings in more recent years I owe more incitement and help than I can express or repay.

Peirce was touched by this. Nonetheless, he doesn't have much good to say about James's essay. He tells James in a 1909 letter: "I thought your *Will to Believe* was a very exaggerated utterance, such as injures a serious man very much ..." (*CWJ* 12: 171; 1909).[22] He scorned what he took to be James's view: "Oh, I could not believe so-and-so, because I should be wretched if I did" (*CP* 5. 377; 1877).

We have seen that Peirce is very interested in what he calls "regulative assumptions." His account of truth turns on the idea that a regulative assumption of inquiry is that there would be an answer to the question at hand. As he thinks his way through the implications of that idea, he speaks to the nature of regulative assumptions more generally. We have seen that some of his examples resonate with James's alpine climber. For instance, Peirce talks of a general who "has to capture a position or see his country ruined." He "must go on the hypothesis that there is some way that he can and shall capture it" (*CP* 7. 219; 1901).

But for Peirce, the essential point to make about regulative assumptions is not one about their truth or about whether we should believe or assert them. His is a point about the successful continuation of a practical matter—making friends, preventing your country from being ruined, jumping the chasm, continuing to inquire. If we want to succeed in any of these endeavors, we need to make assumptions—assumptions that allow the practice to go on in the way that is desired.

Peirce seems to be suggesting that there is a propositional attitude, alternative to belief, which is appropriate in certain circumstances. It is of course an open question whether adopting this kind of attitude towards the proposition "this chasm is jumpable" or "we can capture this position" would be sufficient to instill the confidence required to successfully jump the chasm or capture the position. The attitude that Peirce thinks is warranted towards such beliefs is that we should hope that they are true. And in so hoping, we should act on them. He is very clear that this is a different matter from believing or asserting. In 1908 he distances himself from the Jamesian brand of pragmatism, which he attributes to James, Schiller, and "the pragmatists of today":

It seems to me a pity they should allow a philosophy so instinct with life to become infected with seeds of death in such notions as that of ... the mutability of truth, and in such confusions of thought as that of ... willing to control thought, to doubt, and to weigh reasons ... with ... willing to believe.

[*CP* 6. 485; 1908]

---

[22] Peirce was even more scathing about the proofs of James's *Pluralistic Universe*. In comparison to *Will to Believe*, Peirce calls *Pluralistic Universe* "far more suicidal" (*CWJ* 12: 171; 1909). He suggests that the view of truth James advances in those proofs is "careless" and needs to be altered lest it "flatly condemn all human reasoning" (*CWJ* 12: 171–72; 1909).

That is, Wright's worry that James is too "epicurean" remains standing. A belief about what exists in the world might make one happy or give one peace of mind, but that does not constitute a reason for believing that a particular thing exists. Recall Wright's 1867 distinction between "the desirableness of a belief and the evidence thereof." The debate between James and his fellow founders of pragmatism is a debate about whether desirable outcomes are linked to the ideas of evidence and true belief. James at times seems to suggest that they are. Wright and Peirce were not in the slightest tempted to conflate these phenomena.[23]

Here is one of James's staunchest defenders—Howard Knox—in 1909 supporting this reading of "The Will to Believe":

> All that Prof. James had actually contended was that certain risks had to be taken by faith by both parties; but it was tempting to treat this doctrine merely as intended to revive the apologetics of Pascal's wager, and to glorify faith by the sacrifice of Reason. His essential purpose was, however, to challenge the very conception of 'pure Reason' which created the antithesis, and to mitigate their divergence by showing that Reason, no less than Faith, must be justified by works.
>
> [2001 [1909]: 5]

All beliefs, on this reading of James, are made true by being good to believe. Science and faith are not separate spheres of activity, one the province of reason and the other the province of what is desirable. Religious belief is in the same camp as scientific belief, true if it "pays," false if it does not. For reason and truth themselves are inextricably linked to what pays. Neither is it the case that our passional natures must decide between propositions only when they can't be decided on intellectual grounds. James wants to broaden the scope of "intellectual grounds" so that they include the passional. Hence his rejection of "The Will to Deceive" or "The Will to Make-Believe" as alternative titles (suggested by D. S. Miller)[24] for "The Will to Believe." James was speaking about fully believing that *p* is true, not about some other kind of propositional attitude, such as self-deception, or pretending to believe. For James, non-epistemic or pragmatic criteria,[25] such as making one more comfortable or one's life more harmonious, are relevant to truth and hence to belief acceptance. His point is not that belief acceptance is tied to prudence or benefit rather than to truth.[26] His point is that prudence or benefit is tied to truth. That is the very radical nature of

---

[23] To complete the picture of the classical pragmatist response to "The Will to Believe," here is Dewey: the happy consequences for a believer of a belief in God "can not prove, or render more probable, the existence of such a being, for, by the argument, these desirable consequences depend upon accepting such an existence" (*MW* 4: 106; 1908). Note that in moral and political matters, a belief's making life go better might indeed be relevant to its warrant. For there the inquiry might well be about what makes life go better.

[24] See Miller (1898) for the suggestion, and James (1975 [1907]: 124) for the rejection of it.

[25] These terms are from debates in mid-1900s empiricist philosophy of science, in which one camp thinks that science can only appeal to observational evidence and the other camp thinks that science can appeal to non-observational criteria for theory choice—"non-epistemic" or "pragmatic" criteria.

[26] See Jackman (1999: 1) for a clear account of this distinction.

James's proposal. He could not be clearer than in the preface to the collection *The Will to Believe*:

If religious hypotheses about the universe be in order at all, then the active faiths of individuals in them, freely expressing themselves in life, are the experimental tests by which they are verified, and the only means by which their truth or falsehood can be wrought out. The truest scientific hypothesis is that which, as we say, "works best"; and it can be no otherwise with religious hypotheses.

[1979 [1896]: 8]

For James, religious hypotheses, like all hypotheses, need to be verified. He is a "complete empiricist" (1979 [1896]: 22). He is in agreement with T. H. Huxley's stance in "A Modern 'Symposium' "[27] and Clifford's in "The Ethics of Belief" that we cannot simply will ourselves to believe something—that Lincoln's existence is a myth, for instance (1979 [1896]: 15, 18). We need to verify our beliefs. But verification can take the form of seeing how the hypothesis plays out in people's lives.

We shall see in Part II of this book that James's radical proposal has continued to attract criticism. For now, let's simply note J. B. Pratt in 1909, taking on James's view that religious hypotheses can be believed to be true if so believing would be good for one:

Pragmatism . . . seeks to prove the truth of religion by its good and satisfactory consequences. Here, however, a distinction must be made; namely between the "good", harmonious, and logically confirmatory consequences of religious concepts as such, and the good and pleasant consequences which come from believing these concepts. It is one thing to say a belief is true because the logical consequences that flow from it fit in harmoniously with our otherwise grounded knowledge; and quite another to call it true because it is pleasant to believe.

[2001 [1909]: 186–87]

Whatever the Jamesian position is, one thing is clear. The Peircean pragmatist seeks to prove the truth of a hypothesis by its good and satisfactory consequences—those that are empirically confirmed, fit with our otherwise grounded knowledge, etc. That this is Peirce's view is made very clear when we remember how he handled the question of whether it is rational to believe in God. He was just as keen as James on inquiring whether theism is a legitimate doctrine, but he thinks there is one and only one way to show that the hypothesis is belief-worthy—to show that it is such that we can get publically available kinds of evidence for or against it. The consequences relevant to belief cannot be of the sort "it is satisfying to me" or "it has a commanding influence on my life." For Peirce, truth is not linked to this kind of consequence. For James, it is. Peirce's objection to James's line of thought is that passional evidence—that one cannot, for instance, emotionally or psychologically do without the belief—is pertinent to the question of whether or not religion is good for human beings, but not

---

[27] The remainder of the title is "The Influence upon Morality of a Decline in Religious Belief," Huxley (1877).

pertinent to the question of whether God exists. Hypotheses about God's existence are hypotheses about the world. Hence they need empirical verification of the usual sort.

We have seen that one way of thinking of James's view has it being compatible with evidentialism—with the view that one should believe in accord with one's evidence. But he has a view of evidence that is so expansive that it is anathema to the evidentialist. James says in "The Sentiment of Rationality," published in the same volume as "The Will to Believe," that we must not go merely on the "literal evidence" or the "scientific evidence" (1979 [1897]: 76, 80). We shall see below that he thinks that experiments in living, experiences that we might have in séances, and like might be evidence for a belief. All the hard work now needs to be done. How do we delimit good/undistorted/legitimate evidence from bad/distorted/illegitimate evidence? This must be part of any pragmatist project. What we do in fixing belief is interrogate experiences. Of course we only have our own standards to work with. Nonetheless, in asking questions—in the very business of inquiring—we assume that we can make such distinctions and that we can make them in a principled manner.

4.5 The Breadth of Experience

James was continually gripped by the idea that beliefs about God might be verifiable, despite the fact that he seemed not himself a believer in a biblical God who sits on high.[28] He frequently returned to the ideas in "The Will to Believe." In 1897 he says that the scientist thinks "that there is something called scientific evidence by waiting upon which they shall escape all danger of shipwreck in regard to truth."[29] But in thinking this, the scientist disregards all sorts of other kinds of evidence, and does so at his peril (1979 [1897]: 7). James made at least two additional sustained attempts at making the argument that religious experience could count as scientific evidence and in these attempts we see just how radical his empiricism really is.

The first is in the 1901–2 Gifford Lectures, delivered in Edinburgh and published as *The Varieties of Religious Experience*. The aim of these lectures is to show that it is experience, not abstract rationalist philosophy, that provides the motivation for and justification of religious belief. The rationalist offers the theist "a metaphysical monster"—"an absolutely worthless invention of the scholarly mind" (1985 [1902]: 353). We would do better to look to the "religious propensities of man" (1985 [1902]: 12). Religious belief is grounded in experience.

He sets out to rehabilitate the term "mystical" as a label for a category of experiences (1985 [1902]: 301, 336; 301–2). Just as a dog whistle is a legitimate perception of fact

[28] His wife, however, did have strong beliefs in a Christian God and was keen on this line of her husband's inquiry. See Gunter (2009).

[29] In the 1909 Hibbert Lectures, he revisits "The Will to Believe," invoking a "faith-ladder," moving from "it might be true" to "it would be well if it were true" to "it shall be held as if true, for you" (1977 [1909]: 148). In *Pragmatism*, we find him asserting that "I myself believe that the evidence for God lies primarily in inner personal experiences" (1975 [1907]: 56).

for a dog, despite the fact that James cannot hear it, mystical experiences are legitimate and "important" perceptions for those who have them, despite the fact that James himself is shut out from such experiences. He is talking here about a wide range of experiences, from déjà-vu, trances, and dreams to the meditative and heightened states of consciousness cultivated by adherents to various religions. He also includes experiences had under the influence of alcohol and nitrous oxide, which "stimulate the mystical consciousness in an extraordinary degree" (1985 [1902]: 307). And he includes the paranormal. He was active in the British and the American Society for Psychical Research.

James is ever committed to considering *all* forms of experience; ever committed to "sportsmanlike fair play in science" (1979 [1897]: 9). He was dead set against any closed-minded approach. When this methodological point is what he is getting at, as it is in the following passage from "The Will to Believe," it is eminently sensible: "Why do so few 'scientists' even look at the evidence for telepathy, so called? Because they think, as a leading biologist, now dead, once said to me, that even if such a thing were true, scientists ought to band together to keep it suppressed and concealed" (1979 [1896]: 19).

But he does not always stick to such fine methodological thoughts about not being close-minded against certain kinds of evidence. He has a more positive point in mind. Mystical experience, James argues, is the province of the subconscious and is as telling for the perceiver as is the experience of ordinary, mundane consciousness. Indeed, our vision is limited by ordinary consciousness. We need to try to get beyond "the pretention of non-mystical states to be the sole and ultimate dictators of what we may believe" (1985 [1902]: 338).

Sometimes James links this suggestion to a substantive position about the nature of religion and its connection to the world. At one juncture we find him arguing that all religions believe in the same core. As an example, he suggests the feeling of uneasiness: "a sense that there is *something wrong* about us as we naturally stand." Another is the belief that "*we are saved from the wrongness* by making proper connection with the higher powers" (1985 [1902]: 400). This implies that the universe includes both the physical or "visible" world and an unseen spiritual order. During prayer, energy flows between them so that there are effects in the physical world (1985 [1902]: 338, 382).

Mystical states, he thinks, "break down the authority of the non-mystical or rational consciousness, based upon the understanding and the senses alone. They show it to be only one kind of consciousness" (1985 [1902]: 335). Some mystical states or "kinds of truth" "relate to this world—visions of the future, the reading of hearts, the sudden understanding of texts, the knowledge of distant events" (1985 [1902]: 325). But "the most important revelations," James says, are theological or metaphysical—they are, for instance, experiences of "God's touches" (1985 [1902]: 327). They relate to a world that goes beyond the earthly one. Mystical consciousness, that is, delivers us insights that have "metaphysical significance" (1985 [1902]: 308).

James asks himself whether experiences had in mystical states "furnish any *warrant for the truth*" of the conclusions to which they point or whether they merely seem to do so. His answer is that mystical states do "open out the possibility of other orders of truth." But such mystical states are authoritative only to those who have them, licensing faith, but not requiring the belief of those who do not have the mystical states themselves (1985 [1902]: 335). Mystical experience, that is, is not a "superior authority"—it is just one authority amongst equals (1985 [1902]: 338). It offers "possibility and permission" to believe, not a duty to believe (1985 [1902]: 339). This is of course consistent with the final version of "The Will to Believe," as is the statement in *Varieties* that "the uses of religion, its uses to the individual who has it, and the uses of the individual himself to the world, are the best arguments that truth is in it" (1985 [1902]: 361). James notes that we find both the "mean" and the "noble" amongst the religious and the non-religious, so there is no obvious practical advantage in being religious—religion does not obviously work best for the world (1985 [1902]: 383). So the religious man's experience is indeed "evidence," but not indefeasible evidence and not evidence for everyone.

In 1903, James Leuba, in *The International Journal of Ethics*, takes against James's view:

If . . . we are to abide by these conclusions, the judgment of absurdity and irrationality commonly passed by the ordinary consciousness upon mystical, insane, and drunken dreams would have to be declared altogether irrelevant, for the reason that they would belong to other aspects of consciousness. Each aspect of consciousness would be its own judge of reality.

[1903: 331]

Leuba's point is one that we shall see is made repeatedly against the successors of Jamesian pragmatism: on James's view, we have no way whatsoever of adjudicating any claim. As long as statements about mystical states are taken to be entirely subjective—as long as they are taken to "describe immediate experiences and nothing more"—then, quite rightly, they are not open to criticism. James's mistake is to take them to be evidence for objective matters. Leuba's argument is that as soon as statements are made about the world—"that the ecstatic feelings are due to God's descent into the believer; that Christ was actually, bodily, present; that the feelings of repose, of vastness, of illumination and the increased ethical power, imply the existence of a world of spiritual existences"—then they must be open to criticism. We can, for instance, use the "canons of logic" such as the "principle of logical contradiction" and we can test mystical or drug-induced experiences against one's ordinary experiences (Leuba 1903: 331–34). James is wrong to not see this.

Leuba's view is precisely Peirce's view. Peirce, like James, wants to have a broad account of experience, but Peirce thinks that there has to be some basis for dividing experiences into those that are relevant for truth claims and those that are not. His attempt is as follows. If statements about God are about the world, then they are subject to the kinds of requirements that all statements about the world are subject to—verification by the senses and the usual standards of belief and theory choice. James, on the other hand, when he asks himself "where the differences in fact which are due to God's existence come in" offers "prayerful communion," which "exerts an influence" by raising our personal energy and producing "regenerative effects" (1985 [1902]: 411–12). These are of course internal effects on a person, not on the world.

In the 1909 Oxford Hibbert Lectures, James is still at it. His radical empiricism has it that "the only things that shall be debatable among philosophers shall be things definable in terms drawn from experience" and part of his aim in these lectures is "to unite empiricism with spiritualism" (Perry (1976) [1935] 2: 443). His position is that "We have so many different businesses with nature that no one of them yields us an all-embracing clasp"—and so we find ourselves in the business of reconciling all of the types of experience that have us in their clasp, including religious experiences (1977 [1909]: 19). He says: "there *are* religious experiences of a specific nature . . . I think that they point with reasonable probability to the continuity of our consciousness with a wider spiritual environment from which the ordinary prudential man (who is the only man that scientific psychology, so called, takes cognizance of) is shut off" (1977 [1909]: 135).

If Russell, the hard-headed atheist and empiricist, was in the audience, he must have been unimpressed. The Hibbert Lectures, piled on top of *Varieties of Religious Experience* and "The Will to Believe," will have sealed his view of James's brand of empiricism as being completely off the mark. We shall see in Part II how devastating this reaction was to the fortunes of pragmatism.

To summarize, James's empiricism is in step with very early American philosophy and with his pragmatist contemporaries in trying to make the concept of experience go beyond the physical senses. He also in step with those others in thinking that the empiricist must scrutinize our beliefs, not the origins of them. He notes with approval that Jonathan Edwards thought that it was by the fruits not the roots that we must test beliefs (1985 [1902]: 25). He also, with Peirce, is very clear that the analytic-synthetic distinction must go:

> Some readers may expect me to plunge into the old debate as to whether . . . truths are 'analytic' or 'synthetic'. It seems to me that the distinction is one of Kant's most unhappy legacies, for the reason that it is impossible to make it sharp . . . There is *something* 'ampliative' in our greatest truisms . . . The analytic-synthetic distinction is thus for us devoid of all significance.
>
> [1981 [1890]: 1255]

But he is decidedly out of step with Peirce and Wright in that he thinks that mystical and drug-induced experiences are as good for speaking to claims about the world as are the experiences delivered by our senses. Peirce and Wright would agree with James that philosophy must deal with "the data of life" (1978 [1876]: 5). What they would not agree with is the qualifier James uses: the "personal look at all the data of life." They would agree with James that all beliefs must be open to verification by experience. But they would not agree with James that all experience, however subjective, can be included in that verification.

Hence, James is right when he says the following: "If one should make a division of all thinkers into naturalists and supernaturalists, I should undoubtedly have to go . . .

into the supernaturalist branch" (1985 [1902]: 409). He is a naturalist in that he wants only to take experience into account. But he characterizes experience so broadly that his naturalism is very precarious.

4.6 Ethics

James quite rightly takes the most important paper in *The Will to Believe* volume to be "The Moral Philosopher and the Moral Life."[30] In this paper we find a lucid exposition of a more objective pragmatist theory of truth, even though that is not its primary topic. James asserts in this essay that "truth supposes a standard outside of the thinker to which he must conform." He offers us a view of truth on which truth is not what works here and now for an individual thinker. Truth is what works in the long run for the community of thinkers. It is clear that James toggled between a radically subjective pragmatism and a pragmatism of the more objective stripe.

The primary topic of the essay is to carve out and argue for a theory of ethics. That theory walks hand in hand with the more objective pragmatist account of truth and inquiry. Here are the first couple of sentences:

> The main purpose of this paper is to show that there is no such thing possible as an ethical philosophy dogmatically made up in advance. We all help to determine the content of ethical philosophy so far as we contribute to the race's moral life. In other words, there can be no final truth in ethics any more than in physics, until the last man has had his experience and his say.
>
> [1979 [1891]: 141]

James takes on a wide array of opponents, including the idealist, the intuitionist, the evolutionist, the skeptic and the "pure" empiricist who thinks that the entirety of our moral lives can be explained by utility (1979 [1891]: 141–42).

The idealist comes in for especially intense treatment. As Timothy Sprigge notes, James's objection to absolute idealism often had a moral focus (2006: 402). Idealism seems to hold that the world is a perfect Whole and everything in it, if understood properly, is a contribution to that perfection. James could not stomach the idea that human suffering was to be thought of in this way. Moreover, under the influence of the French philosopher Charles Renouvier (1815–1903), James was unable turn his back on the idea that human beings have free will. He thought that the idea of the Absolute entailed a block universe—a universe "whose parts have no loose play" and where there is no room for freedom of the will (1979 [1897]: 216). The absolute idealist cannot satisfactorily account for the regret of this or that particular event nor for genuine and difficult moral decision. All we can do, on the idealist view, is regret the whole universe in which particular events are necessary or become relentless optimists who hold that all evils are really good or lead to something good.[31]

---

[30] See Perry (1976 [1935] 2: 263, 263 n. 1).
[31] See James (1979 [1884]).

But in "The Moral Philosopher and the Moral Life," James attacks the idealist on different grounds: it is a superstitious view with an incoherent metaphysics. The terms "good" and "bad," James argues, only have application in relation to thinkers or to sentient beings. Judgments of something being good or bad "cannot float in the atmosphere . . . like the aurora borealis" (1979 [1891]: 147). At worst, the idealist is engaged in spurious metaphysics, ungrounded in anything that is linked to experience. At best, the idealist brings "good" and "bad" not down to earth but up to heaven in holding that one of the thinkers in the universe is divine while all the rest are human. But if that were the case, then it would follow that the divine judgments must be the model for the judgments of the others. James is puzzled about "the ground of obligation, even here." Why should we think "that we should conform our thoughts to God's thoughts, even though he made no claim to that effect, and though we preferred *de facto* to go on thinking for ourselves" (1979 [1891]: 148)? James asks us to assume that there is a universal or divine consciousness. He then points out that in this, our own "queer world," we happen to have a tendency to not respect the demands of that or any other consciousness. Whether the idealist thinks of God as something a priori and abstract or whether he thinks of God as a personal God, the fact that we are not always or even generally responsive to God's claims is a problem for the view.

It turns out that "the only force of appeal to *us*, which either a living God or an abstract ideal order can wield, is found in the "everlasting ruby vaults" of our own human hearts, as they happen to beat responsive and not irresponsive to the claim" (1979 [1891]: 149). Ethics deals only with "life answering to life" (1979 [1891]: 149). This is the profound insight at the center of James's ethical theory. Every claim or demand, however slight, made by any creature, however weak, creates an obligation. No God need be present in this picture:

were there left but one rock with two loving souls upon it, that rock would have as thoroughly moral a constitution as any possible world . . . while they lived, there would be real good things and real bad things in the universe; there would be obligations, claims, and expectations; obediences, refusals, and disappointments . . . there would, in short, be a moral life . . . We, on this terrestrial globe, so far as the visible facts go, are just like the inhabitants of such a rock. Whether a God exist, or whether no God exist, in yon blue heaven above us bent, we form at any rate an ethical republic here below.

[1979 [1891]: 150]

James also objects to much empiricist ethical theory. The "pure" empiricist does not make the mistake of the idealist, for he sees that ethics is about human demands and claims. But the pure empiricist goes wrong in trying to explain everything in terms of association or utility. While a "vast number of our moral perceptions . . . are certainly of this . . . brain–born kind," once you look beyond the "coarser and more commonplace moral maxims," the explanations become less straightforward. The "sense for abstract justice," the "passion for music" or for philosophy, the "feeling of the inward dignity of certain spiritual attitudes, as peace, serenity, simplicity, veracity," and the aversion to "querulousness, anxiety, egoistic fussiness" are "quite inexplicable except by an innate preference"—a feature not well explained by the psychology of the pure empiricist (1979 [1891]: 143). "Purely inward forces are . . . at work here," and constitute a kind of evidence in morals not available to the standard empiricist (1979 [1891]: 144).

The "presumptions of utility" are also flawed if they are taken to be the single determinant in moral matters, for they may fly in the face of the evidence. The concept of utility as a moral barometer gets much right: it takes morality to be about sentient beings who have needs and desires, which in an ideal world, would all be satisfied. But in our imperfect world, these needs and desires clash with those of others and some of them must be "butchered" in order to have a maximum number of needs and desires satisfied. A "specific and independent sort of emotion" tells us that it would not be right were "millions . . . kept permanently happy on the one simple condition that a certain lost soul on the far-off edge of things should lead a life of lonely torture" (1979 [1891]: 144). The emotions or "inward forces" that tell us that this would be wrong, despite its maximization of utility, are not purely the products of past "couplings of experience" and they are at work everywhere in our moral lives. They cannot be accounted for by the pure empiricist or utilitarian, but they must be taken seriously as evidence for (or against) ethical claims and theories.

The intuitionist is better off, as he both respects the psychological facts and can account for inward forces. The intuitionist takes the good to be what is "recognized by a special intuitive faculty" (1979 [1891]: 152). It is interesting that, although James doesn't want to think of himself as being perfectly aligned with the intuitionist, he brings to bear in this paper no good arguments against the position—just the general complaint that the intuitionist tends to be dogmatic and intent on putting forward abstract rules garnered from those intuitions. Such rules, James says, help "less in proportion as our intuitions are more piercing" (1979 [1891]: 158). But James's position is not terribly far off that of the intuitionist, if we can subtract the special faculty idea. Both think that emotions or feelings or reactive attitudes count as evidence in moral deliberation.

He is also in this paper critical of the apparently relativist view of truth that he seems to promote in other moods. He imagines a world with two sentient beings, each of whom ignores the other's attitudes about good and evil, indulging his own preferences. This world, James says, would be "without ethical unity" in that "the same object is good or bad there" depending on who is measuring it (1979 [1891]: 146). It is worth quoting him at length, to see how he was not always tempted by the subjective view to which we have seen him at times succumb:

Nor can you find any possible ground in such a world for saying that one thinker's opinion is more correct than the other's, or that either has the truer moral sense. Such a world, in short, is not a moral universe but a moral dualism. Not only is there no single point of view within it from which the values of things can be unequivocally judged, but there is not even a demand for such a point of view, since the two thinkers are supposed to be indifferent to each other's thoughts and acts. Multiply the thinkers into a pluralism, and we find realized for us in the ethical sphere something like that world which the antique sceptics conceived of—in which individual minds are the measures of all things, and in which no one "objective" truth, but only a multitude of "subjective" opinions, can be found.

[1979 [1891]: 146–47]

In such a world, we cannot make sense of obligation. We cannot make sense of the normative. James, at times, was fully on board for the Peircean kind of pragmatist project—for attempting to get genuinely normative concepts of good, right, and truth out of our human, fallible practices.

On the view we find James putting forward in "The Moral Philosopher and the Moral Life," all we have to go on are the demands, claims, and judgments of humans, but he thinks that we can nonetheless get some normative principles out of that. The "guiding principle for ethical philosophy" is to "satisfy *as many demands as we can.*" "That act must be the best act, accordingly, which makes for the *best whole*, in the sense of awakening the least sum of dissatisfactions" (1979 [1891]: 155). This would be a straight-up utilitarian view, were it not for the intuitionist addition we have seen above and the pragmatist spin that James gives it. He argues that society may be seen as a long-running experiment aimed at identifying the best kind of conduct. Its conventions thus deserve respect. Our background beliefs, while remaining fallible, capture the experience of generations. James thinks that "ethical science is just like physical science, and instead of being deducible all at once from abstract principles, must simply bide its time, and be ready to revise its conclusions from day to day" (1979 [1891]: 157). This is the James that is completely in step with Peirce about truth.

He is also in step with modern Rawlsian views, even presaging Rawls's use of the term "reflective equilibrium":

The course of history is nothing but the story of men's struggles from generation to generation to find the more and more inclusive order. *Invent some manner* of realizing your own ideals which will also satisfy the alien demands—that and only that is the path of peace! Following this path, society has shaken itself into one sort of relative equilibrium after another by a series of social discoveries quite analogous to those of science.[32]

For instance "slavery, private warfare and liberty to kill, judicial torture and arbitrary royal power have slowly succumbed to actually aroused complaints." They have succumbed to experience. But "there is nothing final in any actually given equilibrium of human ideals"—we must keep the inquiry and deliberation going (1979 [1891]: 156). We can have progress and even revolutions in ethics. Just as in physics, this is how inquiry proceeds. In the meantime, we must go on our current well-grounded beliefs: "it would be folly quite as great, in most of us, to strike out independently and to aim at originality in ethics as in physics" (1979 [1891]: 157).

---

[32] 1979 [1891]: 155–56. This is not quite the Rawlsian notion, which involves reaching a balance between judgments in particular cases, principles, and theoretical considerations. James is more interested in a balance between conflicting interests and ideals.

This is a very powerful view of ethics. Ethical judgments are candidates for truth and falsity and are subject to the force of experience. The experiences and intuitions we have about what is right or wrong, just or unjust are data or evidence for our ethical judgments. For what are ethical judgments about if not about what makes a human life go better? How could we know what makes a human life go better other than by seeing how humans feel about what makes their lives go better?

Nonetheless, the link between what we feel to be right and what is right is not one of straightforward identity. It cannot be that if I feel x to be right, then x is right. In "The Sentiment of Rationality," also published in *The Will to Believe* volume but written earlier than "The Moral Philosopher and the Moral Life," James argues also against the materialist who takes the world to be "a simple brute actuality" in which "the words 'good' and 'bad' have no sense apart from subjective passions and interests" (1979 [1879]: 85). In James's view, I must think that the world is moral. Otherwise at "the mountain precipice" I "will doubt my right to risk a leap" and I will "actively connive at my destruction" (1979 [1879]: 88). The "method of faith" underpins the idea that the world is moral (1979 [1879]: 84).

We need again to think about the options with respect to such regulative assumptions.[33] We have seen that James is tempted to think that if I have to believe p in order to fulfill some aim, then I am justified in believing p. Peirce disagrees, arguing that my need to believe p is not linked to p's rationality or truth. He suggests, rather, that we assume p in order to continue with a practice to which we are committed. If that practice is at the very heart of what we think makes us human—seeking for right answers to our questions; seeking to distinguish the morally right from the morally wrong, then these hypothetical regulative assumptions are going to be hard to dislodge. Nonetheless, they are mere hopes—without which it is true, the human world as we know it is imperiled.

In "The Dilemma of Determinism," also collected in *The Will to Believe*, James moves towards this Peircean position. He argues that we have to act as if we have freedom of the will, if we are to continue in the way we think necessary. Such an appeal to what we need to assume was clearly a major strategic plank for the early pragmatists. It is a plank that we shall see remains in place today.[34] It is a shame that James relies on it only occasionally, preferring more often than not to rest with the idea that the need to assume something legitimizes belief. As Henry Jackman says, James's project is to draw out the consequences of a through-going naturalism. Like Peirce (and we shall see, even more like Dewey) he wants to outline the place for

---

[33] For a concise pulling-together of my line of argument about James and Peirce (and Santayana) on this score, see Misak (2012).

[34] For instance Peter Strawson in *Freedom and Resentment* argues, in fine pragmatist fashion, that we need to assume that we have freedom of will if we are to explain our practices of educating children in matters of right and wrong and our practices of praising, blaming, and resenting those people we treat as full participants in the moral community. This is an assumption that we cannot fail to make without doing such violence to our conception of things that our world would become unrecognizable.

value in that naturalist world.[35] While sometimes his view radiates with insight (such as in "The Moral Philosopher and the Moral Life"), at other times his naturalism seems to be one in which the words "good" and "bad" and "true" and "false" have no sense apart from subjective passions and interests. We shall see that, unfortunately, it is the latter position that became identified with pragmatism.

---

[35] Indeed, Dewey was very impressed by "The Moral Philosopher and the Moral Life," saying "it rejoiced me greatly" and "I think it is the best and simplest statement I have ever seen" (*CWJ* 7: 165; 1891). The thing that pleased Dewey so much about this paper is its commitment to the idea that our ethical theory cannot be determined in advance. It has to come out of our deliberation in the midst of difficult ethical situations.

5

Fellow Travelers

5.1 Oliver Wendell Holmes: Law and Experience

Oliver Wendell Holmes (1841–1935) was one of the founding members of The Metaphysical Club and was good friends in those early days with William James and Chauncey Wright. He had frequent philosophical "palavars" with them,[1] but did not mix as much with Peirce. He and the other lawyer in The Metaphysical Club—Nicholas St. John Green—played critical roles in the birth of pragmatism. Peirce, for instance, credits Green with urging upon the group Bain's definition of belief as that upon which we are prepared to act.[2] Late in life, we find Holmes reflecting on the importance of those early discussions: "Chauncey Wright a nearly forgotten philosopher of real merit, taught me when young that I must not say *necessary* about the universe, that we don't know whether anything is necessary or not. I believe that we can *bet* on the behavior of the universe in its contact with us. So I describe myself as a *bet*tabilitarian."[3]

After serving and being wounded three times in the Civil War, Holmes went on to become one of America's most famous legal theorists and Supreme Court justices. He did not identify himself with the pragmatist movement. This is not surprising, as the debates Holmes was immersed in were not the debates of Peirce, James, Schiller, Royce, or any other thinker associated with pragmatism. Holmes's issues were those of analytical jurisprudence and his primary intellectual interlocutors were the English legal scholars John Austin and Frederick Pollock, as well as German legal scientists. Nonetheless, one can detect a strong current of pragmatism running through his thought. The ideas hammered out in The Metaphysical Club animated the view of law he developed during the late 1800s, a view that did not undergo significant revision during the rest of his long and illustrious career.

---

[1] See Kellogg (2007: 42). This is true of James in particular, with whom Holmes had extensive contact and correspondence upon Holmes's return from a trip to Europe in September of 1866 (*CWJ* 4: 147, n. 1). In a letter to his sister, dated Nov. 14, James cheerfully describes "wrangling" with Holmes (*CWJ* 4: 144; 1866). Correspondence between the two, however, dwindles until, in the last two years of James's life, it appears to cease entirely.

[2] See Fisch (1954). In his (1942: 94) Fisch surmises that pragmatism may even have arisen out of Holmes's prediction theory of law.

[3] Holmes–Pollock Letters (2: 252; 1929).

Holmes was interested in the common law—as Frederic Kellogg puts it, the bottom-up theory of law (2007: 19). Holmes described the common law as starting with cases "and only after a series of determinations on the same subject matter" does it come, "by . . . induction to state the principle" (1995 [1870]: 213). Law is not something that is set in stone or in statute. It is a growing, evolving, ongoing enterprise. It is an enterprise of inquiry, or "successive approximation," that starts from precedent and then is driven by experience, conflict, and unanticipated problems.[4] Holmes was set against taking precedents, legislation, or moral principles as immutable truths. In the first few lines of the 1882 *The Common Law*, which was based on his 1880 Lowell Lectures, he tells us what law is: "The life of the law has not been logic: it has been experience" or "the felt necessities of the time" (1882: 1). The law does not consist of a fixed body of doctrines and syllogisms derived from them, but rather, it is an organic structure that has come together in response to experience. He says that all theories that consider the law "only from its formal side" are failures (1882: 36–37). Whatever code or set of principles or statutes might be adopted, "[n]ew cases will arise which will elude the most carefully constructed formula" and will have to be reconciled (1995 [1870]: 213). "Truth," he says, is "often suggested by error" and that is why we need always to employ "reason and scrutiny" (1882: 37). Law, for Holmes, grows in a fallible way, where doubt, conflict, and disputes about what the law is are resolved under the force of experience.

The reader will recognize how very similar this is to Peirce's doubt–belief conception of inquiry and with all pragmatists' skepticism about top-down theories. Pragmatist epistemology is just as forcefully expressed in Holmes's 1897 "The Path of Law":

Take the fundamental question, What constitutes the law? You will find some text writers telling you that it is something different from what is decided by the courts of Massachusetts or England, that it is a system of reason, that it is a deduction from principles of ethics or admitted axioms or what not, which may or may not coincide with the decisions. . . . The prophecies of what the courts will do in fact, and nothing more pretentious, are what I mean by the law.

[1952 [1897]: 172–73]

The reasons the prophecies of the courts are so important is that people are enabled by them to predict and adjust their behavior accordingly. The Bad Man, for instance, is able to predict what the courts will decide in order to adjust his behavior and avoid sanction. Holmes says: "a legal duty so called is nothing but a prediction that if a man does or omits certain things he will be made to suffer in this or that way by judgment of the court" (1952 [1897]: 169). We can hear Bain's dispositional account of belief operating in the background here. As Max Fisch puts it, Holmes thinks of law in terms of expectancies or predictions and our readiness to act upon them (1942: 366). We act on our best predictions of how rules will be interpreted and maintained by the courts.

---

[4] For the notion of "successive approximation," see (1995 [1870]: 212). Kellogg (2007) is excellent on the topic and on how Holmes's conception of the law is deeply pragmatist.

Those rules and interpretations evolve with new experience, so predictions can never be locked-in.

Courts, for Holmes, are engaged in the business of inquiry. That is, courts and judges are engaged in a fallible search for the best answer we can come to given the time in which we are living and the circumstances in which we find ourselves. The "secret root from which the law draws all the juices of life," Holmes argues, is "the considerations of what is expedient for the community concerned" (1882: 35). Laws are good if they fit with the values of the community, as determined by judges who are looking to experience to decide cases.

There is quite clearly a pragmatist conception of validity or legitimacy at play in Holmes's theory of law. Indeed, we have seen James invoke this very conception of law and truth. With it comes the questions that press in on all pragmatists. Do validity, rationality, truth, and other normative concepts turn on expediency, individual or community will and desire, and hard social facts? Or do they turn on responsiveness to something less contingent and subjective? Is the aim of our inquiries to get answers that satisfy current, local, interests or is it something more? In the following passage, it might seem that Holmes thinks there is nothing more:

It is perfectly proper to regard and study the law simply as a great anthropological document. It is proper to resort to it to discover what ideals of society have been strong enough to reach that final form of expression, or what have been the changes in dominant ideals from century to century. It is proper to study it as an exercise in the morphology and transformation of human ideas.

[1952 [1889]: 212]

Passages such as this encourage the reading of Holmes that has him arguing that because we have no absolute or certain way of settling political and legal conflict, security and stability are best served by taking the people's will as what is right.[5]

But there is some evidence that Holmes was interested in normativity that goes beyond mere description of what has been found to be expedient or dominant. On the occasion of William James's death, he writes to the English legal historian Frederick Pollock in a way that distances his own view from that of James: "His reason made him sceptical and his wishes led him to turn down the lights so as to give miracle a chance."[6] And although Holmes sees that he and James start from "similar premises," Holmes is not warm to the pragmatist label. In 1908 he writes: "*I* think pragmatism an amusing humbug—like most of William James' speculations."[7]

As we have seen, the label "pragmatism" was very much associated with James in the early 1900s. When Holmes rejects pragmatism, it will be James's version he has in mind. There was some tension between these two old friends. James disapproved of what he thought of as Holmes's relentless ambition. And Holmes's remark about James

---

[5] See e.g. Dyzenhaus (1997).
[6] Quoted in Fisch 1942: 98.
[7] Holmes–Pollock Letters (1: 138–39; 1908). Also see *CWJ* 11: 338; 1907, where Holmes takes issue with James's account of truth.

shows that he thought it would have been better if James had kept the lights on full when he was thinking about religion. We do know that when Holmes eventually read Dewey, he was impressed and was struck by how much agreement there was between his own view and Dewey's pragmatism.[8]

A careful reading of Holmes shows him not to hold a skeptical view of the law, on which there is no sense to be made of judgments being better or worse, only a recording of what community ideals are in force here and now. As Kellogg argues, Holmes does not want judges to import their local and subjective values, beliefs, or whims into their judgments. That does not mean that he thinks that custom, motives, and background belief are dismissible in inquiry. Nor does it mean that he thinks that the values that inform law are whatever values happen to be in force in the community. The way that Holmes incorporates background belief and values into his conception of legal inquiry is as subtle as Peirce's. The following passage is illuminating:

Austin said . . . that custom only became law by the tacit consent of the sovereign manifested by its adoption by the courts; and that before its adoption it was only a motive for decision, as a doctrine of political economy, or the political aspirations of the judge, or his gout, or the blandishments of the emperor's wife might have been. But it is clear that in many cases custom and mercantile usage have had as much compulsory power as law could have, in spite of prohibitory statutes; and as to their being only motives for decision until adopted, what more is the decision that adopts them as to any future decision? What more indeed is a statute; and in what other sense law, than that we believe that the motive which we think that it offers to the judges will prevail, and will induce them to decide a certain case in a certain way, and so shape our conduct on the anticipation?

[1995 [1972]: 294]

We look to the law to enable us to predict how our behavior will be received and treated. When conflicts arise, judges resolve them in an inquiry not unlike the kind of inquiry the scientist conducts. Both kinds of inquiry are experience-driven enterprises, with custom and background belief having some real force. But nonetheless, as the passage above suggests, there are external standards. Motives and arguments are *offered* to judges, for their consideration. Law proceeds via "judgment as to the relative worth and importance of competing legislative grounds" (1952 [1897]: 181). Judges have to use their judgment to weigh the claims of custom, background belief about what is right and wrong, statutes, etc. "The law," Holmes says, is the "witness and the external deposit of our moral life. Its history is the history of the moral development of the race/The practice of it, in spite of popular jests, tends to make good citizens and good men" (1952 [1897]: 170). The history of law is a history of *development*, on which we improve our views about what is good. It is not simply a record of what happened to be thought good.

We have seen that Peirce finds external standards by invoking the force of experience— by requiring our beliefs to be not determined by accidental circumstances. Holmes is speaking about the legal and ethical domain and thus faces an especially difficult task in

---

[8] See Fisch (1942).

giving shape to what counts as non-accidental. It is harder to see how values might be determined by something objective, for want of a better word. At least, it is hard to see how there can be external standards if one resists the temptation, as does Holmes, to appeal to God, to Reason, or to some internal logic. If one is a naturalist or a pragmatist, the worry is that one will have to say that we can make sense of only one kind of standard—what the community happens to believe.

Holmes makes an attempt at articulating this problem and its solution. Like Peirce, he pays attention to what makes a belief *well*-settled. In Holmes's words, "a well-settled legal doctrine embodies the work of many minds, and has been tested in form as well as substance by trained critics whose practical interest it is to resist it at every step" (1995 [1870]: 213). A well-settled belief is not simply the belief that fits with the spirit of the times. External standards are employed by those many minds and those many trained critics. For instance, one external standard is found by considering what a reasonable or prudent person, taking into account the weight of experience, would think. If a workman on top of a house tosses a beam into a busy street, he should have foreseen that the beam might have hit someone. The standard of a reasonable man applies to his behavior (1882: 55–56). This is the kind of thing that looking to objective circumstances amounts to in the legal or ethical domain.

In the same vein, we find Holmes gesturing at an aim of our legal inquiries. He says:

The truth is, that the law is always approaching, and never reaching, consistency. It is forever adopting new principles from life at one end, and it always retains old ones from history at the other ... It will become entirely consistent only when it ceases to grow ... However much we may codify the law into a series of seemingly self-sufficient propositions, those propositions will be but a phase in a continuous growth.

[1882: 36–37]

The aim of law is reached when disputes no longer arise. This state is at least conceivable—law might cease to grow and be entirely consistent. But, like Peirce, Holmes does not treat the attainment of this aim as a likely possibility. Its pursuit is supported by what Peirce would call a regulative assumption.

5.2 Josiah Royce: Harvard Idealism vs Harvard Pragmatism

Josiah Royce (1855–1916) grew up in modest economic circumstances in a mining town in California, his feckless father having unsuccessfully chased the gold rush. The highly intelligent boy launched himself into Berkeley for an undergraduate degree, followed by a year of study in Germany in 1875–76. Royce returned infused with Hegel, Schelling, Kant, and Schopenhauer and began graduate work in the brand-new program at Johns Hopkins in 1876. He was taught by Peirce and graduated in the first small class of PhDs. He and James were to become Harvard's two best-known philosophers of the era. He was an intense and unhandsome man. His student

Santayana says of him: "merely to look at him you would have felt that he was a philosopher; his great head seemed too heavy for his small body, and his portentous brow, crowned with thick red hair, seemed to crush the lower part of his face" (2009 [1920]: 64). Royce had a formidable intellect and became a force on the American philosophical scene. His students included C. I. Lewis, George Herbert Mead, Santayana, Henry Sheffer, Arthur Lovejoy, and Morris Raphael Cohen. They tended to be devoted to him but not to follow him down the idealist path, an independence of thought that was encouraged by Royce.[9]

We need to understand Royce if we are to understand the intellectual air the founders of pragmatism breathed. He occupies an unusual place in the pragmatist pantheon. He was an absolute idealist who always felt a pull towards pragmatism. After a short and unhappy stint teaching back at Berkeley, James got him a position at Harvard and he remained intertwined with James and Peirce for the rest of their lives.[10] He was in steady conversation with them about matters of meaning and truth. Peirce was critical of Royce's views, but respected them. For his part, Royce acknowledged a great debt to Peirce (especially to his theory of signs) and rescued his papers after his death.[11] Royce and James were even more closely bound together. They conducted a passionate, public, and on the whole friendly debate over the whole of their time together at Harvard, with James insisting that philosophy stick to experience and Royce insisting that something more—something unifying, something absolute—be above those facts.

Royce gestured often at evolutionary biology, wrote on psychology, and frequently used mathematics and logic in his philosophical reasoning. But he was not trained in science or logic, as were Wright, Peirce, and James. He was deeply interested in religion and wrote much on sorrow, pain, atonement, prayer, and grace. When he used evolutionary ideas it was to unite them with his idealism in an attempt to find a way of reconciling the new science with ethics. Despite Royce's considerable efforts, Peirce thought him substandard in formal logic: Royce is a "powerful and accurate thinker who has been so completely led astray in his argumentation by his Hegelian logic" (CP 8. 130; 1902, also CP 8. 115; 1900).

The influence of Peirce and James can be seen throughout the arc of Royce's thought. In 1880, during what he saw as his year of exile at Berkeley, he received an invitation to send a paper to The Metaphysical Club, which had been revived at Hopkins.[12] That paper, "On Purpose in Thought," is fully engaged with pragmatism. Peirce had recently published "The Fixation of Belief" and Royce agrees with the central idea expressed there: thought "seeks to change uncertainty into confidence" (1968 [1880]: 227). It seeks to portray "an ideal picture of a world of experience" (1968

---

[9] Santayana is an exception here—he was not happy with the thesis topic Royce assigned him.
[10] Royce also engaged Dewey and his work. See e.g. Royce (1891).
[11] See Clendenning (1999: 358).
[12] See Clendenning (1999: 86).

[1880]: 260). Though we can detect the shadow of the Absolute— Royce goes on to say that this world of experience will be portrayed "as One" in thought—the ideas expressed here reveal pragmatist leanings. As John E. Smith remarks, "The crucial factor in Royce's development was his study of several papers written by his contemporary Charles S. Peirce" (2001 [1968]: 3).

But the relationship is far from straightforward and it is important to see the complex interplay between pragmatism and the idealism that Royce champions. He argues that what is present to our minds is our ideas of things or the appearance of things. The external world is to be built out of these ideas. Sometimes he puts this point by saying that "all reality is reality because true judgments can be made about it" (1885: 433). Here we can see why Peirce was inclined to call pragmatism a kind of idealism, for he also at times characterizes reality in this way. But we shall see that Peirce (and James) made it clear that there were important differences between pragmatism and Royce's idealism.

The early Royce's view is on the whole set *against* the spirit of pragmatism. He holds that experience of the Absolute is key to working out the big questions in philosophy. The experience of the Absolute would of course transcend the experiences of finite human beings and hence his is exactly the kind of metaphysics against which the pragmatists set themselves. In 1891, we find Peirce writing to James that he ranks Royce as a philosopher "no higher, certainly, than Abbot," whose philosophy James had just called "scholastic rubbish" (*CWJ* 7: 219–20; 1891).

In the 1885 *The Religious Aspect of Philosophy*, Royce first puts forward his most significant and durable argument. It is an argument about "the logical conditions" of the very possibility of error. Royce is out to answer the skeptic who questions whether our ideas correspond to the real world (1885: 392). He argues that one truth the skeptic must know is that error is possible. For the skeptic asserts that we might be wrong in thinking that our ideas correspond to something external. Royce argues that the very possibility that we might get something wrong shows that there is a perspective that goes beyond what this or that person might think. Otherwise, how could we make sense of someone's being mistaken?

Error, for Royce, is "incomplete thought" and he argues that only a higher thought can see that the error has taken place:

let us overcome all our difficulties by declaring that all the many Beyonds, which single significant judgments seem vaguely and separately to postulate, are present as fully realized intended objects to the unity of an all-inclusive, absolutely clear, universal, and conscious thought, of which all judgments, true or false, are but fragments, the whole being at once Absolute Truth and Absolute Knowledge. Then all our puzzles will disappear at a stroke, and error will be possible, because any one finite thought, viewed in relation to its own intent, may or may not be seen by this higher thought as successful and adequate in this intent.

[1885: 423]

The idea that truth must go beyond what is believed here and now if error is to be possible is an important insight. But the way the insight plays out in Royce's hands—that God, or absolute thought, or an "absolute judge" is required—is not, in the pragmatist's view, the best manifestation of that insight.

Peirce wrote a long review of *The Religious Aspect of Philosophy*.[13] He takes the blows Royce aims at his philosophical punching bag "Thrasymachus" to be aimed at him. Thrasymachus, Peirce says, holds:

> that reality, the fact that there is such a thing as a true answer to a question, consists in this: that human inquiries,—human reasoning and observation,—tend toward the settlement of disputes and ultimate agreement in definite conclusions which are independent of the particular stand-points from which the different inquirers may have set out; so that the real is that which any man would believe in, and be ready to act upon, if his investigations were to be pushed sufficiently far.
>
> [*W* 5: 222; 1885]

Royce had complained that this view "is not merely a moderate expression of human limitations, but jargon . . . honest-seeming nonsense" (1885: 394). Indeed, Royce presents the argument of "Thrasymachus" as "the old-established view of common sense," which errs in appealing to some "possible judge" who would ultimately be able to weigh in on the truth of a matter in a plausibly objective manner (1885: 426–27). Peirce supposes that Royce would say that a belief that was perfectly supported by inquiry and a belief in the mind of God would coincide. But in that case "I fail to understand why he should be so cruel to the childish Thrasymachus; since after all there is no real difference between them."

But Peirce thinks that there is a very significant difference between him and Royce. He identifies the Hegelian "upshot" of *The Religious Aspect of Philosophy* as: "the reality of whatever really exists consists in the real thing being thought by God" (*CP* 8. 40; 1885). Royce imports Hegel's "capital error"—he "ignores the Outward Clash" or the "direct consciousness of hitting and of getting hit" which makes consciousness "mean something real" (*CP* 8. 41; 1885). Royce is also "like Roger Bacon, who after stating in eloquent terms that all knowledge comes from experience, goes on to mention spiritual illumination from on high as one of the most valuable kinds of experiences" (*CP* 8. 43; 1885). Note that Royce on this score is almost indistinguishable from his great opponent James.

Peirce is adamant, with Royce, that we have to preserve a gap in which error can live—a gap between what we happen to believe and the truth. On Peirce's view, the outward clash can let us know that our beliefs are not what they should be. And, of course, truth is that which would fit with *all* of human experience, were we to pursue the gathering of that experience as far as we fruitfully could. Truth is not what we happen to believe here and now. We can explain error and preserve the gap between truth and current belief without, as James put it, "lugging in" the Absolute (Clendenning 1999: 241).

---

[13] It was to be one of the very few philosophical reviews of the book, but the publisher fell through (Clendenning 1999: 124).

What Royce objects to in Thrasymachus's view, is that the end of inquiry is "*barely possible*" and "[b]are possibility is blank nothingness" (1885: 430). Peirce's reply is excellent: "he would seem to be speaking of mere logical possibility" and "while the final opinion . . . may possibly, in reference to a given question, never be actually attained, owing to a final extinction of intellectual life or for some other reason," it is far from being a mere logical possibility. Indeed:

> upon innumerable questions, we have already reached a final opinion. How do we know that? Do we fancy ourselves infallible? Not at all; but throwing off as probably erroneous a thousandth or even a hundredth of all the beliefs established beyond present doubt, there must remain a vast multitude in which the final opinion has been reached. Every directory, guide-book, dictionary, history and work of science is crammed with such facts.
>
> [*CP* 8. 43; 1885]

In 1899 Royce gave the Gifford Lectures, published in two long volumes as his magnum opus *The World and the Individual*. In these lectures, he takes another stab at resolving these disputes. His central questions are "What is an Idea?" and "How can Ideas stand in any true relation to Reality?" (1899: 16) The modern reader will be with Peirce in thinking: "We wish that in place of the vague word "idea" he had substituted *judgment* . . . he is considering cognition in its truth or falsity, and only judgments have truth or falsity" (*CP* 8. 115; 1900).

Royce sets up the problem by noting that an idea (or a judgment) appears to represent or correspond to "a fact existent beyond itself," but it is not clear how it can do that, given that its "primary character" is an internal character of fulfilling a purpose or expressing a will at the time it comes to mind (1899: 24, 41). Realists, or those who insist that an idea corresponds to something external, fail to tell us how an idea can escape the world of the internal and represent something that goes beyond it. As James put Royce's argument against realism in a review of *The Religious Aspect of Philosophy*:

> Turn and twist as we will, we are caught in a tight trap. Although we cannot help believing that our thoughts *do* mean realities and are true or false of them, we cannot for the life of us ascertain how they *can* mean them. If thought be one thing and reality another, by what pincers, from out of all the realities, does the thought pick out the special one it intends to know?
>
> [1987 [1885]: 286]

And those who insist that our ideas are only *our* ideas fail to tell us how we could possibly be mistaken in our beliefs.

At the center of Royce's route out of this quandary lies the pragmatist-sounding thought that we cannot pull apart cognition and volition. Every idea, Royce argues, has its purpose, which he calls its internal meaning (1899: 25). It also has its external meaning or that toward which we direct its purpose or action. The external meaning is the object or referent of an idea. Both are essential parts of what is it to have an idea, to make a judgment, or to hold a belief.

In 1900 Peirce wrote an illuminating review of this "important" book for the *The Nation* (*CP* 8. 100; 1900). He takes Royce's characterization of meaning to be aligned with the general spirit of the pragmatic maxim and in his discussion we find one of Peirce's finest statements of his own theory of signs and meaning (*CP* 8. 119–20; 1902). In what is a bit of a provocation, given that Royce is very much set against James's view during this period, Peirce says: "We can hardly believe that he is so entirely won over to the extreme pragmatism of his colleague, James" (*CP* 8. 115; 1900). And indeed, here is Royce, sounding very much like James:

> There is no purely external criterion of truth ... Every finite idea has to be judged by its own specific purpose. Ideas are like tools. They are there for an end. They are true, as the tools are good ... But let a man ask, Is a razor a better or worse tool than a hammer? Is a steam engine a better mechanism than a loom? Such questions are obviously vain, just because they suggest that there is some one purely abstract test of the value of any and all tools, or some one ideal tool that, if you had it, would be good apart from any specific use. Yet there are philosophers who ask, and even suppose themselves to answer, questions about the truth of ideas that are just as vain as this.
> [1899: 308–9]

Peirce begins his review by summarizing his own account of truth: truth is what would be found "were the inquiry to be prosecuted without cessation." In the book under review, Royce does not spurn this as the view of a silly Thrasymachus.[14] Rather, he takes the reader through three mistaken "historical conceptions of being" en route to his own. The first two—realism and mysticism—are uncompromising in that realism is all about external meaning and mysticism is all about internal meaning. The other two conceptions—critical rationalism and Royce's own "constructive idealism"—are much better, as they find ways of melding together internal and external meaning. Although he does not name Peirce or James, it is the pragmatist who is under scrutiny as the ultimately unsatisfying critical rationalist.[15]

In Royce's telling, this kind of philosopher is enthusiastic about science and about the need for our ideas to be connected to the external, but avoids the realist's mistaken view that our beliefs represent a reality whose essence is that it is entirely independent of knowledge. The critical rationalist holds that the real is the object of possible knowledge. Royce's objection to this view remains steady. His objection remains centered around what he takes to be the problematic nature of the "bare possibility" of "possible experience" (1899: 357, 259ff.). If truth and reality are what would be determined, were we to have all possible experience, then truth and reality are "in a

---

[14]   It is very clear that Royce knows his Peirce. For instance, he says, repeating Peirce almost verbatim, that "the mathematician ... has ... created his world of mathematical objects. This world is there, as it were, by his decree ... But once created, this world ... is as stubborn as the rebellious sprits that a magician might have called out of the deep." And: "like any other student of Real Being," the mathematician "observes and experiments" (1899: 214, 226). At (1899: 254f.), Royce's extended and explicit discussion of Peirce's view of how mathematical reality impinges upon us and how we experiment upon diagrams shows us that the importance of Peirce's idea, of which I have made so much, was noticed and appreciated at the time.

[15]   See Kuklick (1985: 119–20).

measure, indeterminate" (1899: 290). In his review, Peirce answers the objection again: "Professor Royce seems to think that this doctrine is unsatisfactory because it talks about what would be, although the event may never come to pass. It may be that he is right in this criticism; yet to our apprehension this 'would-be' is readily resolved into a hope for a '*will be*'" (*CP* 8. 84; 1891). We hope or assume that there will be a determinate answer to our questions. That is clear enough, Peirce thinks, whereas Royce's qualms about "bare possibility" are not at all clear.

It is interesting that, in his own response to Royce, James delivers one of the most effective responses to objections to his view of truth. He agrees with Royce that facts are facts only if they fall under the scope of consciousness. Where there is no knowing, there is no truth and no reality. That is where the idealism in pragmatism resides. But Royce is wrong in attacking pragmatism on the grounds that it appeals to the possible unfolding of inquiry. James notes that an egg is a possible chicken in that the chicken is expected. "His coming *makes* the truth which doesn't *exist* now; it is an error to say that any proposition about the chicken is either true or false in advance of his actual presence" (1988 [1899]: 206). To talk of possibilities is to talk of expectations. Royce's problem is that he takes the possible chicken to be an actual fact and hence he needs to appeal to the Absolute to explain how something that does not yet exist is actual. James quips that even if there were a completely empty universe, Royce would bring in the Absolute as the knower of the nothingness: "Hegel's logic revives: to posit nothing is to posit being, and so on through the rigmarole" (1988 [1899]: 208).

In *The World and the Individual* Royce continues to propose a solution to this impasse by appealing to a deity—to Absolute Thought or Absolute Purpose (1899: 41). Our "poor fleeting finite ideas" strive after an ideal (1899: 359). "This alone is real,— this complete life of divine fulfillment of whatever finite ideas seek" (1899: 359). We human beings are fragments of or parts of a "conscious whole" and only from that perspective can ideas possess true internal meaning and purpose. It is the "Absolute Will which faces the final meaning and fulfillment of the world" (1899: 459). In Peirce's words: Royce thinks that internal meaning tends towards the limit of "the knowledge of an individual, in short, of God" (*CP* 8. 115; 1900).

Peirce rejects this brand of idealism by turning Royce's argument from the possibility of error back onto its author:

All reasoning goes upon the assumption that there is a true answer to whatever question may be under discussion, which answer cannot be rendered false by anything that the disputants may say or think about it ... This makes an apparent difficulty for idealism. For if all reality is of the nature of an actual idea ... what, then, can be the mode of being of a representation ... unequivocally false? Prof. Royce, however, seems almost to resent the idea that anybody could suppose that he denied the validity of the distinction of truth and falsehood.

[*CP* 8. 126; 1902]

Royce, again, is wrong about what provides for error. Error is made possible by the outward clash of the world on our beliefs and expectations. Peirce says that

Royce "is blind to a fact which all ordinary people will see plainly enough; that it is one thing to *be* and another thing to *be represented*" (*CP* 8. 129; 1902). Absolute idealism "precisely consists in denying that distinction" and hence it denies the possibility of error. In a review of *The Religious Aspect of Philosophy*, Peirce says that what Royce fails to appreciate is that we can indicate the world without describing it as it is independently of our thoughts:

If the subject of discourse had to be distinguished from other things, if at all, by a general terms, that is, by its peculiar characters, it would be quite true that its complete segegation would require a full knowledge of its characters and would preclude ignorance. But the index, which in point of fact alone can designate the subject of a proposition, designates it without implying any character at all. A blinding flash of lightning forces my attention and directs it to a certain moment of time with an emphatic "Now!"

[*CP* 8. 41; 1885]

James also rails against Absolute idealism, especially as expressed by Bradley.[16] He thinks that Royce, like all Absolute idealists, thinks that we either have to "choose the complete disunion of all things or their complete union in the Absolute One" (1977 [1909]: 33). We have seen that James argues that this view has pernicious moral consequences. Royce was sharply aware of this criticism—that the perfection of the Absolute makes all actual evil in the world a part of some perfect and good whole. On this point, Royce is committed: "The world that is, is . . . indeed, as Leibnitz said, the best of possible worlds" (1967 [1892]: 440). But in response to pressure from James, Royce holds that his own kind of absolute idealism does not "rejoice . . . too easily" at the tidy solution to ethics that the Absolute seems to promise. In *Studies of Good and Evil*, Royce argues that evil is necessary, and our only solace is that our sufferings are the sufferings of the divine (1915 [1898]: 14). He thinks also that "one who finds himself . . . close . . . to the gate of the celestial city . . . does, after all, well to tremble" (1967 [1892]: 440). The moral goal is never attainable—finite human beings can never reach the perfection of the Absolute. We can merely approach it like an infinite series approaches its end (Royce *et al.* 1909 [1897]: 346).

In his 1903 Presidential Address to the third annual meeting of the American Philosophical Association, Royce attacks the pragmatism of James, Dewey, and Schiller. His talk is titled "The Eternal and the Practical" and in it he asserts that he had begun his career as a "very pure pragmatist." He also notes, making explicit the argument in *The World and the Individual*, that pragmatism and his own Absolute idealism share a kind of Kantian argument against realism. Both take the world to

---

[16] James objected to Bradley's thought that there is a spiritual Absolute that underlies all appearances. The way this kind of absolute idealist tries to escape the empiricist worry about skepticism (as illustrated by Hume) is to rethink the relationship between the perceiver and the perceived. The perceiver (the human mind) somehow contains the perceived (the universe itself). Royce, on the other hand, tended to think of the Absolute as infinity. Appearances are finite, but that does not mean that they are mere appearances—less than real. It just means that they fall short of the infinite Absolute.

be the construction of human beings rather than a set of facts given independently of human experience.[17]

But he takes the pragmatist account of truth to be inadequate, this time for a different reason. Pragmatism, he says, sticks to "transient, passing, variable" human beings and hence true judgments become "not genuinely true, but only special points of view" (1904: 142). In *The Spirit of Modern Philosophy*, this point is made in even more explicitly Jamesian language. The pragmatist thinks that an idea becomes true when it satisfies some transient finite need. Against this view, Royce claims that "[t]he truth, whenever we get it, must be . . . hard and fast" (1967 [1892]: 17).

So, although we find Royce in the early 1900s saying things like "I admit, in a very large and loose sense of the term, we are all alike more or less pragmatists" (1904: 113), he certainly is not at this stage of his career, happy about being called a pragmatist.[18] By the time the 1908 ethical treatise *The Philosophy of Loyalty* was published, however, Royce was starting to replace the idea of the Absolute with the idea of community, beginning what would be his genuine move to pragmatism. The commitment to the eternal did not entirely go away. Loyalty, for Royce, is "the Will to Believe in something eternal, and to express that belief in the practical life of a human being" (1995 [1908]: 166).

His wariness of the Jamesian pragmatist account of truth did not entirely go away either. In 1908 Royce attended, with Schiller, the Third International Congress of Philosophy in Heidelberg and acrimony broke out between the two men over pragmatism.[19] Royce's paper was titled "The Problem of Truth in the Light of Recent Discussion." It is a sharp attack on James and, to a lesser extent, Dewey, both of whom, he asserts, make truth the successful adaptation to natural and changing environments. "Truth therefore, grows with our growth, changes with our needs, and is to be estimated in accordance with our success. The result is that all truth is as relative as it is instrumental, as human as it is useful" (1951 [1908]: 66–67). He too is not above a bit of mockery: "The sole ground for my assertions is this, that I please to make them" (1951 [1908]: 86).

James and Dewey, Royce notes, take pragmatism to be a rebellion against authority, rigidity, and "pretended finality" (1951 [1908]: 68). That rebellion is fine, but pragmatism illicitly tends to "make the whole problem of truth identical with the problem of the rights and freedom of the individual" (1951 [1908]: 70). His objections are piled one on top of another. Pragmatism might work when we consider empirical truths about the present, but it is useless for thinking about past truths and the ideas of dead thinkers, such as Newton, when such "truths" no longer have any instrumental

---

[17] He asserted the same thing in *The Spirit of Modern Philosophy* (1967 [1892]: 294–300).

[18] There are other points of contact between his view and pragmatism—especially Peirce's version of it. His 1913 "Hypotheses and Leading Ideas" uses Peirce's thoughts on induction as a springboard for the argument that the scientific method makes important use of leading ideas or regulative assumptions (1951 [1913]: 262).

[19] See Clendenning (1999: 307).

value. It is not clear that we can verify our beliefs about the contents of the minds of others. As soon as you try to deny that there is a truth that goes beyond what you can verify here and now, you rely on a notion of truth that goes beyond what you can verify here and now. A theory of truth is surely true, full stop, not true for the moment.

No longer is Royce concentrating his worries about pragmatism on the idea of the possible upshot of inquiry. His conclusion, however, remains the same: pragmatism needs the Absolute. We have to "acknowledge a truth that transcends our individual life" (1951 [1908]: 88). He is silent about Peirce's way of acknowledging the gap between individual belief and the truth—the idea that truth is what would best account for experience and argument.[20] Indeed, Peirce gets mentioned in this paper positively, for his advances in logic. Royce concludes with a plea for his own brand of "Absolute Pragmatism" in which "what we know . . . is always relative to our human needs and activities. But all of this relative knowledge is . . . defined in terms of absolute principles" and "all truth" is "the essentially eternal creation of the Will" (1951 [1908]: 95–96).

From here on, at this late stage in his career, Royce started to become more and more Peircean. In his 1918 *The Problem of Christianity* he says that he owes more to "our great and unduly neglected American logician, Mr. Charles Peirce" than he does to recent idealism or to Hegel himself (1968 [1918]: 39).[21] Most importantly, under the influence of Peirce, the notions of signs, interpretation, and community start to play a major role in his epistemology. In 1912, Royce reread some papers of Peirce's[22] and started to argue that "Man is an animal that interprets; and therefore man lives in communities" (1968 [1918]: 298). His epistemology starts to be laced with talk of a third, mediating idea that allows us to compare our ideas of two things. It becomes laced with Peirce's triadic view of signs and interpretation.[23] Setting the stage for his student Mead's theory of the self and sociology, Royce argues that the "social mind" expresses itself "in language, in customs, in religions"—things that an individual mind is not able to produce (1968 [1918]: 80–81). Royce remarks that "every interpretation, being addressed to somebody, demands interpretation from the one to whom it is addressed" (1968 [1916]: 290). It is interpretation of the signs of others that draws us into discourse, and thus, into a community. The notion of a community also starts to

---

[20] This is particularly interesting given the "special obligation to Mr. Charles Peirce" that Royce records in the preface to the first volume of *The World and the Individual* (1899): xiii). Royce says that he is obligated to Peirce "not only for the stimulus gained from his various published comments and discussions . . . but for the guidance and the suggestions due to some unpublished lectures of his which I had the good fortune to hear' (1899: xiii). We might surmise that Royce was silent on Peirce's account of truth because he did not take it to be a target.

[21] He also claims that he is in agreement with his great friend and opponent James, at least some of the time (1951 [1908]: 78–86). He agrees to the extent that James's pragmatism captures the fact that the search for truth is practical in nature (1908: 324–48). After James's death, Royce remarked that "I long loved to think of myself as his disciple; although perhaps I was always a very bad disciple" (1969 [1911]: 8).

[22] See Clendenning (1999: 349), as well as Royce's *The Problem of Christianity* (1968 [1913]: 275–76).

[23] See 1968 [1918]: 286–90, 298–304. He says that he "freely imitate[s]" Peirce's main thesis of interpretation: "interpretation *is* a triadic relation" (1968 [1913]: 285–86).

play a central role in Royce's account of truth. A community of interpreters who work together will eventually take us in the direction of truth. Royce, however, remains unwilling to go all the way with Peirce. God, for reasons never solidly articulated, remains in the picture as the divine interpreter, somehow undergirding truth.

Royce's attempt to combine absolute idealism with pragmatism is perhaps best summed up in his memorial at the 1916 APA meeting. He asserts that his aim is "to find in the world of the Absolute, elbow room for the individual, to show that the finite and temporal are not by this idealism shorn of the meaning they actually possess in concrete experience."[24] Royce spent his career fighting two battles. One was against realism. Here he always found the pragmatists fighting alongside him and he was happy to join forces. But the other battle was against pragmatism itself. In Royce's view, Jamesian pragmatism left not merely elbow room for the individual, but let the individual elbow out genuine, unchanging truth. He was right about James. But when he saw that Peirce's pragmatist account of truth rested not on the individual, but on the community of inquirers, he put down his sword. Not entirely won over to the pragmatist side, wanting to leave elbow room still for the divine, he at least made peace with the pragmatists.

5.3 The Extreme View of F. C. S. Schiller

Ferdinand Canning Scott Schiller (1864–1937) was a German-British philosopher, educated at Rugby and Oxford. He spent 1893–97 studying and teaching at Cornell, where he discovered James and saw the affinities between James's position and the view he was starting to articulate. He returned to Oxford, where he engaged in highly contentious debates with Bradley and Russell and was very much a part of the public face of pragmatism.

Like James, Schiller took himself to be battling against both the absolute idealists and the realists. Both kinds of "intellectualist philosopher" yearn for a truth "that shall be absolutely true, self-testing, and self-dependent, icily exercising an unrestricted sway over a submissive world, whose adoration it requites with no services, and scouting as blasphemy all allusion to use or application" (1969 [1907]: 9). The pragmatist or "humanist," on the other hand, thinks that meaning and truth cannot be pulled apart from use and application.

Schiller thought that the new pragmatism was a clear, refreshing, down-to-earth view. He also thought it was a revolution in philosophy and engaged in the uprising using his considerable comic talents as a weapon. His 1901 spoof *Mind! A Unique Review of Ancient and Modern Philosophy. Edited by A. Troglodyte, with the Co-operation of the Absolute and Others* is a brilliant parody of the philosophical establishment and the journal *Mind*. No doubt this did not endear him in the hearts of his opponents.

[24] An excerpt was printed in the *Report of the National Academy of Sciences*, while the full memorial was printed in the *Nation*, Nov. 16, 1916.

His debates with Bradley, for instance, are characterized by the following kind of passage. Bradley, he says, makes his debut "by triumphantly dragging the corpse of Mill round the beleaguered stronghold of British philosophy" and exercises "a reign of terror based on unsparing use of epigrams and sarcastic footnotes" (1969 [1907]: 115). In the preface to *Studies in Humanism*, he is similarly undiplomatic:

> It is clear to all who have kept in touch with the pulse of thought that we are on the brink of great events . . . The ancient shibboleths encounter open yawns and unconcealed derision. The rattling of dry bones no longer fascinates respect nor plunges a self-suggested horde of fakirs in hypnotic stupor. The agnostic maunderings of impotent despair are flung aside with a contemptuous smile by the young, the strong, the virile.

> [1969 [1907]: viii]

No wonder Schiller's humanism met with a chilly response. We shall see that even his fellow pragmatists were wary. James veered from cheering on Schiller's "radical" work and his attack on "*professionally*" expressed philosophy (*CWJ* 10: 26) to ruing it. Dewey's Chicago School was critical.[25] And Peirce, while not wanting to turn back any supporters, was privately very disappointed that a position even more extreme than James's was becoming identified with pragmatism.

Schiller adopts as his slogan Protagoras's "man is the measure of all things" (1969 [1907]: xx; 1939: 21, 105), and commits himself to the doctrine of "personalism," which follows the maxim "personality is the supreme value and key to the meaning of reality."[26] These are stronger governing sentiments than James's "the trail of the human serpent is over everything." But we shall see the crevices open between Schiller and others along familiar lines—the very lines that separate James at his most radical and his fellow pragmatists.

The early Schiller was a part of a short-lived movement called "personal idealism," which conceived of itself as a "development of Oxford idealism," opposed to both naturalism and the Absolutist brand of idealism.[27] It held, in Peirce's words, that "enough has not been made of personality in philosophy." It attempts to combine the core principles of empiricism and idealism. As Sturt puts it in his preface to Schiller's volume that announced personal idealism's arrival on the scene: "'Empirical idealism' is still something of a paradox; I should like to see it regarded as a truism" (1902: viii). The view had experience at its core. But this is the experience of individuals—full of interest, personality and other kinds of subjectivity. The similarity with James's "Will to Believe" is vivid.

Schiller uses the labels "pragmatism," "anthropomorphism," "voluntarism," and, most often, "humanism" for his view. His aim is one of "*humanising* Truth" (1969 [1907]: viii). His first careful working out of this view can be found in "Axioms and

---

[25] See Shields (1967: 51) and also Schiller (1939 [1936]: 57–64), in which he tries to put to rest the criticisms that he and James take meaning to be a private as opposed to a social affair; that they are too focussed on subjectivity; and that they fail to pay attention to mathematics and formal logic.

[26] This is R. T. Flewelling's definition.

[27] See Sturt (1902; v–vii).

Postulates," his contribution to *Personal Idealism*. In it, he talks about "the right to postulate" (1902: 90). Knowledge, for Schiller, is a matter of accepting "postulates which had suggested themselves as desirable if true, and had succeeded and survived, for transparent reasons, and could all be traced to the various activities of our will to believe" (1934 [1927]: 100). We assume that something is true because we desire it to be true—it serves an interest of ours. Then we test it to see if it fits with our experience. If it survives, it is indeed true. The will to believe is at the root of knowledge and truth. Put in an even stronger form, Schiller says that "Nothing more is required of a truth than that it should be relevant to a specific situation" (1910 [1891]: 133).

Schiller also brings his humanizing thoughts to the concept of reality. The world is "a *construction*" (1902: 54). Metaphysics, for Schiller, is a personal matter: "the fit of a man's philosophy is (and ought to be) as individual as the fit of his clothes" (1902: 50); "A metaphysic which is true for one man, because it seems to him to synthesize his experiences, may be false for another, because his personality is different" (1939: 178). We seem to have here a pragmatist position at the extreme end of the continuum, on which both truth and reality are "*wholly plastic*" (1902: 61).

Even more so than James, Schiller tends to glide from the idea that there is no sense to be made of trying to have our beliefs correspond to a reality that is entirely independent of human needs and interests to the idea that reality itself is entirely determined by human needs and interests. He starts with the perfectly good idea that we do not have "any independent knowledge of the 'external world'" (1902: 55–56) and moves to:

> there can be neither "things" nor "persons", neither "effects" nor "causes", until the chaotic flow of happenings has been set in order by successful discriminations. Every sort of distinct perceptual object, therefore, alike whether it be a "thing" or a "person", seems to be manifestly man-made, *i.e.*, relative to the human interests which singled it out, and preserve for it its status as a "reality" which it is expedient to take into account.
>
> [1909–10: 226]

While James backs off from such thoughts when challenged,[28] Schiller tends to stand his ground. Hence James's complaint that Schiller is forever delivering a "butt-end foremost statement of the humanist position."[29] But usually James is happy to see Schiller as fighting his battles. He says that a paper of Schiller's seems "to be written with my own heart's blood—it's startling that two people should be found to think so exactly alike" (1920 2: 271; 1907). And in a review of *Personal Idealism*, he seems to

---

[28] Sometimes Schiller presents a less radical view as well. The organism "needs assumptions it can act on and live by, which will serve as means to the attainment of its ends. These assumptions it obtains by postulating them in the hope that they may prove tenable, and the axioms are thus the outcome of a Will-to-believe" (1902: 91). Those that work—the survivors—are held to be true. Nonetheless, "it ill becomes them" to "give themselves airs and to regard their position as immutable and unassailable" (1902: 92). For, although it is highly unlikely that we shall ever want to make a revolution in our thought, we may find ourselves changing some of our axioms (1902: 93–94).

[29] James was so irked that this remark was made publicly, in his lecture "Pragmatism and Humanism" (James 1975 [1907]: 117).

agree with Schiller's metaphysics: "a general outcome" of pragmatism is the kind of "re-anthropomorphised universe" envisioned by Schiller (James 1987 [1903]: 94).

Peirce, on the other hand, thought that Schiller's view of reality was to be resisted. He reviewed *Personal Idealism* for *The Nation*, singling out Schiller's piece as the best in the volume, then holding it up for serious criticism. This is generally Peirce's way with Schiller. For instance, he says that Schiller's logic is "brilliant and seductive" and happily acknowledges that Schiller is part of the pragmatist family. But in the next sentence he says that Schiller's view is "very evil and harmful" (*CP* 5. 489; 1907). The harm, as Peirce describes it in the review of *Personal Idealism*, comes about because:

Mr. Schiller does not believe there are any hard facts which remain true independently of what we may think about them. He admits it requires a hard struggle to make *all* facts suit our fancy, but he holds that facts change with every phase of experience, and that there are none which have been "all along" what history decides they shall have been. This doctrine he imagines is what Professor James means by the "Will to Believe"'.

[1979 [1979 [1903]: 127]

Peirce also objects to Schiller's view that metaphysics ought to be regarded as "a matter of personal fancy" (1979 [1903]: 126). In a direct poke at Schiller, Peirce distinguishes himself from the positivists: "instead of merely jeering at metaphysics, like other prope-positivists, whether by long drawn-out parodies or otherwise, the pragmaticist extracts from it a precious essence" (*CP* 5. 423; 1905).[30]

Schiller and Peirce went back and forth, in friendly letters in 1905, about the nature of the pragmatic maxim, with plenty of misunderstanding due to the fact that Peirce had hardly anything in print. But while their disagreements about the pragmatic maxim might have more or less faded by the end of the correspondence, their disagreement about reality remained entrenched. Peirce insists on the independence of reality and it is this insistence that marks off his position from that of Schiller:

As to whether the real is changed by our thinking about it, I do not think there can be any question . . . my ethics of terminology will not permit me to give it any other meaning than that it is that whose characters do not at all depend upon what any man or men think that they are. I have said (in 1892) that to say that anything is quite real is a postulate, much as if a man went to borrow money of a bank and was asked for his security, he might say "Oh, I have no other security than that I postulate the loan." But I added that many things certainly approach so near to being real that we cannot say they are not so. You seem to think this very ill considered; but that is what we think in the laboratory.[31]

In general, he spells out their differences as thus: "I have no hope of finding you nearer to me because you want your philosophy to be the quintessence of the whole man.

---

[30] Upon the publication of Schiller's *Humanism*, Peirce writes to James: "The humanistic element of pragmatism is very true and important and impressive; but . . . [y]ou and Schiller carry pragmatism too far for me. I don't want to exaggerate it but keep it within the bounds to which the evidences of it are limited" (*CP* 8. 258; 1904).

[31] Unpublished letter quoted in Scott (1973: 372).

I want mine to be no such thing. I want it to be scientific, logical and frigid, with all the falsifications (if you will regard them as such) that are unavoidable in dissections."[32] Peirce most decidedly "cannot turn aside into Mr. Schiller's charming lane" (*CP* 5. 489; 1905). It is bad enough that James has followed him. Of *Studies in Humanism*, Peirce says: "Schiller informs us that he and James have made up their minds that the true is simply the satisfactory. No doubt; but to say 'satisfactory' is not to complete any predicate whatever. Satisfactory to what end?" (*CP* 5. 552; 1905)

Kenneth Winetrout sums up Schiller's place in classical pragmatism nicely: "we may think of pragmatism as having three initial thrusts: Charles S. Peirce represents the analytical thrust; John Dewey, the reformist thrust; and William James and F. C. S. Schiller, the existentialist thrust" (1967: 10). Schiller and James were the ones who took individual freedom, immediate concrete experience, and the personal to be at the centre of their theory of truth and reality. Schiller himself was not unaware of such gulfs in the pragmatist family:

> Its putative parent, Peirce, was so shocked by the fame of the doctrine fathered upon him, and so dismayed by the herculean exploits which it accomplished even in its cradle, that he was actually driven to disown his paternity, and to take refuge in a "pragmaticism" which he said, was ugly enough to be left severely alone . . . Its real progenitor, James, could hardly restrain his nearest and dearest pupils from participating in the congenial labor of misrepresenting what they had never understood.
>
> [1929: 451–52]

There is at least one point made by Schiller that the pragmatist would do well to hold on to. He accepted the pragmatic maxim that all concepts must be understood by their consequences. When applied to the concept of truth, he took the maxim to suggest that the difference between the truth and the falsehood of an assertion must show itself in some visible, observable way. Two theories that lead to precisely the same practical consequences are different only in words (1969 [1907]: 5). His own interpretation of "consequences" aligns him closely with James—both take consequences to be linked to human interest. Schiller says: "Human interest, then, is vital to the existence of truth: to say that a truth has consequences and that what has none is meaningless, means that it has a bearing upon some human interest. Its 'consequences' must be consequences to some one for some purpose" (1969 [1907]: 5). Here is where Schiller gets interesting. He follows James and Peirce in being expansive about the kinds of consequences that we might consider: "Of course the special nature of the testing depends on the subject-matter, and the nature of the 'experiments' which are in this way made in mathematics, in ethics, in physics, in religion, may seem very diverse superficially" (1969 [1907]: 6–7). What he says about this diversity is important:

> In some cases, doubtless, as in many problems of history and religion, there will be found deep-seated and enduring differences of opinion as to what consequences and what tests may be

---

[32] Unpublished letter quoted in Scott (1973: 372).

adduced as relevant: but these differences already exist, and are in no wise created by being recognized and explained. Pragmatism, however, by enlarging our notions of what constitutes relevant evidence, is far more likely to conduce to their amicable settlement than the intellectualisms which condemn all faith as inherently irrational and irrelevant to knowledge.

[1969 [1907]: 155–56]

Schiller's point is that there are many ways we come to believe something and there is bound to be disagreement about the status of some of those ways of fixing belief. The pragmatist declines to pretend that there is one proper, certain, way of fixing belief. Rather, we must attend to the diversity and see whether we can say something about which methods are legitimate and which are not. We have seen that Peirce's attempt to demarcate a principle is to say that our belief must be determined by something not extraneous to the facts. We have seen that James seems unwilling to demarcate any such principle. Schiller, at his best, falls between the two, seeing that some principle is required, but not providing it himself. We will see this debate continue to play out as we explore what became of pragmatism after the classical pragmatists went to their graves.

PART II

The Middle Period

6

The Reception of Early American Pragmatism

6.1 Introduction

It is clear that pragmatism was a topic of heated debate in the decades that ushered in the twentieth century. James and Schiller had introduced a new position to the world of philosophy and it was the object of lively attention. We have seen how that debate was engaged by the idealists—in particular by James's great opponent Royce. But what we have yet to see is how the position was received by the other side—by those of a more realist bent. Their response to pragmatism is especially critical if we are to understand how the fortunes of pragmatism have unfolded.

It will come as no surprise that it is James, not Peirce, who attracts the most commentary. Paul Carus, who penned the thought that pragmatism came like a comet on our intellectual horizon, is one of the few philosophers who actually read and engaged Peirce in the early 1900s.[1] In his influential and critical book titled *Truth on Trial*, he shows that he was attuned to the differences between the two founders of pragmatism:

Our readers may have noticed that since 'pragmatism' has become the watchword of a new and popular movement with which Mr. Peirce, the inventor of the term, does not appear to be in full accord, he has introduced the word 'pragmaticism' as if to point out the difference between his own philosophy and that of Professor James.

[Carus 2001 [1911]: 36]

Carus calls Peirce "the real founder of pragmatism" (2001 [1911]: 114), but he hardly mentions him in the rest of the book. He continues: "[t]he nucleus of the comet is Professor James, brilliant but erratic; and he is attended by a tail of many admirers and imitators, all aglow with the stir of their master's enthusiasm and the world stands open-eyed at the unprecedented phenomenon" (2001 [1911]: 44).

Similarly, James Pratt (2001 [1909]), in his attack on pragmatism, takes James to be the celebrity, with John Dewey and Schiller as supporting cast and Peirce with a mere walk-on part. Like many others at the turn of that century, Pratt doesn't even

---

[1] He was locked in a respectful debate with Peirce about chance and laws in *The Monist*.

spell "Peirce" correctly.[2] William Caldwell also leaves Peirce out of the picture. In *Pragmatism and Idealism*, he tells us that "Pragmatism ... rests in the main upon the work of three men, Professors James and Dewey of America, and Dr. Schiller of Oxford" (1913: 3). He allows that Peirce is "canonized as the patron saint of the movement by James," but hardly references him in the rest of the book.[3]

Bertrand Russell also had little knowledge of Peirce until late in his life. When he acquired that knowledge, his view was that "Beyond doubt ... he was one of the most original minds of the later nineteenth century, and certainly the greatest American thinker ever" (1959: 276). But before he acquired that knowledge, he took a rather dim view of what was happening on the American philosophical scene.

We have seen that two very different versions of the pragmatic account of truth and objectivity arose from applying the pragmatic maxim to the concept of truth—from linking the concept of truth to our practices. One version is Peirce's. He focuses on the practices of inquiry and tries to capture our cognitive aspirations to objectivity. The other is James's, in which truth is not stable or static but, rather, is "plastic." It is James's view that inspired the vitriol.

A few words of caution are required. We have seen that James at his most careful was concerned to characterize truth as something that was of human value, without making a true belief what this or that human found valuable at this or that time. He is prone to expressing regret that he does not always make this clear. He tries to correct any misunderstanding of his position by arguing that, contrary to his critics, he holds that the true is "the expedient," but the expedient "in the long run and on the whole, of course" (1975 [1909]: 4). That is, James too wants to argue that true beliefs are beliefs which survive because they deserve to survive.[4] But the reaction, fair or unfair, to James's *Pragmatism* set the tone for how pragmatism was viewed for decades to come. His critics latched on to the most radical statements of his view. Indeed, there is a uniformity about the view that pragmatism's critics take themselves to be reacting to. They all argue against the ideas that we make truth and that a true belief is one that is useful or works.

Caldwell, for instance, identifies two essential elements of pragmatism. First is the idea that truth and reality are "made," plastic or modifiable; second is the rejection of the distinction between appearance and reality (1913). Carus agrees with this characterization. Pragmatism replaces "the belief in the stability of truth, in its persistence and eternality" with "a more elastic kind of truth which can change with the fashions and makes it possible that we need no longer trouble about inconsistencies; for what is true to one need no longer be true to others, and the truth of to-day may be the real now, and yet it may become the error of the to-morrow" (2001 [1911]: 110). Hence

---

[2] In the Open Court Papers housed at Southern Illinois University, someone has misspelled Peirce's name several times on proofs of his own essays. I thank Doug Anderson for pointing this out to me.

[3] 1913: 3. The defenders of pragmatism also ignored Peirce. See e.g. Murray (2001 [1912]).

[4] See Kappy Suckiel (1982: 105–15) for this way of putting the point.

pragmatism has put truth on trial, with James as the hapless prosecutor. Carus says that James's mistake was that he "calls truth what in Mr. Peirce's language is merely 'the fixation of belief'" (2001 [1911]: 58). Peirce's argument, we have seen, is that were we to settle or fix belief permanently so that it would never disappoint us, then that would be the truth. Carus takes James to hold that if we have a belief that currently does not disappoint us, that is the truth. That is the view that was under attack and the attack, we shall see, was relentless.

6.2 The British Front

James's *Pragmatism* sparked the critical attention of Russell and G. E. Moore, who leveled devastating criticisms. That fatal attention was focused also on Schiller, a frequent target of Russell's scorn. He was, for instance, put into "a state of fury" over Schiller's "impertinence" in writing a piece on logic when "he neither knows nor respects the subject" (1992 [1909]: 292). The work in question seems to have been Schiller's 1902 "Axioms as Postulates," not even his most impertinent attack on logic. That title probably belongs to his 1912 *Formal Logic: A Scientific and Social Problem*.

Russell noted that he too was an empiricist, and so was sympathetic with pragmatism's self-understanding as a method that turns its back on a priori reasoning and turns towards concrete facts and consequences (1992 [1908]). Nonetheless, he thought that James's account of truth was seriously defective. Sometimes Russell is irresponsible in the way he goes about his charge. For instance, he quips: "The scepticism embodied in pragmatism is that which says 'Since all beliefs are absurd, we may as well believe what is most convenient'" (1992 [1909]: 280). Neither James nor Schiller went near that thought.

But some of Russell's objections are more measured and need to be taken seriously. For instance, he turns the pragmatist account of truth on itself and notes that if it is itself to be useful, there must be a way of telling when the consequences of a belief are useful:

We must suppose that this means that the consequences of entertaining the belief are better than those of rejecting it. In order to know this, we must know what are the consequences of entertaining it, and what are the consequences of rejecting it; we must know also what consequences are good, what bad, what consequences are better, and what worse.

[1992 [1908]: 201]

This is a very tall order, which Russell immediately illustrates with two examples. First, the consequences of believing the doctrine of the Catholic faith might be that the belief makes one happy "at the expense of a certain amount of stupidity and priestly domination" (1992 [1908]): 201). It is unclear how we are to weigh these benefits and burdens against each other. Second, the effects of Rousseau's doctrines were far-reaching—Europe is a different place from what it would have been without them.

But how do we disentangle what the effects have been? And even if we could do that, whether we take them to be good or bad depends on our political views. The question of whether the consequences of believing something are good or bad is an extraordinarily difficult one.

In a related objection, Russell points out that one can take "works" or "pays" in two very different ways. In science a hypothesis works if we can deduce a number of well-confirmed consequences from it. But for James, a hypothesis works if "the effects of believing it are good, including among the effects . . . the emotions entailed by it or its perceived consequences, and the actions to which we are prompted by it or its perceived consequences." As Russell goes on to note, "This is a totally different conception of 'working', and one for which the authority of scientific procedure cannot be invoked" (1992 [1908]: 210).

Moore reviewed James's *Pragmatism* in the 1907 *Proceedings of the Aristotelian Society*. The review is harsh and rather labored, with Moore identifying James's main assertions as things that he is "anxious" to say; picking them apart at length; and in the end finding them to be, despite James's protests to the contrary, "silly" (1992 [1907]: 161, 174). He strikes a theme and a tone present in many of the commentaries on James:

He may protest, quite angrily, when a view is put before him in other words than his own, that he never either meant or implied any such thing, and yet it may be possible to judge, from what he says, that this very view, wrapped up in other words, was not only held by him but was precisely what made his thoughts seem to him to be interesting and important.

[1992 [1907]: 174]

Here is a catalogue of Moore's objections to James's view. First, he points to a problem that dogs all pragmatist views of truth. If truth is tightly connected to what we can verify, how do we think of statements for which the evidence has been destroyed, or statements that are so trivial that no one has bothered to collect any evidence for them, or statements the evidence for which lies buried deep in the past? (1992 [1907]: 165, 179) Second, with Russell, Moore probes the linkage between the true and the useful. If usefulness is a property that may come and go (in James's own words), then, Moore says, "a belief, which occurs at several different times, may be true at some of the times at which it occurs, and yet untrue at others" (1992 [1907]:183). The truth of a belief, that is, will vary from time to time and from culture to culture. Truth is not a stable property of beliefs. That is an anathema, in Moore's view. And finally, Moore takes on James's claim that we make the truth: "I think that he certainly means to suggest that we not only make our true beliefs, but also that we *make* them true" (1992 [1907]: 191). Moore thinks that it is crazy to suggest that my belief that *p* makes it true that *p*. My (correct) belief that it rained today did not make it rain today.

It is no wonder that even Wittgenstein, who was attracted to pragmatism, felt that he had to distance himself from it. He read James's work (especially *Varieties of Religious Experience* and *Principles of Psychology*) intently and was clearly influenced by it, as was

Ramsey.[5] He says: "So I am trying to say something that sounds like pragmatism. Here I am being thwarted by a kind of *Weltanschauung*" (1975 [1969]: s. 422, 54e). He cannot align himself with James's view: "But aren't you a pragmatist? No. For I am not saying that a proposition is true if it is useful" (1980: s. 266, 54e).

Under a barrage of well-formed criticism such as this, pragmatism's reputation across the Atlantic was heavily damaged. It came under similar stress in America.

6.3 The Home Front

James Pratt is the critic who takes the most care with James's view. He sees two ambitious claims at the heart of pragmatism. The first is about truth: "in morality and metaphysics and religion, as well as in science, we are justified in testing the truth of a belief by its usefulness" (2001 [1909]: 13). A true claim is a "verified human claim" (2001 [1909]: 83). The second is about meaning: "the meaning of any philosophical proposition can always be brought down to some particular consequence in our future practical experience" (2001 [1909]: 25).

Pratt, like Russell, asked whether the pragmatist account of truth was itself true. It is certainly thought to be useful to pragmatists, he says, but not to all other philosophers (2001 [1909]: 127). The fact that pragmatists will want to respond by saying that the truth of pragmatism consists in something more robust than whether it is thought to be useful to this or that philosopher shows that they too think that there is some more transcendental account of truth in play. The pragmatist is "making use of the very conception of truth which he is trying to refute" (2001 [1909]: 129).

Pratt also tackles James's view that religious hypotheses are true if they are good for us to believe. Here he echoes Moore's distinction between the two senses of what works or what is good. Pragmatism, Pratt says:

seeks to prove the truth of religion by its good and satisfactory consequences. Here, however, a distinction must be made; namely, between the 'good', harmonious, and logically confirmatory consequences of religious concepts as such, and the good and pleasant consequences which come from believing these concepts. It is one thing to say a belief is true because the logical consequences that flow from it fit in harmoniously with our otherwise grounded knowledge; and quite another to call it true because it is pleasant to believe.

[2001 [1909]: 186–87]

With two caveats, the difference between the views of Peirce and James can be nicely summarized by Pratt's distinction. Peirce holds that "a belief is true because the logical consequences that flow from it would fit in harmoniously with our otherwise

---

[5] See Goodman (2002), and Misak and Bakhurst (forthcoming). The story of Frank Ramsey's place in the history of pragmatism is one that begs to be told. Ramsey was a brilliant philosopher, who also founded two branches of economics and one branch of mathematics. He died at the age of twenty-six. He was heavily influenced by Peirce, much more than he was influenced by James, and left an unfinished but deeply interesting manuscript on truth. See Misak (forthcoming).

grounded knowledge," and James at times seems to hold that a belief is true "because it is pleasant to believe." The first caveat is that we have seen that Peirce insisted on a subjunctive formulation: a belief is true if the logical consequences *would* fit harmoniously with our otherwise grounded knowledge, *were* we to pursue our investigations as far as they could fruitfully go. The second is that James, as his protests suggest and as we have seen, sometimes put forward a more careful and subtle account of truth, one that was much closer to Peirce's.

Pratt brought an equally damaging set of objections, again echoing Moore, against James's claim about meaning—that the meaning of a sentence consists in its consequences for future experience. He notes that it is not clear whether "our experience" means my own experience, the experience of all human beings at all times, or the experience of any possible rational or sentient being. On any of these options, sentences buried in the past (e.g. "an ichthyosaurus, who perished ages before the birth of the first man, suffered pain") seem to be meaningless, as they do not have any future experiential consequences (Pratt 2001 [1909]: 25ff.).[6] We have seen how this issue absorbed Peirce and we have seen how he tries to resolve it. James does not address the matter.

James railed against these often harshly put objections, claiming that they have a "fantastic" and "slanderous" character and are based on willful misinterpretation (1975 [1909]: 8, 99). He responded, for instance, to Russell by asserting that it would be an "obvious absurdity," one that never tempted him, to hold that someone who believes a proposition *p* must first determine that its consequences are good, and then fix his belief so that the consequences of *p* are good (1975 [1909]: 272). His protests, however, had very little impact. We have already seen Moore's treatment of James's disclaimers. Carus is similarly left cold by them: "He seems to be in the habit of sometimes saying what he does not mean and then blames the world for misunderstanding him" (2001 [1911]: 23). He argues that if James is misunderstood, the misunderstanding can be laid at the feet of "his own carelessness" (2001 [1911]: 127). He is glad to hear that James does not hold the view attributed to him by Russell, "but I cannot help thinking that his explanations of the meaning of pragmatism go pretty far to justify Professor Russell in thinking so" (2001 [1911]: 128).

William Caldwell, in his not unsympathetic *Pragmatism and Idealism*, notes that even in America, pragmatism encountered in its first decade of life "at least something of the contempt and the incredulity and the hostility that it met with elsewhere, and also much of the American shrewd indifference to a much-advertised new article" (1913: 49). Of its second decade Caldwell says that the reaction in America is "the sharpest kind of official rationalist condemnation of Pragmatism as an imperfectly proved and a merely 'subjective' and a highly unsystematic philosophy" (1913: 51). Carus,

---

[6] Pratt concludes that pragmatism must be interpreted broadly, as taking into account any experience—actual or possible and past, present, or future. Then he says that it is indistinguishable from idealism (2001 [1909]: 37f.).

who dedicates his *Truth on Trial* to the memory of James, and who says that James "was a fascinating personality, original and interesting in his very vagaries, genial and ingenious, versatile and learned," also says: "Exactness of method seems to have hampered his mind and naturally appeared to him as pedantry. He loved to indulge in the *chiaroscuro* of vague possibilities, and so he showed a hankering for the mysteries of psychic phenomena, whether due to telepathy or spirit communication" (2001 [1911]: 42–43). "With all my admiration for Professor James I . . . must openly confess that his loose way of philosophizing does not exercise a wholesome influence on the young generation" (2001 [1911]: 42). As Dewey says of James in 1912: "among professional philosophers it was rather the fashion to speak in a tone of amused disparagement of his philosophic attempts" (*MW* 7: 142; 1912).

Hence, pragmatism's reputation at the beginning of the twentieth century was, in Pratt's words, a reputation for "a looseness of thought" (2001 [1909]: 245). He says, with a bit of a sneer, that pragmatists will call his objections " 'logic-chopping'—a simple and useful device when one has been reduced to unavoidable self-contradiction" (2001 [1909]: 128). Such objections were so strenuously put that pragmatism has never been able fully to shake off the reputation it attracted in the early 1900s. The effect of James was cemented in. He caused "pragmatism" to be a household word in the abodes of philosophers and not many wanted his kind of pragmatism to move in permanently.

7

John Dewey (1859–1952)

7.1 Introduction

John Dewey grew up a grocer's son in a middle-class, educated, Calvinist family in Vermont. He attended the University of Vermont at the age of fifteen, then after a few years of high school teaching and private study in philosophy, went in 1882 "to Johns Hopkins . . . to enter upon that new thing, 'graduate work'" (*MW* 5: 150; 1930). His career flourished. He secured a job at University of Michigan directly after graduating from Hopkins and sped up the ranks there. His moves were to Minnesota; then back to Michigan; then to head of department at the University of Chicago where from 1894 to 1904 he reigned over The Chicago School, a hotbed of naturalism and pragmatism. His reputation in educational theory soared, he started an experimental elementary school, and he became widely known and sought-after.

Dewey resigned from the University of Chicago in April of 1904, after an unpleasant set of disagreements with the University over whether his wife would remain principal of the experimental school. He had no position secured elsewhere and Columbia University leapt at the opportunity to make him an offer. He formally retired from Columbia in 1930, but continued to work in a prodigious way. His most substantial book in epistemology, *Logic: The Theory of Inquiry*, was written in 1938, when he was in his late seventies.

Dewey was (albeit briefly) a student in Peirce's class at Johns Hopkins, yet he outlived Peirce and James by four decades, becoming the long-standing standard-bearer for pragmatism and shepherding the tradition through major changes in the intellectual landscape. He was also America's most famous and wide-ranging thinker. His work in educational theory and child development is legendary: he was at the forefront of the move to educate the whole child and of the idea that children learn by doing. He was also engaged in high-profile political discussions and opined on the merits of a wide range of current trends, from Freudian psychoanalysis to the Alexander Technique.

Intellectuals have always spoken to the social, political, and ethical issues of their day, but the mid-twentieth century was a particularly political time for American academics. Debates about communism and Stalinism raged and in the height of paranoia during the Cold War, a university professor could be interrogated and lose his job on a whiff of communism. Dewey was omnipresent in these debates, almost always taking the stance of a progressive reformer and liberalizing force. Alan Ryan aptly describes him as having fought for the radical center (1995: 244). He battled for non-communist social democracy or the anti-Stalinist left; he chaired the Commission of Inquiry that found Leon Trotsky not guilty of the charges in the Moscow Trials; and he vigorously opposed McCarthyism. *The New York Times*, on the occasion of his ninetieth birthday, proclaimed him "America's philosopher." He took his views around the world, giving lecture tours in China, the Soviet Union, Japan, Turkey, and Mexico—to name only those that would have seemed the most exotic. His written work ranges across a vast number of topics over seventy years, filling thirty-seven volumes.

Given Dewey's reputation, pragmatism's fortunes must have seemed entirely secure. But they were not. Ryan notes that "Dewey's reputation sank upon his death" in 1952 (1995: 328) and Bruce Kuklick remarks that none of his students went on to outstanding careers in academic philosophy in which they promoted pragmatism (2001: 191). Dewey is thus of special interest to anyone who wants to find out just what happened to pragmatism during the twentieth century.

One reason for the waning of pragmatism, once Dewey was no longer alive to promote it, is surely due to his own writing style. It lacks the sizzle of James's (and even Peirce's) pen, making a genuine understanding of his views rather heavy going. Oliver Wendell Holmes quipped of Dewey's *Experience and Nature* that it was "incredibly ill-written," but had "a feeling of intimacy with the inside of the cosmos . . . So me-thought God would have spoken had He been inarticulate but keenly desirous to tell you how it was" (1942 2: 287). But we shall see that the story of the fading of pragmatism has more complex and interesting causes. Dewey put forward a version of pragmatism grounded in what he took to be the lessons of the new biology, tinged with Hegelian metaphysics. Aspects of this version of pragmatism were not attractive to what was to become modern analytic philosophy.

It is mostly Dewey's work in epistemology and ethics that will occupy me here. In these domains, Dewey is concerned with the same philosophical issue that concerned Royce, James, and Peirce. How are we to think of the world, given that *we* bring so much to it? How are we to understand truth, given that we cannot have unfettered access to the subject matter of our beliefs and theories? Dewey initially thought, with Royce, that the answers to these questions were to be found in Hegel. As his attempts to hammer out a fully Hegelian solution faltered, he moved gradually to pragmatism, albeit a pragmatism with a residue of Hegelianism.

Dewey's overriding mission is to encourage scientific thought in all branches of philosophy. In epistemology this means that, with Peirce and James, he thinks that inquiry must be at the very heart of our theories about truth and knowledge. In aesthetics, education, political and social philosophy, and ethics, this means that he characterizes these domains as empirical or as experimental sciences. He thinks of himself as "continuing the tradition of David Hume," despite the fact that Hume is taken to be a skeptic (1983 [1930]: 228). Perhaps Dewey could see that a much better reading of Hume has him looking like the pragmatist's predecessor. While in his study,

Hume finds skepticism compelling, but as soon as he leaves that secluded place of theoretical philosophizing, skepticism loses any force it might have had.[1] The skeptic's doubts, as Peirce would put it, are paper doubts. As Hume remarks in the *The Enquiry Concerning Human Understanding*, the "remote considerations" of philosophy have "little efficacy": natural sentiments felt immediately in experience "are not to be controlled or altered by any philosophical theory or speculation whatsoever" (1975 [1777]: §80). But we shall see that it would be a mistake to classify Dewey as straightforwardly continuing in the tradition of Hume. His position is a complex mix of views, and that complexity defies any attempt to set it out in simple terms. I shall, in what follows, stick to the questions that surround the ideas of truth and knowledge, and hope that I am clear enough.

7.2 Dewey, Peirce, and James

Dewey's graduate work coincided with Peirce's brief tenure at Johns Hopkins. In 1879, while at Hopkins, Peirce revived The Metaphysical Club. Dewey participated in these meetings, in which a broad range of topics were discussed—philosophical, psychological, and biological.[2] But Dewey was not a fan of Peirce and his technical approach. He sided with another of his professors, George Sylvester Morris, in thinking that "real logic" was Aristotelian or Hegelian logic, not the formal systems that were just beginning to appear on the philosophical horizon.[3]

We have seen that absolute idealism was the dominant philosophy in America during Dewey's graduate student days. Dewey started off as a Hegelian: it was "the vital and constructive" movement in philosophy (*MW* 5: 152f.; 1930; and 1939: 522). He took Royce's use of evolutionary ideas even closer to idealism, arguing that the organism–environment relationship is a parallel to the Hegelian dialectic. He was heavily influenced by the work of the Victorian utilitarian philosopher Herbert Spencer, who popularized the term "environment" and coined the expression "survival of the fittest." Here is James on the interweaving of biology, psychology, and idealism in Dewey:

Like Spencer, . . . Dewey makes biology and psychology continuous. "Life" or "experience" is the fundamental conception; and whether you take it physically or mentally, it involves an adjustment between terms. Dewey's favorite word is "situation". A situation implies at least two factors, each of which is both an independent variable and a function of the other variable. Call them E (environment) and O (organism) for simplicity's sake. They interact and develop each other without end; for each action of E upon O changes O, whose reaction in turn upon E changes E, so that E's new action upon O gets different, eliciting a new reaction, and so on

---

[1] See Misak (1995: 78) for a more sustained account.
[2] See Fisch and Cope, (1952), Behrens, (2005) and Pearce (forthcoming).
[3] See Jane Dewey's biography in Schlipp (1939: 18).

indefinitely. The situation gets perpetually "reconstructed", to use another of Professor Dewey's favorite words, and this reconstruction is the process of which all reality consists.

[James 1977 [1904]: 2][4]

We have also seen that debates about absolute idealism were interwoven with those of pragmatism, with James (the anti-idealist) and Royce (the idealist) battling for supremacy. Just as Royce eventually found his idealism evolving towards pragmatism, so did Dewey. In 1930 he wrote a kind of intellectual autobiography. Its title speaks volumes: "From Absolutism to Experimentalism." Here Dewey tells us that he was drawn to absolute idealism because it is a unifying philosophy. It is a bringing together of fact and value and of object and subject. This unifying philosophical aim, we shall see, outlasts Dewey's idealism. It persists throughout his long career, making an understatement of Dewey's claim that he drifted away from Hegel over the course of almost two decades (*LW* 5: 154; 1930). What caused the gradual shift? Perhaps it was partly that Dewey started to be confronted everywhere with arguments against his Hegelian position, including James's onslaughts.[5] Perhaps it was partly caused by Dewey's own unsuccessful struggles to try to naturalize Hegelianism by adding to it a biological functionalism.

In any event, he was a Hegelian in his graduate student days and he was on an intellectual collision course with the irascible Peirce. In his first year, he wrote to an old teacher at the University of Vermont:

I am not taking the course in Logic. The course is very mathematical, & by Logic, Mr. Peirce means only an account of the methods of physical sciences, put in mathematical form as far as possible. Its more of a scientific, than philosophical course. In fact, I think Mr. Peirce don't think there is any Phil. outside the generalizations of physical science.

[*CJD* 1: 00415; 1882.10.05, grammatical mistakes Dewey's own.
See also *CJD* 1: 00429; 1884.01.17]

We should thus not be surprised at Peirce's view of Dewey. Peirce is careful in reviews and in public to commend Dewey as a fellow pragmatist, but in letters and in private he was harsh. Matters were not helped by the fact that Peirce had been shortlisted for the job that Dewey ended up getting at the University of Chicago.[6]

Peirce is concerned with what he fears Dewey is doing to pragmatism's name. He writes to Dewey in 1904 saying that while he is "strongly in favor" of Dewey's "Pragmatistic views," he finds his account of inquiry and knowledge "penetrated"

---

[4] See Pearce (forthcoming) for an excellent account of the role of evolution in The Metaphysical Club; the influence of Spencer on the early pragmatists; the role of Samuel Alexander in making the Hegelian-evolutionary biology link; and for the argument that Spencer was more important to Dewey than was Darwin.

[5] We have seen that James thought that the metaphysics of absolute idealism paralyzed action. We shall see when we turn to Dewey's ethics that he felt the force of this argument.

[6] See Dalton (2002: 64).

with a "spirit of intellectual licentiousness" (*CP* 8. 241; 1904). In a complaint very similar to those he made against James, Peirce wishes that Dewey had more rigor:[7]

> But I must say to you that your style of reasoning about reasoning has, to my mind, the usual fault that when men touch on this subject, they seem to think that no reasoning can be too loose, that indeed there is a merit in such slipshod arguments as they themselves would not dream of using in any other branch of science.
>
> [*CP* 8. 239; 1904]

Dewey, in Peirce's view, indulges in "a debauch of loose reasoning" (*CP* 8. 240; 1904).

Dewey eventually came to an appreciation of Peirce. In 1903, we find him softening in a letter to James:

> I must say, however, that I can see how far I have moved along when I find how much I get out of Pierce[8] this year and how easily I understand him, when a few years ago he was mostly a sealed book to me, aside from occasional inspirations. It is an awful pity that he cannot be got to go ahead consecutively.
>
> [*CWJ* 10: 221; 1903.7.27]

In 1908, we find him acknowledging that it was Peirce who identified pragmatism's guiding thought: that "the laboratory habit of mind" be "extended into every area where inquiry may fruitfully be carried on" (*MW* 4: 100; 1908). This is precisely how Dewey envisions pragmatism: it is an application of the scientific method, properly conceived, to every domain of inquiry or subject matter. In the 1930s, when Dewey started to read Peirce very seriously, one can see in his writing a new and deep knowledge of Peirce's work on experience, the categories, and inquiry. In 1935, in a comment on Tom Goudge's work on Peirce, Dewey defends Peirce as putting forward an excellent view of experience that brings in both human psychology and nature (*LW* 11: 86ff.; 1935). It is clear at this later stage in Dewey's thought that he sees how Peirce's view of inquiry turns on the idea of "actuality, taking the word in its most literal and brute sense" (*LW* 11: 482; 1937). We shall see that it is this very topic of actuality where the views of Peirce and Dewey threaten to part ways.

Also in 1935, in a glowing review of the first volume of Peirce's collected papers, Dewey says, perhaps trying to excuse his former neglect of Peirce's work: "His thought is nearer the mind of today than it was to the mind of thirty years ago" (*LW* 11: 422; 1935). There is also the unfortunate fact that Peirce "flung abroad many stones, pebbles, sometimes boulders, while he was sowing germinal ideas" (*LW* 11: 478; 1937). Many of those boulders, in Dewey's view, are caused by that "extraordinarily technical approach" (*LW* 11: 481; 1937). But by 1938, he is nonetheless crediting Peirce for the basics of his own view of inquiry, as a social activity that transforms a problematic doubt-laden situation into an unproblematic one (*LW* 12: 3, 484 n. 3; 1938).

---

[7] Royce seems to have been of the same view. See Lamont (1959: 38–39). It is not clear whether Peirce sent this unpleasant letter.

[8] The misspelling of Peirce's name here is a typist's error, not Dewey's (James *CL* 10: 221 n. v).

Again unsurprisingly, both because of James's gentler character and distaste for formal reasoning, Dewey's relations with James were much easier.[9] Although James was not one of Dewey's teachers, his work, especially *The Principles of Psychology*, had a great impact on the young Dewey. They conducted a mutually respectful correspondence from 1891 until 1909. For instance, James writes:

What you write of the *new school of truth* both pleases and humiliates me. It humiliates me that I had to wait till I read Moore's article before finding how much on my own lines you were working. Of course I had welcomed you as one coming nearer and nearer, but I had missed the central root of the whole business, and shall now re-read you (I had read *all* the articles you quote with great pleasure (but with this semi blindness still)) and try again a hack at Mead and Lloyd of whom I have always recognized the originality, but whom I have found so far unassimilably obscure. I fancy that much depends on the place one starts from—you have all come from Hegel and your terminology *s'en ressent,* I from Empiricism, and though we reach much the same goal it superficially looks different from the opposite sides.

[James *CL* 10: 217; 1903.3.23][10]

For his part, Dewey thinks that James is the only one to see the point of his 1891 *Outlines of a Critical Theory of Ethics* (*CJD* 1: 00459; 1891.05.10). He also understands James so well that he is able to sweep aside James's "inconsistencies" and his "fear of system-making" to see the best of his thought (*LW* 12: 471; 1938). He says the following about "The Will to Believe":

The underlying conception, I should say, is that the individual after all must have some vital connection with the universe in which he lives and that this connection can ultimately be but of two kinds. It is either such as to depress the individual or such as to support and invigorate him. Morally, we are entitled to adopt the latter attitude for the purpose of action even though rational proof of its validity be lacking. Short of the existence of overwhelming evidence of the invalidity of the belief, we may choose to live, to act, heroically, upon the assumption that something in the universe feeds our ideal aspirations and is actively on the side of their realization.

[*LW* 12: 475; 1938]

One wants to say that if James had stuck to this argument for optimism—for acting as if, or assuming that, the world is a moral place—instead of sometimes trying to secure the rational underpinnings of a belief in God, he would have been much more persuasive.

Indeed, Dewey makes it clear that he does not go in for the contentious Jamesian idea that "any good which flows from the acceptance of a belief" can be treated as "evidence" for the truth of that belief (*MW* 4: 109; 1908). He reviewed James's *Pragmatism*

---

[9] Dewey seems not to have met Schiller, but in a memorial to Schiller's work delivered at the New School in 1937, he is full of praise for his work (*LW* 11: 155ff.; 1937). He also seemed perfectly comfortable in aligning himself publically with Schiller's pragmatism and in a review of *Humanism* he vigorously defends Schiller against those who want to charge him with being far too subjectivist (*MW* 3: 313ff., 1904).

[10] The "Moore" James is referring to here is Ernest Carroll Moore, who had been a student of Dewey's and was among the contributors to the volume *Studies in Logical Theory*, which was dedicated to James (and for which Dewey had just sent James proofs). The other article Dewey had suggested to James was Alfred Henry Lloyd's "Dynamic Idealism" (1898).

in 1908, in an important piece titled "What Pragmatism Means by Practical." He takes exception to the fact that when James speaks of Dewey's view of truth, he tends to try to bring him into the Jamesian fold by imputing to him the following: "Truth consists in a character inclosed within the 'situation'. Whenever a situation has the maximum of stability, and seems most satisfactory to its own subject-fact, it is true for him" (1977 [1904]: 105). But Dewey is quick to correct this misperception of his position:

Since Mr. James has referred to me as saying "truth is what gives satisfaction", I may remark (apart from the fact that I do not think that I ever said that truth is what *gives* satisfaction) that I have never identified any satisfaction with the truth of an idea, save *that* satisfaction which arises when the idea as working hypothesis or tentative method is applied to prior existences in such a way as to fulfill what it intends.

[*MW* 4: 109; 1908]

Dewey is alert to how James can move too easily between "since true ideas are good, any idea if good in any way is true" (*MW* 4: 108; 1908). Dewey clearly has James in mind when he distinguishes his own position from a "voluntaristic" one. Dewey says that he is advancing "a type of pragmatism quite free from dependence upon a voluntaristic psychology. It is not complicated by reference to emotional satisfactions or the play of desires" (*MW* 8: 22; 1915).

Dewey often calls his view "instrumentalism." But it is clear from the above that he did not want to be seen, as he often was, as the kind of instrumentalist who says that whatever works for us—whatever hypothesis satisfies our individual desires, or is an instrument enabling us to get something we value—is warranted or true. He sees that if we take truth to be bound up with desirable consequences then we are "face to face . . . with the only serious question a . . . wisely pragmatic philosophy need fear" (*MW* 6: 54; 1911). That is the problem of elevating what is currently desired and believed to what ought to be desired and believed: "equating . . . the intellectually satisfactory with the personally agreeable, or . . . the authentic with what happens to be authorized . . . the legitimate with the legal" (*MW* 6: 5; 1911).

Dewey, though, is a careful reader of James and he sees that James's considered opinion is not that beliefs that satisfy you or me personally are true. "His real doctrine is that a belief is true when it satisfies both personal needs and requirements of objective things" (*MW* 4: 112; 1908). This lines up nicely, Dewey thinks, with his own position. A belief has to satisfy the inquirer's needs and it has to satisfy the situation. It is bound to the personal or the psychological but it also has to meet what the situation demands of it. Since the psychological cannot be kept out of questions about truth, it is better to recognize and accept responsibility for it than to try to ignore it (*MW* 4: 114; 1908).

Dewey is also distinguished from James and Peirce in that he replaces the religion of his youth with a faith in democracy and non-parochial education. He is suspicious of organized and doctrinal religion partly because religion is full of supernatural ideas in tension with his resolute naturalism and partly because he thinks that organized religion is morally dangerous. He is not inclined to immerse himself in debates for and against the existence of God: "I have not been able to attach much importance to religion as a philosophic problem" (*MW* 5: 153; 1930). His 1934 *A Common Faith* explores the possibility of a non-supernatural religion. He thinks that what is valuable in religion is, as Michael Eldridge puts it, "inclusive, intensive allegiances" that transform a person together with "intelligent, passionate participation in society" (2004: 59). Religion should amount to "a fund of human values that are prized and that need to be cherished" (*LW* 9: 54; 1934). There are also, in Dewey's view, "religious values implicit in the spirit of science" (*LW* 14: 79; 1939) and we can have a godless religious experience when we encounter good art: "[t]he sense of communion generated by a work of art . . . take[s] on a definitely religious quality" (*LW* 10: 275; 1934). Like James, however, Dewey thinks that talk of God can be useful—it "might protect man from a sense of isolation and from consequent despair or defiance" (*LW* 9: 36; 1934). That is, he was not a militant or aggressive atheist.

7.3 The Theory of Inquiry

Dewey reacts from an early age against what he takes to be the empiricist idea that perceivers passively absorb inputs from the external world. We have seen that this reaction is entirely in line with his pragmatist predecessors. He takes the great insight of Kant and Hegel to be that we impose human categories on experience. He says in his 1884 "Kant and Philosophic Method" that Hegelian logic is an account of experience "internal and external, subjective and objective, and an account of them as a system, an organic unity in which each has its own place fixed" (*EW* 1: 44; 1884). Subject and object merge in experience.

Thus, in the mid-1880s, when Peirce was working through his own Kantian views in "On a New List of Categories," the even younger Dewey was publishing similar views on the same topics.[11] In addition to the paper cited above, he placed two articles on psychology in *Mind* and one on Kant in the *Journal of Speculative Philosophy*. These pieces together attack both the empiricist and the idealist understanding of knowledge.

In "The Psychological Standpoint," he argues against the empiricist view of mind and world. He thinks that it is a shame that British empiricism seems to have captured the flag of empiricism. Locke, Berkeley, and Hume start with the laudable aim of explaining mental phenomena by experience and hence from the psychological standpoint. Dewey likes their idea that "nothing shall be admitted into philosophy which does not show itself in experience, and its nature . . . shall be fixed by an account of the process of knowledge—by Psychology" (*EW* 1: 124; 1886). But he thinks that the British empiricists give up quickly on this standpoint. They let metaphysics, or a psychology-independent reality, enter their pictures at some point or another (*EW* 1: 124; 1886). This "dogmatically presupposed ontology," an unknowable "thing in

---

[11] He was also publishing heavily on Spinoza, Leibniz, and on topics such as the soul, sex education, and the health of women.

itself," is their ruin (*EW* 1: 144f.; 1886). They would have done better to examine how our practices of discrimination and selection for relevance shape the experiences we have. Dewey was to retain this aversion to any mention of a psychology-independent reality throughout his life. It is what distinguishes his position from that of Peirce and, as we shall see, his contemporary C. I. Lewis.

Dewey also argues that the pragmatist's account of experience is consistent with the development of biology, whereas British empiricism is "completely exploded" by it (*MW* 12: 127–28; 1920). No longer can we think that "mental life originated in sensations which are separately and passively received, and which are formed, through laws of retention and association, into a mosaic of images, perceptions and conceptions" (*MW* 10: 12; 1917). We must think of experience, rather, as an active relationship between an organism and its environment. Moreover, pragmatist empiricism "does not insist upon antecedent phenomena but upon consequent phenomena; not upon the precedents but upon the possibilities of action. And this change in point of view is almost revolutionary in its consequences" (*LW* 2: 12; 1925). We have seen similar criticisms of British empiricism formulated, in similarly compelling ways, by Peirce and James.

In "Psychology as Philosophic Method" Dewey turns his critical attention also to the British idealist understanding of mind and world, as expressed by philosophers such as Green and Caird. Again, he insists that the science of psychology must be the driver of philosophy. This time the metaphysic shown to be spurious by science is the metaphysic of the Absolute. But Dewey was starting to become impressed by the idealists' idea that Hegel and evolutionary biology go hand in hand. In 1887, he brought his thoughts together in a book titled *Psychology*. It is an attempt at merging the best in idealism and empiricism. It did not go over well with many of the empirical psychologists. Dewey's old teacher, G. Stanley Hall, opined that "it might have been written half a century ago, and have been poorer only by a number of pat physiological illustrations" (1888: 157). James, too, was not impressed. He was "sorely disappointed" with the mixture of psychology and German idealism (James *CL* 6: 187f.; 1886.12.27).

Dewey does in fact take himself to be latching on to something in the past. But he wants to go farther back than half a century. He is with the Greeks in taking experience to be intimately bound up with action. He mourns the fact that Locke and the other British empiricists brought to philosophy the idea that experience could be defined as observation. This "spectator theory of knowledge" is wrong-headed.[12] We must return to Aristotle in holding practical activity at the centre of experience. But neither empiricism nor idealism fully gets right the relationship between the mind and the world. His aim, from very early on, is to reconcile the insights of the two. In doing so,

---

[12] Dewey's first denunciation of this view of knowledge appears in *Democracy and Education* (*MW* 9: 347–48; 1916), but the phrase "the spectator theory of knowledge" first occurs in the *The Quest for Certainty* (*LW* 4: 19; 1929).

he finds himself moving towards pragmatism. By 1903, the move is complete. That was the year that saw the publication of *Studies in Logical Theory*, a joint effort with Dewey's Chicago philosophy colleagues, with four introductory chapters by Dewey forming its core. It was seen by James as the foundation for pragmatism in America (1975 [1907]: xiv).

In *Studies in Logical Theory* Dewey offers us his first sustained account of inquiry, an account he had been mulling over for the previous three or four years. He starts with the thoughts expressed in his work on psychology. In the Preface, he sets out the framing idea:

judgment is the central function of knowing, and hence affords the central problem of logic; that since the act of knowing is intimately and indissolubly with the like yet diverse functions of affection, appreciation, and practice, it only distorts results reached to treat knowing as a self-enclosed and self-explanatory whole—hence the intimate connections of logical theory with functional psychology . . .'

[*MW* 2: 296; 1903]

Knowledge and human psychology are inextricably interwoven. We have seen that this is a mainstay of pragmatism: to know something, or to have a belief about what you experience, is bound up with our human capacities and categories. Once we bring an experience into the realm of comprehension, or understanding, or belief, we can no longer make sense of the idea of an experience of something unaltered by us. An understood or comprehended experience is always a joint effort between reality and the experiencer.

Dewey states that reality "must be defined in terms of experience" (*MW* 2: 296; 1903), citing James for inspiration (*MW* 2: 296; 1903). Similarly, logic is "the logic of experience" (*MW* 2: 314; 1903)—it is about "the genesis and functioning in experience of various typical interests and occupations with reference to one another" (*MW* 2: 315; 1903). Logic, that is, is about human inquiry. It should be no surprise that Russell is unhappy with this way of thinking about logic. He says of Dewey: "What he calls 'logic' does not seem to me to be a part of logic at all; I should call it a part of psychology" (1983 [1919]: 134).

A very large part of Dewey's contribution to *Studies* is taken up with a detailed criticism of Hermann Lotze's own attempt to construe logic as a part of inquiry. He says: "we have followed Lotze through his torturous course of inconsistencies" (*MW* 2: 330; 1903). Peirce and other critics took this to be a fruitless side excursion. What they took to be important was Dewey's positive view of inquiry, one which has a decidedly Peircean feel to it, although there is no mention of Peirce in *Studies*.[13] This view of inquiry has it that thought is an activity sparked by a problem that needs solving or

[13] The 1900 "Some Stages of Logical Thought" (*MW* 1: 151ff.; 1900) is very much a precursor to *Studies in Logical Theory*. Here too Dewey is interested in the role of doubt in inquiry, but again there is no mention of Peirce and "The Fixation of Belief."

settling. The measure of the success of thought is the degree to which it solves the problem or settles doubt.

Peirce reviewed *Studies* for *The Nation* and wrote two letters to Dewey about the book. Some of the strong language quoted in section 7.2 above comes from these letters. What Peirce is so upset about is what he calls Dewey's "genetical" reasoning— Dewey's idea that knowledge, logic, and reality can be understood by looking at how human beings think; the idea that logic is "a natural history of thought" (*CP* 8. 190; 1903). Dewey defines "genetic study" thus: "When we deal with any process of life it is found to be a great aid to understanding the present conditions if we trace the history of the process and see how present conditions have come about" (*MW* 5: 8; 1908). In the early 1900s he frequently says that "the experimental method is entitled to rank as a genetic method; it is concerned with the manner or process by which anything comes into experienced existence" (*MW* 2: 5; 1902). The "necessity of the *genetic* method" tells us that the meaning of philosophical concepts is a matter of "their origin in typical crises or junctures of immediate experience" and the "*validity*" of these concepts is a matter of "their relative success in their further career" (*MW* 3: 316; 1904). Dewey sometimes sounds a lot like James: "The pragmatist says that since every proposition is a hypothesis referring to an inquiry still to be undertaken (a proposal in short) its truth is a matter of its career, of its history: that it becomes or is made true (or false) . . . " (*MW* 6: 38–89; 1911). Thus, a "genetic" theory of truth holds that truth is generated rather than found and evolving rather than static. This is what Peirce was wary of and what James[14] and Dewey were not.

Ernest Nagel, perhaps Dewey's best graduate student, puts forward his own version of Peirce's worry in a retrospective on Dewey's work. He says: "There is perhaps only a hair line which divides a sound application of the principle of contextual analysis from a commission of the genetic fallacy." The worry is that Dewey's philosophy "confounds questions of validity and logical order with questions of origin and development" (Nagel in McGilvary *et al.* 1939: 578). This hairline marks the divide between the two kinds of pragmatists I trace in this book. One kind of pragmatist thinks that our history and evolution make us into the interpretative engines we are and, although we cannot completely pry apart interpretation from the truth of the matter, there nonetheless is a matter that we are interpreting. That is Peirce and, we shall see, C. I. Lewis. The other kind of pragmatist thinks that not even by abstraction can we say that there is something that stands apart from our interpretation of it. That is Dewey and, in a different sort of way, James and Schiller.

Peirce and Nagel weren't the only ones to think that Dewey's view of science was wrong-headed. Dewey's student Morris Raphael Cohen charges that by focusing on human psychology and interests, his teacher ignores the "disinterested curiosity" that is

---

[14] James tells us that the "scope of pragmatism" is "first, a method; and second, a genetic theory of what is meant by truth" (1975 [1907]: 37). This is in the context of describing his "plastic" and "living" account of truth.

at the core of science. Cohen argues that "detachment and a critical attitude are the special duties of those who as scientists or philosophers have to maintain the canons of intellectual integrity. Too often has devotion to temporal causes turned philosophical light into partisan heat" (1949 [1940]: 175).

It is interesting that Peirce's vitriol settles on Dewey's view of inquiry, since Dewey is following in Peirce's footsteps in characterizing logic as part of inquiry and inquiry as an activity in which doubt is replaced with a better belief. But for Peirce, while logic is indeed part of inquiry, it is also a formal and rigorous discipline that provides norms for inquiry. Its job is to "pronounce one proceeding of thought to be sound and valid and another to be otherwise" (CP 8. 190; 1903). And we have seen that Peirce thinks that science is a method of settling belief that looks for explanations that are not extraneous to the facts. As far as Peirce is concerned, *Studies in Logical Theory* "certainly forbids all such researches as those which I have been absorbed in for the last eighteen years" (CP 8. 243; 1905).

The view of logic and inquiry presented in *Studies in Logical Theory* persists through- out the great span of Dewey's thought, receiving its most sustained formulation in the 1938 *Logic: The Theory of Inquiry*. These topics were the subject of what Nagel describes as a "very famous" graduate course that Dewey taught at Columbia between 1914 and 1928 (Nagel 1986: 533). In fact, Dewey was still working through these ideas in 1949, contemplating yet another book on the subject (Nagel 1986: 544).

Logic: The Theory of Inquiry is written long after the deaths of Peirce and James. Finally, Dewey is able to gesture properly at Peirce as the author of the account of inquiry that Dewey uses as the building block for his own work.[15] But despite the book's being "thoroughly pragmatic," Dewey does not call his position "pragmatism": "so much misunderstanding and relatively futile controversy have gathered about the word that it seemed advisable to avoid its use" (LW 12: 4; 1938). Whatever labels Dewey chose to use and not use, one thing is clear. He again starts off with Peirce's account of inquiry and then, inspired by evolutionary theory, transforms it in ways that Peirce would have loathed.

Logic: The Theory of Inquiry starts off by accepting Peirce's doubt–belief model of inquiry almost word for word, duly acknowledged (LW 12: 17 n. 1; 1938). The following could have just as easily been taken from "The Fixation of Belief":

Doubt is uneasy; it is tension that finds expression and outlet in the processes of inquiry. Inquiry terminates in reaching that which is settled. This settled condition is a demarcating characteristic of genuine belief. In so far, belief is an appropriate name for the end of inquiry.

[LW 12: 15; 1938]

Dewey starts with Peirce's idea that inquiry is the resolving of a doubt. A trial, he says, is an example of a problematic situation requiring inquiry (LW 12: 123; 1938). Its formal

---

[15] On the topics of logic and inquiry, Dewey says that he has learned the most from those he disagrees with—"with the outstanding exception of Peirce" (LW 12: 4; 1938).

conceptions (misdemeanor, crime, torts, contracts, etc.) arise out of "ordinary transactions"—they are not imposed "from on high or from any external or a priori source" (*LW* 12: 106; 1938). "But when they are formed, they are also *formative*; they regulate the proper conduct of the activities out of which they develop" (*LW* 12: 106; 1938). When problems arise, our theories will likely be revised in light of new insights prompted by the problem.[16] That is, when a problematic situation or a doubt arises, we work to revise our beliefs until we have a settled belief that provides "a decisive directive of future activities" (*LW* 12: 124; 1938).

We have seen that Peirce's "Fixation of Belief" was concerned to answer the question that presses in on this account of inquiry. Are settled beliefs then true? Dewey does not feel the immediate pressure of this question, but we will see that he takes it more seriously elsewhere, when we turn in the next section to his thoughts on truth and certainty. In the book under discussion, he rests with the idea that warranted assertibility (as opposed to truth) is that at which we aim. That is what closes off a particular inquiry (*LW* 12: 15; 1938).

To another question that dogs the pragmatist—is this not a confusion of "is" with "ought"?—he says:

> The way in which men *do* 'think' denotes . . . simply the ways in which men at a given time carry on their inquiries. So far as it is used to register a difference from the ways in which they *ought* to think, it denotes a difference like that between good and bad farming or good and bad medical practice. Men think in ways they should not when they follow methods of inquiry that experience of past inquiries shows are not competent to reach the intended end of the inquiries in question.
>
> [*LW* 12: 107; 1938]

Peirce locates the normative in future inquiry. A belief or a method is not good if it would be overturned by inquiry as inquiry improves. Dewey also has norms arising out of inquiry, but he locates them in the past. A belief or method is not good if inquiries have shown it to be not good and the inquirer fails to notice that.

Despite the similarities between Peirce and Dewey, there is one particularly salient difference. An inevitable objection with respect to the example above is that while this might be an excellent way of viewing the law (as Oliver Wendell Holmes saw), it seems to work not as well for the physical sciences. For there, we think, and Peirce certainly thought, something external is in play. Of course, Dewey's conception of inquiry has more than our own principles and desires in play—whether methods of farming, for instance, have proven to be good will depend on the land, on what is planted, and so on. Nonetheless, whenever anyone mentioned the world and its constraints, Dewey thought they were trying to push him towards what he took to be an unreconstructed

---

[16] A modern, Rawlsian, way of putting the point would be to say that theory and experience are in reflective equilibrium. In considering ethical questions, we have to do a kind of "moral geometry" (Rawls 1971: 121).

correspondence theory of truth.[17] It is certainly the case that those pragmatists who want to talk about the world and its constraints need to work hard to show how there is some space between their view and that of their realist opponents. We have seen that Peirce opens us that gap by arguing that we have no cognitive access to the world of independent objects—it is only by abstracting the forceful element from experience that we can get an inkling that the world is there. Dewey, on the other hand, needs to work to say why his view remains sufficiently far away from his idealist opponents who have a hard time making sense of the ideas of improvement, mistakes, and standards. The divide between Peirce and Dewey may be hairline, but it is a divide that structures the history of pragmatism and the challenges that present themselves to the varieties of pragmatism. We shall see below that Dewey is not altogether successful in meeting his challenges.

7.4 Dewey's Metaphysics

We have seen that Dewey, with all pragmatists, argues that knowing is not a relationship that can be characterized as a passive seeing of the object by the subject. There is no such thing as an encounter between a subject and the world that is unmediated by interests, values, culture, and psychology. Everything that we experience comes laden with active cognition. My suggestion will be, however, that Dewey's way of arguing for this plank in the pragmatist platform is laden with difficulty.

Dewey's biological twist on the Peircean account of inquiry is that he takes inquiry to be a matter of an organism trying to maintain stability or harmony in its environment. The organism faces a problematic situation—instability or lack of equilibrium—and tries to resolve it. The importance of biology, for Dewey, cannot be overstated. He thinks that the biological facts that have shaped us are critical in analyzing the concepts of knowledge and truth. Biologically-based imperatives such as the drive to survive and the necessity of cooperation are the only imperatives that can drive inquiry.

Peirce also thinks that the biological origin of our capacities is relevant: our objectives and capacities are human objectives and capacities, shaped by evolution. But he thinks that one of those human objectives is an interest in getting things right, rather than merely seeming to be right. Our human interests include a desire to have our beliefs checked by the force of experience; a need to have our beliefs caused by something not

---

[17] I say "unreconstructed" because at other times, Dewey maintains that he holds "a 'correspondence' theory of truth" and is merely articulating "the sense in which I hold it" (*LW* 14: 179; 1941). We have seen that Peirce too thought that he could accept the correspondence definition and then expand on it. See Schwartz (2012) for an account of Dewey that takes these infrequent statements more seriously than I do and for the suggestion that Dewey was happy to adopt Tarski's definition of truth. My reading relies on the following. In a 1944 letter to Bentley, in which Dewey says: "I dont know Tarski at all" (*CJD* 3: 1944.09.11, 15371) and in 1946 he says to Chisholm: "I haven't read Tarski or any of the other recent effusions. Either the 'emptyists' are badly off the track or I am indurated with old age." (*CJD* 3: 1946.02.16, 13952). Similarly: "I never answered about Tarski—that material is so out of my line I gues Id better continue to lay off" (*CJD* 3: 1948.05.08, 15698). (All typographical eccentricities are in the originals.)

extraneous to the facts. At first glance, Dewey seems to agree. Experience is "an affair of the intercourse of a living being with its physical and social environment" (*MW* 10: 6; 1917). Knowledge is a process—a process involving an inquirer and his or her environment (*MW* 10: 10; 1917). But Dewey does not take the organism and the environment to be two interacting things. The organism and the environment are meshed together in a more complex, more Hegelian, way.[18]

One way Dewey expresses this complexity is to say that reality "possesses practical character" (*MW* 4: 128; 1908). The world is not a world of fixed forms. Dewey thinks that the new physics vindicates his view. Heisenberg's uncertainty principle shows, he says, that the worlds that different inquirers inquire about are, quite literally, different worlds: "What is known is seen to be a product in which the [individual] act of observation plays a necessary role" (*LW* 4: 163;1929).[19] Another way he expresses it is to say that organisms and the environment are one thing. And so it can seem that for Dewey, as Robert Talisse (2002) argues, the situation has the doubt, not the inquirer. When we experience a situation as vague or confused, then it *is* vague and confused. Dewey could not be clearer: "It is the *situation* that has these traits. *We* are doubtful because the situation is inherently doubtful" (*LW* 12: 109; 1938). Dewey seems to offer us a metaphysics in which a mental state (doubt) is ascribed to a situation that is a merging of the natural world and human inquirers who are freighted with beliefs, needs, desires, and psychological makeups.[20]

The idea of "the situation" is Dewey's attempt to humanize the world. He wants to articulate a view in which humans and the world are one. So far, so good. Everyone must be happy to acknowledge that humans are part of the world or in Dewey's terms, that organisms are part of the environment. It is also well and good that Dewey tries to not leave externality out of his metaphysical picture. After he tells us that it is the situation that is doubtful, he continues: "Personal states of doubt that are not evoked by and are not relative to some existential situation are pathological"; they are a "withdrawal from reality" (*LW* 12: 109: 1938). "Nature" is a part of the problematic situation that calls for inquiry—it interacts with the organism or the self (*LW* 12: 110; 1938). The situation is the "interaction of organic responses and environing conditions" (*LW* 12: 111; 1938).

Indeed, in his review of Peirce's first volume of *Collected Papers*, Dewey commends Peirce for disapproving of "subjective idealism" and links his own idea of a problematic situation with Peirce's idea that experience is that which surprises us: "Experience teaches us, Peirce says, by means of a series of surprises. It is through the conflict of our expectations with what happens in actuality that we learn" (*LW* 11: 423; 1935). His

---

[18] In a paper titled "Dewey's New Logic," Russell detected the Hegelianism and objected to it (1996 [1939]: 146).

[19] I thank Jennifer Welchman for pointing this out to me.

[20] Dewey's elucidations tend to be unhelpful. He describes a situation as a "qualified existential whole which is unique . . . extensive, containing within itself diverse distinctions and relations which in spite of their diversity, form a unified qualitative whole" (*LW* 12: 125; 1938).

reading of Peirce during the mid-1930s is sophisticated. It is hard to think that Dewey disagrees with Peirce when he gets the first two of Peirce's three categories this right:

> The "proof" of existence in general and in particular is found in the fact that we are forced to react and that things react upon us for our reaction to them. It is the non-intellectual, the non-rational element in our experience. It cannot be explained, much less explained away. It simply *is*; we cannot leave it because we must take it. It cannot even be described in its own terms; it can be experienced and then indicated to others . . .
>
> [*LW* 11: 482; 1937]

Dewey's view is that subject and object merge in experience and this, one wants to say, is something very like Peirce's categories. But his way of bringing in the external world is awkward, to say the least. Peirce is surely right that it is believers who have beliefs and doubts, not a metaphysical concoction that is somehow composed of believers and something external to those believers. Dewey's attempt at bringing Hegelian insights to the empiricist or naturalist picture seems always less than satisfactory. As Richard Gale argues, there is a tension between the empiricism and the Hegelianism in Dewey's position (2010: 119–20; 186).

Nagel put the question to Dewey forcefully in 1929:

> The question naturally arises how Professor Dewey comes to have a metaphysics. How does he *know* that specificity, interaction, change, characterize all existence, and that these distinctions are not merely logical, made for purposes of getting along in this world, but characters of an independent existence? Why does he impute the features presented in human experience to a nature embracing, but containing more than, that experience?
>
> [1929: 707]

Nagel thinks that we need to distinguish "symbols from the subject-matter to which they point" (1929: 477). We have seen that Peirce agrees, although his way of distinguishing these two things is as minimal as possible—*all* we can do is point or gesture at the subject matter.

Russell also could not make sense of Dewey's "process of 'inquiry' . . . in which subject and object change."[21] Dewey, he says, tells us that the situation is an "existential whole which is unique" (*LW* 12: 125; 1938), but never tells us "just what 'existential' is supposed to mean here" (Russell *CP* 10. 147; 1939). He also never tells us how we are to individuate situations:

> How large is a "situation"? . . . It is obvious that, in an inquiry into the tides, the sun and moon must be included in the "situation". Although this question is nowhere explicitly discussed, I do not see how, on Dr. Dewey's principles, a "situation" can embrace less than the whole universe . . .
>
> [Russell *CP* 10. 147; 1939]

---

[21] Russell (*CP* 10. 146; 1939). Russell, as usual, is not a very careful reader here. There is much in Dewey that he gets wrong. See Burke (1994). But, also as usual, he shows real insight into what is indeed problematic. And whatever their philosophical disagreements, Dewey was a passionate defender of Russell when his appointment at the City College of New York was revoked after public protest in 1940.

But Russell's main reservation is that Dewey's account of inquiry seems not to be inquiry at all. It is not a "search for truth" or for right answers, but, in Dewey's words: inquiry is the "controlled or directed transformation of an indeterminate situation into one that is so determinate in its constituent distinctions and relations as to convert the elements of the original situation into a unified whole" (*LW* 12: 108; 1938). Russell notes that on this conception of inquiry, a drill sergeant who converts raw recruits into a regiment or a bricklayer who transforms a pile of bricks into a structure must be said to be successfully conducting inquiries. In inquiry, though, we are inquiring *into* something—we are trying to find answers to questions. We are not trying to transform one existential situation into another.

Even James says, in an otherwise positive commentary, that Dewey and his disciples have "a peculiar view of 'fact'" on which:

A fact and a theory have not different natures, as is usually supposed, the one being objective, the other subjective. They are both made of the same material, experience-material, namely, and their difference relates to their way of functioning solely.... It is "fact" when it functions steadily; it is "theory" when we hesitate.

[1977 [1904]: 104]

James, of course, will be more sympathetic to Dewey than most. But James sees that one of the "great gaps" in Dewey's system is that there is "no account of the fact...that different subjects share a common object-world" (1977 [1904]: 105). For Dewey, the object of knowledge is not something that exists before we inquire. Inquiry creates the object of knowledge. Things emerge out of our inquiries. We construct them, rather than discover them.

Perhaps William Savery summed it up best in 1939, in his on the whole positive and generous account of Dewey's place in pragmatism for the Dewey volume of the *Library of Living Philosophers*:

There is a very important problem in philosophy which Dewey leaves unsolved, and which, at times, he does not seem to regard as a problem at all. This is the problem of the nature of the external world. Dewey frequently writes as if he were a natural realist...He is, however, a perspective realist, and he holds that our perspectives are natural events which are added to, although continuous with events already existent.

[1951 [1939]: 508]

Savery cannot make sense of this view.

It is thus not surprising that two kinds of realism came into being the early 1900s, in direct opposition to Dewey. The "new realism" had Ralph Barton Perry and William Montague at its center and "critical realism" had James Pratt, C. A. Strong, Durant Drake, Roy Wood Sellars, Arthur Lovejoy, and Santayana as its main proponents. All of these philosophers argued that there is an external world and we can have knowledge of it. They took Dewey to deny this core realist tenet.

It is interesting that Perry, a student of Royce and James, was so prominent in the new realist movement. For Perry was a sensitive interpreter of pragmatism and wrote an excellent intellectual biography of James.[22] Perry took aim at idealism's "cardinal principle" that "to know is to generate the reality known" and he worried that pragmatism came too close for comfort to that idealist view (1910: 326). In his 1907 "A Review of Pragmatism as a Theory of Knowledge," he remarks that "The pragmatist together with the idealist has done well to insist upon [the] proposition" that "truth in knowledge is always relative to a particular intention" (1907a: 369). In a second 1907 article, "A Review of Pragmatism as a Philosophical Generalization," he cautiously concludes that "Unless I have greatly mistaken the temper of pragmatism, this doctrine is primarily empiricist and only secondarily relativist" (1907b: 428). Perry's worry is that when this secondary character of pragmatism comes to the forefront, pragmatism must "abandon its empiricism for some form of transcendental idealism" (1907b: 427).

The critical realists were dualists, which made their view even more set against Dewey. They argued that there are perceivers and objects perceived and that we must distinguish between the acts of perceiving and knowing (which are mental) and what is perceived and known (which may not be mental). The distinction allows mental events but denies the need for a substratum of mental substance, enabling the realist to avoid positing mental entities to explain how perception functions. We have seen the pragmatists call for an explanation of how this is supposed to work. They find none.

But, with Dewey, these critical and new realists were all naturalists. They agreed with him that to talk of a belief's correspondence with its object "is to take refuge in confusion" (Perry 1907a: 374). Indeed, they took themselves to have so much in common with Dewey that Sellars asserted: "My agreement . . . is so fundamental that any outstanding divergence on minor points must be capable of amendment" (1907: 432). But the amendments did not turn out to be easily made. Lovejoy, for instance, pressed upon Dewey the perennial problem of statements about the past and the future. How can we have knowledge about the past and future if knowledge is what is verifiable? He found Dewey's attempts at response unclear and unsatisfying (1922: 506).

When Dewey turns his mind to these realist objections, he is at his best in his attempt to capture what is right in each of what he takes to be the two discredited positions—idealism and realism. In "The Problem of Truth," he tells us that truths are bound up with the social process of inquiry. But that process of inquiry is also responsive to something. His "definition of truth through reference to consequences" brings in the way things "really are"—for the "things are causes" (*MW* 6: 47; 1911). There are "objective truths" (*MW* 6: 53; 1911). But even when Dewey gives us such clear and compelling accounts, he characterizes objectivity in a way that seems hardly deserving of the word. He concludes the paper as follows:

---

[22] It is marred, as Kuklick (1977: 340) notes, by the tendency to see James as merely anticipating new realism.

I do not profess to be offering more than a hypothesis . . . Its status is socially determined. The conception of objective truth which I am proffering—that objective truth means interpretations of things that make these things effectively function in liberation of human purpose and efficiency of human effort—has not itself been yet subjected to the tests of social use, which it exacts as the measure of any truth.

[*MW* 6: 66; 1911]

That is, he concludes by saying that social use is the test of truth, including the truth of his conception of truth. It is no wonder that Dewey was and is taken to be less interested in the objective and more interested in the subjective.

We might characterize these objections as all suggesting that when one calls for the dissolution of a dualism, one is under an obligation to replace the mistaken picture with an account that does better. Dewey calls for abandoning the "gratuitous dualisms" between "objective and subjective, the real and apparent, the mental and physical" (*LW* 14: 9; 1939). But he needs to replace them with something that makes good sense. Sometimes he comes close. Philosophical thought would have been better, Dewey says, had empiricism not spoken of "givens" or what is given to us as raw data. It would be better to speak of "takens" or what we select from the subject matter that confronts us (*LW* 4: 142; 1929). Here he seems to be acknowledging that there is something that stands externally to us, which we take from and interact with. But on the whole, he stays away from such thoughts, as he feels that they reproduce the dualisms inherent in the spectator theory of knowledge and the correspondence theory of truth.

We have seen that all the early pragmatists thought that Bain was right in taking a belief to be or to involve a directive to action. Peirce and James want this aspect of belief to coexist with the fact that a belief is a state of a believer; they want belief to be something that can be true or false; they want belief to be something that is warranted or unwarranted. It might be that all the pragmatists are unclear on the matter of how belief can be all of these things: a mental state, something for which there is evidence for and against, and something that can result in action or a propensity to action. But Dewey seems to be the most muddled of all the pragmatists on this score. For he adds to this already heady mix the bizarre idea that a belief is a state of a situation. One surmises that what he was really after in attributing belief and doubt to the situation was something entirely reasonable. The idea of experiment is the key to understanding his important insight. In inquiry, we do something. We change the world as well as our beliefs. He was also, I suggest, trying to distinguish himself from James on the matter of the will to believe. In response to Russell's trying to make sense of his conception of a situation, he says:

Mr. Russell proceeds first by converting a doubtful *situation* into a personal doubt, although the difference between the two things is repeatedly pointed out by me. I have even explicitly stated that a personal doubt is pathological unless it is a reflection of a *situation* which is problematic. Then by changing doubt into private discomfort, truth is identified with removal of this discomfort. The only desire that enters, according to my view, is desire to resolve as honestly and impartially as possible the problem involved in the situation. "Satisfaction" is satisfaction of the conditions prescribed by the problem. Personal satisfaction may enter in as it arises when any job is well done according to the requirements of the job itself; but it does not enter in any way into the determination of validity . . .

[*LW* 14: 156; 1939]

This is a telling response. It provides us with a glimpse of Dewey's motivation for shifting the emphasis away from the doubts and beliefs of the inquirer and onto the doubtfulness of the situation. But in trying to distance himself from the Jamesian view that the easing of personal doubts and needs is linked to truth, Dewey twists himself into metaphysical knots.

Notice, though, how Dewey's metaphysics is less problematic for ethics. The ethical world is constantly changing over time, partly as a result of our own actions. In ethics, we try to maintain an acceptable equilibrium between our changing needs, interests, and capacities and our changing social environments, which we produce. We shall see in section 7.6 that, indeed, one of Dewey's signal contributions to pragmatism is in ethics. But first, we need to see how Dewey introduces a revolutionary thought into pragmatism.

7.5 Truth and the Quest for Certainty

Dewey is set against the "intellectualist" account of truth, on which truth is "*antecedent* to any process of verification" (*MW* 4: 76; 1909). One version of this, he says, is held by contemporary idealists such as Bradley and Royce. Another version is the correspondence theory of truth on which truth is a "self-contained" property of ideas that "consists in their relation of agreement or correspondence to things" (*MW* 4: 77; 1909). The problem with the intellectualist is that he cannot make sense of his "dualism" between mind and matter or between consciousness and objects "where each of these terms is supposed to refer to some fixed order of existence" (*MW* 4: 79; 1907). Instead, the intellectualist's "idea-ism," which Dewey warns us "not to dignify . . . with the title of idealism" is a commitment to "self-luminous" ideas advertising their truth or falsity. The problem, Dewey says pointedly, is that "such phosphorescence is notoriously lacking," with the result that the truth or falsity of an idea bears no discernible connection with reality, the very connection intellectualists of both stripes prize. Dewey hits the nail on the head:

Then, of course, comes up the question of the nature of the agreement, and of the recognition of it. What is the experience in which the survey of both idea and existence and their agreement are recognized? Is it an idea? . . . Then what has become of the postulate that truth is agreement of idea with existence beyond idea? Is it an absolute which transcends and absorbs the difference? Then . . . what is the test of any specific judgment? What has become of the correspondence of fact and thought? Or, more urgently, since the pressing problem of life, of practice and of science is the discrimination of the relative, or superior, validity of this or that theory, plan or interpretation, what is the criterion of truth . . . ?

[*MW* 4: 79; 1907]

These are good questions and Dewey clearly thinks they cannot be answered by the intellectualist.

Neither can truth be correspondence of a thought with an antecedent reality or with how things "really are" (*MW* 6: 34; 1911). For we cannot get at how things really are: "we seem to require a third medium in which the original proposition and its object are surveyed together, are compared and their agreement or disagreement seen" (*MW* 6: 34; 1911).

The two theories of truth most prominent in Dewey's time do not stand up. No wonder, he says, that "a third party has finally been rash enough to intervene" (*MW* 6: 33; 1911). That third party is the pragmatist, or the "instrumentalist," who holds "a functional theory of knowledge" or a "philosophy of experience" (*MW* 4: 50; 1907, *MW* 4: 78; 1907). On this view we do not look, with the idealist and the realist, to a "ready-made" truth. We look to the future: we look to "the differences" a proposition "makes in further experience" (*MW* 6: 38; 1911). The job of our theories is not to mirror an absolute nor is it to mirror the world as it really is. The job of our theories is to enable us to predict and act and solve problems with success.

In *Logic*, Dewey is happy to "define" truth as what would be agreed to by all who investigate (*LW* 12: 50; 1938). We find him saying, in this later period, that he is one with Peirce in thinking of truth in terms of "continued inquiry" (*LW* 14: 56; 1939). "I should say that the stability of truth, like 'reality' as defined by C. S. Peirce, represents a *limit*" (*LW* 5: 215; 1930). While we have seen that this is not really Peirce's view (he did not define truth as a limit), it is interesting to see Dewey reach for a notion of truth on which the truth of a belief is stable.

In 1929, Dewey delivered the Gifford Lectures in Edinburgh, the third American after James and Royce to do so. The series was titled *The Quest for Certainty*. A considerable amount of the material in these lectures is drawn from Dewey's preparations for *Logic*. So it is unsurprising that *The Quest for Certainty* only strengthens the case for thinking that Dewey and Peirce speak with one voice on the matter of truth. They both argue that truth adheres to human judgments or beliefs, not to abstract propositions. What we are really interested in, as Tom Burke puts Dewey's point, is "warranting a judgment by concretely acting in accordance with its dictates to see how it actually stands up" (1994: 238). *The Quest for Certainty*, that is, has it that any search for absolute truth is not merely bound to be fruitless, but that absolute truth is not in fact what we take ourselves to be seeking. No one investigating a particular problem aims for certainty. Rather, they aim at "security"—at a reliable solution to the problem at hand (*LW* 4: 3f.; 1929). We aim at getting beliefs that would stand up to all the evidence; we aim at getting beliefs that will work well. We are always immersed in a context of inquiry, where the decision to be made is a decision about what to believe from here, not what to believe were we able to start from scratch—from certain or infallible foundations. Dewey and Peirce ask their readers, as Alan Ryan puts it, to turn away from the desire for certainty and accept that security, in the midst of uncertainty, is enough (Ryan 1995: 233). Traditional faith is to be replaced by "nature, including humanity, with all its defects and imperfections . . . as the source of ideals" (*LW* 4: 244; 1929).

But Dewey, for better or worse, takes this thought a step further than Peirce. He calls for a comprehensive reconstruction of philosophy in which traditional problems of philosophy, and the concepts upon which they rely, will be discarded. We don't "solve" the traditional problems of philosophy, we "get over them" (*MW* 4: 14; 1909). Dewey, that is, is a revolutionary. He wants to turns his back on philosophy. This is why he tends to dismiss objections to his view rather than take them head on, to escape questions rather than answer them. Many of those questions, he thinks, arise only if you are in grip of a completely wrong-headed philosophy.

One must ask, though, whether such a revolutionary stance is in tension with the pragmatist project. That project has us starting with where we find ourselves. We have our concepts and our ways of thinking through philosophical problems. We cannot simply toss them in the dustbin and start again. Even if one wants to argue, as does Dewey, that many of our philosophical concepts came into being in a mistaken, pre-Darwinian way, they are nonetheless embedded in our practices and one might well argue that the pragmatist cannot make the revolutionary move. We shall see, however, that the revolutionary spirit of Dewey remains strong in some quarters of pragmatism. His reconstructionist idea is picked up by Richard Rorty in the 1970s. Rorty agrees with Dewey that philosophers ought to be engaged in showing how philosophy's past is composed of a series of mere "puzzles" (*LW* 1: 17; 1925) to be discarded as "chaff" (*LW* 1: 4; 1925). They both advocate an overthrow of "the industry of epistemology." Rather than try to say what knowledge in general is, we should try to solve the "problems a-plenty" of knowledge in particular. For "there is no problem of knowledge in general" (*MW* 10: 23; 1917).

Peirce, on the other hand, thinks that there is a problem of knowledge and truth in general. While we always have in mind the proximate aim of getting the solution to some particular problem, were we to find a solution that stood up to whatever further problems and experience we encountered, that solution would be the right solution. It would be true. Although we have seen that Dewey sometimes says that "truth is the end and standard of thinking" (*MW* 4: 64; 1907), more often he prefers to say that "warranted assertibility" is that at which we aim (*LW* 12: 15; 1938). He tends to shy away from speaking to what a belief would have to do in the future to show itself to be true and sticks, rather, with a belief's ability to solve a problem in the present.

Another way of putting this disagreement between Peirce and Dewey is to ask whether truth is a static phenomenon. Both reject the idea that truth is static in the sense that our beliefs either mirror the world of the Absolute (and are hence true) or fail to do so (and are hence false). But Peirce thinks that truth is static in the sense that a belief either would or would not survive the rigors of inquiry. Again, Dewey usually stays away from this thought. His interest ends with beliefs that show themselves to resolve a particular, local problem.

7.6 Ethics and Inquiry

Sidney Morgenbesser, who arrived to teach at Columbia in 1953 and later held the John Dewey Professorship there, thinks that it was Lovejoy who quipped that Dewey hated the number 2: not only did he dislike dualisms, but he disliked any kind of distinction (Morgenbesser 1977: xxxi). While that is of course an exaggeration, Dewey most certainly is determined to break down one purported hard-and-fast distinction— that between fact and value. The pragmatist, he says, "has at least tried to face, and not to dodge, the question of how it is that moral and scientific 'knowledge' can both hold of one and the same world" (*MW* 4: 132; 1908).

Dewey sees Darwin's evolutionary theory as a cause of a "crisis"—the very crisis that gripped Wright, Peirce, and James. It seems to make a mockery of ethics and any other values involved in human conduct: "This effect of modern science, has, it is notorious, set the main problems for modern philosophy. How is science to be accepted and yet the realm of values to be conserved?" (*LW* 4: 33; 1929). Idealism, Dewey thinks, provides us with no satisfactory answer. He joins James in being appalled by what he took to be the ethical view inherent in it. He says of Green's position, that there is a "helplessness" "when it comes to action" (*EW* 3: 163; 1892). The Absolute stands off to one side and says, "No matter what you do, you will be dissatisfied. I am complete; you are partial. I am a unity; you are a fragment, and a fragment of such a kind that no amount of you and such as you can ever afford satisfaction" (*EW* 3: 163; 1892). He could not sound more like James in his disparagement of the consequences of idealism.

Ethics must provide us with practical guidance. Dewey is the first of the pragmatists to really follow through on the idea, implicit in Peirce, and explicit but not always fully developed in James, that ethical matters fall under the scope of inquiry and knowledge. Inquiry or the method of science must be imported into domains such as ethics and politics:

Failure to institute a logic based...on the operations of inquiry has enormous cultural consequences. It encourages obscurantism; it promotes acceptance of beliefs formed before methods of inquiry had reached their present estate; and it tends to relegate scientific (that is, competent) methods of inquiry to a specialized technical field. Since scientific methods simply exhibit free intelligence operating in the best manner available at a given time, the cultural waste, confusion and distortion that results from the failure to use these methods, in all fields in connection with all problems, is incalculable. These considerations reinforce the claim of logical theory, as the theory of inquiry, to assume and to hold a position of primary human importance.

[*LW* 12: 527; 1938]

Like Peirce and James, Dewey wants to offer a "unified theory of inquiry"—a single way of thinking about how we resolve problematic situations in science, ethics, politics, and law (*LW* 12: 102; 1938). He describes coming to that idea as follows:

as my study and thinking progressed, I became more and more troubled by the intellectual scandal that seemed to me involved in current (and traditional) dualism...between something called "science" on the one hand and something called "morals" on the other. I have long felt that the construction of a logic, that is, a method of effective inquiry, which would apply without abrupt breach of continuity to the fields designated by both of these words, is at once our needed theoretical solvent and the supply of our greatest practical want.

[LW 5: 156; 1930]

In 1903, in "Logical Conditions of a Scientific Treatment of Morality," Dewey tries in a systematic way to resolve the crisis posed by the new science and to counter the "assertion that there is something in the very nature of conduct which prevents the use of logical methods in the way they are employed in already recognized spheres of scientific inquiry" (MW 3: 5; 1903). He dismantles assorted reasons for thinking that there is a "gulf" between science and ethics. For instance, he joins James's attack on the idea that science is about general facts whereas ethics is about particular, individual acts. The general and the particular are part of both science and ethics (MW 3: 7ff.; 1903). This move is a recurring one in Dewey's thought. Just as Peirce argues that every experience contains aspects of each category (quality, brute interaction, and norm-laden interpretation), Dewey argues that the normative and the factual are mixed into the situation itself.[23]

Dewey's insight here can be articulated independently of his metaphysical account of the situation. We can say that inquiry (as opposed to the situation) is not purely descriptive. It is a rule governed activity—an activity of developing hypotheses, predictions, and explanations; of assessing what is to count as evidence for or against a hypothesis or prediction; of deciding which explanations should be adopted and acted upon, and so on. Inquiry is threaded with methodological principles or norms about how it ought to conduct itself and it is shot through with our psychological makeup and values. We are taken to the central pragmatist thought that the "oughts" of inquiry do not come from outside of human inquiry, but that does not prohibit them from being binding.

In ethics, Dewey argues, we aim to transform a doubtful or problematic situation into one in which "confusion and uncertainty" are resolved (MW 14: 144; 1922). There are "objective truths," in Dewey's sense of "objective," in ethics as well as in science. For Dewey, we have seen, this means that they are not subject to the whim of individuals:

That there are truths independent of individual wish and learning; that these truths are so graded as to supply rules by which individuals may regulate the formation of their private judgments and conclusions—these facts stare us in the face. They are as influential in every phase of experience as they are in the region which, more or less arbitrarily, we mark off as moral.

[MW 6: 53; 1911]

Dewey's account of ethics was more warmly received than was his account of science. The widely used textbook Ethics (1908) written by Dewey and James Tufts,[24] for

---

[23] See e.g. MW 12: 117; 1920, LW 1: 13; 1925.
[24] Tufts wrote Part I, a kind of history of the practice of ethics. Dewey wrote the more theoretical Part II. Part III, on contemporary problems, had chapters written by each. Dewey and Tufts had been colleagues at Michigan and then again at Chicago, where they were mainstays of the Chicago School.

instance, was seen to mark "the end of the abstract, speculative treatises and the beginning of the positive studies of established human values" (Wilde 1908: 636). The book begins by setting out the "moral situation," similar to any problematic situation which calls for inquiry. "The problems of men" must be brought into the ambit of science or inquiry:

if we can discover ethical principles, these ought to give some guidance for the unsolved problems of life which continually present themselves for decision. Whatever may be true for other sciences it would seem that ethics at least ought to have some practical value . . . Man must act; and he must act well or ill, rightly or wrongly. If he has reflected, has considered his conduct in the light of the general principles of human order and progress, he ought to be able to act more intelligently and freely, to achieve the satisfaction that always attends on scientific as compared with uncritical or rule-of-thumb practice.

[*MW* 5: 10; 1908]

We have seen how, in *Logic*, Dewey takes a legal trial to be an instance of a problematic situation that is resolved by inquiry. He also says there that inquiry or "deliberation" into moral matters is another instance of judging a problematic situation with the aim of resolving it—resolving it into one that is "morally satisfactory and right" (*LW* 12: 170; 1938).

Dewey acknowledges that there are differences between ethics and science, despite both being subject matters for inquiry. He takes the distinguishing feature of morals to be that it involves voluntary conduct or behavior that manifests the agent's character (*MW* 5: 188; 1908). A moral problem or situation is thus: "Which shall he decide for and why? The appeal is to himself; what does *he* really think the desirable end? What makes the supreme appeal to him? What sort of an agent, a person, shall he be? This is the question finally at stake in any genuinely moral situation: what shall the agent *be?*" (*MW* 5: 194; 1908). Choices about what to do or what to value are choices that make up our very selves.

Lest that sound rather individualistic for pragmatism, it must be emphasized that Dewey, and as we shall see, the rest of his Chicago School, think that "[w]e cannot think of ourselves save as to some extent *social* beings. Hence we cannot separate the idea of ourselves and of our own good from our idea of others and of their good" (*MW* 5: 268; 1908). Lovejoy in 1909 was unimpressed with this aspect of *Ethics*, thinking that it remained mired in Hegelian metaphysics:

The moral criterion at which the author arrives is not . . . so thoroughly distinct from the "self-realization" standard of Green and his disciples as it seems meant to be. The crucial transition in the argument seems to depend upon the observation that the individual's real good or happiness demands social well-being because the self is essentially a social self . . . a characteristically abstract, loose, and shifty piece of neo-Hegelian phraseology . . .

[1909b: 143]

If this is Hegelianism, it is certainly a Hegelianism found in some form or other in all the pragmatists. We have seen, for instance, that the idea of the social self is at the heart of Peirce's view of reasoning. But Lovejoy is right that a substantial problem for Dewey resides in the idea of self-realization. The following question stands out for him: if moral deliberation is a matter of my making choices that will determine who I shall be, how am I to make sense of the ideas of accuracy, error, getting a better belief, making a mistake, etc? The difficulties do not go away by linking the self to the community. For it is not clear how Dewey has anything to say to those who think that the height of self-realization is to forge a homogenous community by eliminating "the other" or all who are different. A community, that is, might well exclude any who would question the current idea of self-realization, or the dominant cultural norms, or the current authority. Must we say that whatever such a community thinks right is right? Morton White, fellow-pragmatist and contemporary of Dewey, thinks that Dewey must indeed say this. White thinks that Dewey makes what he takes to be Mill's mistake and conflates what is desirable with what is desired (White 1996: 230ff.).

Dewey felt the force of this problem and tried throughout the entire span of his work to solve it. At times he is skeptical about giving any content at all to the ends of inquiry outside particular situations and contexts.[25] But he often feels that he has to say something about how we determine which acts are good, how we can make sense of a right answer, and how we adjudicate between beliefs.

At an early stage of his thinking, it is that the judgment *feels* right—the conflicting impulses are resolved in a way that seems to agree with the reality of our experience. In *The Study of Ethics* he says that we can tell that a conclusion is misguided even when we are aiming at self-realization, for the result will be internal conflict, discomfort, and "compunctions" (*EW* 4: 298; 1894). We can query our desires, aims, and conceptions of ourselves if we see that they lead to disharmony. But this seems less than adequate. For not all evil-doers experience such discomfort. Jennifer Welchman articulates the difficulty:

One might object, however, that although ordinary deliberation can proceed along the lines Dewey suggests, the reflective deliberation that issues in remorse, regret, and the effort to reform oneself cannot. An act that is "right" because it is true to myself may still be wrong because the sort of self I am is a wrong or bad self.

[1995: 109]

The Nazi or the child molester may find meaning or self-realization in vile and odious acts. Without some kind of check that goes beyond the individual and beyond the current, local, possibly homogenized community, there is nothing critical that can be said. Even in ethics, we need a thought like Peirce's: we must respond to something that is not extraneous to the facts.

In *Human Nature and Conduct*, Dewey takes another crack at answering the question of validity. If we are merely constantly solving problem after problem, "learning and then relearning the meaning of our active tendencies," then "[d]oes this not reduce moral life to the futile toil of a Sisyphus who is forever rolling a stone uphill only to have

---

[25] See Richardson (1995).

it roll back so that he has to repeat his old task?" (*MW* 14: 144; 1922). Dewey answers that moral life is like this only from the perspective of someone looking for fixed definitive answers to questions. It is not futile from the perspective of one who sees that "continual search and experimentation to discover the meaning of changing activity, keeps activity alive, growing in significance" (*MW* 14, 144–45; 1922). That is, we need to see that there is no certainty to be had and there is no pre-set meaning or purpose to life. Deliberation goes on and the aim of all that deliberation is "learning the meaning of what we are about and employing that meaning in action" (*MW* 14: 194; 1922). Deliberation is the construction of meaning for ourselves and for our societies.

But it is not merely the construction of any old meaning. We are trying to realize better selves and societies. That is, Dewey invokes the aim of meliorism or progress in ethical deliberation.

[We] convert strife into harmony, monotony into a variegated scene, and limitation into expansion. The converting is progress, the only progress conceivable or attainable by man. Hence every situation has its own measure and quality of progress, and the need for progress is recurrent, constant.

[*MW* 14: 195; 1922]

In the 1920 *Reconstruction in Philosophy* he puts it thus:

the process of growth, of improvement and progress, rather than the static outcome and result, becomes the significant thing. Not health as an end fixed once and for all, but the needed improvement in health—a continual process—is the end and good. The end is no longer a terminus or limit to be reached. It is the active process of transforming the existent situation. Not perfection as a final goal, but the ever-enduring process of perfecting, maturing, refining is the aim in living.... Growth itself is the only moral "end".

[*MW* 12, 181; 1920)]

In the absence of certainty, we go forward, trying to do better and better. Conflicts should not be seen as a threat; they should not be seen as destructive of harmony. Rather, they are opportunities to inquire and to come up with a better situation—an enlarged morality. Growth, for Dewey, is an increased capacity for dynamic action. It is living in a richer more interesting environment.

Unfortunately, Dewey's way of unpacking the idea of "getting better" or of improvement leaves much to be desired. As Matthew Festenstein says, criteria for these aims:

appear to be undefined in his philosophy, or defined only in notoriously vacuous ways: as what is conducive to "growth", to the coordination of activities and interests, or to consummatory experience. Rational or "intelligent" agency, it seems, is viewed as instrumental and goal-directed, but the goals to which it is or should be directed have been left out of the picture of inquiry and practical judgement.

[2008: 89]

We have seen that Peirce was also attracted to the idea of harmony and growth—he appealed to it in a fruitless attempt to say how we could verify the existence of God.

There are plenty of problems with the idea. Not only is it very difficult to unpack the idea of "harmony," but as Sidney Hook, Dewey's student and fellow-pragmatist, put it, growth is not in itself a good. It can be dangerous—"we sometimes find ourselves wishing not only that something wouldn't grow but that it had not come to be" (1959: 1013). Hook notes that Dewey never addresses the questions that arise from this fact.

On Peirce's view of truth, in which he stays away from the idea of growth that attracted him elsewhere, there is something that we are aiming at. Despite the fact that we can never be certain that we have it, we are aiming at a belief that would forever stand up to experience and deliberation. On occasion, we have seen that Dewey seems to opt for Peirce's general view of truth. He sometimes does so when he speaks of ethics as well "a truly moral (or right) act is one which is intelligent in an emphatic and peculiar sense: it is *a reasonable* act. It is not merely one which is thought of, and thought of as good, as the moment of action, but one which will continue to be thought of as 'good' in the most alert and persistent reflection" (*MW* 5: 278–79; 1908). The "outcome" is "moral knowledge" (*MW* 5: 279; 1908). But notice the "will be," rather than the Peircean "would be." Peirce was the only pragmatist to insist on the subjunctive formulation of the pragmatist account of truth, hence placing it more on the objective as opposed to the subjective end of the continuum. A right or a true belief is not one that will continue to be thought of as right or true. It is one that would continue to be thought of as right or true, were we able to consider all the evidence and argument.

But more often than not, Dewey does not take us to be aiming at any end point. So it is not at all clear what progress means for him. It seems that Dewey's efforts to assert the contrary notwithstanding, our ends are whatever standards are prevalent in any culture.

It is when Dewey leaves the problem of validity and gets down to the details of an examination of how inquiry works in ethics that the tangential insights for moral philosophy flow in a steady stream. For instance, he follows Peirce in taking thought experimentation to be crucial in inquiry in general, but especially in ethical inquiry. In ethics, experiment:

is a process of tentative action: we "try on" one or another of the ends; imagining ourselves actually doing them, going, indeed, in this make-believe action just as far as we can without actually doing them. In fact, we often find ourselves carried over the line here; the hold which a given impulse gets upon us while we are "trying it on" passes into overt act without us having consciously intended it.

[*EW* 4: 251; 1894]

Dewey thinks that we can learn something in thought experimentation. We can learn something about ourselves, about how we react to certain moral scenarios, and, if we try on other people's shoes, we can learn something about how those others might react.

Moral deliberation and experimentation involve what Dewey calls "intuition." We propose potential solutions to the ethical problems that press on us; we try to predict the consequences of those solutions; and we ask whether our reactions to those consequences would be positive or negative. Once a solution has withstood the challenge of testing in thought experiment or experiment in the imagination, we can go with it in real life:

Deliberation is a process of active, suppressed, rehearsal; of imaginative dramatic performance of various deeds carrying to their appropriate issues the various tendencies which we feel stirring within us. When we see in imagination this or that change brought about, there is a direct sense of the amount and kind of worth which attaches to it, as real and direct, if not as strong, as if the act were really performed and its consequences really brought home to us.

[*MW* 5: 292; 1908]

Part of the reason that thought experimentation is so vital in the moral domain is that, as Dewey, James, and Peirce all argue, ethical judgment is not identical to judgment in physical science. So it is no surprise that the kind of evidence relevant to the confirmation of these different kinds of judgments would vary. Dewey says: "Every sort of judgment has its own end to reach; and the instrumentalities (the categories and methods used) must vary as the end varies" (*MW* 3: 20–21; 1909).

While this does not fully solve the validity problem faced by the pragmatist, it takes us a considerable distance to *understanding* validity in the moral domain. Ethical judgment is bound up with human wants, needs, and culture. It is only to be expected, then, that what we find when we examine possibilities in thought experiments is our reactions to things—our feeling that *x* is desirable, loathsome, salutary, etc. It is also only to be expected that those reactions will not be uniform across inquirers, across communities, and across times. We might add that it is not appropriate to look for tidy answers in an area of inquiry such as ethics in which the subject matter is so tied to human needs. It is also not appropriate to look for tidy answers in a subject matter in which many issues are indeterminate or not answerable without a residue of regret that one could not act on other competing but legitimate concerns.

Nonetheless, we try to do ever better. Like James, Dewey argues that we have learned from experience that beliefs in ethics can fail in the face of scrutiny. Dewey takes this point and makes it do serious work in opening up the gap between "is" and "ought". He tells us that "Every person in the degree in which he is capable of learning from experience draws a distinction between what is desired and what is desirable" (*LW* 13: 219; 1939). We have desires as they first appear to us and then we revise or transform "the first-appearing impulse." He says:

The "desirable", or the object which *should* be desired (valued), does not descend out of the a priori blue nor descend as an imperative from a moral Mount Sinai. It presents itself because past experience has shown that hasty action upon uncriticized desire leads to defeat and possibly catastrophe. The "desirable" as distinct from the "desired" does not . . . designate something at large or a priori. It points to the difference between the operation and consequences of unexamined impulses and those of desires and interests that are the product of investigation of conditions and consequences.

[*LW* 13: 220; 1939]

Here again, we see the influence of Peirce—our perceptions arrive uncritically and then we subject them to scrutiny.

As Ryan (1995: 337) puts it, at the heart of Dewey's view is that our moral judgment is just that: *judgment*. We consider, reflect, experiment, get more information, and scrutinize our desires. We ask whether what we desire really is desirable. We put some distance between the two. The problem of adjudication and validity now persists in a more manageable form. An individual might examine and revise her own desires very carefully and still be wrong. But being genuinely engaged in the effort of improving one's ethical beliefs is half the battle.

Elizabeth Anderson (1993: 2) has recently resurrected Dewey's ethical theory in a compelling way. She notes that when I judge something to be valuable I judge that it is properly valued, not that I happen to value it on some occasion or another. In ethics, we are interested in what *is* right or wrong, valuable or worthless, not what *seems to me* or even *what seems to most people* to be right or wrong, valuable or worthless. She says:

> emotional experiences have a special tie to normative force. Feelings of admiration are *evidence* of admirability, as desire is evidence of desirability. Of course, such feelings are defeasible.
>
> [Anderson 2006b: 6]

One takes the experience of finding oneself resenting *x* or admiring *y* as prima facie evidence for the truth of corresponding ethical judgments. What we learn, on Dewey's view, is what options are attractive, repugnant, etc. to us. Then we weigh and evaluate those feelings, sometimes finding that other reasons defeat them. Our judgments, put in place largely through experience, can be subject to disillusionment through further experience, reflection, and argument (Anderson 2004: 8). In its finest form, Dewey's view is that we do not know what we value or what is valuable until we engage in inquiry.[26] This is one of his signal contributions to philosophy.

7.7 Democracy and Political Philosophy

Another important contribution of Dewey's is the idea that democracy walks hand in hand with inquiry. Democracy, he argues, is the use of the experimental method to solve practical problems; it is an application of "cooperative intelligence" or inquiry (*LW* 13: 187; 1939); it is the space in which we can "convince and be convinced by reason" (*MW* 10: 404; 1916). He is interested in our capacities for and practices of intelligently initiating action, deliberating, consulting, and experimenting. Democracy, he suggests, is a precondition of these practices in every domain of inquiry, from physics to politics. Inquiry (or the scientific method) requires the unimpeded flow of information and the freedom to offer and to criticize hypotheses (*EW* 3: 33; 1895, *LW* 11: 375; 1936). It requires, that is, a democratic underpinning.

---

[26] See Welchman (1995: 189) for this way of understanding Dewey.

We have seen the roots of this idea in Peirce and James—if a true belief is one that accounts for all the evidence, then everyone must be able to have his say. This is an epistemic justification of a democratic method of inquiry and Dewey expands on it. In *Ethics*, he argues that the community of inquirers must be one in which people pursue harmonious, egalitarian, and stable forms of conduct. In "Freedom and Culture," he argues that the community of inquirers will, by democratic means, identify "values prized in common" (*LW* 13: 71; 1939).

One might ask again: what about the political views of those who do not choose to engage in democratic inquiry or deliberation? What can we say about those who when they deliberate, pay no mind to the views and feelings of others and who conclude that the way forward is to eliminate those others? What about those who inquire and then decide that ethnic cleansing is the way forward for their society? Morton White restates his worry: on Dewey's view, the "most obnoxious ends and means" could be defended by a unified community (1957: 201). Matthew Festenstein articulates it thus: "Whatever Dewey's personal moral or political commitments . . . his experimentalism is vulnerable to appropriation by whatever social forces are most powerful" (2008: 90).

While there may be a way of answering these questions,[27] Dewey struggles with them in an especially pressing way. There is a direct link between the conception of truth of Pierce and James (when, that is, James shares it, as he does in "The Moral Philosopher and the Moral Life") and democracy. When Dewey declines that conception of truth, the questions press in on him. Sometimes he simply asserts that participation in democracy is an essential part of what it is to lead a good life, or to achieve self-realization, or to pursue growth and improvement. It is required for a "truly human way of living" (*LW* 11: 218; 1935). These suggestions remain open to the question of what we say about those who assert the opposite: that the good life centers around a violent nationalism, for instance.

Much of the highly visible criticism of Dewey's political philosophy (the criticism that made its way out of the halls of professional philosophy departments and journals and into the publically accessible realm) revolved around a similar issue. Dewey seemed naïve and optimistic to many of his readers. Randolph Bourne attacked him by noting that societies are not the rational impartial entities that Dewey seems to assume.[28] Walter Lippmann, in *Public Opinion* (1922) and *The Phantom Public* (1925), argued that human beings are simply not as rational as Dewey makes them out to be. Passions and emotions drive them, not a commitment to scientific inquiry, if they even know what that means. If rationality is to be the driver, then an elite of those interested

---

[27] I have tried to answer them on the pragmatist's behalf in my *Truth, Politics, Morality: A Pragmatist Account of Deliberation* (2000), as has Rob Talisse (2005, 2007). By the very act of engaging or arguing with others and by the very act of believing or asserting something, we commit ourselves to the idea that we aim at getting the right answer. And if (as the Peircean pragmatist has it) the right answer is the answer that would stand up to all the reasons and evidence, we also commit ourselves to the idea that we must expose our beliefs to all the available and relevant reasons and evidence. We commit ourselves to the idea of deliberation and the democratic idea that all views and experiences must be part of that deliberation.

[28] Bourne (1997 [1913]) also argued that Dewey's emphasis on science, intelligent inquiry, and "the experimental way of life" was stifling of creativity and had dangerous consequences.

in and able to engage in such inquiry would be required. And that runs against the grain of democracy.

Dewey was also charged with a different kind of optimism, in both his moral and political theory. His view seemed to leave no room for tragic choices; for situations with no happy or even reasonable ending; for the "inexorable" (Bourne 1964 [1917]: 59). Royce is perhaps the first to articulate this objection. In 1891, he says that the trouble with Dewey lies in an "untroubled optimism . . . in the presence of all the harder problems of ethics," which he "rather too gayly ignores" (1891: 505). For Dewey, problems in ethics and politics will be resolved by inquiry.

In a letter to Scudder Klyce in 1915, Dewey responds to the charge by saying that it is not his job, in putting together an ethical theory, to solve all the hard problems in ethics: "my only claim is that the objection . . . is true. I have not given or tried to give any 'solutions'. But it doesn[']t seem to have occurred to the objectors that to say that moral life is a s[e]ries of problems and that morality *is* their solution as they arise would naturally preclude me from proffering solutions" (*CJD* 1: 03522: 1915.05.06). The moral or political *philosopher* is first and foremost engaged with setting out a compelling account of what rightness or validity amounts to. Once that is done, the philosopher might well be engaged in the project of saying what is right or wrong in particular sets of circumstances. And, of course, Dewey was not merely interested in theory—he was always engaged with hard ethical and political issues. He amplifies his response in his 1920 *Reconstruction in Philosophy*, though, in a way that makes the charge seem warranted. There are no insoluble problems. Inquiry will solve them one by one. Since the mechanism of inquiry can do this, "The great need is the organization of cooperative research, whereby men attack nature collectively and the work of inquiry is carried on continuously from generation to generation" (*MW* 12: 100; 1920).

Sometimes Dewey tries to answer the charge by focusing on the idea of a community and the interests that bind them:

The problem is to extract the desirable traits of forms of community life which actually exist, and employ them to criticize undesirable features and suggest improvement. Now in any social group whatever, even in a gang of thieves, we find some interest held in common, and we find a certain amount of interaction and cooperative intercourse with other groups. From these two traits we derive our standard. How numerous and varied are the interests which are consciously shared? How full and free is the interplay with other forms of association?

[*MW* 9: 89; 1916]

The "education" of a gang of thieves is "partial and distorted," as their shared interests are not numerous and varied and they have an inevitably limited harmonious interplay with other groups. Democratic and liberal forms of association are much better, Dewey argues, as they maximize our abilities to expand our shared interests and to develop our society's possibilities:

A democracy is more than a form of government; it is primarily a mode of associated living, of conjoint communicated experience. The extension in space of the number of individuals who participate in an interest so that each has to refer his own action to that of others, and to consider the action of others to give point and direction to his own, is equivalent to the breaking down of those barriers of class, race, and national territory which kept men from perceiving the full import of their activity.

[*MW* 9: 93; 1916]

These noble sentiments are again ineffective against those who would argue that they are deeply uninterested in living amongst, or associating with, a minority class, race, or different territorial group and would much prefer to do away with them. But in situations short of that extreme case, we can start to see that one thing that is especially valuable about democracies is that they encourage understanding of those who are not like the majority.

His best answer to the charge of optimism follows Peirce. He, like all the pragmatists, accords a central role to "'guiding' or 'leading' principles of inquiry" (*LW* 12: 19; 1938). Peirce takes this notion from Kant's account of regulative assumptions, although we have seen that he does not follow Kant in maintaining that such assumptions are necessarily true. The principles that guide inquiry have been ascertained during the process of inquiry to be necessary contributors to its success—principles that are *practically* necessary to the business of inquiry. Inquiry can bootstrap not the truth of its principles, but at least the reasonableness of assuming the principles upon which inquiry must rest.

One of those principles is that we have to go on the assumption that there is a solution to the problem at hand, otherwise we cannot go forward. There are indeed evils and tragic situations, but philosophy's job, Dewey says, is to contribute "in however humble a way to methods that will assist us in discovering the causes of humanity's ills" (*MW* 12: 181; 1920). Philosophy must see that if it is to discharge this duty, it cannot be a philosophy that leaves no room for success. "Pessimism is a paralyzing doctrine" (*MW* 12: 181; 1920). We must, as Peirce put it, go on the hope of success. "Wholesale optimism," or the attempt to explain all evil away, would of course be just as wrong-headed. What Dewey's pragmatism offers is "meliorism." It offers not practical solutions to our problems, but "confidence and a reasonable hopefulness" (*MW* 12: 182; 1920).

Another of those principles, Dewey might well argue, concerns democratic inquiry. If we are to have any hope of success in reaching beliefs that stand up to all experience, we must take the experience of others seriously. The best way of taking them seriously is some form of democratic representation and collective decision-making.

8

Fellow Travelers

8.1 George Herbert Mead (1863–1931) and the Chicago School

The University of Chicago was just a few years old when Dewey arrived to head its department of Philosophy. It was on a steep upward trajectory and Dewey was able to build something very impressive there. He brought his friend George Herbert Mead (1863–1931) with him from Michigan and proceeded to find and develop a network of like-minded philosophers, educationalists, psychologists, and sociologists. In 1903, James says the following of the intellectual culture he saw Dewey had built:

Chicago University has during the past 6 months given birth to the fruit of its 10 years of gestation under John Dewey. The result is wonderful—a *real School*, and *real Thought*. Important thought, too! Did you ever hear of such a city or such a University? Here [at Harvard] we have thought, but no school. At Yale a school but no thought. Chicago has both.

[*CWJ* 10: 324; 1903]

The Chicago School included Dewey's students and colleagues who contributed to *Studies in Logical Theory*—Helen Bradford Thompson, Simon Fraser McLennan, Myron Lucius Ashley, Willard Clark Gore, William Arthur Heidel, Henry Waldgrave Stuart, and Addison Webster Moore. But the most prominent and important members were George Herbert Mead and Jane Addams.

Mead published no books and his work has been known largely through posthumously published lecture notes. He had studied at Harvard with Royce and had lived in James's house while tutoring at least one of the James children. So he was well prepared to become Dewey's intellectual soul-mate. He was not, however, prepared to call himself a pragmatist.

Mead was immersed in the debates about idealism and realism as a student, especially as impacted by the new biology. His honor's exam topic asked "How large a share has the subject in the object world?" Following Royce, he held idealism and evolution to be a perfect pair. Modern science and the theory of evolution do not lead directly to materialism, empiricism, and loss of value in the world.[1] On the contrary, they lead to a

---

[1] Pearce (forthcoming) is excellent on this matter.

kind of idealism. With Dewey, Mead put forward the argument that an organism responds to a problematic situation in its environment, trying to reach homeostatic equilibrium. The two of them also agreed on the fundamental principle that experience is social experience or experience had in communities.

Mead's contribution to Dewey's program was to think about how such communities come into being and how individual selves are formed within them. The starting point of his thought is the idea of an act. We act in the world and from our actions emerge self-awareness, mind, and society. These seemingly abstract, mysterious, inexplicable phenomena come into being through democratic relationships and communication. He is the founder of the school of symbolic interaction in sociology and an originator of the idea (found also in James's *Principles of Psychology*, which Mead had read) that the self is a social construction.

A less well-known connection to pragmatism is found in Mead's analysis of signs, which is extraordinarily similar to Peirce's, although it is thought that Mead had not read Peirce.[2] Peirce's *Collected Papers* appeared only at the time of Mead's death, but perhaps the material from Peirce in Ogden and Richards's influential 1923 *The Meaning of Meaning* provided an entry point. At the very least, we have the connection that Mead's student Charles Morris saw himself as attempting to "carry out resolutely the insight of Charles Peirce that a sign gives rise to an interpretant and that an interpretant is in the last analysis a 'modification of a person's tendencies towards action'" (1946a: 27–28). All three—Peirce, Mead, Morris—take the meaning of a sign to be a disposition or habit of the interpreter.

Mead begins with a "sign situation" in which the acts of one agent affect another. A gesture is a simple kind of sign situation—the growling and teeth-baring behavior of a dog, for instance, affects other dogs. Mead suggests that in this kind of sign situation, we have only a conversation of gestures—the growling dog is not intending to cause fear in the other dog, he is just routinely chasing away a rival. He is focused on his own mental states. The dog does not really understand how his gestures affect the other dog—he does not imaginatively respond to his own gestures from another perspective. The participants respond from their own perspectives only, with no awareness of the social phenomenon of which they are a part.[3]

Although gestures produce behavioral responses in others, only when you know what response you will produce are you engaging in symbolic interaction. These "significant symbols" are a special kind of gesture—the kind that produce the same response from person to person. The user of a symbol takes on the role of the other in that he tends to respond to the gesture in the same way that others respond. Once one starts to anticipate how a symbol will elicit a response, one becomes reflexively aware of the meaning of the symbol. Mind consists in the functioning of these significant symbols.

---

[2] See DeWaal (2008: n. 6).   [3] See DeWaal (2008: 155) for this example.

Meaning, for Mead, as for Peirce, is not a ghostly thing. It is the response created by a sign. For instance, dark clouds mean that people run or are prepared to run inside, anticipating rain. In Mead's words, "the relationship between a given stimulus—as a gesture—and the later phases of the social act of which it is an early (if not the initial) phase constitutes the field within which meaning originates and exists" (1967 [1934]: 76). There is nothing more to the meaning of a sign than that: "language simply lifts out of the social process a situation which is logically or implicitly there already" (1967 [1934]: 79). To say that one sign means the same as the other is to say that it causes the same kind of responses or dispositions to respond in others. These responses can be either an overt behaviors or inward responses that are a sort of "imagined behavior."

This might all be a page directly from Peirce's book. Mead, though, takes Peirce's view two interesting steps further. First, he joins Dewey in hooking up the theory of signs to advances in biology. Overt behavior, he argues, has a corresponding analogue in the central nervous system. A disposition to respond to a sign is present in the central nervous system as a potential response. It doesn't have to become overt; nor does it have to even be likely to become overt. There is simply a corresponding pattern present, to be potentially activated in response to stimuli. Mead thus takes the pragmatist theory of signs into the new world of neurobiology.

Second, we have seen that Mead argues that the self comes into being within the process of symbolic interaction. The individual chooses a response from the catalogue of possible responses. It is in this way that the self is born. The way in which this choosing occurs is critically important for Mead. The distinctive feature of humans, he thinks, is found in the phenomenon of reflexive behavior. We evaluate and check our impulses to act. We have some internal interaction with ourselves—some to-and-fro that might result in acting on our impulses or in holding back. This is how "mind" comes into being. It is the internalization of the social process—thinking is social interaction internalized. It is like a conversation with oneself.

Mead goes on to argue that our understanding of meaning is enhanced by role-playing in which one tries on the roles of others and responds to them. In this kind of thought experiment and in actual games, the self is shaped. Role-playing deepens and broadens one's sense of self, as it adds perspectives on which to draw. If you take on the roles of others, you provide yourself with "material" out of which you can "build up" your consciousness (1982: 61). The self emerges in the context of the socialization process of a community, where we internalize patterns of behavior and learn to anticipate the responses of others. In doing so, the "unity of the self" comes into being. We incorporate the "generalized other" into an ongoing dialogue with oneself:

The organized community or social group which gives to the individual his unity of self may be called 'the generalized other'. The attitude of the generalized other is the attitude of the whole community.

[1934: 154]

With Dewey, Mead concludes that this kind of human activity—the social activity of language—is important in "making our world."

While Mead seems to have thoroughly imbibed pragmatist views, the other members of the Chicago School tended to be less systematic in their expression of such ideas. But each of them added to the texture of the emerging democratic/pragmatist position. Jane Addams (1860–1935), for instance, was influenced by both James and Dewey, and influenced Dewey in turn. She was a reformist social worker, a pioneer of the urbanist/city movement, and a vigorous supporter of radical causes. In 1931 she was the first woman to win the Nobel Peace Prize. Addams ought to be considered a major contributor to pragmatism, but her influence has been faint. Her *Democracy and Social Ethics* is a brilliant attempt to show that since ethics is social in nature, we need to adopt a democratic method in our moral reasoning. James calls it "one of the great books of our time" (*CWJ* 10: 124; 1902).

Addams was taken with the idea of following through on pragmatism—of having the philosophical theory of pragmatism play out in practice, especially for social problems. The pragmatist says that problems are solved by experimentation and that is precisely what Addams did. She co-founded Hull House in 1889, an organization devoted to a democratic cooperative experiment for impoverished immigrants. It attracted great attention. Dewey was on its first board of trustees. In "A Function of the Social Settlement," Addams cites both James and Dewey, and talks about the university and settlement as dividing up labor. The university generates ideas, and the settlement tries them out: "Having thus the support of two philosophers, let us assume that the dominating interest in knowledge has become its use, the conditions under which, and ways in which it may be most effectively employed in human conduct." An ideal living laboratory to further this interest is the settlement: "The settlement stands for application as opposed to research"; it "is an attempt to express the meaning of life in terms of life itself, in forms of activity" (1965 [1899]: 186–86).

Addams adopts the broad conception of experience that we have seen is characteristic of the pragmatists. She then focuses on the implications for ethics. Her argument is that in ethics, just as in science, we need to seek out as diverse a set of experiences as we can. If morality is social (and what else could it be?), then "it is inevitable that those who desire it must be brought in contact with the moral experiences of the many" (1907 [1902]: 5). Addams is alert to the problem that plagues Dewey (and we might add, all those who would offer a moral theory). We can come up with arguments that those who desire to be moral ought to do such-and-such. But we struggle to know what to say about those who do not desire to be moral.

Addams does not solve the problem. But for those who do desire to be moral, she can say the following. Our ethical standards are:

not attained by traveling a sequestered byway, but by mixing on the thronged and common road where all men must turn out for one another, and at least see the size of one another's burdens. To follow the path of social morality results perforce in the temper if not the practice of the democratic spirit, for it implies that diversified human experience and resultant sympathy which are the foundation and guarantee of Democracy.

[1907: 6-7]

With James and Peirce, Addams argues that moral intuitions are the cumulative result of our experiences and that "We do not believe that genuine experience can lead us astray any more than scientific data can" (1907: 7). If we are not to be led astray, however, we need to have as much contact as possible with the experience of others, for "such contact is the surest corrective of opinions concerning the social order, and concerning efforts, however humble, for its improvement" (1907: 7). In addition, newspapers and literature can help us learn about the experience of others and "discover truth by a rational and democratic interest in life" (1907: 11). She says:

Thus the identification with the common lot which is the essential idea of Democracy becomes the source and expression of social ethics. It is as though we thirsted to drink at the great wells of human experience, because we knew that a daintier or less potent draught would not carry us to the end of the journey, going forward as we must in the heat and jostle of the crowd.

[1907: 11]

Ethics requires us to engage with the experience of others. If we fail to engage with the wealth of human experience, we will never get answers to what is right or wrong, just or unjust. In Addams, one gets the best of Dewey and the other pragmatists' view of ethics in a distilled, clear, and unmetaphysical format. Modern moral philosophers would do well to return to her.

In the early 1930s, the University of Chicago was in the hands of a new President—Robert Hutchins—who brought Mortimer Adler to the department of philosophy with an eye to reshaping it.[4] This was the end of the heyday of the Chicago School and the locus of pragmatism shifted to New York. Nonetheless, Chicago retained a pragmatist feel—Manley Thompson and Charles Hartshorne, for instance, were both Peirce scholars who remained in the Chicago Philosophy Department well after the Chicago School was no more.

8.2 George Santayana (1863–1952) and the Realists

George Santayana (1863–1952) was a Spaniard, born in Madrid and raised in Boston from the age of nine. After an undergraduate Harvard education, he did his PhD under Royce and James, then two sparring junior professors. Santayana was kept on in the Harvard philosophy department and became a successful teacher. In 1912, after sustained pining for Europe, he moved there, abandoning professional academic philosophy and spurning offers from Columbia and Oxford to re-enter university life.

Like James and Dewey, Santayana was spread over much of the intellectual land-scape, not just the philosophical regions. His autobiography and novel were bestsellers and he was a poet, art theorist, and literary critic of great stature. In 1936, he appeared on the front cover of *Time*. A considerable number of his one-line insights live on, such as "Those who cannot remember the past are condemned to repeat it" (1962 [1905]

---

[4] See Gross (2008:106–7).

1: 184). His lyric style made his philosophy an enigma to many in the professional philosophical ranks. It seemed to them that he was elusive, both as a person and "in the natural texture of his thinking" (Brownell 1951 [1940]: 35).

Santayana wrote with pragmatism hovering in the background. He was a friend of James's and he valued his open, spontaneous warmth. But their intellectual relationship was strained. Santayana makes clear his dislike for his Harvard education in his lectures *Character and Opinion in the United States* (2009 [1920]: 21ff.). He is sometimes abusive about what he sees as relentlessly capitalist America, and can only have irritated James and later Dewey with his characterization of pragmatism. He thinks that "in their hearts and lives," Americans are all pragmatists: "Their real philosophy is the philosophy of enterprise." They are optimists who "turn their scorn of useless thought into a glad denial of its existence" (1951 [1940]: 248–49). He did not want to be associated with the American "business intellect" way of thinking (1925: 677). He preferred the intellectual company of Spinoza and the ancient Greeks.

Santayana thought James's conception of experience put forward in *Principles of Psychology* to be superb, but he was not keen on much else in his thought.[5] He cast James's "excursions in philosophy" as "not consecutive" "raids" (2009 [1920]: 52) and he joins the chorus of disagreement with respect to the Will to Believe thesis. He found the idea that we should live "boosted by an illusion" to be unpalatable. Rather than believe when it is desirable to believe, we must, he thinks: "Believe, certainly; we cannot help believing; but believe rationally, holding what seems certain for certain, what seems probable for probable, what seems desirable for desirable, and what seems false for false" (2009 [1920]: 60). James returned the barbs, calling Santayana's view on poetry and religion "the perfection of rottenness" (Santayana 1951 [1940]: 498).

Schiller came in for even rougher treatment by Santayana. James writes in a letter to Dewey in 1903: "Santayana reported the book at a 'Conference' the other night very sneeringly, & told me afterwards that he 'hated' Schiller & his thought" (*CWJ* 10: 336; 1903). The book in question is Schiller's *Humanism*. Santayana was also not impressed by Dewey. In a review of *Experience and Nature*, he characterizes Dewey as having a "quasi-Hegelian tendency to dissolve the individual into his social functions" (1925: 675). Santayana saw very clearly the tension in Dewey's view between naturalism and the metaphysical conception of "events" in which mind and nature are somehow brought together (1951 [1940]: 250).[6] He thought that Dewey's naturalism was "half-hearted and short-winded" (1925: 680). He alludes to the two shortcomings in Dewey's philosophy—the awkward metaphysics and the inability to adjudicate—in

---

[5] See 2009 [1920]: 52. and Kerr-Lawson (1991).

[6] This is from a revised version of Santayana's review of Dewey's *Experience and Nature* for the *Journal of Philosophy*. Glenn Tiller pointed out to me that when Santayana submitted the review, he stated: "Never did I tackle anything so stiff," but also: "I hope [it] may amuse Dewey and not offend him, because I have come away from reading his book—twice, most attentively—liking him better than ever" (*Letters*, 3: 261). Dewey was not amused—he was surprised and angry to find himself attacked by someone he thought of as an ally. Much later Santayana wrote that if he were to re-review Dewey he would be "more sympathetic" (*Letters*, 6: 291).

one harsh sentence. Dewey remains an idealist with Emerson, Schelling, and Hegel: "romantic, transcendental, piously receiving as absolute the inspiration dominating moral life in their day and country" (1925: 680).

But despite Santayana's attempts to distance himself from the pragmatists, his view is strikingly like theirs. He is a part of the great wave of naturalism that rose up in the early 1900s. Santayana aligned his naturalism with the realist movement. He was a mainstay of the short-lived school of critical realism, which we have seen vied with new realism as the replacement for what was seen as Dewey's naturalist, but overly subjective, view. The critical realists staked their claim in a 1920 volume called *Essays in Critical Realism*. They knew a lot about pragmatism. We have seen, for instance, that Pratt was a careful critic of James. Lovejoy in 1908 wrote a paper called "The Thirteen Pragmatisms" which painstakingly pulled apart and enumerated the different and often conflicting views that the various pragmatists expressed at one time or another.

Drake puts the critical realist position thus. The two familiar "starting points for knowledge" are too extreme. The objectively-minded argue that "the data of perception are the very physical existents which we all practically believe to be surrounding and threatening our bodies" (1920: 3). These physical existents "somehow get within experience." The subjectively minded argue that "the data of perception are psychological existents." The data of perception are "shut in" the world of ideas or representations of objects (1920: 3). Critical realism tries to combine the insights of the two extreme positions while escaping their flaws. It avoids saying, with other kinds of realism, that perceptual knowledge is some kind of special, inexplicable intuition or insight into the non-mental and it avoids the idealist assertion that to be is simply to be perceived (Sellars 1920: 188).

This, we have seen, is precisely pragmatism's aim as well. Both the critical realists and the pragmatists hold that the assertion that we know reality in an unmediated way leads to "intellectual cramp," and a false skepticism (Santayana 2000 [1922]: 216). The appropriate (and limited) skeptical attitude is rather to note that all knowledge is fallible and layered over with human abilities and values. Whenever we know, perceive, or recognize something we bring to it concepts, or what Santayana and many other of the critical realists call (less than felicitously) "essences." These essences are "irresistibly taken to be the characters of the existents perceived."[7]

The critical realists then employ a distinctly pragmatist argument. Objects are independent. We try to say true things about them. But we do not need to (and should not) believe that we are accurate in our attempts to assert true statements about objects (Santayana 1920: 163f.). All we can say is that "this instinctive (and practically inevitable) belief in the existence of the physical world about us is pragmatically justifiable" (Drake 1920: 4). We find that our belief "works." We have no proof that our "little private 'movie'" is a movie of things that actually exist. But we have to

---

[7] See Drake (1920: 4 n.1) and Santayana (1920: 167).

assume it nonetheless (Drake 1920: 5f.). "Without assuming realism it would be impossible to prove realism or anything else" (Santayana 1920: 183).

The critical realists sometimes see how closely aligned their position is to pragmatism. Lovejoy cannot make sense of the way pragmatism swings between realism and idealism and he locates the problem at the juncture in which pragmatism went the way of James's view that it "can recognize no objects or relations that are 'trans-experiential'" (Lovejoy 1920a: 41). Under the influence of James's radical empiricism, on which subject and object are part of the same "stuff," pragmatism, Lovejoy thinks, has strayed from its principles. A "true pragmatism" looks very much like critical realism (1920a: 76ff.). He concludes his piece for *Essays in Critical Realism* with:

Thus the doctrine commonly put forward as "pragmatism" may be said to be a changeling, substituted almost in the cradle . . . I invite all loyal retainers to return to their true allegiance. If they do so, they will, I think, find that there need be—and . . . can be—no quarrel between their house and that of critical realism.

[1920b: 80–81]

The critical realists do not like the ways that James and then Dewey try to combine object and subject; organism and environment. They each take a different stab at explaining the relationship between mind and world—for instance, Sellars argues (with Peirce) that the relation is indexical. But they all—critical realists and pragmatists alike—want to avoid representationalist views on which the mind represents the world as it is.

Santayana is an excellent example of how close these new naturalists (In this case, the critical realists) were to what they were starting to see as the old naturalists (the pragmatists). He takes himself to be arguing against Dewey, but in fact his position is very much in step with the general direction of Dewey's view. His 1923 *Scepticism and Animal Faith* starts off in a manner that appears to be antithetical to pragmatism. He states that he wants to "push scepticism as far as I logically can" (1923: 10). Similarly, in the Santayana volume of the *Library of Living Philosophers*, he says that he invites skepticism to "do its worst" (1951 [1940]: 18). Russell was not unusual in thinking that Santayana "is himself a sceptic, but believes that mankind in general has need of myths" (1951 [1940]: 474).

But Russell is wrong. Santayana is perfectly in step with the pragmatist's anti-skeptical argument. As Glenn Tiller (2008: 133f.) has argued recently and Milton Munitz (1951 [1940]: 192) argued at the time, Santayana's purpose here is aligned with Peirce's. Skeptical moves ought to be shunned as prompting only paper doubts—we ought to liberate ourselves from skepticism. Santayana argues that skepticism, at best, results in solipsism of the present moment. Like Hume, he concludes that when skepticism does it worst, the result is the inability to assert or believe anything at all. This state of suspended belief is impossible to maintain and soon the skeptic will find himself adopting some beliefs and adhering to some principles for adjudicating beliefs. He concludes *Scepticism and Animal Faith* as follows:

I have imitated the Greek sceptics in calling doubtful everything that, in spite of common sense, any one can possibly doubt. But since life and even discussion forces me to break away from a complete scepticism, I have determined not to do so surreptitiously nor at random, ignominiously taking cover now behind one prejudice and now behind another. Instead, I have frankly taken nature by the hand, accepting as a rule in my farthest speculations, the animal faith I live by from day to day.

[1923: 308]

This is the very response that Peirce gives to the skeptic. Our beliefs, as Santayana puts it, are "radically incapable of proof" (1923: 35). It is a good thing, then, that proof is not required. We go on instinctive reason or faith in a world that we take ourselves to perceive and sometimes change. As Peirce would say, it is a regulative assumption of inquiry, and indeed of living, that there is a world which influences us and which we influence. We simply cannot doubt as the skeptic advises. He and Santayana (and Santayana's fellow critical realists) are in full agreement that:

In regard to the original articles of the animal creed— that there is a world, that there is a future, that things can be sought and found, and things seen can be eaten—no guarantee can possibly be offered. I am sure these are often false; and perhaps the event will some day falsify them all; and they will lapse altogether. But while life lasts . . . this faith must endure.

[Santayana 1923: 180]

As we have seen, Peirce argues that we have to start with where we find ourselves, laden with a body of belief, which we could not abandon even if we wanted to. Philosophy must begin in the middle of things. We assume that many of our beliefs are true and we need not be pushed into trying to prove those beliefs or show that they are certainly or infallibly true. We do not need Cartesian requirements for certainty. Try as we might to suspend beliefs that are in want of guarantees, life and the need to act get in the way of that suspension. Either Santayana or Peirce could have made this remark: "I stand in philosophy exactly where I stand in daily life; I should not be honest otherwise." It happens to come from Santayana's pen (1923: vi). Indeed, the first sentence of *Scepticism and Animal Faith* tells us that the philosopher is compelled to "plunge in *media res*" (1923: 1). "You cannot prove realism to a complete sceptic or idealist; but you can show an honest man that he is not a complete sceptic or idealist, but a realist at heart" (Santayana 1920: 184).

Santayana is at pains to distinguish his position on this matter from James's thoughts about the will to believe. He notes that James "overlooked the fact that I too relied on animal faith in science and common life"; on "the fundamental presuppositions that I cannot live without making" (1951 [1940]: 499, 505). But Santayana does not infer from the fact that we have to accept some beliefs as they come that we can simply choose the beliefs we should accept. Despite some surface similarities between the idea of animal faith and the will to believe, he shuns James's voluntarism about belief. James's view that sometimes "faith in success could nerve us to bring success about, and so justify itself by its own operation" is "a thought typical of James at his worst—a worst in which there is always a good side" (Santayana 2009 [1920]: 60).

Santayana and Peirce struggle mightily to articulate the good side of this thought. They both argue that we must accept the bulk of our beliefs, but always keep them open to recalcitrant experience and never believe them on grounds extraneous to facts and reasons. This last point is important. Like Peirce, when Santayana uses the word "faith," he does not mean to mark something that is unbacked by reasons. He says that instead of using "so brutal a term as animal faith," he might have used "cognitive instinct, empirical confidence, or even practical reason" (1951 [1940]: 586). Each of these alternatives makes it clear that there is something normative or non-arbitrary in what we need to assume. Again to distinguish himself from James on this topic, he says:

> Why does belief that you can jump a ditch help you to jump it? Because it is a symptom of the fact that you *could* jump it, that your legs were fit and that the ditch was two yards wide and not twenty. A rapid and just appreciation of these facts has given you your confidence, or at least has made it reasonable . . . otherwise you would have been a fool and got a ducking for it.
>
> [2009 [1920]: 61]

Santayana also imports the related idea, which we have seen the pragmatists adopt from their very early American predecessors, that experience comes by way of "*shocks*" to which we must pay attention (1923: 139f.). "In the tangle of human beliefs," he says, one can distinguish "a compulsory factor called facts or things from a more optional and argumentative factor called suggestion or interpretation" (1923: 3). The encountering of "brute fact" is the "ground" for Santayana's realism (1951 [1940]: 504–5). The "experience of shock" "establishes realism"—it establishes "a world of independent existences" (1923: 142). Santayana does not want to be associated with the pragmatists because he thinks that a pragmatist such as Dewey is "a philosopher of the foreground" (1925: 680), too content with the surface of things. But Santayana is in fact one with Peirce in arguing for a pragmatist view that takes not just the foreground seriously, but also the fact that what is not in the foreground has its surprises for us.

When Santayana turns his attention to questions of truth and knowledge, his pragmatist tendencies come into even sharper focus. He thinks that the label "metaphysics" "has rather lost its glue and may harmlessly flutter down upon anything" (1951 [1940]: 519). He, with the pragmatists, wants a low-profile kind of metaphysics. The philosopher must make "God, matter, Platonic ideas, active spirits, and creative logics" "totter on their thrones":

> They may be excellent in an instrumental capacity . . . but it would be sheer idolatry to regard them as realities or powers deeper than obvious objects, producing these objects and afterwards somehow revealing themselves . . . to the thoughts of metaphysicians.
>
> [1925: 675]

Truth and knowledge must be non-metaphysical notions. Truth is a matter of "valid ideation, verified hypothesis, and inevitable, stable inference" (1962 [1905] 1: 134). Knowledge "is true belief grounded in experience, I mean, controlled by outer facts. It is not true by accident; it is not shot into the air on the chance that there may be something it may hit" (1923: 180).

A pragmatist sensibility is also brought to the concept of reason. Santayana argues that reason is the animating pulse of all distinctively human activity. But this is not "reason" in the sense that others may have used the term—which is identified with a special power of intuition and used to spread a comforting rationale over religion and other favorite theses. There is a place for religion, poetry, psychology, and ethics—"if only they are content with their natural places" (1925: 674). They are stretches of the imagination (1951 [1940]: 499)—deeply important and interesting fictions based on "bodily life" (1951 [1940]: 504).

Dewey was not so sure about Santayana's anti-metaphysical credentials.[8] He found the 1905–6, five-volume, *The Life of Reason* a frustrating work, which showed signs of "hankering after the flesh-pots of 'metaphysics'" and said so in a review (*MW* 4: 233; 1907). Indeed, at first glance, Santayana does indeed seem to be an old-school metaphysician. He is, for instance, fond of the concept of "substance." But as John Lachs notes, he uses the term in an idiosyncratic way and does not mean by it a changeless, enduring, ultimate constituent of the world (Lachs 2003: 159). He also seems overtly metaphysical in that he sets out a system of categories or an ontology that separates matter, essence, spirit, and truth into distinct kinds. But here too Santayana tries to make it clear that his categories are simply useful ways for us to structure our experience:

My system . . . is no *system of the universe*. The Realms of Being of which I speak are not parts of a cosmos, nor one great cosmos together: they are only kinds or categories of things which I find conspicuously different and worth distinguishing . . . my system . . . is *not metaphysical*.

[1923: vi–vii, emphasis his]

He says that he will "wait for the men of science to tell me what matter is, insofar as they can discover it" (1923: viii). His job is to try to outline the categories that we human animals spontaneously employ. It is "ordinary reflection systematized" (1942: 827).[9]

Sometimes Dewey sees that Santayana's thought fits nicely with his own intention of providing a "union of naturalism and idealism" (*MW* 3: 322; 1906). But on the whole, he is critical. He, with Russell, thinks that Santayana fails to find a way to combine subjectivism and objectivism and this drives "him into complete scepticism, tempered by a sudden and unmediated practical jump of pure faith into the things of nature—a kind of arbitrary pragmatism from which I shrink" (1939: 526).

But Dewey and Russell do not have Santayana right. We have seen that Peirce, James, and Santayana all hold in high esteem the idea that we need to hope or believe certain things. Santayana and Peirce unpack this thought by arguing that some general

---

[8] Neither were others. Munitz (1951 [1940]), for instance, also takes Santayana to task for putting forward a metaphysics full of essences. For Santayana has another concept of truth at play—the truth is the set of essences that are, were, or will be embodied in matter. See e.g. 1942 [1938]: 404. It is not clear how this is consistent with his pragmatist account of truth.

[9] See Tiller (2008: 129–36) and (2002).

presuppositions need to be assumed if we are to investigate, act, live, or have beliefs about the world. We need to presuppose that there is a world independent of our thought about it and that there is some possibility of coming to a view that would stand up to all experience and evidence. It is James who tends to develop this idea by arguing that an inquirer is entitled to presuppose any belief that serves him well. Dewey and Russell conflate James and Santayana, suggesting that both advocate believing whatever happens to work in this or that circumstance or that both advocate believing in myth.

If Santayana breaks from the classical pragmatists anywhere it is in his belief that philosophy has lost its way and that it needs to return to its proper job of setting out the possibilities of happiness and articulating and celebrating what it is to lead a good life. "Knowledge of what is possible," he opines, "is the beginning of happiness" (1910: 204). Our practices are evaluated by seeing how well they lead to human happiness. As Russell, who was a friend and admirer of Santayana, puts it, his thought is "fundamentally ethical" (1951 [1940]: 454). But here too, as Lachs has argued, Santayana's ethics are naturalist. Value is "situated in the life cycle of animals making their way in a difficult, sometimes even hostile, environment" (Lachs 2003: 160).

8.3 The New York Naturalists and the State of Pragmatism at the End of the Classical Era

Dewey moved to Columbia in 1904. Naturalism thrived there as well, in the hands of Fredrick Woodbridge, William Montague, and Wendell Bush and it only gained in strength while Dewey was in New York. A snapshot of some of the New York naturalist activity in the 1940s can be seen in a volume containing essays by some of the leading philosophers of the day—the 1944 *Naturalism and the Human Spirit*, edited by Y. H. Krikorian. The very title indicates that the project is the pragmatist one of trying to find a place for value in a scientific world-view. Many of the contributors explore the place in naturalism of what appears to be a non-empirical domain of inquiry. Ernest Nagel offers a view of how logic can be pried apart from a spurious metaphysical ontology; Sidney Hook considers politics; Abraham Edel, ethics; Sterling Lamprecht, religion; and George Boas and Edward Strong, history. Dewey wrote the introductory essay. The two most influential contributors were Hook and Nagel. Both had been undergraduates at City College with Dewey's student and critic Morris Raphael Cohen and then had gone on to do graduate work with Dewey.

Nagel was the paradigm of an analytic, logically inclined, philosopher of science in America. In 1954 he became the first John Dewey Professor in Philosophy at Columbia. His 1961 *The Structure of Science* was a major work in philosophy of science. In it, Nagel plays down any pragmatist bent. He takes Dewey's position to be an instrumentalism about truth and wants to distance himself from it (Poulos 1986: 540). Nonetheless, the very premise of the book betrays the influence of Peirce and Dewey.

He starts with the idea that inquiry is ignited by a problem and he replaces the notion of truth with "reliably warranted conclusions."

Hook, on the other hand, became a through-and-through Deweyan—so much so that he was often called "Dewey's bulldog." He is mostly remembered for his controversial and fiery engagement in the political debates of his day. He started off as a passionate Marxist, attempting to unite pragmatism and Marxism. He ended up a passionate anti-communist, reacting to the rise of Stalinism and notoriously approving of some of the sentiments lying behind McCarthyism. The later Hook took the view that the scientific experimentalist methodology put forward by Dewey will result in "the end of ideology" and make it possible for America to put in place a democracy that will thwart communism.

Dewey's legacy thus appeared secure, with his students Hook and Nagel continuing to put forward views very much along their teacher's lines. But in fact, his intellectual estate was precarious. By the time Dewey's career was drawing to an end, pragmatism had ceased to be a sharply delineated position. The naturalist middle ground between idealism and realism that he had been so intent on clearing and then occupying was becoming crowded by positions that shared much with each other, whether they acknowledged it or not. This of course, is not an unheard-of phenomenon. When a philosophical theory starts to become established, newcomers can want to set themselves against it, even though the ideas of the established theory have permeated the intellectual consciousness. Thus it was with pragmatism in the 1940s. Many philosophers who shared a set of principles and values with the pragmatists preferred the label "naturalism," or "realism," even though it is hard to see what distinguished their view from pragmatism. This was the atmosphere that awaited the logical empiricists, as they made their great migration out of a politically fraught Europe to the shores of the New World.

PART III

The Path to the Twenty-First Century

9

The Rise of Logical Empiricism

9.1 Introduction

We have seen that in the early decades of the 1900s the dominant intellectual force in America was pragmatism. A great and unbroken lineage could at that time be traced from Dewey back to the founders of pragmatism. Dewey had engaged with Peirce at Johns Hopkins and had been a steady interlocutor of James. He was the most prominent philosopher in the land. We have also seen that pragmatism was viewed with some suspicion by philosophers both within America and abroad. William James's view of truth, especially, had done the position no favors. Nonetheless, the speed of the near-demise that ensued for pragmatism is staggering. How could the dominant discourse have so quickly become moribund?

The received view is that when logical empiricism hit the shores of America in the 1930s it became the mainstream, pushing pragmatism into the backwaters. The logical empiricists, who arrived from Germany and Austria after Dewey's retirement from Columbia in 1929 but while he was still very active, simply flooded over him. As Richard Rorty puts it:

Along about 1945, American philosophers were, for better or worse, *bored* with Dewey, and thus with pragmatism. They were sick of being told that pragmatism was the philosophy of American democracy, that Dewey was the great American intellectual figure of their century, and the like. They wanted something new, something they could get their philosophical teeth into. What showed up, thanks to Hitler and various other historical contingencies, was logical empiricism, an early version of what we now call "analytic philosophy".

[Rorty 1995c: 70]

Rorty takes the new analytic philosophy to have been a damaging force in American philosophy departments and he is followed in this way of thinking by many contemporary pragmatists. But the idea that pragmatism was simply eclipsed by logical empiricism is not held merely by those who think that such an eclipse was a terrible thing. Those who thought that logical empiricism was a force for the good tend to adopt the same view of the fortunes of pragmatism. They think that pragmatism was justifiably eclipsed by analytic philosophy.

The eclipse view, as Talisse[1] calls it, is thus well entrenched: pragmatism and logical empiricism did battle, with pragmatism quickly finding itself on the losing end. But this is not, I shall argue, an accurate account of the engagement between logical empiricism and pragmatism. We shall see that the eclipse view has some fatal, if deeply interesting, flaws. My argument will be that there were remarkable similarities between pragmatism and logical empiricism. When the logical empiricists arrived in America, they found a soil in which their position could thrive. They did not arrive in a land that was inhospitable to their view, nor did they need to uproot the view they found already planted there.

It may be true that those in 1930s America who worked primarily in the history of philosophy extended chilly greetings to the logical empiricists upon their arrival. But the pragmatists had an altogether different attitude. As George Reisch puts it, there was a "golden age" in which the logical empiricists and the pragmatists were engaged in a collaborative project (1995: 23). Pragmatism had real affinities with logical empiricism and these affinities were well recognized. Ruth Barcan Marcus, for instance, says of her time as a graduate student in Sidney Hook's NYU Philosophy department: "pragmatism thrived in harmony with logical positivism and its variants, logical empiricism and scientific empiricism."[2]

What is now known as "analytic" philosophy is a rigorous style of philosophy that can be found as early as the Stoics and Aristotle. But its modern incarnation was born with Frege and Russell's delivery of a new and powerful logic in the 1930s; spent its youth in the optimistic excitement of logical empiricism in the 1930s and 1940s; became a kind of linguistic analysis in the hands of Russell and others at around the same time; went through a period of disillusionment when the most strenuous version of logical empiricism started to unravel and linguistic analysis started to fade; and came into maturity with the likes of Quine. A less severe version is now perhaps showing itself to be immortal as the dominant methodology of philosophy. The thread running through all of the stages in my potted history is that analytic philosophy is a *way* of doing philosophy. The term now, if anything, marks a method that has argumentative rigor, logic, and a respect for science and its methodology at its centre. And here at least one of the classical pragmatists—Peirce—is completely at home, while the others are at the very least frequent houseguests.

More striking though, is the fact that the epistemology and the view of truth that dominated analytic philosophy from the 1930s logical empiricism right through to Quine's reign in the 1950s was in fact pragmatism.[3] In 1932 Otto Neurath put the

---

[1] Talisse (2007: 131). He is as set against this interpretation of the history of pragmatism as I am.

[2] This is from her 2010 Dewey Lecture (Barcan Marcus 2010: 5).

[3] It was pragmatism of the Peircean variety. Other varieties were also on the scene. Suzanne Langer kept alive the Dewey-Mead idea that life must be seen as a continuous process in which we make meaning through symbolic transformation of experience. Alain Locke, who studied with James and Royce, kept alive Dewey's progressive political pragmatist focus, arguing that race is a form of social solidarity. But these views were more often than not in the background, not the foreground of philosophy departments.

insight at the heart of his view of truth and knowledge in terms of a classical metaphor. It was to become a famous image:

There is no way to establish fully secured, neat protocol statements as starting points of the sciences. There is no tabula rasa. We are like sailors who have to rebuild their ship on the open sea, without ever being able to dismantle it in dry-dock and reconstruct it from its best components.

[1983 [1932]: 92]

This metaphor delivers the same message as Peirce's central metaphor: inquirers are walking on a bog, saying only "this ground seems to hold for the present. Here I will stay till it begins to give way" (*CP* 5. 589; 1898). Knowledge is fallible and we make revisions when the force of experience causes a particular belief or theory to be thrown into doubt.

Hans Hahn, also in the early days of logical empiricism, is happy to explicitly throw his lot in with the pragmatists on the general matter of truth and knowledge: "As against the metaphysical view that truth consists in an agreement with reality—though this agreement cannot be established—we advocate the pragmatic view that the truth of a statement consists in its confirmation" (1987 [1933]: 43). We can already see that the explanation for the downturn in pragmatism's fortunes has to be far more interesting than that promoted by the eclipse view.

9.2 Logical Empiricism

Logical empiricism (or logical positivism, or the Vienna Circle) came into being in the mid-1920s when a group of philosophers, physicists, mathematicians, social scientists, and economists in Vienna gathered around Moritz Schlick and another group in Berlin gathered around Hans Reichenbach. The impending Second World War scattered this talent. Reichenbach, Rudolf Carnap, Carl Hempel, Herbert Feigl, Philipp Frank, and others emigrated to America in the 1930s. Schlick was shot dead in 1936 in Vienna by a mentally ill student. Neurath eventually ended up in England, joining the convert A. J. Ayer, who had visited the Vienna Circle as young man.

Germany lost more than the war and millions of lives. It lost its brain trust and lost it mostly to America. The lifespan of these expatriate philosophers extended into the 1970s and their reach extended even farther: many of their students are today still at the top of the profession. The logical empiricists ignited excitement in American philosophy departments. Their positions were were crisp and clear; their knowledge of logic and science was unassailable; they were driven by a sense of purpose and a mission to clean up the metaphysical squalor in which they thought philosophy lived; and they thought that progress is possible only if all inquiry is scientific. Tensions and differences of opinion eventually opened up fissures within the logical empiricist ranks and there was a Kantian theme, promoted by Carnap, pulling against the core story I tell below. That story focuses on the *empiricist* face of logical empiricism after its proponents arrived in North America. But we shall see that the Kantian thoughts embedded in logical empiricism are also important, certainly as its engagement with pragmatism unfolds.[4]

The logical empiricists aimed to unify all inquiry under the umbrella of science. Neurath started, edited, and nurtured *The International Encyclopedia of Unified Science* and this, teamed with a set of influential conferences, was for a long time the official forum for logical empiricism—its "organized contemporary expression" (Neurath *et al.* 1938: 2). The unification of inquiry was to proceed with a new and important resource—the formal or symbolic logic that was developed by Frege. It was also to proceed along the lines of the verifiability principle, which held that all meaningful sentences are reducible, via deductive logic, to statements that are empirically verifiable. Thus, no meaningful question is in principle unanswerable by science. Inquiry is unified and progress is possible if all branches of investigation are carried out in the same straightforward, logical, observational language. The statements of metaphysics, ethics, and religion are cast into suspicion on this view.

But one group of statements—the analytic—is kept safe from the verifiability criterion. The criterion holds that a meaningful statement is either analytically true or verifiable. The distinction between these two kinds of statements is old and venerable. In Kantian terms, analytic statements such as "All brothers are male" are true solely in virtue of their very meaning or by relations between concepts. Synthetic statements such as "Oliver Wendell Holmes had two brothers" are made true or not by the world. A similar distinction is cemented into Hume's philosophy as well, under the terms "relations of ideas" and "matters of fact." The distinction is deeply embedded in logical empiricism. Analytic truths, such as the statements of mathematics and logic, lack content—they are tautologies or true solely in virtue of their meanings. They need not be exposed to the verificationist test.

One version of logical empiricism has it that deductive axiomatic theories are given empirical meaning by definitions that hook up primitive terms in the formal language with observables in the world. This project is to devise an ideal language in which we can reconstruct the statements we find in science using only the clear and certain tools of formal logic and experiential predicates. Carnap's 1928 *The Logical Structure of the World* (the *Aufbau*) for instance, tries to show how we can give precise definitions or rational reconstructions of all scientific terms. These definitions bottom out in a primitive language—the "thing-language" or the language of physics. But even in this early work, Carnap produced two formal languages (the thing-language and the language of sense data) and argued that one can reduce discourse to either language,

---

[4] Michael Friedman has been one of the tracers of this Kantian lineage (see also Alan Richardson 1998). Friedman suggests that this line of thought was submerged by Russell's and Ayer's radical empiricist, reductionist interpretation of what the Vienna Circle was up to (Friedman 1999: xiv). One way of understanding my story is that when the reductionist, empiricist strain in logical empiricism petered out, the Kantian/pragmatist strain became prominent.

depending on what one's interests are. We shall see that this introduction of the idea of choice into logical empiricism aligns him with the pragmatists.

Another version is the "operationalism" of the physicist Percy Bridgman. A concept is fixed when the operations by which it is measured are fixed. For example: "the concept of length involves as much as and nothing more than the set of operations by which length is determined . . . *the concept is synonymous with the corresponding set of operations*" (1960 [1927]: 5, emphasis in original). The meaning of a concept lies in the operations of its verification.

On all versions of logical empiricism, philosophy must put itself into scientific language and render itself clear. Most of the purported answers to age-old questions will be shown to be fruitless and meaningless, by showing that they are not reducible to observation statements. They are not empirically verifiable and so they are "pseudo-propositions." Statements about essences, the Absolute, the thing-in-itself, etc. are to be put into the dustbin of metaphysics. Ethics and politics are also put in a precarious state. They are either to be reimagined or imperiled. Statements about what is right or wrong are either: (i) statements about what people actually approve of, not what they ought to approve of—that is, ethics is an empirical science; or (ii) they express emotions or feelings—to say that an act is odious is to say "Boo-hiss!" to it and to say that an act is good is to say "Hurrah!"; or (iii) they are meaningless. Carnap spells out the options as he sees them:

The word "Ethics" is used in two different senses. Sometimes a certain empirical investigation is called "Ethics", *viz.* psychological and sociological investigations about the actions of human beings . . . Ethics in this sense is an empirical, scientific investigation; it belongs to empirical science rather than to philosophy. Fundamentally different from this is ethics in the second sense, as the philosophy of moral values and moral norms, which one can designate normative ethics. This is not an investigation of facts, but a pretended investigation of what is good and what is evil, what it is right to do and what it is wrong to do.

[1935: 23]

He goes on to argue that a norm or a rule such as "killing is evil," is "merely an expression of a certain wish," not an assertion that can be true or false. In his *Problems of Ethics*, Schlick makes the same point: "When I recommend an action to someone as being 'good,' I express the fact that I *desire* it" (1962 [1939]:12). In *Language, Truth and Logic*, Ayer agrees:

Thus if I say to someone, "You acted wrongly in stealing that money", I am not stating anything more than if I had simply said, "You stole that money". In adding that this action is wrong I am not making any further statement about it. I am simply evincing my moral disapproval of it. It is as if I had said, "You stole that money", in a peculiar tone of horror, or written it with the addition of some special exclamation marks.

[1936: 107]

We have seen that pragmatists want to retain a place for value in legitimate inquiry. They opt for a version of (i) above—ethics is an empirical science, but experience must be conceived not merely as what is given by our senses and the conclusions of ethics issue in 'ought' statements, not 'is' statements. Some of the logical empiricists most committed to the unity of science idea agreed with the pragmatists. Indeed, the *Encyclopedia of Unified Science* contained a volume of Dewey's on ethics in which he argued for this view. Volumes were also planned for education and law. These and more subject matters, were to have a welcome place in the unity of science movement.

Some of the logical positivists wanted to pull ethics and the other human sciences out of scientific methodology—they opted for (ii) and (iii) above.[5] Reichenbach (1938) distinguishes between the context of justification and the context of discovery. The politics, sociology, and psychology of how scientists come to their decisions are part of the project of discovery, not justification. Notice that this is a move away from one of the very fundamentals of pragmatism: all pragmatists take as a fundamental insight the idea that the justification of beliefs and theories cannot be fenced off from human elements. We have seen that some pragmatists (the Jamesians) take the context of discovery to include an individual's needs and wants, and others (the Peirceans) restrict the context of discovery to the norms and standards of inquiry. But neither kind of pragmatist would agree with Reichenbach.

There were debates within logical empiricism. Carnap and Neurath most famously differed in their styles of reasoning. The former was more technical and interested in logic as an essential and metaphysically neutral tool for philosophy. Neurath was more interested in the unity of science movement and politics. There were also disputes about the concept of truth. Carnap ended up siding with the Tarskian or "semantic" view. Alfred Tarski was a brilliant logician who fled Poland and emigrated to the US in 1939. He shared the logical empiricists' view about what constitutes a rigorous theory (a rigorous theory is a logical theory) and devised a definition of truth for formal languages.[6] A theory of truth must have the following as theorems for all sentences p of the language for which truth is being defined: "p" is true if and only if p. Truth, that is, is extensionally defined as an infinite string of sentences of the sort: "snow is white" is true if and only if snow is white. Tarski's adequacy condition and account of truth proved and still proves attractive to many.

Neurath was not so inclined. He thought that the semantic view of truth commits one to a metaphysics that, like all metaphysics, is spurious. It establishes two orders of facts—a language and a world, with a comparison between the two implicit in the account. He argues, rather, for a coherence view of truth in which the truth of a statement is agreement with our accepted statements.[7] The acceptance of "protocol

---

[5]   It is interesting to note that the following argument, often kept implicit, has a long history in empiricism: ethics, politics, and (especially) religion are not sciences; hence propositions in these domains are not refutable by science; hence I am free to believe whatever appeals to me. There is more than a whiff of William James here.

[6]   See 1983 [1956]: 154–65. Tarski saw how strong Peirce was in logic. He calls Peirce the "creator of the theory of relations" and goes on to say that "It is . . . rather amazing that Peirce . . . did not have many followers" (1941: 73–4).

[7]   But see Uebel (2004) for the argument that Neurath was only taking about belief acceptance, not truth.

statements" that serve as the basis or jumping-off point for a vocabulary is practically determined: "There is no way to establish fully secured, neat protocol statements as starting points of the sciences" (1983 [1932–33]: 92). This means that for Neurath, as for the pragmatists, there are no first principles. As Cartwright *et al.* show, Neurath puts everything on the "same earthly plane," as he was fond of saying (1996: 208). His naturalism is resolute.

There were also important controversies about the nature of the experience in which meaningful statements were supposed to be grounded. Some of the logical empiricists (the phenomenalists) held that observation reports are about private sensations and others (the physicalists) held that they were about public physical events. The problem for the phenomenalists is that it seems impossible to communicate such private qualitative content to others—the experiencer seems to be trapped in his or her own world. The problem for the physicalists is that they seem to be grounding knowledge in something about which we could be mistaken. That is, they seem to not be able to achieve their aim of epistemological security.

Despite the differences, the verifiability principle was at the heart of all of these views[8] and it was under sustained pressure. It faced some formidable objections and was constantly undergoing revision and liberalization in light of them. One set of objections centers around the strength of the verifiability required. If a meaningful statement is one that can conclusively be shown to be true or false, then there are few, if any, candidates for meaningfulness. For it turns out that all kinds of discourses are in trouble on this stringent criterion. Statements about the past, about the future, and about the mental states of others are not conclusively verifiable by observation and thus are swept away as meaningless on the strong verifiability criterion. Even "Blue, here, now!" when presented with a patch of blue, is not conclusively verifiable. I might, for instance, be hallucinating or suddenly become color blind. In order for the statement to carry certainty with it, it has to be reframed so it reads: "It seems to me that blue, here, now." Hence, the statement, if it is to be conclusively verified, is a statement about my mental state—about how the world seems to me—not a statement about the world.

Even more disconcerting was that scientific laws and dispositional hypotheses seem not to meet the bar. A scientific law is a universal generalization ranging over an infinite domain and hence no finite number of positive instances will conclusively verify a law. Statements containing dispositional terms such as "soluble," "temperature," "mass," "heat" and "force" are analyzable only by counterfactual or subjunctive conditionals—"were x to be placed in water, then it would dissolve" or "were a thermometer to be in contact with x, it would register y degrees." This kind of statement is also not subject to conclusive verification.

---

[8] Schlick was an early advocate of a verifiability principle, whereas others, such as Carnap, adopted one later.

Another set of objections centers around the nature of the observation required. Much of science seems to fail the test, if what we are asking for is observation by the senses. For instance, hypotheses about unobservable entities, such as subatomic particles, cannot be meaningful statements that are either true or false, but at best useful instruments. An instrumentalism about theoretical terms and statements seems to follow straight on from the verifiability principle.

Many attempts were made to try to overcome these challenges. The verifiability principle underwent liberalizations such as: not requiring conclusive verifiability; not taking verifiability to be the entirety of meaningfulness; beefing up deductive logic with inductive logic, each move taking the principle farther away from the goals of straightforwardness and certainty. Tempering the criterion in these ways amounted to abandoning some of the very ideals of clarity, rigor, and precision that drove the reductionist program of analyzing meaningful sentences via logic and observational predicates. The strong program, that is, seemed to collapse in light of the contortions required to save sentences that seem to be worth saving. In 1953, Nelson Goodman could say to Ayer's colleagues at the University of London: "Surely I need not in this place and before this audience recount the tragic history of the verification theory of meaning" (1983: 1953: 31). What is most interesting as far as the topic of this book is concerned is that, as we shall see, many of the logical empiricists abandoned the strong program and moved towards pragmatism.

At the same time, many of the logical empiricists drifted away from the broad unity of science movement, on which all kinds of inquiry can show themselves to be sciences. These empiricists gravitated instead towards the view that the physical sciences and logic were the only domains of knowledge.[9] The social and political vision promoted by Neurath, Frank, and Charles Morris lost ground to the more hard-edged vision promoted by Carnap, Feigl, and Reichenbach. But we shall see that both these branches of logical empiricism had a strong gust of pragmatism blowing through them.[10]

9.3 Peirce and Logical Empiricism

We have seen that pragmatism has always had a hearty verificationist strain. Arthur Lovejoy remarks on it in 1909, speaking of James. Pragmatism, he says, is "a modern expression" of the positivism of Comte and others, reducing meaning and truth to the

---

[9] See Reisch (2005: 21f., 167ff., 168ff.) for a sustained account of the move away from the value-laden unity of science idea and towards a more austere value-free philosophy of the hard sciences. While there is much that is fascinating in Reisch's account, his claim that the cause of the shift was largely due to McCarthyism and cold war politics seems to me to be only a small part of the story. The swing to volition and value and then away again plays out through the whole of the history of verificationism.

[10] So did Popper's view. He heatedly set himself against logical empiricism, but shared its emphasis on science, logic, probability theory, and anti-metaphysical attitude. His falsificationism (make bold conjectures; try to falsify them; theories then get closer and closer to the truth) also has parallels with pragmatism. See Popper (1963).

pointing to particulars in concrete experience (1909a: 577). In 1968, Ayer wrote a book on how logical empiricism is a modern expression of pragmatism—on how pragmatism was a precursor of logical empiricism. He states that Peirce's position "allows no truck with metaphysics. Its standpoint is closely akin to that which was later to be adopted by the logical positivists. Peirce's pragmatic maxim is indeed identical ... with the physicalist interpretation of the verification principle" (1968: 45).

Lovejoy and Ayer were not quite right. We have seen that pragmatism does not seek to *reduce* meaning and truth to the pointing to particulars—Peirce, at least, was very clear that he was talking about an aspect of meaningfulness, not the whole of it. Pragmatism also offers a much broader account of experience than the physicalist interpretation of the logical empiricists' verification principle. It does not want to exclude all metaphysics, ethics, etc. from the realm of the legitimate. But Lovejoy and Ayer are onto *something*. Peirce, Wright, and James argued that if you try to divorce philosophical concepts from experience and practice, you lose contact with what is real and you sink into useless metaphysics.

The similarity between Peirce and the logical empiricists was not merely noticed after the heyday of logical empiricism. Neurath, in the first volume of the *Encyclopedia*, says this in setting out the history of logical empiricism:

The connection between modern logic and empiricism did not arise instantly ... A few of the modern logicians, such as Peirce, and, later on, Bertrand Russell, combined the interest in logic with an interest in empiricism. Traditional idealistic philosophers did not discuss carefully or look with favor upon this new combination of logicalization and empiricalization. The fact that Peirce was a logician and simultaneously interested in empiricism was in turn important for the preparation of modern scientific empiricism in the United States.

[1938: 17]

This introductory volume of the Encyclopedia—Volume 1, Number 1—has the connection between pragmatism and logical empiricism as a theme running throughout it.

Peirce was also the subject of a talk at the fifth International Conference for the Unity of Science, which Charles Morris organized at Harvard in 1940. This was the first of the conferences held in the United States. Ernest Nagel, the Columbia philosopher of science who didn't like to call himself a logical empiricist or a pragmatist, but who had strong connections with both camps, gave a masterful paper titled "Charles S. Peirce: Pioneer of Modern Empiricism." Nagel pointed out the affinities between logical empiricism and pragmatism: the antipathy to metaphysical speculation, the emphasis on cooperative scientific research, and the fact that the pragmatic maxim "was offered to philosophers in order to bring to an end disputes which no observation of facts could settle because they involved terms with no definite meaning" (1940: 73). Nagel, as Andrew Jewett (2011), argues, tried to convince all parties that logical empiricism and American pragmatism were made for each other.

Reichenbach saw the connection as well. He remarks that the founders of pragmatism showed "great merit" in coming up with an anti-metaphysical theory of meaning at a time when the "logical instruments" that the positivists took to be required for that theory were not yet developed (1938: 69). He admired Peirce's work on induction, saying that "There is no doubt that the contributions of Peirce mark the first forward step towards a solution of this problem since it had been pointed out so seriously by David Hume...Reading Peirce's collected papers has always been for me a high intellectual enjoyment combined with the suspicion of a personal tragedy behind all these scattered utterances of a brilliant mind" (1939: 187–88).

Reichenbach sees his own vindication of induction as walking hand in hand with pragmatism. He gives us an argument on which "[i]nductive inference cannot be dispensed with because we need it for the purpose of action" (1938: 346). The only way of justifying induction is as follows: "if success is possible at all it can be obtained by continued application of the principle of induction" (1939: 190). Reichenbach sees this as a "development of ideas which originated in pragmatism." Rather than try (fruitlessly) to show that inductive inferences are valid, Reichenbach, with Peirce, argues that if we are to know anything at all, we must rely upon inductive inference. In Peirce's terms, the belief that induction is reliable is a regulative assumption of inquiry. This does not give us certainty, but gives us all we need (Reichenbach 1939: 190).

Peirce revered logic as much as did the logical empiricists. And all the pragmatists had a deep respect for science, some brand of verificationism at the core of their view, a suspicion of metaphysics, and an emphasis on practical consequences. As Morton White put it in 1957: "Pragmatism, logical positivism, and operationalism all encouraged a tighter, more scientifically oriented, less monumental conception of philosophy" (2005 [1957]: 146).

Pragmatism, though, expressly included value in its ambit, whereas not all of the logical empiricists were so enthusiastic about that project. This lack of enthusiasm lead Randall to describe Carnap as a "Prussian systematizer," "relatively insulated from the main currents of American experience and thought." This is in contrast to Dewey's democratic, engaged philosophy, as the canonized patron saint of American democracy (Jewett 2011: 91–2). But, as we have seen, the logical empiricists were not all set against bringing ethics under the scope of scientific inquiry. Morevoer, they were also deeply political and engaged, more often than not with Dewey on the progressive left.

9.4 Dewey and the Unity of Science Movement

The similarity between pragmatism and logical empiricism is only amplified when we turn to Dewey's philosophy. Dewey's aim is identical to that of the unity of science strain of logical empiricism: to unify all inquiry—physics, ethics, aesthetics, etc. via the experimental method. His 1922 *Human Nature and Conduct*, for instance, is an attempt to make ethics a science. This similarity was well recognized by the logical empiricists and their allies. Russell saw Dewey's pragmatism as marked by a "very genuine scientific temper," in contrast to "the will to believers."[11] Reichenbach asserted that, despite his worries about Dewey's blurring of the subjective and the objective, the two of them are very much in the same camp (1939: 160). Once the logical empiricists hit the shores of America in the 1930s, Dewey, who was then in his seventies, was seen as a kindred spirit.

Charles Morris (who was part of Dewey's Chicago School), Sidney Hook, Ernest Nagel, and Otto Neurath persuaded Dewey to join forces with the logical empiri-cists.[12] Dewey was at first suspicious and reluctant. He did not even respond to Neurath's initial invitation to be a part of the planning committee for the *Encyclopedia*. The turning point seems to have been when Nagel and Hook accompanied Neurath to Dewey's house with the intention of asking Dewey to contribute to the *Encyclo-pedia*.[13] Dewey was wary, as he wanted nothing to do with the logical empiricist's atomism—with the view that bits of language hook on to discrete parts of the world, either getting the world right or wrong. Nagel recounts that Neurath's English was at this point poor and he was having a hard time articulating the platform of logical empiricism to Dewey: "When he realized that his efforts at explanation were getting him nowhere, he got up, raised his right hand as if he were taking an oath in a court of law (thereby almost filling Dewey's living room), and solemnly declared, 'I *swear* we don't believe in atomic propositions'" (Lamont 1959: 12).

Dewey was won over, although perhaps only to Neurath, who he considered the most pragmatist of the logical empiricists (Lamont 1959: 13). He agreed to be on the *Encyclopedia*'s Advisory Committee and he wrote a section of the introductory first volume, alongside Neurath, Carnap, Russell, Morris, and Niels Bohr. His section is titled "Unity of Science as a Social Problem" and in it he is happy to stand with the founders and mainstays of logical empiricism against the "numerous and organized" "enemies of the scientific attitude" (*LW* 13: 274; 1938). He tells us that the scientific attitude can be manifested in every walk of life, for the scientific attitude is the attitude that is freedom from dogma, unexamined tradition, and self-interest. It is a commit-ment to inquiry, the gathering of evidence, and the drawing of conclusions based only on evidence: "It is the intention to reach beliefs, and to test those that are entertained, on the basis of observed fact" (*LW* 13: 273; 1938). He then tells us that science deals with actual problems and that "The home, the school, the shop, the bedside and hospital, present such problems as truly as does the laboratory." His metaphysics is absent in this piece and Dewey is quite wonderfully clear and persuasive.

In 1939 Dewey was the sole author of a volume of the *Encyclopedia*. This volume was titled *Theory of Valuation* and in it he brings values under the scope of science. He tries

---

[11] See Russell (1983 [1919]: 147). C. I. Lewis also saw the differences between Dewey and James (1939: 574).

[12] See Reisch (2005: 84f.).

[13] This meeting most likely took place in 1936–37.

to show how propositions about what is good or right are "empirically grounded propositions about desires and interests" (LW 13: 242; 1939). Inquiry into values produces verifiable conclusions: we can verify "what individuals and groups hold dear or prize and the grounds upon which they prize them" (LW 13: 243; 1939). "Valuation-phenomena," Dewey argues, "have their immediate source in biological modes of behavior" and "owe their concrete content to the influence of cultural conditions" (LW 13: 249; 1939). All of this can be studied.

It is not surprising that some of the attacks on Dewey were identical to those on the logical empiricists. The reaction to Dewey's 1929 *The Quest for Certainty*, for instance, was that he was too enamored of science. It was said that he illicitly applied science to questions of value.[14] Indeed, reviews of the 1908 *Ethics* had already seen Dewey as contributing to positivism.[15]

It is pretty clear that Dewey was not out of step with the ideas of the new philosophy. He was, however, out of step with the new analytic way of *doing* philosophy. The other contributors to the introductory volume of the *Encyclopedia* take logical empiricism to be, in Charles Morris's words, "the union of formal logic and empiricism" (1938a: 66). But within the halls of what was becoming mainstream philosophy, it was thought by anyone who knew any logic that Dewey was no logician.

Dewey argues that logic must be seen in a "naturalist" manner. It grows out of organic, human activities, rather than out of "a mystical faculty of intuition." Logic is social in that it arises in communities where there is language and inquiry (LW 12: 26; 1938). It is "a subject falling within the domain of social inquiry" (LW 5: 166; 1929). Logic is about the operations of inquiry and hence it is about inquirers and their ways of organizing and going about their inquiries. He presents logic as a set of "postulates" or as "conditions, discovered in the course of inquiry itself, which further inquiries must satisfy if they are to yield warranted assertibility as a consequence" (LW 12: 24; 1938). Subsequent investigations can result in a revision of these postulates of logic.

We have seen that Peirce also spoke about logic as the theory of inquiry. But that view traveled alongside his remarkable advances in mathematical logic. During his time, the new formal logic was just coming into being and only a small handful of philosophers could claim to know what was going on at the frontier. Peirce was one of them. Dewey, though, was skeptical of formal logic. In 1912, he published an interesting review of Schiller's rather silly *Formal Logic: A Scientific and Social Problem*. The review, titled "A Trenchant Attack on Logic," applauds Schiller's "demolishing hand" (MW 7: 131; 1912).

---

[14] See both Burke (1930) and Bixler (1930). In the latter, titled "Professor Dewey Discusses Religion," Bixler criticizes Dewey's treatment of value and remarks that "James's view is the one which really fits the notion of a changing world" (1930: 220).

[15] See e.g. Wilde (1908: 636).

By the time Dewey wrote *Logic: The Theory of Inquiry* in 1938, mathematical logic had ceased to be new. It was now a serious matter if you were weak in formal logic, especially if you were weak in logic and writing treatises on it. The idea that logic is the theory of inquiry had become antiquated. Dewey looked less and less to the new breed of philosophers like someone who was speaking their language and wrestling with their set of problems. Indeed, just as he tried to avoid Peirce's technical course on logic at Johns Hopkins, Dewey advised his own students to not take courses in symbolic logic, lest they become taken with the logical empiricists' brand of empiricism (Lamont 1959: 13). It is no surprise that we find Nagel, Dewey's younger and formal-minded Columbia University colleague, writing: "there is a tendency among those interested primarily in formal problems to deny that he was a logician, and to classify him as perhaps a descriptive psychologist or anthropologist" (1986: xiii). Nagel adds to Dewey's defects in logic a lack of technical facility in science as well:

Dewey's physics and even mathematics was at best second-hand, and he relied very heavily for his information on what are essentially popularizations.... I confess I never felt entirely at ease when Dewey talked about physical theory (even though his comments were often full of insight), for he didn't exhibit a mastery over this material that comes only from a first-hand knowledge of the subject.[16]

There were also significant points of substantive disagreement between Dewey and those of the logical empiricists who were physicalists. In Dewey's contribution to the introductory volume of the *Encyclopedia*, he includes a sentence set against Carnap's idea that we can define the terms of all sciences by defining the terms of physics. Any such project, Dewey says "is doomed in advance to defeat" (*LW* 13: 276; 1938). Letters flew back and forth. Dewey's main objection to this branch of logical empiricism is that it denies that ethics falls under the scope of science. We have seen that Carnap opted for the view that a statement in ethics is an expression of a desire, not an assertion that might be true or false. In *A Theory of Valuation*, Dewey criticizes emotivism—the "ejaculatory" view on which to say something is good is to exclaim your approval and to say something is bad is to exclaim your disapproval (*LW* 13: 196; 1939). On this theory, Dewey notes, value statements are not such that we can disagree about them. You say "boo" to fraudulent ponzi schemes, I say "hurrah," and all we are left with is a difference in our likes and dislikes, with no way of adjudicating between them. In Dewey's view, value expressions are human expressions, but they aim at transforming an existing situation into a better one—an outcome that Dewey thinks can be tested (*LW* 13: 201–939). We have seen, however, that he was less than successful in showing how testing and adjudication is possible on his view.

It is important to see that this is a substantial but interfamilial argument. It is an argument within the circle of those who insist that value judgments, if they are to be

---

[16] Ernest Nagel interview Oct. 10, 1966, John Dewey Papers Collection 102. See also Nagel in McGilvary *et al.* (1939: 575ff.).

legitimate, must be empirical. But interfamilial relations, where there is more similarity than difference between the siblings, can be intense. Dewey's remark caused some upset between Carnap and Neurath. Carnap read a draft of Dewey's volume for the *Encyclopedia* and objected that no logical empiricist continued to hold the ejaculatory view. Perhaps Schlick had held it, but even Schlick, Carnap protests, thought merely that there was a non-cognitive component to value judgments, not that value judgments were devoid of cognitive content and hence mere expressions of "boo" or "hurrah." Neurath also told Dewey that he had misrepresented the logical empiricists' view here. Dewey replied that it was Ayer whom he had in mind. He left the disputed sentence in his monograph, but added a note that tried to be more subtle about the views of his brethren.[17]

Perhaps Dewey did unfairly set up certain of the logical empiricists' views of ethics. But he is surely right to spot the following difference between those views and his own brand of empiricism. His aim is to *find a place* for value in a scientific world-view. The project of the logical empiricists, on the whole, is to work out the implications of what they take to be the scientific world-view, without a commitment to keeping a place open for value. Some of them, notably those on the physicalist branch, hold firm to the idea that "the field of scientifically warranted propositions is exhausted in the field of propositions of physics and chemistry" (*LW* 13: 193; 1939). Value judgments are either made to fit or left out in the cold. That is, some logical empiricists did indeed think that ethical and political claims could not be scientifically tested and hence they were a second-class kind of claim. A hallmark of pragmatism, in contrast, is that our ethical and political claims can indeed be tested—they can be tested in living.

In a related objection, Dewey was also upset at the logical empiricists for being responsible for what he saw as the loss of philosophy's relevance to the world's problems. In the 1948 introduction to the new edition of *Reconstruction in Philosophy* he bemoaned contemporary philosophy's concern "for the improvement of techniques" and a "withdrawal from the present scene" (*MW* 12: 257; 1948). Philosophy, Dewey argues, must be connected to real-life problems, including ethical and political problems. By the end of his life, he was warning his students that logical empiricism was the "new scholasticism"—a set of difficult exercises that the clever student will be put through, to no clear end (Randall 1953: 7).

But the logical empiricists did not think that their views were unconnected to ethics and, especially, politics. They thought that they were freeing ethics and politics from the dangerous religious and cultural forces that had done the world so much ill. Neurath, for instance, is very much in tune with Dewey on this score. As Alan Richardson (2008) puts it, Neurath and Dewey both think that an increasingly scientized world is one which will be socially progressive.[18]

---

[17] See Reisch (2005: 87–97) for a full account of this incident.
[18] See also Philipp Frank and Charles Morris.

9.5 Charles Morris and the Resurrection of Peirce's Theory of Signs

Charles Morris (1901–79) played an important role in bringing together Dewey and the logical empiricists. Indeed, he was a broad and sturdy bridge between the whole of pragmatism and logical empiricism. He completed a PhD under Mead in Chicago on the symbolic theory of the mind and thought of himself as taking the next step in developing Mead's pragmatist theory of language, communication, and self. He was a follower of Dewey, wholeheartedly embracing the view that science must be the core of philosophy and of democratic politics. Pragmatism, they both argued, is an expression of the values that are built into a healthy democracy.

Morris had met and been impressed by many of the Vienna Circle while on sabbatical in Europe in 1934 and then again at the 1938 Prague meeting of the International Congress of Philosophy. He became a kind of agent for them in America—encouraging and helping them to emigrate; bringing Carnap to the University of Chicago; and offering advice and support. Once the empiricists arrived, he became enmeshed in their project. He, Neurath, and Carnap were editors in chief of the *Encyclopedia of Unified Science* and he organized the 1940 Harvard meeting of the International Congress of the Unity of Science. His logical empiricist pedigree was unassailable, even if there was some hearty suspicion of his extra-philosophical excursions into neo-Buddhist religion, a study of body types and temperaments, and so on.[19]

Morris's bridge between pragmatism and logical empiricism is formed by two planks. First, he highlights the fact that pragmatism and logical empiricism share a commitment to the scientific spirit. His 1938 prelude to the Harvard conference—"The Unity of Science Movement and the United States"—puts it as follows. Pragmatism and logical empiricism are both philosophies focused on science. While Americans, with the great exception of Peirce, have not been the leaders in logic or in thinking about the scientific method in a formal way, they have been leaders in bringing the scientific attitude to the social sciences and the humanities (1937a: 26–27). The "whole temper of the country is against the sharp separation—so easy for Europeans—of the natural sciences and the 'mind' sciences." American intellectuals seem to be "singularly prepared" to incorporate the human sciences into the unity of science movement (1938b: 27). Hence the only real difference between the logical empiricists and the pragmatists is in the scope they take science to have. He says:

The pragmatists have, without exception I believe, wished philosophy to become as scientific as possible, but have not limited philosophy to the philosophy of science. A scientific philosophy need not be a philosophy of science—unless one decides to define 'philosophy' is this way.

[1963: 96–97]

---

[19] E.g. see Morris's 1942 *Paths of Life: Preface to a World Religion*, a survey of possible responses to the "agony" that Morris sees as an inherent and inescapable feature of human life.

In his own volume for the *Encyclopedia*, the 1938 *Foundations of the Theory of Signs*, Morris again cited the tradition of pragmatism as an important part of the movement in philosophy towards science and its unity (1938a: 9). He notes that Peirce seems to be an outlier—of all the classical pragmatists, he was least interested in thinking about matters such as democracy and value. We have seen that this is only half right. While Peirce was indeed not concerned with theorizing about democracy, he conforms nicely to the pragmatist tradition of bringing all kinds of inquiry, such as mathematics, metaphysics, and morals, under the naturalist-pragmatist tent. But it is not surprising, given how little of Peirce's work was available in the 1930s, that Morris and others would have missed this.

The other plank in Morris's bridge comes straight out of Peirce, who he says was "second to none in the history of semiotic" (1938a: 31). Morris thinks that the theory of signs is the mechanism by which the physical and the human sciences can be integrated (1937a: 28). On Morris's Peircean theory, there are three interrelated and interdependent features of language, each of which demands study. "Meaning," if the term must be used, does not reside in any one of these features, but is to be characterized by the whole of the sign process, taking its objective, subjective, and inter-subjective aspects seriously (1938a: 45). The first aspect of the sign process is syntactics—the formal study of how signs relate to each other. Morris rightly sees Peirce as a pioneer here—he developed a first-order quantified logic that shows how various classes of signs follow syntactical rules of formation and transformation. Both Peirce and Morris argue that logic rests on a general theory of signs, in which we trace the relations of signs within a formal language (1938a: 47).

Morris sees parallels between Peirce's theory of signs and Carnap's project of arriving at a precise language for science (1938a: 14ff.). A central issue that engaged Carnap is the idea that the formal or objective study of signs is required for scientific clarity.[20] Science demands a "special and restricted" language (1938a: 12). It demands "the formal point of view" (1938a: 13). Morris summarizes and commends this aspect of logical empiricism as follows: "the formalized languages studied in contemporary logic and mathematics clearly reveal themselves to be the formal structure of actual and possible languages of the type used in making statements about things; at point after point they reflect the significant features of language in actual use" (1938a: 21).

The formalist deliberately neglects the other features of language, so as to isolate a particular object of interest—syntactics (1938a: 21). But Morris and Peirce think that those other features are just as important. The second dimension to language is

---

[20] Carnap adopts Morris's sytanctics-sematics–pragmatics distinction in his own contribution to the *Encyclopedia*, the 1939 *Foundations of Logic and Mathematics*: "Morris made [a trichotomic structure] the basis for the three fields into which he divides semiotic... namely, pragmatics, semantics, and syntactics. Our division is in agreement with his in its chief features" (1939: 4–5). Carnap invokes this distinction again in *Introduction to Semantics* (1942: 9, 239). He also adopts a pragmatist view of language: "A language is a system of... habits... The elements of the language are signs... produced by members of the group in order to be perceived by other members and to influence their behavior" (1939: 3).

semantics, which studies the relationship between signs and what they denote—the relation of signs to things. At its most theoretical, it asks questions such as "is the structure of language the structure of nature?" and at its most particular or empirical, it asks what the actual conditions are under which certain signs are employed (1938a: 22). Here part of Morris's work is to examine the semantic rules involved in the use of different kinds of signs—Peirce's trio of icons, indices, and symbols.

But Morris, again with Peirce, wants to draw special attention to the third and under-recognized feature of signs: pragmatics. He takes himself to be attempting to "carry out resolutely the insight of Charles Peirce that a sign gives rise to an interpretant and that an interpretant is in the last analysis 'a modification of a person's tendencies toward action'" (1946a: 27–8). In his view, pragmatism's major and lasting contribution is that it has directed our attention to and made profound insights into to the study of how signs relate to their users and interpreters (1938a: 29). Morris is responsible for labeling what subsequent generations of linguists and philosophers still call "pragmatic criteria": "all the psychological, biological, and social phenomena" which occur in the functioning of signs and inquiry (1938a: 30).

Morris also follows Peirce in identifying the interpretant as an important "dimension" of the meaning of a sign or of "sign functioning" (1938a: 31). He is the only one of his generation who sees that Peirce's pragmatism was about aspects of meaning, not the whole of meaning.[21] We have seen that Peirce argues that the interpretant of a sign is the modification of the interpreter's tendencies in rational conduct *or thought*. Morris opts to emphasize the former, not the latter, hence making his position more behavioristic than Peirce would have liked. Here he is following his teacher Mead, who "was especially concerned with the behavior involved in the functioning of linguistic signs and with the social context in which such signs arise and function" (1938a: 31). The effect on the interpreter is an overt behavioral effect or a disposition to behave in a certain way. The pragmatic dimension of meaning, on the Mead/Morris account, is largely a matter of stimulus and response. Such behavioral responses are much more accessible, observable, and simple than Peirce's complex effects a symbol might have on its interpreter and Morris thinks that his own view provides a cleaner theory for science to work with (1946a: 289–90). He recognizes that he and Mead differ from Peirce on this score (1946a: 7).[22] But there is much more in common than

---

[21] He also approves of the way Peirce brings the mental into the sign relation by insisting that the irreducible triadic sign relation has, as one of its three components, the mediation of a mind or intention. Morris repeats Peirce's analysis of the concept of "giving" to make this point. "Giving" cannot be reduced to two dyadic relations: one hand extending an object to another person and the other person taking the object from that hand. An intention or desire that the recipient have and keep the object is involved.

[22] Morris is subtle on this point. While he does not intend to "deny private experiences," he does want to deny that "such experiences are of central importance or that the fact of their existences makes the objective study of semiosis . . . impossible" (1938a: 6). But Morris also thinks that "recent formulations of behavior theory have in their own way accepted Peirce's position in so far as they recognize that the conditioning of one response to a stimulus which previously produced another response is mediated by a third factor, a 'reinforcing' state of affairs" (1946a: 288).

not. In science, Morris argues, signs stand in specific relations to each other, to objects, and to practice. He echoes Peirce beautifully when he says: "The very statement that science walks on three legs of theory, observation, and practice will call out opposition in a certain type of mind—the statement is more frequent with 'practice' omitted" (1937a: 67).

Dewey's response to Morris is interesting. Despite the affinities between their views, despite Morris's desire to promote those affinities, and despite a shared interest in a scientific democratic politics, Dewey is rude to and about Morris[23] and he attacks Morris's account of Peirce in a harsh and undeserved way.[24] In his 1946 "Peirce's Theory of Linguistic Signs, Thought, and Meaning," Dewey argues that Morris gets Peirce's account of signs badly wrong. He says that Morris's introduction of an "interpretant" is "gratuitous" if one already has the interpreter in the relation and it is the latter that has to be abandoned (*LW* 15: 142; 1946). Peirce, he says, would object with "scorn" to the presence of the interpreter as part of the sign relation.

This seems a terribly unfair criticism. Morris is clear that the sign relation is "triadic" (1938a: 6). The three components of a semiotic relationship are the sign, the object, and the interpretant. He suggests, without investing much in the idea, that "the interpreter may be included as a fourth factor" (1938a: 3). Dewey's point seems to be that, for Peirce, meaning is not an effect *on* an interpretER, but rather, *is* an interpreTANT. The interpretant is always another linguistic sign and it is a mistake to bring the notion of an arbitrary "sign receiver" into the equation. It is fair enough to note that Morris is too concerned with action and with particular sign receivers than with the further development of signs and thought. But he is not deserving of the reprimand Dewey delivers. Dewey accuses Morris of giving us an "inverted report of Peirce"—one that needs Dewey to step in and "rescue Peirce's theory . . . before an Ersatz takes the place of what [he] actually held" (*LW* 15: 141; 1946).

In his 1948 "Signs about Signs about Signs," Morris responds to Dewey's charge by pointing out that Dewey has taken only a partial view of his position (apparently ignoring Morris's 1946 *Signs, Language, and Behavior*), and a faulty one at that (1948: 124ff.). To support the latter point, Morris cites lengthy passages from his own work alongside that of Dewey and Peirce, and rightly concludes that his position in *Signs, Language, and Behavior* "is very close indeed to that of Peirce and not at an inversion of his position" (1948: 126).

Morris is fully alert to the normative challenge that faces pragmatism. He says that the pragmatic dimension of sign functioning is prone to abuse. Aggressive acts of individuals and groups, can for instance, "drape themselves in the mantle of morality"

---

[23] See Reisch (2005: 334ff.). As I will note when I talk of the response to C. I. Lewis, this is a period in the history of philosophy that could do with some further sociological scrutiny.

[24] The debate still rages amongst semioticians. A depressing snapshot of it is contained in Deledalle (2001). I think that Seth Sharpless, who was a student of Morris's, gets the matter exactly right. He asserts that Morris read Peirce carefully and understood him well, but he wonders whether Dewey returned the favor when it came to reading Morris. See Reisch (2005: 334).

(1938a: 40). Their stated purpose and their intended effect can be dishonest. Similarly, he says that dishonesty comes through the door if we say that truth is fully pragmatic— "so that any sign which furthers the interest of the user is said to be true" (1938a: 40–41). He notes that only some of James's statements "taken in isolation might seem to justify this perversion of pragmatism" and "Dewey has specifically denied the imputed identification of truth and utility" (1938a: 41). Nonetheless, Morris is worried that both philosophers are prone to be overly subjective. He has some normative principles hovering above his own view that would prevent, he thinks, truth and utility from being confused. These are principles that he would invoke to criticize those acts and interests he thinks are morally suspect. Normative scrutiny of the purposes and effects of signs must be part of a pragmatist analysis. Although Morris does not set out what these principles are and how they can be justified, he does very clearly see that purposes and effects must be evaluated.

9.6 Logical Empiricism Turns to Pragmatism

We have seen that affinities between pragmatism and logical empiricism abound. But the relationship between the two positions is stronger than one of mere affinity. Pragmatism influenced the evolution of logical empiricism in underappreciated ways.

Charles Morris was already stating in 1937 that the theory of truth held by Carnap, Hahn, Reichenbach and Frank "has become very similar to the position of Dewey and Lewis" (1937a: 4). Carnap writes in the *Library of Living Philosophers* volume dedicated to him: "Morris is certainly right in pointing out that, since I came to America, my philosophical views have clearly been influenced by pragmatist ideas"—those of C. I. Lewis, Morris, Nagel, and Hook (1963: 860–61). He says that as a result of these pragmatist influences, he puts more emphasis on the social factor in knowledge and on the idea that a "conceptual system" involves practical decisions (1963: 861).

As the doctrines of the logical empiricists came under stress and as the logical empiricists became more familiar with the positions in their new country, they became clear about the pragmatism running deep in their views.[25] Here is Philipp Frank:

The physicist in his own scientific activity has never employed any other concept of truth than that of pragmatism. The "agreement of thoughts with their object", which the school philosophy requires, cannot be established by any concrete experiment. . . . In reality, physicists compare only experiences with other experiences. They test the truth of a theory by what it has become customary to call "agreements".[26]

Frank, with Neurath, is a meaning holist, arguing that the meaning and the truth of a statement are matters of the statement fitting into a system of statements—into a

---

[25] Alex Klein (forthcoming) has suggested that the logical empiricists modified the views they had carved out in Europe to fit their new, not fully secure, academic home.
[26] See 1949 [1930]: 101–2. Also see Frank (1950).

theory. He argues that theories are under-determined by the data—more than one theory can account for what we experience. Hence the choice of theory involves considerations such as social utility (1951: 19).

Carnap too had an acknowledged and strong tendency towards pragmatism. Indeed, he is perhaps the most interesting of the logical empiricists, as far as pragmatism is concerned. In the 1950 "Empiricism, Semantics, and Ontology," he distinguishes between external and internal questions. Internal questions, which can only be raised from within a linguistic framework, must be straightforwardly verifiable. An external framework of abstract concepts, beliefs, methodological principles, and what Peirce would have called regulative assumptions, on the other hand, is chosen on pragmatic grounds. This external framework is as close to metaphysics as the logical empiricist will allow. The question of truth does not arise for these statements, for the framework does not consist of verifiable assertions. We accept a framework on the grounds of whether it is "expedient, fruitful [or] conducive to the aim for which the language is intended" (1956 [1947]: 214). Carnap's Principle of Tolerance, which he held from very early on, states that "*It is not our business to set up prohibitions, but to arrive at conventions*" (1937: 51). The "proper way" of framing external questions is to ask: "'How shall we construct a particular language? Shall we admit symbols of this kind or not? And what are the consequences of either procedure?'" (1937: 164). These choices are a matter for "pragmatics," a term he adopts from Morris.[27]

Carnap's empiricism was influenced by Kant. We have already seen that the Kantian idea that we arrive at regulative assumptions and construct ways of theorizing about the world resonates throughout the history of pragmatism. Carnap is very much in step with this pragmatist theme, especially as it manifests itself in Peirce. Carnap's empiricist, pragmatist, twist on Kant is to have our frameworks tested "by their success or failure in practical use." What we take to be necessary or analytic truths are found in this external framework. Hence these truths and the truths of metaphysics are free of "religious, mythological . . . or other irrational sources."[28]

This pragmatic conception of necessary truth rankles with Russell. He responds that "many questions have turned out to be linguistic . . . but I think this is not so often true as many logical positivists suppose" (1997 [1945]: 154). Russell thinks that Carnap over-applies the principle of tolerance because he underestimates "the dependence of language upon the matters of which it speaks" (1997 [1945]: 155). He also notes that Carnap's tendency to this kind of relativism about the framework is in tension with the aim of coming to objective and grounded true beliefs. It unhooks truth from reality: "Various questions which I should regard as questions of fact are, for [Carnap], questions as to the choice of language" (1997 [1945]: 154). Russell, that is, complains about the logical empiricists in just the way he complains about the pragmatists.

---

[27] See Richardson (2007: 296).
[28] Carnap (1950: 40). Richardson (2007: 302f.) makes this point very well and very clearly.

One thing ought to be very clear by now. There is no clean break between pragmatism and logical empiricism. The story of pragmatism's fate does not turn on its being displaced by a radically different kind of view. The similarities between pragmatism and logical empiricism were there (and were recognized) from the beginning. By the late 1950s and 1960s the strong program of logical empiricism was unraveling and it was no longer obvious what logical empiricism's distinctive claims were, given the liberalizations it had piled up. It moved even closer to pragmatism.

But if the debate between pragmatism and logical empiricism was not about fundamental breaches in philosophical view, what was it about? Was it that logical empiricism, as Dewey asserted, was irrelevant to the issues that pressed in on mankind? The logical empiricists certainly did not think that they were putting forward a sterile and irrelevant philosophy. They had fled horrors in Europe and thought that their way of doing philosophy was progressive. We have seen that some of them argued, with Dewey, that ethics and politics must be brought into the scientific way of thinking. Others took their intensely held moral and political views as matters of choice, outside of (and hence protected from) science and logic. The pragmatists quite rightly reviled emotivism, but this was a minority view amongst the logical empiricists. As Joel Isaac puts it, "the claim that early analytic philosophy in America, under the purported sway of the logical positivists, repudiated normative issues in ethics and politics" is "dubious" (2011: 269).

Morton White had a front-row view of the debates. He tells us that much of the disagreement was a continuation of the political debates in which Dewey and others were immersed. The 1940s, White says, were marked by polemics in which "liberalism, Communism, pragmatism, and positivism often did battle with each other on political and personal levels" (1999: 87). Some of the personal skirmishes involved disputes over who was to be hired and tenured and some of them were more personal. All of this might be an unattractive reflection on the state of the academic personality, perhaps, but there is nothing in these wars to suggest that pragmatism and logical empiricism themselves are at odds.

There was another kind of battle occurring in academic philosophy in 1930s and 1940s America. Historians of philosophy were appalled by the ahistorical methods of the logical empiricists, who thought of themselves as forward-looking and committed to progress, not backward-looking with interests in their intellectual forbearers. That progress, they thought, was going to be guided and enabled by the new formal logic and they disdained those who were not expert in it. We have seen that Dewey returned that disdain, despite the fact that his own mantra was that the job of philosophy is to effect the progress of humankind by bringing the problems of men under the umbrella of science.

Because pragmatism was so intimately linked to Dewey, it was in danger of seeming to swim against the tide. That tide was to turn into a tsunami. The story that unfolds in next two chapters is particularly fascinating. For we shall see that the pragmatism of Peirce survives the storm in Lewis's capable hands, only to have Lewis himself later disappear under the seas.

10

Clarence Irving Lewis (1883–1964)

10.1 Pragmatist Pedigree

C. I. Lewis, even more substantially than Charles Morris, was a bridge between classical pragmatism and logical empiricism and he too puts paid to the idea that pragmatism withered away because it was never fully entrenched in the new professionalized philosophy departments.[1] An undergraduate and later a graduate student at Harvard, Lewis did not come by his pragmatism through the Chicago School. After teaching at Berkeley, he returned to Harvard in 1920 and became one of the most prominent philosophers of his time. He taught (and influenced) much of the next generation of first-rank philosophers: Quine, Goodman, Sellars, Firth, and Chisholm.

In his intellectual biography, Lewis illustrates just how his undergraduate education was shaped by classical pragmatism:

In my third and final year, I took the famous course in metaphysics which James and Royce divided between them and in which each gave some attention to shortcomings of the other's views. It was immense. . . . It also impressed me that James and Royce had more in common— particularly the voluntaristic strain—than either of them recognized; and I was later gratified by Royce's reference to what he called his "absolute pragmatism". I should be glad to think that the "conceptual pragmatism" of *Mind and the World-Order* had its roots in that same ground; indeed the general tenor of my own philosophic thinking may have taken shape under the influence of that course.

[1968a: 5]

Pragmatism might have seemed the order of the day while Lewis was an undergraduate, but when he returned to Harvard as a graduate student, idealism and pragmatism were under attack by Perry, Santayana, and other realists. He began a serious engagement with Kant, under Perry's tutelage, and found himself "in the middle" of what he took to be exciting and important debate about the place of the human mind in the world (1968a: 10; 1968b: 663). He could not accept idealist metaphysics, but he thought that the differences between idealism, pragmatism and the new realism were exaggerated (1968a: 10).

---

[1] See Campbell (2006) for the view that pragmatism did not thrive in the new professionalized philosophical world.

When he arrived at Harvard as a faculty member in 1920, he "practically lived with" the "manuscript remains" of Peirce for two years. This massive bulk of papers had been left to Harvard in a state of disarray by Peirce's widow and there was some hope that Lewis would start to put them into order (1968a: 16).[2] He was already on a Peircean path, guided there by Royce.[3] Lewis dipped in and out of the Peirce papers for those two years, coming to the opinion that the "originality and wealth" of this "legendary figure" was not fully evident in Peirce's meager published writings and not well represented by those who were influenced by him (James and Royce) (1970 [1930c]: 78). It is very clear that he studied these papers closely. His writing teems with Peirce's language and thoughts.[4]

Lewis was a contemporary of Dewey's and the two were conversant with each other's work. Dewey might seem to be the closest of the pragmatists to Lewis. Both want to bring ethics (and aesthetics)[5] under the scope of the cognitive while avoiding foundationalism. But they are less happy with each other's work than one might expect. In a review of *The Quest for Certainty*, Lewis acknowledges that he shares Dewey's rejection of the impossible goal of certainty: "Man may not reach his goal of the quest for security by any flight to another world—neither to that other world of the religious mystic, nor to that realm of transcendent ideas and eternal values which is its philosophical counterpart" (1970 [1930b]: 66). He agrees with Dewey that "reality can not be an alien and imposed somewhat, or a net of tight-bound circumstances in which we are caught, because the only reality there for us is one delimited in concepts of the results of our own ways of acting" (1970 [1930b]: 68).

What Lewis is unimpressed by is Dewey's "preoccupation" with the "forward looking function of knowledge" to the neglect of the "backward looking ground or premises" of knowledge (1970 [1930b]: 69). He is as keen as every pragmatist on the idea that we need to look to the "anticipation of future experience" if we are to understand the ideas of knowledge and truth (1956 (1929): 195). But he is also insistent that the very possibility of knowledge suggests that there is "some continuing stability which extends through past and future both" (1970 [1930b]: 71). "If knowledge is to be other than a random leap in the dark, a belief must have some ground or warrant" and that warrant cannot merely be its working out in the future as a good guide to action (1970 [1930b]: 71). It has to be something prior.

---

[2] As I write, Peirce scholars are still working at this project.

[3] As Eric Dayton pointed out to me, not only was Lewis supervised by Royce (and Perry), but he was Royce's assistant in his logic class, in which Peircean themes were worked through.

[4] To take but one example, compare Lewis's fallibilist point about the foolishness of wagering one's life, or the future welfare of all humanity, on something that you are sure about with Peirce's identical point and language. Lewis (1970 [1936]: 287]); Peirce (*CP* 1. 150; 1897).

[5] Lewis treats aesthetic value much as he treats moral value, with an insight separating the two. Aesthetic judgments do not "set one man against another"; possession of aesthetic value "is free of entanglement with questions of the moral relation to others" and from practical care and action. The enjoyment of them can thus be "serene" (1971 [1946]: 449–50).

Dewey's mistake is that he fails to acknowledge the critical role of "the given data of sense" and the stable world that we infer it to indicate (1970 [1930b]: 71). Lewis is after something more substantial than Dewey's idea that the "whole end of man" is to "make a difference in nature." He muses that perhaps Dewey "will allow us moral holidays, for the celebration of scientific insight as an end in itself'" (1970 [1930b]: 74). He worries that Dewey is too close to James. Here is his astute verdict on the two:

It was the besetting sin of James's pragmatism to confuse [human] validity with truth; and of Dewey's to avoid the issue by the near absence of any clear distinction of the two. James's "human truth", by suggesting that the best we can do in the way of knowledge is good enough, and that unchanging truth is a transcendental myth, subtly belittles the human cognitive enterprise and its unchanging goal. Even Dewey's more judicious phrase, "warranted assert-ability",—obviously descriptive of *valid* or *justified* belief, but often functioning as a substitute to "truth"—holds some danger of offering those short-range problems which are solved by achieving some more comfortable adjustment as paradigm for human knowledge, and suggesting that verification is a matter of muddling through.

[1968a: 11]

Lewis is after something more than human truth or muddling through. He is happier with Peirce's account of truth and rues coming so late to him (1970 [1930a]: 12; 1968a: 11). He is one with Peirce on the point that true beliefs are stable (indefeasibile, as Peirce put it): they are not merely "altered reactions to altered problems" (1968a: 11). Human knowledge is not just a matter of believing what one will, nor is it just a matter of solving some local problem for some short period of time. He is unwavering in his view that "When we determine truth, we determine that which it is correct to believe and that upon which it is desirable (not merely desired) to act" (1970 [1940]: 111). Lewis is interested in what is *really* desirable to believe.

Lewis too thought that Dewey misconceived logic (1970 [1930a]: 12) and Dewey sees that Lewis is his superior in this regard. But on the whole simply ignores Lewis.[6] In a letter to Arthur Bentley, Dewey says of his lack of engagement with Lewis's work: "My reason for leaving Lewis out was like yours; I thought he wasn't that important. I did have hopes for him after his early work; he seemed to be the one who was expert with logistic symbolism who knew its limitations. But I couldn't make his later stuff add up" (*CJD*, 3: 1945.08.08 [15494]). In a letter to James T. Farrell he acknowledges that his own lack of facility with the new logic may have kept him from appreciating a new book on the subject, and points to Lewis's opinion on the matter as authoritative: "Of course the fact I'm not up on symbolic logic, may cause it to be sour grapes with me. But C I Lewis at

---

[6] Dewey at times shows some appreciation of Lewis. In a 1943 letter to Bentley, he points to Lewis's notion of "fact" as being on the right track—and allows that Lewis "isn't by any means as bad generally as in the article on introspection I criticized" (*CJD*, 3: 1943.09.01 [15268]).

Harvard who is up on it, perhaps the best man in the country, doesn't think it covers the whole of philosophy" (*CJD*, 3: 1941.03.02 [09727]).

In 1929 Lewis read a paper at the American Philosophical Association's annual meeting titled "Pragmatism and Current Thought," in which he argued that Dewey and Peirce are empiricists nicely in step with logical empiricism (1970 [1930c]: 79). He sees Dewey as an operationalist who holds that a concept is good if it is effective as an instrument of action and control (1970 [1930c]: 85). And he notes that Peirce's pragmatic maxim has "a kind of empiricism" implicit in it, an empiricism of the following sort:

What can you point to in experience which would indicate whether this concept of yours is applicable or inapplicable in a given instance? What practically would be the test whether your conception is correct? If there are no such empirical items which would be decisive, then your concept is *not* a concept, but a verbalism.

[1970 [1930c]: 79]

Lewis devotes much of his career to working out for himself the details of this pragmatist empiricist project.

10.2 Lewis and the Logical Empiricists

Like Morris, Lewis was intimately connected to logical empiricism. He and the logical empiricists were engaged with each other both personally and professionally. Lewis was a first-rank logician, making major contributions to modal and intensional logic. The fact that his interests went beyond first-order predicate logic was, one suspects, no accident. They were backed by the pragmatist thought that logic needs to meet the needs of practice. In 1918 he published the first modern logic textbook in America, *A Survey of Symbolic Logic* and in 1932 he authored half of the famous Lewis and Langford text *Symbolic Logic*.

But it is not only a shared interest in logic that aligns Lewis with the logical empiricists. As Robert Sinclair (2012) suggests, Lewis perhaps had a better grip on Carnap than Quine did. Indeed, Carnap says in "Testability and Meaning": "It seems to me there is agreement on the main points between the present views of the *Vienna Circle* ... and those of *Pragmatism*, as interpreted e.g. by *Lewis*" (1936: 427). Schlick agrees. He replies to Lewis in the *Philosophical Review*, asserting that "It will be easy to show that there is no serious divergence between the point of view of the pragmatist as Professor Lewis conceives it and that of the Viennese Empiricist" (1936: 344). He finds Lewis's position to be in "perfect agreement" with his own (1936: 344). Ayer writes that his own 1936 *Language, Truth and Logic* was influenced by Lewis's 1929 *Mind and the World Order*. Ayer "adopted" Lewis's "pragmatic view that all empirical statements, including those ostensibly about the past, were hypotheses the content of which was taken to be equated with what would count as the present or future evidence bearing upon them which was available to their interpreter" (Ayer 1992: 18).

Lewis was also alert to the similarity between pragmatism and logical empiricism.[7] He suggested in "Pragmatism and Current Thought" that physics is based on the pragmatic test and that Bridgman's idea that a concept is synonymous with its operations is a pragmatist idea (1970 [1930c]: 83). In papers such as "Logical Positivism and Pragmatism" and "Experience and Meaning" he expands on verificationist-pragmatist parallels. Towards the end of his life, he tells that in the early writings of the logical empiricists "I found an empiricism and an analytic method which were congenial to my own persuasions. I still find them so" (1968b: 664).

It will thus be unsurprising that Lewis seemed to many philosophers to be a part of the great verificationist train driven by logical empiricism. But he is eager to point out that his *Mind and the World Order*, which already contains his empiricist thoughts, was published the year that the Vienna Circle was founded (1968b: 664). His empiricism is not the verificationism of the logical empiricists, but is, rather, a "pragmatic empiricism" born with Peirce (1968b: 664; 1929: xi). Indeed, rather than advocating logical empiricism, Lewis contributed to the onslaught of objections that caused the gradual refinement and then demise of the strong foundationalist project.

Lewis's most serious concern is the knife blade of the verifiability criterion, as sometimes wielded by the logical empiricists. The pragmatists do not ignore, by eliminating as meaningless, the difficult problems of philosophy (1970 [1940]: 99). The logical empiricist is mistaken in wanting to "logicize all problems," thereby getting rid of some of the most important problems in philosophy (1970 [1940]: 96). Meaning, Lewis argues, is a more complex thing than that envisioned by the verifiability criterion. One impact of living with Peirce's manuscript remains is that in Lewis's thought we find the view about different aspects of meaning that we have seen in Peirce. Meaning, for Lewis, involves each of Peirce's three categories: imagery, the force of experience, and interpretation. There is more to meaning than the early Carnap's logic and experience: "words and sentences without associated imagery are marks or noises without significance."

Lewis also criticizes logical empiricism on the grounds that it tries to terminate knowledge claims in what is actually present to a person here and now. Knowledge and meaning, on that view "collapse into the useless echo of data directly given to the mind at the moment" (1970 [1934]: 263). He argues that such solipsism of the present moment has to be avoided by any theory, if it is to be compatible with the idea of the validity of knowledge. It is a mistake to think that empirical knowledge is confined to what we observe—knowledge rests also in the ability to correctly anticipate further possible experience (1970 [1934]: 268).

Lewis struggles throughout his career with the question that has troubled every empiricist. Experience is supposed to ground knowledge or validity. But because we interpret what is given to us in experience, those interpretations are subject to error and

---

[7] See Murphey (2005: 219–20).

revision. What is given to us in experience cannot give us certainty. Lewis is identified in many people's minds as promoting the idea of "the given" and many have assumed that he must have been a foundationalist about it. But we shall see that his student Nelson Goodman is right: "Lewis is actually more vitally concerned with the directness and immediacy and irreducibility of this relation between sensory experiences and sentences describing it than with the certainty of these sentences" (1952: 164). He does not share the logical empiricists' aim of securely grounding knowledge in experience.

But the most critical difference, for Lewis, is the way logical empiricism treats value statements (1970 [1934]: 260). We will see below that he thinks that these expressions are not to be tossed into the dustbin of meaninglessness. He thinks that value judgments are assertions about value experiences.

10.3 Anti-foundationalism and the Given

Roderick Firth begins his contribution to the *Library of Living Philosophers* volume on Lewis as follows: "There is probably no philosophical doctrine more closely associated with the name of C. I. Lewis than the doctrine that our knowledge of the external world can be justified, in the last analysis, only by indubitable apprehensions of the immediate data of sense."[8] This association between Lewis and foundationalism is frequently made, but it is terribly unjust.

Lewis notes that all philosophers who think about knowledge and belief must try to deal with the distinction between, on the one hand, "immediate data, such as those of sense which are presented or given to the mind" and, on the other hand, a belief about or an interpretation of that data (1956 [1929]: 38). One approach is to argue that the very distinction is misguided. Lewis does not want to take that easy route out. Neither does he want to join the foundationalist in holding that the data of sense provide an indubitable grounding for belief and knowledge. What is given to us in experience does not *justify* beliefs. Something that is not a belief cannot stand in a justificatory relationship to a belief. "There is no knowledge merely by direct awareness" (1956 [1929]: 37). The foundationalists, he thinks, overemphasize what is given to us in experience (1956 [1929]: 43). The "New Realists", too, overemphasize what is given to the mind (1956 [1929]: 39). Lewis takes them to argue that observation involves a direct, causal, and mirroring relationship between what is given, and our beliefs about what is given (1956 [1929]: 42f.). He argues that the new realists or "representationalists" construe this bond too tightly and make error impossible. He notes that "we cannot both of us see reality as it is when we do not see it alike" (1956 [1929]: 166). The mind, for Lewis, cannot mirror reality. Rather, reality "is relative to the knower" (1956 [1929]: 167).

---

[8] Eric Dayton (1995) begins his excellent paper on Lewis with this quote.

He is equally unhappy with the idealist, who thinks that the distinction between the given and belief is a distinction that must be drawn entirely within thought. Lewis opines that the denial that there is something external which is given to us is enough to "put any theory beyond the pale of plausibility" (1956 [1929]: 48). Color, he argues, is relative to the sun's spectrum, or the color pyramid, or the sensory apparatus of the kind of animal perceiving it. This does not mean that color, when perceived, is not a property of a real object. It varies when we vary illumination, we can predict our altered visual experience under different conditions, and so on. The idealist's "fallacy" is to begin with the perfectly good thought that "the nature of the thing as known always depends on the mind" and then move to the illicit conclusion that "the object cannot exist or have character independently of the mind" (1956 [1929]: 188). On the contrary, "Relativity is not incompatible with, but *requires*, an independent character which is thus relative" (1956 [1929]: 172).

He calls his own attempt at making sense of the distinction between what is given to us and our beliefs about it "conceptual pragmatism." It is a kind of combination of Peirce and Kant.[9] We have something given to us in brute experience, which we then interpret:

> [W]e confront what is presented by the senses with certain ready-made distinctions, relations, and ways of classifying. In particular, we impose upon experience certain patterns of temporal relationships, a certain order ... It is by interpretation that the infant's buzzing, blooming confusion gives way to an orderly world of things.
>
> [1970 [1926]: 250]

The point about the infant is from James. There is no making sense of the stream of experience without interpretation (1956 [1929]: 195). As soon as one makes a statement or forms a belief about what one observes, the statement or belief contains much more than what is given to us by our senses. Interpretation is constrained by what is given to us in experience and it is "subject to the check of further experience." But this does not "save" or guarantee an interpretation's validity, for we bring a wealth of concepts to what is given in experience. Moreover: "what experience establishes, it may destroy; its evidence is never complete" (1956 [1929]: 195). Firth is wrong. Lewis makes no appeal to the notion of certainty—he makes no attempt to argue that what is given to us in experience is a foundation for belief. Indeed, he explicitly denies the foundationalist thought.

Lewis sees that "various metaphysical issues gather about" any talk of the given (1956 [1929]: 48). When one talks about what is immediately present, it is easy to give it "a dubious metaphysical status" (1956 [1929]: 61). He tries to be as straightforward as he can about the "tangle" of issues he finds here. He distinguishes between the given and the "sense data" which he thinks philosophers in his day want to misuse as explanatory concepts in epistemology. In Lewis's view, the given is "the

---

[9] One might say that Lewis's position is Kant's position, filtered through Peirce.

thin experience of immediate sensation" not the interpreted "thick experience of everyday life" (1956 [1929]: 30). Only the thick judgment of experience, not the thin given of immediacy, can be used to explain and justify beliefs (1956 [1929]: 53). Thick experience incorporates interpretation. The thin given is everything minus interpretation.

Lewis thinks that we "prescribe the nature of reality," while we "cannot prescribe the nature of the given" (1970 [1930a]: 16). This is precisely Peirce's distinction. Reality is what we come to believe of it, those beliefs shaped by the forceful, pressing experience that indicates an external world. That experience—that given—is what it is, whatever we think of it. Once we are presented with what is given to us in experience—James's blooming buzzing confusion—we interpret it or, if you like, we turn it into our view of reality. Lewis puts the distinction between the given and our beliefs about it as follows. "There is, in all experience, that element which we are aware that we do not create by thinking and cannot, in general, displace or alter. As a first approximation, we may designate it as 'the sensuous'" (1956 [1929]: 48). As soon as we try to describe this element or report on it, we bring to it our concepts, our categories, and our interests. We "select from it, emphasize aspects of it, and relate it in particular and unavoidable ways" (1956 [1929]: 52). Here is Peirce's vivid way of making the point about how thin the given of experience is: "think of it, and it has flown!"[10] He is adamant that there is not much more we can say about the given than that it is what impinges upon us.[11] In Lewis's words, the given is "ineffable, always" (1956 [1929]: 53). Both argue that we can get at the given only through the method of "abstraction"—we can get a grip on it only by the method which tries to isolate elements of what comes before the mind. The given is an "excised element," says Lewis, for "a state of intuition utterly unqualified by thought is a figment of the metaphysical imagination" (1956 [1929]: 66). The given "never exists in isolation in any experience or any state of consciousness" (1956 [1929]: 55).

With Peirce (and with Kant), Lewis takes the given to be that which is not under our control—that which is independent of the mind's constructive activities. We make an assumption that what is given to us in experience is provided by the world. In doing so, we can make sense of the ideas of reality, validity, knowledge, and truth. But what the mind meets is not reality—that only comes with "further ado" (Dayton 1995: 266). "The world of experience," Lewis argues, "is not given in experience": "This reality which everybody knows reflects the structure of human intelligence as much as it does the nature of the independently given" (1956 [1929]: 29).

---

[10] Peirce uses this phrase with respect to the first category of "pure quality." But it applies to the second category as well. It applies to everything pre-interpretation.

[11] Lewis, unlike Peirce, is not always steady on this matter. He usually is clear that anything we try to say about the given involves us in interpretation. But sometimes, to his disadvantage, he tries to say more about simple awareness. He adds to Peirce's minimalist account the idea that the given has a certain feeling to it. Hookway, though, argues persuasively that Lewis's two thoughts about the given can be pulled apart (2008: 280). The given is that which impinges upon us or resists our attempts to change it and thus constrains our opinions (this is the set of thoughts he shares with Peirce). There is no need to add that the given is something that has a certain structure or quality.

Hookway (2008: 277) identifies the central worry for this view: how can we make sense of a non-conceptual thin given so that some interpretations of it are legitimate and others not? Lewis's answer starts with the idea that the given puts us in touch with the objects of knowledge, but the given does not provide foundations or justification for our beliefs (2008: 281). All of our beliefs are interpretations of the given. They are hence all fallible. But the given provides a brute reality check for us, as in Peirce's idealist who is "lounging down Regent St.... when some drunken fellow unexpectedly lets fly his fist and knocks him in the eye" (CP 5. 539, 1902).

In 1951 there was a seminar at the American Philosophical Association meetings on "The Experiential Element in Knowledge," in which Hans Reichenbach and Nelson Goodman attacked what they took to be Lewis's concept of the given. Goodman argues that it makes no sense to ask whether what is given to us in experience is true or false: "truth and falsity and certainty pertain to statements or judgments and not to mere particles or materials or elements" (1952: 162). We have already seen that well before 1951, Lewis had put forward just this thought and we have seen that Goodman recognized that Lewis was more concerned with immediacy than with showing that what is immediate is true. What Lewis argues is that there must be something constraining the truth and falsity of our statements and beliefs. He says, in reply to Goodman:

either there must be some ground in experience ... which plays an indispensible part in the validation of empirical beliefs, or what determines empirical truth is merely some logical relationship of a candidate belief with other beliefs which have been accepted. And in the latter case any reason ... why these *antecedent* beliefs have been accepted remains obscure.

[1970 [1952]: 324]

We need the given as a touchstone, even if it is so thin that we can say nothing about it. Otherwise, we must abandon standards and norms to the vagaries of history and personal wants or needs. The coherence theory of truth, even in its most sophisticated probabilistic form, such as that put forward by Reichenbach, is a matter of supposing that "if enough probabilities can be got to lean against one another they can all be made to stand up." But, alas, "on the contrary, unless some of them can stand alone, they will all fall flat" (1970 [1952]: 328).

Lewis himself said that he regretted much of what he had written about the given. He saw the matter as "the most difficult—the most nearly impossible—enterprise to which epistemology is committed" (1968a: 18). He could see that in talking about the given, one runs the risk of being taken for a foundationalist, despite one's disclaimers. Because he was engaged with the logical empiricists in these debates, his language was theirs—it was one of sense data and terminating judgments. His interpreters, perhaps, can be forgiven for not always seeing what he trying to get at.

10.4 Value

Lewis's treatment of value as part of what is given to us in experience should have made those who wanted to paint him as a foundationalist think twice. With every pragmatist before him, Lewis wants to expand the boundaries of what is given to us beyond what our senses deliver: "the pleasantness or fearfulness of a thing may be as un-get-overable as its brightness or loudness" (1956 [1929]: 57).[12] Value judgments are under our cognitive scope. They "are a form of empirical cognition, directed upon facts as obdurate and compelling as those which must determine the correctness of any other kind of knowledge" (1971 [1946]: 407).

Lewis argues that we experience value in more or less the same way we experience a thing's being green or hard. Something impinges upon us or is given to us. When we make a judgment or form a belief about what impinges upon us, the given in its initial form flies away (1956 [1923]: 403). The mystic and the intuitionist might be "out-raged" at this view, as it stands against anyone who would see us "sinking ourselves in the presentation itself and putting thought to sleep" (1956 [1923]: 406). But if we are to have any knowledge at all of value then, just as with any kind of experience, we must bring to immediate presentations of value our network of thought structures.

Lewis recoils from the emotivist branch of empiricist ethics. Indeed, he locates the subject of ethics as the site of the divide between pragmatism and logical empiricism. He thinks that "one of the strangest aberrations ever to visit the mind of man" is the idea that value-predictions are not about matters of fact but are merely expressions of emotion and hence are not true or false.[13] Non-cognitivism about ethics, he thinks, implies that "one belief would be as good as another." It results in "both moral and practical cynicism" and makes action "pointless" (1971 [1946]: 366). If it were not better to be right than wrong in what one believes, why bother about your belief or your grounds for it? As Peirce puts this point, aiming at the truth is a regulative assumption of genuine belief and inquiry. As Lewis puts it, the idea that judgments are not candidates for truth and falsity, validity or invalidity—"is an absurdity in view of the plainest facts of life." If our observations of value did not have any connection whatsoever to "the objective value-properties of things, then it would be totally impossible for us to learn from experience how to improve our lot in life."

Lewis wants to occupy the ground that Dewey is interested in—a "naturalistic" conception of values (1971 [1946]: 398). Human beings are the judges of what is right and wrong. But that does not mean that "the evaluations which the fool makes in his folly are on a par with those of the sage in his wisdom." Human beings "stand in need of all that can be learned from the experience of life in this natural world" (1971 [1946]: 398–99). Lewis, that is, thinks that "empiricism in epistemology and naturalism in ethics do not imply . . . relativism and cynicism" (1971 [1946]: viii). This is a promising theory of ethics and it warrants a book-length treatment itself. I will merely give its outline, as it appears in Lewis's 1946 *An Analysis of Knowledge and Valuation*, a now nearly and unjustly forgotten book in which Lewis builds his account of ethics on a pragmatist account of meaning and knowledge.

---

[12] Lewis also suggests that we broaden ethics so as to take into account the values of animals.
[13] See 1971 [1946]: 365–66, 399; 1970 [1934]: 259.

Underlying Lewis's account of ethics is the pragmatist idea that knowledge, action, and evaluation "are essentially connected." Meaning is connected to action in that we need to be able to apply or verify a meaningful expression in action—either physical or imaginative (1971 [1946]: 134–35). As we have seen, Lewis argues that our verifications are not "categorically determinable"—we do not aim at the false grail of certainty when we verify a hypothesis. What we need to do in order to show that we grasp meaning is to say what *would be* further evidence for or against the hypothesis in question (1971 [1946]: 136–37).

There are two especially interesting twists on this pragmatist account of meaning, both of which Lewis shares with Peirce. First, the idea that value judgments might be verifiable in the imagination suggests that thought experiments are on a par with other kinds of experiments. Second, "even what is analytically true and knowable a priori is to be assured by reference to sense meanings."[14] Although Lewis prefers to talk about the a priori–a posteriori and not use the language of the analytic–synthetic distinction, he is speaking about the issue that both distinctions share. We shall see that he takes analytic statements to be such that they too can fall to experience, as well as to changes in the way we classify and think about things. We shall see, that is, that he does not accept the distinction between that which is immune from overthrow by experience and that which is subject to such overthrow.

Knowledge is also tied to action. Truths and falsities are "independent of our supposition or our wish," but they have "imperative significance for belief and for sensibly taken action" (1971 [1946]: 399). Action, for its part, "is rooted in evaluation." Deliberate action would be pointless if we did not have something that we have evaluated as being good or worthwhile at which we were aiming.

Lewis distinguishes three kinds of value predication. First we have expressive statements of the sort "This is good," said at the table, where the speaker intends merely to express her immediate impression about the food, not to make a statement that is verifiable by others. This is "apparent value" or "felt goodness" or a sense that something is "prized" (1971 [1946]: 374, 398). This kind of value judgment is the data for the other two kinds of value statements. "Without the experience of felt value and disvalue, evaluations in general would have no meaning" (1971 [1946]: 375). Here we see the makings of a distinction in Lewis's thought between what seems to me to be good and what is good. Expressive statements about what seems to me to be good are not subject to error. They are only true or false in the sense that we can tell lies about what we experience. They do not fall into the category of knowledge. There is a distinction to be made between what is prized, on the one hand, and what is judged or "appraised" on the other. Only the latter fall under the scope of knowledge.

---

[14] That is not to say that there are no distinctions whatsoever to be found between different kinds of statements. Analytic statements may "assert some relations of meanings amongst themselves" and non-analytic statements may require a relation to some particular experience (1971 [1946]: 171).

The second kind of value predication consists of evaluations that are verifiable by the course of experience. Although we can never verify these (or any other kind of empirical judgment) with certainty, some of them are "terminating judgments" (1971 [1946]: 375). We predict a course of experience and that prediction is "decisively" verified or falsified. We set a test and the test is passed or not passed. These statements are predictions that a course of action will be good or bad, or will cause enjoyment or pain. We have here "a form of empirical knowledge, not fundamentally different in what determines their truth or falsity, and what determines their validity and justification, from other kinds of empirical knowledge." These evaluations are either true or false and they are verified or falsified in the same way as other predictions—they "will be disclosed in experience." They speak to what we should do and they give rise to "rational conduct." If we judge falsely, that can have "devastating consequences" (1971 [1946]: xi). Sometimes these terminating judgments are easily and decisively verified—if my aim is to get pleasure and I predict that doing A will bring me pleasure, the truth or falsity of my prediction might be a relatively straightforward matter. But if my purpose "is to make the world safe for democracy," that will not be easily verifiable (1971 [1946]: 368–69). No limited set of experiences is going to be sufficient to exhaust the empirical significance of such a statement.

The third kind of evaluative judgment is also a form of knowledge—it too falls under our cognitive scope. We often evaluate things, actions, and states of affairs as good or bad—we attribute a value to them, just as we attribute the property of red to an object. These evaluations are diverse and complex, but they are also subject to verification—this time in "non-terminating" experiences. They cannot even sometimes be decisively verified: further experience might always turn out to be relevant (1971 [1946]: 365, 375f.). They are never more than probable. But we might have so much to go on that they are "practically certain," a term right out of Peirce (1971 [1946]: 376). Complex statements in normative ethics, such as "Torture is odious" or "It is right to help others" are not unverifiable expressions of desires or emotions (1970 [1941a]:111; 1970 [1941b]: 166). These judgments are such that further experience may always come into play. But that is just to say that they continue to be responsive to experience and continue to subject themselves to the possibility of being disconfirmed.

The issues surrounding these thoughts are complex and it will repay the reader to go through Lewis's accounts of them carefully. I will confine myself to expanding on the question of how Lewis thinks of validity—on the question of how he manages to make sense of right and wrong answers in ethics. He takes on the issue just as we have been describing it for Dewey, and addresses it at precisely the point where Morton White would later (and unfairly) judge that Dewey's account goes wrong: with respect to "Mill's assertion that the only proof that a thing is desirable is its being desired." This is an "unguarded" assertion, Lewis thinks. What is valuable is not equivalent to what is immediately perceived as valuable by this or that person. Lewis notes that he might get enormous satisfaction from a cartoon on his desk, but he can nonetheless see that it is a trivial, not very valuable, matter (1971 [1946]: 381).

The absence of a tight connection between what someone values and what is truly valuable goes in the other direction as well: the goodness of a good object is not dependent upon that goodness being experienced by someone (1971 [1946]: 388). Nonetheless, it is a "peculiarity" of value judgments that "expressive meaning" (what is felt to be valuable) drives "objective meaning" (what is in fact valuable). Like Peirce, Lewis moves to subjunctive conditionals to articulate his position. Something may be beautiful even if no human were ever to behold it. What is important is how "it *would be* beheld if it ever *should be* beheld under conditions favorable to realization in full of the potentialities for such delight which are resident in the thing" (1971 [1946]: 389).

Lewis thinks that an important test for goodness is that some people find or experience the thing or trait as good, but that other tests can come into play as well. "Objective goodness *is* to be defined by relation to goodness disclosed in experience," but that does not mean that "immediate satisfaction" is all that is relevant. Something might be good because it produces other good things down the line, for instance (1971 [1946]: 389). Moreover, one can discover that something is of value without actually experiencing it for oneself:

> one may easily find evidence that a thing is valuable otherwise than through experiences of positive value. Just as one may find evidence that a thing is round or is hard in other ways than by seeing it round or feeling it hard, so too the objective value of a thing may be confirmed 'indirectly' in other ways than by what would be called "experiencing the value of it".
>
> [1971 [1946]: 376]

He gives the example of coming to believe that his neighbor is a good musician through his rendition of difficult passages, even though the music leaves him cold. One might add to Lewis's own examples that one can learn something about the moral rightness or wrongness of a practice by reading first-person reports of those who have been subject to the practice, by listening to the argument on either side, and so on.[15] For Lewis, value ascriptions are subjective in the sense that they boil down to how human beings would experience a thing or an act. But they are not subjective in the sense that if I value *A*, then *A* is valuable or in the sense that only if I value *A* is *A* valuable.

Any naturalist account of value must find a way of coping with the difficulties that were thrust upon Dewey. What about those whose idea of what is valuable is inconsistent with the ideas of others? What of those whose aim is to ensure substantive homogeneity so as to put in place a uniform set of values? Lewis's attempt at answering such questions is to make the Peircean move that we have to hope, if there is to be any chance of improvement in the quality of our lives, that there is an answer to our questions and that there is enough commonality in the experience of value so that inquiry will converge upon that answer. This is a critically important theme in Lewis's

---

[15] See Misak (2008b) for the argument that we can learn about what is right and wrong from the narrative reports of others, as well as from thought experimentation.

work. It is the Kantian strain in the brand of pragmatism he shares with Peirce. We need to assume that we would find enough agreement or "community" in our judgments of value, else there is no point in making them:

if there were a complete absence of community in our value-findings on given occasions, or if communities of value-apprehension in the presence of the same object should be mere matters of chance, then no one could, with the best will in the world, learn how to do anybody else any good—or for that matter, how to do him harm.

[1971 [1946]: 423–24]

Some very important practices—practices that we cannot imagine giving up—make sense only on the assumption that our value judgments are in principle able to reflect what is really valuable or not, as the case may be. Sometimes Lewis makes the point in Peirce's very terms. We must go on the hope that there is a truth of the matter: "If there is any hope that we can, by our reasonably directed efforts, effect any improvement in the quality of living, for ourselves or for anybody else, then there must be a solid core of what is both veridical and common, underlying the personal and the inter-personal variabilities of our value-findings in the presence of external things" (1971 [1946]: 424).

Naturalist conceptions of value must also cope with the fact that experience of value is less constant, less regular, than experience of physical properties, such as hardness and redness. Lewis sees that, in comparison with some other kinds of empirical statements, value judgments are likely to encounter "more variation from person to person" and more variation for an individual from one time to another. Our very likes and dislikes also seem particularly sensitive to our own attitudes—to "how one goes out to meet" objects and situations (1971 [1946]: 418). He is of the view that this distinguishes value judgments from sensory judgments by degree, not by kind. All data are influenced by "internal" and interpretative factors. In other kinds of empirical matters, we simply don't look as often to these factors as explanations for why our judgments diverge. We tend to look rather to differences in the external set-up to explain differences of opinion (1971 [1946]: 422–23). Most significantly, we tend to emphasize divergence of belief in ethics because it is important for us to do so. It is critical to note the disagreements of others when we diverge about whether, for instance, assisted dying is permissible, whereas it is less important with garden-variety judgments of greenness or hardness. Disagreements tend to matter more when it comes to value (1971 [1946]: 419).

Lewis thus builds validity into his account of value by showing us how the notions of disagreement, error, and getting things right play a vital role in our ethical deliberation. He identifies ways we can be mistaken about our value judgments and speaks to how we can learn from experience so that we improve our value judgments. For instance, I can be mistaken about my felt judgments—I might mistakenly think that my experiencing A as valuable on one occasion means that I will experience it as valuable on every occasion. Or I might be wrong in inferring that because I take A to be good, others will also take it to be good. That is, my experiencing A as valuable need not be connected to *A*'s really being valuable. There could be another explanation of my taking *A* to be valuable:

the *reason why* this presentational content has this immediate value-quality may be a reason to be found in our personal make-up or personal history or personal attitude on this occasion, or it may be a reason in which nothing which is merely personal or peculiar to us has preponderant influence, but is to be found in the nature of the objective situation confronting us and in those capacities of apprehension which are common to humans in general.

[1971 [1946]: 416]

The reader will be reminded of Peirce's central idea: if a belief is caused by circumstances extraneous to the facts, we ought to be suspicious of it.[16] Much of inquiry, especially into ethical matters, will be an attempt to discern whether my belief is caused by things particular to me or whether my belief is connected to what is valuable in some more robust sense.

In his 1950 "The Empirical Basis of Value Judgments," Lewis continues to work his way through the problem of validity. He tells us that if someone is convinced that he really ought to destroy humanity with atom bombs because humanity has sinned in the eyes of God, he is acting according to a moral standard if he tries to live up to his conviction. It is "his judgment of values" that we must deplore (1970 [1950]: 175). And what makes us justified in deploring someone's judgment of values is a matter of how his acts will affect the lives of others. That is an empirical question, which, in the example Lewis gives above, will be answered in a straightforward manner. Good intentions must be accompanied by good judgment about what is in fact valuable and what is not (1970 [1950]: 177).

One might think from the above example that Lewis's answer to the question about what good living amounts to goes in the direction of utilitarianism. But it would be more accurate to say that it centers around Kantian notions of the moral autonomy of the person.[17] In his view, the good comes down to equality with respect to liberties allowed and restraints imposed. The final sentences in *An Analysis of Knowledge and Valuation* tell us that, while valuation is always a matter of empirical knowledge, what is right and just can never be determined by empirical facts alone (1971 [1946]: 554). Perhaps this is in tension with James and Dewey, who seem not to want to go beyond empirical facts. Perhaps some will think that Lewis's argument for going beyond the facts is in tension with the pragmatist/naturalist impulse itself.

One thing is clear, though. In trying to say what the nature of value is—what "good" and "bad" amount to—Lewis does not mean to appeal to principles that are written in stone or given to us from on high. While we need to have an a priori framework that tells us that "Pleasure is good" or "A thing is good if it is the subject of an interest," this idea is

---

[16] Jonathan Adler, in his own account of belief, makes a similar but stronger point. Not only ought we be suspicious of such a belief, but if we consider that belief in full awareness of the circumstances that gave rise to it, we simply will in fact doubt it: "The compulsion [to doubt] is due to our recognition, when attending to any particular belief, that we are entitled to the belief only if it is well founded" (2002: 27).

[17] See 1971 [1946]: 488ff. for his argument against utilitarianism.

not as anti-pragmatist or as anti-naturalist as it looks on the surface. We shall see below that Lewis thinks that beliefs in our a priori framework can be false—they are subject to revision and can be overturned. Our beliefs about the very nature of the good have no glow of certainty about them. They may simply be disguised empirical generalizations about the customary usage of the word "good"; they may be "hortations to accept one such convention, to the exclusion of other usages"; or they may be explications of the meaning of the word in order to try to make the term more lucid and thus try to "delimit the essential nature" of the good (1971 [1946]: 378–79). Our a priori framework will include some principles of rationality or thought. For instance, a principle of consistency needs to be assumed, else "life in general would be free of any concern; and there would be no distinction of what is rational from what is perverse or silly." But with Peirce, Lewis brings any thought of Kantian necessity down to human earth:

> To act, to live, in human terms, is necessarily to be subject to imperatives; to recognize norms. . . . To repudiate normative significances and imperatives in general, would be to dissolve away all seriousness of action and intent, leaving only an undirected floating down the stream of time; and as a consequence to dissolve all significance of thought and discourse into universal blah. Those who would be serious and circumspect and cogent in what they think, and yet tell us that there are no valid norms or binding imperatives, are hopelessly confused, and inconsistent with their own attitude of assertion.
>
> [1971 [1946]: 481]

The very practices of assertion, of acting with intent, and, I would add, believing, require that we hold ourselves up to standards and norms.[18] Lewis thinks that we can add to this imperative the following: "Be consistent, in valuation and in thought and action; Be concerned about yourself in future and on the whole."[19] We need to abide by these requirements if we are to make sense of the life we live. The abandonment of these standards is barely conceivable, and even if we could do it, we would be crippled in making sense of a human life. We can only repudiate these norms if we are willing to repudiate all norms and the distinction between validity and invalidity itself.[20] And we can't do that while remaining the kinds of beings we are and think important to be (1971 [1946]: 483–84). This is the Kantian pragmatist position of Lewis and Peirce.

---

[18] I have made this argument in numerous places, taking Peirce to be the precursor of it. See e.g. Misak (2000). But Lewis is much more explicit than Peirce and he also makes the argument in the context of moral value, which is the context I invoke. If I could begin afresh, Lewis would figure prominently.

[19] He is also enthusiastic about Kant's "No rule of action is right except one which is right in all instances, and therefore right for everyone." This is implicit in the distinction between right and wrong, he thinks. It is a part of the moral sense to be presumed in humans (1971 [1946]: 482). I have relegated this point to a footnote because it seems, in Lewis's hands, to be the least well-argued for.

[20] He adds the "ultimate aim": to lead a self-conscious and active good life (1971 [1946]: 500ff.).

10.5 A Pragmatic Conception of the A Priori

In 1923 Lewis made his views about the status of our framework very clear in "A Pragmatic Conception of the A Priori." He argues against traditional conceptions of the a priori in which "the mind approaches the flux of indeterminacy with some godlike foreknowledge of principles which are legislative for experience" (1970 [1923]: 231). With all other pragmatists, his view is that we have no "natural light," no "self-illuminating propositions," no "innate ideas," no first principles of logic from which other certainties can be deduced.

Lewis's alternative account builds on the Peircean idea that what is compelling is what we find in the brute resistance of experience. An a priori truth is necessary, but not in the sense that we are compelled to accept it and only it:

> What is *a priori* is necessary truth not because it compels the mind's acceptance, but precisely because it does not. It is given experience, brute fact, the *a posteriori* element in knowledge which the mind must accept willy-nilly. The *a priori* represents an attitude in some sense freely taken, a stipulation of the mind itself, and a stipulation which might be made in some other way if it suited our bent or need. Such truth is necessary as opposed to contingent, not as opposed to voluntary ... That is *a priori* which is true, *no matter what*. What it anticipates is not the given, but our attitude toward it: it concerns the uncompelled initiative of mind or, as Josiah Royce would say, our categorical ways of acting.
>
> [1970 [1923]: 231]

For Lewis, it is experience—not logic, not conceptual truth—that is brute and compelling: "no conscious being ... can fail to be aware of that element in his experience which he finds, willy-nilly, as it is and not otherwise; or to recognize that, without this, we could have no apprehension of an external world at all" (1968b: 665). The a priori, on the other hand, is the "uncompelled initiative of human thought" (1970 [1923]: 238). It is needed in order to understand or "interrogate" what is given to us (1970 [1923]: 237). Lewis offers us this nice metaphor: "we cannot capture the truth of experience if we have no net to catch it in" (1956 [1929]: 271). The a priori is that net of categories and definitive concepts.

Lewis thinks that there is more than one net that we might employ. He argues, for instance, that we have discovered that there are several logics, each self-consistent on its own terms. The choice of which to adopt is a "pragmatic" one. Here Lewis uses the term "pragmatic" to signal a matter of choice, the criteria for which will be drawn from our "human bent and intellectual convenience" (1970 [1923]: 233). We have seen this usage employed also by Morris and most famously by Carnap, over a decade after Lewis's own presentation of the idea. To illustrate, Lewis says that the law of excluded middle merely:

> formulates our decision that whatever is not designated by a certain term shall be designated by its negative. It declares our purpose to make, for every term, a complete dichotomy of experience, instead—as we might choose—of classifying on the basis of a tripartite division

into opposites (as black and white) and the middle ground between the two. Our rejection of such tripartite division represents only our penchant for simplicity.

[1970 [1923]: 232]

The laws of logic are "principles of procedure, the parliamentary rules of intelligent thought and speech" (1923 [1970]: 232). Definitions, analytic truths such as "all brothers are male," categories that underlie science such as that of absolute space and time, and the laws of inference are "addressed to ourselves" and "represent no operations of the objective world, but only our categories of mind." Our conceptual frameworks, that is, "are peculiarly social products, reached in the light of experiences which have much in common, and beaten out, like other pathways, by the coincidence of human purposes and the exigencies of human cooperation" (1970 [1923]: 239). Our conceptual framework both has the feel of a "fiat" and of "deliberate choice" (1956 [1929]: 213).

It should be clear that Lewis is a fallibilist about beliefs in our conceptual framework. One way so-called "analytically true" beliefs can be false is that we "are capable of failing to observe what is involved in our own intentions and of mistaking our own meanings through inconsistency." With Peirce, he notes that we can also make mistakes when we construct proofs in logic and draw inferences (1971 [1946]: 25, 31). But more importantly, our a priori categories and definitions "are subject to alteration on pragmatic grounds when the expanding boundaries of experience reveal their infelicity as intellectual instruments."[21] Our "categorical modes of interpretation may be subject to gradual transition and even to fairly abrupt alteration" (1956 [1929]: 228). These changes might be brought on by facts of social history, but also by the developing mind.

This fallibilism about the a priori is Lewis's pragmatic twist on Kant. As Nelson Goodman puts it, Lewis's treatment of the analytic makes it something that we can *work on*: "wistful speculation concerning forever inaccessible realms of being or consciousness gives way to investigations in logic, to the analysis of concepts, to the examination of the nature, varieties, and functions of symbolic systems" (1964: 1972: 419). We investigate, revise, and perhaps even re-invent our framework.

Lewis makes it clear that he does not intend his position to entail that "the a priori is . . . arbitrary in the sense of being capriciously determined" (1956 [1929]: 237). The fact that our framework is not predetermined does not mean that it answers to no criteria. Mathematics, he suggests, answers to the criterion of self-consistency. And since knowledge has "a practical business to perform," our concepts and interpretations answer to "our need to understand, in the face of an experience always more or less baffling, and . . . our need to control" (1956 [1929]: 237). It is also the case that the human mind is a "social product," forged by the fact that "the needs of individual humans are mostly served by cooperation with others." Our categories must answer to those requirements as well (1956 [1929]: 229).

Lewis, that is, thinks that some pragmatic considerations "occupy a place . . . much higher, for the long-run satisfaction of our needs in general," than others. "In the popular mind especially, pragmatism too often seems to connote the validity of rather superficial and capricious attitudes—for instance, the justification of belief from no deeper ground than personal desire." This kind of (Jamesian) pragmatism must be eschewed, in favor of a pragmatism that understands that the human ends and purposes that are relevant are not desires, but rather values such as "intellectual consistency and economy, completeness of comprehension, and simplicity of interpretation." It is "high-plane purposes," not "low-plane motives" that the pragmatist must take as the human ends that drive our choice of beliefs as well as truth and validity (1956 [1929]: 267).

As we have seen, Lewis joins Peirce in maintaining that the distinction between concept and immediacy is important. These two great pragmatists do not hold that this distinction, or that between analytic and synthetic, must be dissolved, as if dissolution itself would solve all the problems with which the distinctions are trying to cope. On the contrary, Lewis says that the trouble with some of his classical pragmatist predecessors is that they have neglected to make these distinctions at all. The result is that they introduce a tension in their view: they "seem to put all truth at once at the mercy of experience and within the power of human decision" (1956 [1929]: 266).

In the same vein, Lewis rejects the idea, again sometimes found in James, that "new truth" replaces "old truth." When a new belief replaces an overturned belief, that should suggest to us that the old belief was false, not an old truth. Lewis is crystal clear that what we accept as truth is not identical with the truth. That would be a pragmatist view that ought to make anyone "uncomfortable" (1970 [1936]: 285). The beliefs we adopt on the evidence to date, or on grounds of simplicity, or convenience, or coherence are temporary working hypotheses, "at the mercy" of future experience (1970 [1936]: 285–86). An assertion always "outruns" our current evidence and best thinking. It reaches into the future and makes a prediction that the evidence and best thinking will continue to support the assertion (1970 [1936]: 288). This, of course, is the Peircean conception of truth.

Lewis ends "A Pragmatic Conception of the A Priori" with this brilliant statement, in effect siding with Peirce over James:

Pragmatism has sometimes been charged with oscillating between two contrary notions: the one, that experience is "through and through malleable to our purpose"; the other, that facts are "hard" and uncreated by the mind. We here offer a mediating conception: through all our knowledge runs the element of the *a priori*, which is indeed malleable to our purpose and responsive to our need. But throughout, there is also that other element of experience which is "hard", "independent" and unalterable to our will.

[1970 [1923]: 239]

Lewis's conception of the a priori is deep and subtle. It explodes the old distinctions between a priori–a posteriori and analytic–synthetic. A priori and analytic statements, like a posteriori and synthetic statements, are fallible and answerable to experience. Nonetheless, in 1947, when Quine, Nelson Goodman, and Morton White were writing to each other, gearing up for a sustained attack on the analytic–synthetic distinction, they identified both Lewis and the logical empiricists as their principal enemies. An early volley was an article written by White in 1949: "The Analytic and Synthetic: An Untenable Dualism." One of the holders of the untenable dualism is identified as Lewis.[22]

As we turn to Quine's view, the reader would benefit by keeping in mind the following quite stunning passage from Lewis:

the whole body of our conceptual interpretations form a sort of hierarchy or pyramid with the most comprehensive, such as those of logic, at the top, and the least general such as ["all swans are birds"] etc, at the bottom; that with this complex system of interrelated concepts, we approach particular experiences and attempt to fit them, somewhere and somehow, into its preformed patterns. Persistent failure leads to readjustment . . . The higher up a concept stands in our pyramid, the more reluctant we are to disturb it, because the more radical and far-reaching the results will be . . . The decision that there are no such creatures as have been defined as "swans" would be unimportant. The conclusion that there are no such things as Euclidean triangles, would be immensely disturbing. And if we should be forced to realize that nothing in experience possesses any stability—that our principle, "Nothing can both be and not be," was merely a verbalism, applying to nothing more than momentarily—that denouement would rock our word to its foundations.

[1956 [1929]: 305–6]

This is from *Mind and the World Order*, written in 1929, long before Lewis's philosophical progeny started to use these very sentiments against a rather stern teacher for whom they had few warm feelings.

A second passage is also worth remembering. Lewis says that pragmatism has the following at its heart:

because of the complexity of the total body of accepted principles, and the consequence that we can test no one of them in isolation, there is, therefore, some room for choice in what we shall keep and what we shall throw out when confronted with a new fact which does not fit our system as a whole—that therefore there is a pragmatic factor in the determination of what, at any given moment, we accept as truth.

[1970 [1936]: 285]

We shall see in the next chapter these very sentiments expressed, almost word for word, by Quine.

---

[22] See White (1999: 338ff.). Goodman fired the first shot with his 1949 paper "On Likeness of Meaning."

Lewis sees that he and Quine "are very much less far apart than many others who are interested in these questions."[23] But Quine is not inclined to admit this. We find ourselves at a deeply interesting turning point in the history of pragmatism. In the late 1950s, towards the end of Lewis's era, pragmatism was still going strong. Lewis was offering an alternative to Dewey's pragmatism, and trying to steer the position in a more Peircean direction. He was a major player in current philosophical debates. He was the teacher of the next generation of philosophical superstars, and yet those students wanted to put some distance between themselves and Lewis. It would be interesting for someone to undertake a study in the sociology of knowledge during this time, as I suspect many of the explanations are to be found there. I will merely start to describe this generational battle, which dovetailed with a withdrawal of interest in Dewey. Richard Bernstein puts the matter thus: "When I wrote my dissertation on John Dewey in the 1950's, interest in Dewey and pragmatism seemed to be at an all-time low among academic philosophers. The pragmatists were thought to be passé and to have been displaced by the new linguistic turn in analytic philosophy . . . " (2010: ix). But the pragmatist views that were falling from grace were those of James and Dewey. Peirce was still going strong in Lewis's capable hands and his view would continue to dominate philosophy in America. For that view is also Quine's view. It is just that Quine did not fully understand or did not want to acknowledge his own pedigree.

---

[23] Quoted in Murphey (2005: 327) from Lewis's 1952 class lecture notes. One point of difference lies in the fact that Lewis is a champion of intensional logics and concepts, whereas Quine is passionate about a "sparse" landscape in which only extensional concepts were allowed. This difference might have been what made Quine minimize the similarity between his view and Lewis's.

11

Willard van Orman Quine (1908–2000)

11.1 Introduction

W. V. Quine is a turning point in the fortunes of pragmatism. He is one of the most eminent philosophers America has ever produced. He was a relentlessly analytic thinker, making great contributions in logic and philosophy of language, with a sparse writing style and an even sparser metaphysics. He is also famous for putting forward a naturalized epistemology very much in the pragmatist spirit. But he was wary of the pragmatist label (1981d: 32).

Quine arrived at Harvard in 1930 as a graduate student in philosophy, with a BA in mathematics. Two of his courses during his short, intense graduate study were taught by C. I. Lewis and it was here that he acquired his introduction to pragmatism.[1] Quine was never really interested in studying the texts of past masters and he seemed especially uninterested in the history of pragmatist ideas. He told Morton White, for instance, that reading Royce was like going through muck (White 1999: 121–4).

Quine did read some Peirce and he was impressed by him. But unsurprisingly, given the amount of reading of bits and pieces of manuscripts it would have taken, he says he "never succeeded in getting a unified picture" of Peirce. He learned much about Peirce's advances in logic and probability theory, but when he speaks of Peirce's account of truth, it is clear that he has not gone into it in any depth—he takes Peirce to hold that science will march toward a limit (Quine 2008 [1999]: 165).[2] With respect to the other classical pragmatists, Quine asserts that he departs "radically" from James's theory of truth and his argument about the will to believe, "which seems to me to be a way of giving aid and comfort to wishful thinkers." James's idea that one can will to believe strikes Quine as a distortion of the notion of belief (1987: 18f.).

But he does see the similarities. For instance, in 1968 he gave the inaugural John Dewey Lectures at Columbia, later published as "Ontological Relativity," and says:

---

[1] See Quine (1990: 292) and Quine (2008 [1999]: 60).

[2] Quine shows that he was not a scholar of Peirce: "And Peirce was never, to my knowledge, one to question the law of excluded middle" (Quine 2008 [1999]: 165). We have seen that Peirce was a great questioner of the law of excluded middle.

Philosophically I am bound to Dewey by the naturalism that dominated his last three decades. With Dewey I hold that knowledge, mind, and meaning are part of the same world that they have to do with, and that they are to be studied in the same empirical spirit that animates natural science. There is no place for a prior philosophy.

[1969: 27]

He also notes that his behaviorist account of meaning is very like the pragmatist account of meaning as a social product, requiring more than one speaker, and cashing out in action.[3] But we do not need to look to Dewey retrospectives to find Quine acknowledging the lineage. In the first paragraph of his famous "Two Dogmas of Empiricism," he asserts that one upshot of the paper is "a shift towards pragmatism" (1980 [1951]: 20).

I have already foreshadowed the striking similarity between Quine and Lewis. Donald Davidson, one of Quine's most influential students, says the following in an interview:

I do think that C. I. Lewis had a tremendous influence on Quine, but Quine doesn't realize it. The explanation for that is that Quine had no training in philosophy and so when he took Lewis's course in epistemology, he took for granted that this is what everybody knows about epistemology. Quine didn't realize that Lewis was any different from everyone else; pretty soon he worked out that there are some things he didn't agree with Lewis about, like the analytic-synthetic distinction. I don't think Quine would put it this way. As I said, I don't think he realized any of this, but you can find most of Quine's epistemology in C. I. Lewis minus the analytic-synthetic distinction. Epistemology naturalized is very close to the heart of C. I. Lewis. I don't think that Quine knows the extent to which there really is a sequence that starts with Kant and goes through C. I. Lewis and ends with Quine.

[Davidson 2004: 237]

We shall see that Davidson is wrong in only two respects. First, Lewis and Quine had more or less the same (pragmatic) conception of the analytic–synthetic distinction. The difference is only that Lewis thinks it is important to hold a place for this pragmatic conception of the analytic in the theory of knowledge, whereas Quine, seeing that the pragmatic conception is not the pernicious version of the distinction between analytic and synthetic, thinks that he has killed off the distinction. But Quine, as I have suggested, not only declines to associate himself with Lewis's view—he attacks it. Perhaps he wanted not to seem to be simply repeating the views of his teacher, although that is just what he did. Perhaps he felt that James had captured the pragmatist flag and wanted to distance himself from the position that had attracted so much scorn from Russell, Moore, and others.[4]

Second, while Kant is indeed one of the fathers of this kind of pragmatism, Peirce cannot be left out of the sequence. This kind of pragmatism takes the best from the empiricist tradition (the naturalist epistemology) and leaves the worst of it (the

---

[3] Quine's behaviorism was forged in conversation with his friend and colleague, B. F. Skinner—an important figure in the history of American functionalism, of which Dewey and Mead are critical.

[4] In 1992 he says that his hesitation over whether to classify himself as a pragmatist "was only my uncertainty over what distinguishes a pragmatist from any other empiricist" (Quine 2008 [1992]: 213).

reductionism and the atomism). It also takes the best from the Kantian tradition (the idea that we need to assume certain norms or principles if we are to carry on in ways that we seem to need to carry on) and leaves the worst of it (the idea that these norms and principles are necessarily true).

Unfortunately, Quine's desire to underplay his pragmatist lineage did serious damage to the tradition. His followers tend not to identify themselves as pragmatists. So although there is a very tight line that goes from Peirce to Lewis to Quine, the position these three giants of philosophy shared was in the end no longer called pragmatism. While pragmatist philosophy did not disappear from the philosophical landscape, that philosophy ceased to call itself pragmatist. Quine for most of his career abandoned the pragmatist camp, leaving the ground wide open to be taken over by a new Jamesian in the person of Richard Rorty.

11.2 The First Dogma of Empiricism and A Pragmatic Conception of the Analytic

Quine had an affinity for logical empiricism. As a newly minted PhD on a Harvard traveling fellowship, he attended Schlick's lectures and some meetings of the Circle in Vienna; sat in on Carnap's lectures in Prague; and visited Tarski and other outstanding Polish logicians in Warsaw. Once ensconced at Harvard as a junior faculty member, he was instrumental in bringing Tarski to the Unity of Science meeting and then persuading him to remain, saving him from the horrors that would have been in store for him on his return (Quine 1986: 19). He and Carnap carried on a life-long correspondence and were in constant discussion over matters of analyticity and choice of language. Quine says that the logical empiricism of the Vienna Circle was the "main influence" on him (Quine 2008 [1999]: 36). Yet he never thought of himself as belonging to the movement and he delivered some of the most devastating objections to it.

From their first meeting in Prague in 1932, Quine and Carnap disagreed about the status of the analytic–synthetic distinction. We have seen that every empiricist needs to expend some effort to deal with, for instance, statements of mathematics and logic. How can they be true or false, given that they are not directly verifiable by the senses? Or putting it the other way: why have empiricists given an exemption to mathematical and logical statements in not requiring that they pass the verificationist test? Most empiricists, from Hume to the Vienna Circle, respond by asserting that statements of mathematics and logic are special because they are necessarily true, or analytically true, or always true, or true by virtue of their very meaning. They are not made true by contingencies in the world. They are hence let off the verificationist hook and do not need to prove themselves meaningful or legitimate by passing the tests of experiment and observation.

Mill is one of the very few empiricists whose answer is that mathematics and logic should not be hived off into a special category of their own, immune from the rigors of the empiricist criterion. But as I have noted, he did not put forward an account of how they were empirical that made mathematicians very happy. He suggested that "2 + 1 = 3" is an empirical generalization, discovered and verified by moving things around to see how many of them it takes to get to 3. We have also seen that Peirce is one of that small handful of empiricists who requires all statements to be connected to experience; one of those empiricists who is happy to do without the analytic–synthetic distinction. He does better than Mill, in that he does not require mathematical and logical statements to be verifiable by the senses. He takes such statements to be empirical in that they are subject to the force of surprise and possible overthrow of experience in diagrammatic or proof contexts.

Quine is the third in this triumvirate of great empiricists who attempt to bring mathematics and logic under the scope of experience and verification. In 1950 he gave a talk at the APA in Toronto titled "Two Dogmas of Empiricism," which he published the next year in the *Journal of Philosophy*. Some think that it is "perhaps the most-famous paper in twentieth century philosophy" (Creath 2004: 47). His attack on the dogmas of logical empiricism is an attack from within the empiricist camp. It was the knockout punch to an already staggering opponent.[5]

The first dogma is the analytic–synthetic distinction. Quine asserts that it is an empiricist article of faith, with no rational grounding or explanation. It rests on the idea of synonymy—on the idea that "brother" and "male sibling" mean the same thing, making "All brothers are male" true by the very meanings of the words. But all the purported ways of explaining synonymy invoke concepts such as "definition," "possibility," or "contradiction," each of which stands in as much need of explanation as the concept of synonymy itself.[6] How can Kant, for instance, explain the metaphor that one concept contains another without somehow relying upon the notion of sameness of meaning? Similarly, there is no contradiction in the statement "No brothers are siblings," unless one is already relying on the notion of synonymy, which is exactly what is to be explained.

Quine thinks that the chain of circularity must be broken by adopting an empirical account of meaning for all statements. The only genuine way to understand the ideas of meaning, synonymy, necessity, or analyticity is to invoke an empiricist or behaviorist criterion. Quine, that is, explains the apparent necessity of so-called analytic statements in an empiricist way: they are such that everyone would assent to them. He argues that we learn a language by observing other people's verbal behavior and by having our own behaviors observed by others and reinforced or corrected. "There is nothing in

[5] This is despite the fact that Carnap also put forward a kind of holism on which one could choose where to make revisions—even in the fundamental propositions of logic and mathematics. See Friedman (2007: 10).

[6] White mounts the same argument: the idea of synonymy, on which the idea of analyticity rests, has not itself been defined except in a circular way (1950: 320). Philosophy, which was supposed to be the preserve of unpacking analytic truths, will no longer be sharply separated from science, the supposed preserve of discovering synthetic truths. A chasm thought to have been unbridgeable will no longer divide those who seek meanings or essences and those who collect facts (1950: 330).

linguistic meaning beyond what is to be gleaned from overt behavior in observable circumstances" (1992 [1990]: 38).

Quine is a holist. Statements about mathematics and logic have empirical content or pull their weight in our interconnected body of knowledge through the indirect structural support they provide. They are not of a different kind from other statements in our webs of belief. They are not true or false solely in virtue of their meanings. But that does not mean that each and every statement can be empirically tested or verified on its own. Quine argues that the sentence is too small a unit to be the vehicle of empirical meaning. Rather: "The unit of empirical significance is the whole of science" (1980 [1951]: 42). What carries empirical meaning, or what has testable consequences, is a scientific theory taken as a whole: "our statements about the external world face the tribunal of sense experience not individually but only as a corporate body" (1980 [1951]: 41). Our entire belief system, that is, must be seen as one interconnected web. Mathematics and logic are at the center, gradually shading into the theoretical sentences of science, and then to specific observation sentences at the periphery. When faced with recalcitrant experience, we must choose where to make adjustments in our web of belief. No sentence is protected from revision. We could, and on very rare occasions do, choose to revise some part of our most cherished mathematical and logical assumptions.

Quine thinks that our choices about what to revise, when faced with recalcitrant experience, are based on "pragmatic" choices. Theories, he argues, are underdetermined by the evidence. Hence, theory choice, once the evidence has run out, boils down to considerations of simplicity, elegance, and avoiding massive destruction of our well-grounded beliefs. This is not quite the Jamesian idea that when the evidence falls short of determining a belief, we can choose to believe as we will. For Quine and James differ about what kinds of non-evidential grounds can be brought to bear on an underdetermined theory choice—Quine would never allow for a positive effect of the theory on its believers. One surmises that it was the whiff of similarity to James on this matter that motivated Quine to distance himself from the pragmatism so clearly manifest in his view. But Quine's view is pretty much a repetition of Lewis's position. Lewis's pragmatic conception of the a priori is that the a priori is what we tend to take to be "true, *no matter what.*" Quine's conception is: "an analytic sentence is one held true come what may." We have also seen that Carnap argued that we can choose logics and "conceptual systems." So what did this debate amount to? Why did Quine attack a distinction that was embedded in his own position? One part of the answer has to do with Quine's year in Vienna and Prague, which focused Quine on an early version of the distinction—the one he found in Carnap's *Aufbau.*[7] The disagreement remained in place, if watered down. Carnap says in 1963:

Quine shows...that a scientist, who discovers a conflict between his observations and his theory and who is therefore compelled to make a readjustment somewhere in the total system

---

[7] Don Howard pointed this out to me.

of science, has much latitude with respect to the place where a change is to be made. In this procedure, no statement is immune to revision, not even the statements of logic and mathematics. There are only practical differences, and these are differences in degree, inasmuch as a scientist is usually less willing to abandon a previously accepted general empirical law than a single observation sentence, and still less willing to abandon a law of logic or of mathematics. With all of this I am entirely in agreement. But I cannot follow Quine when he infers from this fact that it becomes folly to seek a boundary between synthetic and analytic statements. I agree that "any statement can be held true come what may." But the concept of an analytic statement . . . is not adequately characterized as "held true come what may."

[1963: 921]

He goes on to say just what Quine says: a change in logic would be a "radical alteration" or even a "revolution" in the history of science, whereas a change in a single observation sentence "occurs every minute." Carnap's concept of analyticity is of course not about this latter kind of change.

But the question about Quine's treatment of Lewis looms even larger. Quine says that Lewis "stopped short" of abandoning the analytic-synthetic distinction altogether (Quine 1981d: 34). He focuses on the fact that Lewis retains the distinction in name rather than on the fact that what he retains under that name is really an exploded distinction. Lewis might not have acknowledged that the distinction he was holding onto had disintegrated in his hands, but nonetheless, his was no longer the analytic–synthetic distinction that relied on a notion of synonymy or sameness of meaning.

Davidson again throws light on the matter. He says that the demolition of the analytic–synthetic distinction is distinctly pragmatist and that Quine must have known this:

The important thing in Quine, and certainly in me too, is abandoning the analytic/synthetic distinction. And Quine could not have failed to recognize in this an element of pragmatism . . . To deny the analytic/synthetic distinction is to suppose that you cannot make a strong division between the architectonics of thought and its content. You can choose your own structure, which was already Lewis' idea.

[Borradori 1994: 44]

We might add that it was already Carnap's idea as well. But Quine prefers to cite Pierre Duhem, the French physicist and mathematician, as his fellow holist. At around the same time that Peirce and Wright were developing their holism, Duhem was arguing that no hypothesis is tested alone, but always with a set of auxiliary hypotheses.[8] Here is Lewis, in 1936, putting forward precisely what is known as the Quine/Duhem thesis:

In testing one hypothesis, we make use of other and better established hypotheses, in order to determine what consequences should follow if the hypothesis tested is true . . . The important consideration here is that no one hypothesis can be tested in isolation. We test the hypothesis H by reference to its consequence C. C, however, is not a consequence of H alone, but of

---

[8] See Duhem (1954 [1914]) and (1990 [1917]).

H together with J and K. If C fails to occur, we attribute this to the falsity of H, because J and K are better established . . . all that we can be sure of . . . is that there is something false in the compound statement, HJK.

[1970 [1936]: 282–83]

We have seen this point also made by Chauncy Wright. But while Quine can be easily forgiven for not knowing that, it is less easy to understand how he could not have known that the Lewis brand of pragmatism was his own. One would be hard pressed to guess from whose pen—Quine's or Lewis's—the following sentence flows: "We are likely, for obvious reasons, to choose that revision which requires the smallest total alteration, or is most easily accepted for some other reason of the same general type—a kind of reason which is likely to be labelled 'pragmatic.'" The words happen to be Lewis's (1970 [1936]: 283).

11.3 The Second Dogma and the Pragmatist Theory of Truth

Quine identifies the second dogma of empiricism as reductionism. He wants nothing to do with the project of showing how every legitimate belief is reducible to something secure:

The naturalistic philosopher begins his reasoning within the inherited world theory as a going concern. He tentatively believes all of it, but believes also that some unidentified portions are wrong. He tries to improve, clarify, and understand the system from within. He is the busy sailor adrift on Neurath's boat.

[1981d: 28]

Here too Quine's pragmatism shouts from the rooftops. He argues that we act on our settled beliefs until some surprising experience throws them into doubt. Then we inquire until we have another, better, settled belief upon which to rely. It is a mistake to think that epistemology gives us an independent standpoint from which to evaluate science and its theories. Rather, epistemology must be the study of how we come, in science and inquiry, to our beliefs. Epistemology must be naturalized. Science (Quine) or inquiry (Peirce) is our theory of what exists. We don't need fruitless philosophies that try to stand over and above first order inquiry and tell us what *really* exists. We don't need that kind of metaphysical theory.

Inquiry, of course, is a fallible enterprise and it might turn out that what science now tells us—even its most general claims such as that there are physical objects that have an impact on our sensory apparatus—gets overturned. That, is, the skeptics might be right. There may be no physical objects about which we are busily theorizing. But we have no better option than to believe what science now tells us.

As must every naturalist, Quine tries to answer the charge that he is conflating the descriptive with the normative—the "is" with the "ought." He says:

The normative is naturalized, not dropped. The crowning normative principle of naturalized epistemology is nothing less than empiricism itself; for empiricism is both a rule of scientific method and a scientific discovery. It is natural science that tells us that our information about the world comes only through impacts on our sensory surfaces. And it is conspicuously normative, counseling us to mistrust soothsayers and telepathists.

[1990: 229]

Our norms are the norms of science. This does not eliminate normativity altogether, but it does makes science is the sole measure of it. Quine's detractors will not think that he has wrestled hard enough with this question, but that is as Quine intends it. The matter, he thinks, is straightforward.

It seems that, on this view, truth must be naturalized as well. Indeed, here we see Quine on the verge of adopting a pragmatist account of truth:

We can improve our conceptual scheme, our philosophy, bit by bit while continuing to depend on it for support; but we cannot detach ourselves from it and compare it objectively with an unconceptualized reality. Hence it is meaningless, I suggest, to inquire into the absolute correctness of a conceptual scheme as a mirror of reality. Our standard for appraising basic changes of conceptual scheme must be, not a realistic standard of correspondence to reality, but a pragmatic standard.

[1961 [1950]: 79]

Indeed, the following passage in "Two Dogmas of Empiricism" could not have failed to bring James and Dewey to mind:

As an empiricist I continue to think of the conceptual scheme of science as a tool, ultimately, for predicting future experience in the light of past experience. Physical objects are conceptually imported into the situation as convenient intermediaries—not by definition in terms of experience, but simply as irreducible posits comparable, epistemologically, to the gods of Homer. For my part I do, qua lay physicist, believe in physical objects and not in Homer's gods; and I consider it a scientific error to believe otherwise. But in point of epistemological footing . . . both sorts of entities enter our conception only as cultural posits. The myth of physical objects is epistemologically superior to most in that it has proved more efficacious than other myths as a device for working a manageable structure into the flux of experience.

[1980 [1951]: 44]

The objects of our best concepts and theories, from the most abstract to the most concrete, are what is real.

What follows is the passage that is the key to the transition from logical empiricism to the Peircean/Lewisian pragmatism of Quine:

theories and concepts, like language itself, are man-made, and reification is part of conceptualization. Brute fact intrudes only amorphously in the impacts of light and molecules on our sensory receptors. Thus I see the whole of science as Carnap saw the pragmatically adopted framework of science. He saw the reification of numbers and other abstract objects as a matter of framework rather than fact: I see all reification on a par, even to sticks and stones.

[Quine 2008 [1999]: 220]

Carnap thought that some of our beliefs—the framework beliefs or the analytic beliefs—were determined on pragmatic grounds. Scientific beliefs are determined in a more objective, empirical, way. Thus, his position has only a gust of pragmatism blowing through it. The true or complete pragmatist thinks that none of our beliefs are exempt from the test of experience and none of our beliefs are exempt from the influence of pragmatic or human factors.

Quine (mistakenly) takes Peirce to put forward a "limit theory of truth" on which theories undergo a successive approximation towards the truth. This, he rightly points out, is a flawed account of truth, as theories do not march in a linear fashion towards some perfected form and we have no criteria on which we can compare theories to see which are positive developments of others. It should be clear to the reader, however, that Peirce's actual account of truth is remarkably like Quine's, right down to the brute intrusion of the external world on our human-made theories and the naturalism which tells us that what is real is what science says is real. Where they differ is that Quine often wants to restrict science to physical science, whereas Peirce was a more liberal naturalist.

Because he misunderstands Peirce's position, Quine would rather identify himself with Dewey. He does not, however, think that Dewey gets truth right either. Quine is adamant about "dissociating truth from warrant" (1987: 56). He does not want his holism to suggest that truth is what we are warranted in taking to be true. So Quine makes a move that has reverberations throughout the subsequent unfolding of pragmatism. He adopts a disquotationalist theory of truth:[9]

John Dewey proposed, in the interests of naturalism, simply to avoid the truth predicate and limp along with warranted belief. Otto Neurath in his last years took a similar line. But surely neither Dewey nor Neurath could have denied that the truth predicate is rendered crystal clear by disquotation, and presumably both philosophers subscribed to "p or not p". So they did not circumvent the problem, they just did not sense it.

[Quine 2008 [1999]: 165]

Quine was impressed by Tarski's definition of truth for formal languages: any adequate theory of truth must entail, for every sentence p of a language L, that: "p" is true if and only if p. The well-worn example of an instance of this schema is: "snow is white" is true if and only if snow is white. When the quotation marks are used, it is the sentence that is being talked about. When we drop the quotation marks, we are talking about snow itself. Quine suggests that all there is to say about truth is an infinite run of sentences of this sort (1987: 214). A number of modern pragmatists have very happily followed him down the parallel set of rails on which truth is somehow both disquotation and the best that inquiry and assertion could do.

---

[9] Frank Ramsey, in Cambridge, England in the late 1920s, was the first to bring together disquotationalism and the pragmatist account of truth. But Ramsey's excellent brand of pragmatism was and is under-noticed and under-appreciated. I will try to rectify this in Misak (forthcoming).

My own attempts[10] at trying to reconcile pragmatism and disquotationalism have revolved around the argument that the insight of disquotationalism is precisely the insight of pragmatism. Both hold that when we assert that p is true, what we are doing is asserting p. The Peircean pragmatist modifies this shared thought slightly, not wanting to limp along with warranted belief. When we assert that p is true, what we are doing is asserting p and asserting that p would remain assertible. There is nothing more to saying that p is true than saying that we would be justified in asserting p—that p is indefeasible. Both pragmatism and disquotationalism, that is, keep us focused on first-order inquiry. As Huw Price puts it: "Our theoretical gaze never leaves the world" (2011: 14).

We have seen that Peirce also offers us a nominal definition of truth that runs parallel to his pragmatist view: the correspondence definition. I have argued (2007b) that he would have been happy replacing correspondence with the disquotationalist definition. For the disquotationalist is making a point very close to Peirce's: there is nothing more to saying that p is true than saying that p is assertible. But Peirce would be insistent about taking a step further. When you have some things to say about what makes a belief worthy of assertion, you have some things to say about truth—about what it is that true beliefs have in common. That is, Peirce's adoption of the nominal definition of truth does not split his view of truth into two. When we say that p is true, all we are doing is asserting p. But when we unpack what it is to assert p, we are taken directly to the idea of a belief that stands up to experience and argument. Quine thinks that the disquotationalist account of truth is useful in that it allows us to say general things such as "libel laws do not apply to true statements," and "I will tell the truth," while staying well away from any over-blown metaphysical speculation about the very nature of truth.[11] He thinks that the disquotational theory of truth has "a significant residue" of the correspondence theory, but he takes it to be innocuous (1987: 213). While he does not want a metaphysical theory about the very nature of truth, he does want to say that there is something about truth that transcends "man's faltering approximations."[12] The disquotational theory gives us this without reference to metaphysically spurious facts, states of mind, or correspondence to reality. He says:

[U]sage dictates that when in the course of scientific progress some former tenet comes to be superseded and denied, we do not say that it used to be true but became false. The usage is rather that we thought it was true but it never was. Truth is not the product of science, but its goal. It is an ideal of pure reason, in Kant's apt phrase.

[Quine 2008 [1999]: 164; Hahn ed. 1999: 79]

---

[10] Misak (1998) and (2007b).

[11] One of his reasons for adopting the disquotational theory of truth is that he wants to preserve, not as a "fact of life," but as a "norm governing efficient logical regimentation," the law of the excluded middle (1987: 57). This of course, makes Quine very much like Peirce, who thinks that the law of the excluded middle is a regulative assumption of inquiry.

[12] Føllesdal and Quine (2008: 165); Hahn ed. (1999: 79).

What an interesting passage. It is a poke at James's view that what was false one day can be true the next; it is an affirmation that our use of "is true" is paramount in understanding the concept of truth; and it is a clear statement that we use "is true" to mark something objective, for want of a better term, and something we aim at. We shall see that the thoughts expressed in this passage distinguish Quine from one of the next major pragmatists to arrive on the philosophical scene: Richard Rorty. But the commitment to disquotationalism is shared by both. The question will be whether these two ideas—disquotationalism and pragmatism—pull against each other or can live together in harmony.

Quineans might answer by saying that pragmatist epistemology is about knowledge (or warranted belief or the best that we could do) and that Quine thinks there is a gap between knowledge and truth. Quine, that is, is not really a pragmatist when it comes to truth. Perhaps that would be fair enough. But as we shall see when we turn to Rorty's view, Quine's move has been adopted by pragmatists who want to obliterate any gap between warranted assertibility and truth and, for these philosophers, the question cannot be answered so lightly.

11.4 Holism without Ethics

There is one vast chasm between Quine and other pragmatists. Quine recoiled from extending his holism to matters of value. As his friend and colleague Morton White puts it: "Although Quine was a pragmatist and an empiricist in his approach to mathematics, logic, physics, and ontology, his pragmatism and empiricism virtually disappeared when he dealt with ethics" (White 2002: 53). Quine thinks that "apart from a salient marker or two" one finds only "uncharted moral wastes" in moral matters (1987: 5). Science and ethics do not have enough in common to think of them as both being a part of legitimate inquiry:

[O]ne regrets the methodological infirmity of ethics as compared with science. The empirical foothold of scientific theory is in the predicted observable event; that of a moral code is in the observable moral act. But whereas we can test a prediction against the independent course of observable nature, we can judge the morality of an act only by our moral standards themselves.

[1981 [1979]: 63]

It interesting to note that Quine's early characterization of experience is certainly broad enough to bring moral judgments into the fold. Observation sentences:

can be roughly distinguished from others by a behavioural criterion, involving no probing of sensations. For this is characteristic of them: witnesses will agree on the spot in applying an observation term, or in assenting to an observation sentence . . .

[2008 [1975]: 230]

He suggests that if sensory irritations are such that they prompt the same assent and dissent patterns in everyone, we have a basis on which to distinguish the impact of external things from our interpretations that are built up from these impacts.[13] This behaviorist criterion of an observation sentence unlinks observation from our senses and leaves room for the possibility that some ethical statements will be observational—"that's odious" upon seeing a sexual assault of a child, for instance.[14]

In his later work, Quine backed off of this generous characterization of experience. He started to argue that experience is the stimulation of our sensory surfaces. This effectively ruled out ethics for him, although one might argue that it should not have ruled out ethics, given that Quine also thought that all observation is theory-laden. As Macarthur (2008) argues, science is full of norms of rationality, norms that Quine cannot provide a scientific account of.

That is, one might well argue that Quine, like it or not, has all the elements of the pragmatist position in place, including plenty of room for the legitimacy of ethics. But for one reason or another, he balks at this last pillar of pragmatism. He was adamant about keeping philosophy restricted to being about logic and science. He did not want to extend his view to include norms and, indeed, this fact might be significant enough to withhold judgment on whether Quine can really be called a pragmatist.

---

[13] Hookway 2008: 284f.

[14] Quine does not want to make anything of the possibility. In a response to Morton White he says "That's outrageous" cannot be considered an observation sentence even in the case where everyone in the linguistic community would assent to it on observation of a certain act. It depends too much, he says, on collateral information that need not be shared by other witnesses of the act. But Quine admits that the observational status of sentences is a matter of a degree (Quine 1986: 664). See Sinclair (2011) for the use of this last point as the basis of a qualified defense of White against Quine's rejection of the idea of moral observation sentences.

12

Fellow Travelers

12.1 Morton White's Full-time Holism

Morton White (1917–), with Lewis and Quine, is another clear counterexample to the claim that American pragmatism was drummed out of the academy during the 1950s and 1960s. He was an enormously successful pragmatist, deeply knowledgeable about the history of pragmatism, and vigorously engaged with the epistemological and political debates of his time.

White was a graduate student at Columbia, where he wrote an MA thesis on Peirce and probability and a PhD thesis titled "The Origins of Dewey's Instrumentalism." He taught at the University of Pennsylvania and then moved to Harvard in 1948, where he was chairman of the department for four years. In 1970 he moved to the prestigious Institute for Advanced Study at Princeton. He was of the view that the logical empiricism that was all the rage in America was no foreign import. It was, rather, an integral part of the new scientific philosophy, of which pragmatism was one major expression. The two views, walking hand in hand, encourage "a tighter, more scientifically oriented, less monumental conception of philosophy" (2005: 146).

It is important to see that the line of American pragmatism that I am tracing in this book was unbroken when White went to Harvard. Lewis, who was taught by Royce and James, was still in the Harvard department and Henry Sheffer would "reminisce charmingly about Royce, James, Santayana" (White 1999: 101). White and Quine are the next generation in the Harvard family of pragmatists. They both went to war against the analytic–synthetic distinction, trying to mark themselves off from logical empiricism and from Lewis. While this move did distinguish them from many of the logical empiricists, their epistemology was pretty much identical to Lewis's. And unlike Quine, White never wavered in calling himself a pragmatist.

White agrees with Lewis, Quine, and Peirce that logical and mathematical statements are subject (indirectly say Lewis and Quine, more directly says Peirce) to verification. The paper in which White first articulated this view is his contribution to Sidney Hook's celebratory volume for Dewey on his ninetieth birthday in 1950, the same year that Quine published "Two Dogmas of Empiricism." White's paper was titled "The Analytic and the Synthetic: An Untenable Dualism." White comes to his antipathy to the distinction, he says, through Mill's empiricism and through

Dewey's general destructive attitude towards dualisms.[1] This is despite the fact that Dewey sometimes seems to disagree with White on this particular issue and despite the fact that their "manner and method" are "quite foreign" to each other. Dewey explicitly "shunned" White's argument that the distinction between analytic and synthetic does not stand up to scrutiny (White 2005 [1950]: 97–98).

In 1956, White published *Toward Reunion in Philosophy*, which built on his argument against the analytic–synthetic distinction and articulated a sustained pragmatist view. It is set out as a pragmatism that turns away from the excesses of logical empiricism while still retaining empiricism's concern for practice and experience. With all his pragmatist predecessors, White abandons what Dewey called the quest for certainty and the spectator theory of knowledge. Free of these dogmas, his empiricism is one that offers us a naturalist view of "the roles of reason, sensory experience, and sentiment" in knowledge and inquiry (1956: xiii).

We have seen that the logical empiricists and the pragmatists think that all inquiry must be thought of as being part of a seamless whole. Once this general point is made, these holists go in one of two directions. Peirce, Holmes, James, Dewey, Lewis, and White think that ethics, politics, art, religion, and law are part of the world-view that is responsive to experience. Quine and many of the logical empiricists think that these domains fail to be responsive to experience. They take science and logic to be the totality of our legitimate aspirations to knowledge. As I have suggested, it may be that this is enough to withdraw the label "pragmatism" from Quine's position.

White, on the other hand, adopts Quine's epistemology and tries to bring ethics, politics, and art into the naturalist tent. All of our inquiries and deliberations are empirical disciplines, but they are empirical in different ways. Like Lewis, White thinks that ethics "may be viewed as empirical if one includes feelings of moral obligation as well as sensory experiences in the pool or flux into which the ethical believer worked a manageable structure" (2002: xi). He argues that the anti-rationalisms of Hume, Duhem, Dewey, and James were "part-time" (2002: 3). In some form or another, they each retained a distinction between beliefs that must face the tribunal of experience (the empirical) and those that need not (the analytical; the ethical). White wants to be a full-time naturalist. All of our statements are answerable to experience. He remakes the Quinean "web of belief," so that ethics and other subject matters become a part of it.

This kind of holistic pragmatism, White says, sets itself against the classical rationalist view that "we have knowledge that is not tested by experience" (2002: 2). One distinction—between beliefs that are subject to the tribunal of experience and beliefs that are not subject to that tribunal (because they are logically true, or they are tautologies, or they are self-evident)—must be abandoned. There are no beliefs that need not be responsive to or answerable to experience. There is nothing that can serve

---

[1] See White (2005 [1950]: 97).

as a certain foundation for knowledge. Another distinction—that between beliefs that are subject to the tribunal of experience and those that are not (because they are about our feelings of what is desirable or good)—must also be abandoned.

Inquirers, White argues, deal with both normative and descriptive beliefs. Moral sentiments, say, of obligation and repulsion, are among the experiential inputs that we need to account for (White 2005: 189; 1981: 30–31, 39–42). They can be recalcitrant—they can jar with what is already held true in our web of belief.[2] As with the scientific inquirer, the ethical deliberator has a number of options open to her in dealing with recalcitrant experience. She may question the experience that does not fit, she may question existing beliefs, or she may even, if she cannot resolve the matter in these less extreme ways, reject underlying logical laws (1981: 31; 2005: 190). This insight is generally attributed to Dewey and it is being resurrected in fruitful ways in contemporary moral philosophy. White, though, with Lewis, is its forgotten champion. White brings Dewey to Quine—he brings Columbia naturalism to the new Harvard naturalism, taking us back to the first Harvard naturalism of The Metaphysical Club.[3]

12.2 Nelson Goodman: Induction and World-making

Nelson Goodman (1906–98) is also part of the twentieth-century great Harvard pragmatist juggernaut. He completed his BA at Harvard in 1928 and his PhD in 1941. He ran an art gallery in the 1930s, setting himself up nicely for his important work in aesthetics. This meant that, although he was only two years older than Quine, he finished his PhD twelve years later. Much of his academic career was at the University of Pennsylvania, where he taught the budding pragmatists Hilary Putnam and Sidney Morgenbesser. He returned to teach at Harvard in 1968. As with Quine, there is very little to suggest that he read and understood the classical pragmatists—his pragmatism also must have been imbibed from his teacher, C. I. Lewis.

I have noted that Goodman was part of the trio who got together in the late 1940s and hammered away at the analytic–synthetic distinction. His 1949 "On Likeness of Meaning" sets out his view of the matter: there are no criteria on which we can judge that one bit of language has the same meaning as another, and without the concept of sameness of meaning, there can be no concept of analyticity. This, we have seen, was

---

[2] White takes John Rawls to be a holistic pragmatist. Rawls, in *A Theory of Justice*, argues that bringing judgments into reflective equilibrium is a matter of bringing them into agreement with each other in what White sees as an empiricist or pragmatist process of justification. Ethical judgments are not justified by an appeal to first principles or to what is self-evident. Rather, we make piecemeal adjustments between rules and our considered judgments. We are to regard a moral theory as we would regard any other theory. It presupposes truths in mathematics, logic, economics, and psychology, with fundamental principles at the top and anchoring confirmations—considered judgments—at the bottom. Just like the physicist, White says, the Rawlsian deliberator balances the claims of theory and observation (1981: 67).

[3] Rob Sinclair suggested to me that I put the point this way.

Quine's argument in "Two Dogmas." Goodman also shared with Quine a passion for nominalism and extensionalism, views on which only individuals, not classes, exist.

Goodman is not always seen as a pragmatist and, for the most part, he does not see himself as one. Like so many others of his generation, he tends to associate pragmatism with the Jamesian "libertine doctrine that anything goes." This "perverse maxim that whatever you can get away with is right" or "whatever works is clear" is, he says, a kind of "crude pragmatism" (1983 [1953b]: 32). He does sometimes acknowledge that a more sophisticated kind of pragmatism permeates his work. For instance, in the 1973 introduction to the book that brought him the most lasting recognition—*Fact, Fiction and Forecast*—he is clear that he is offering a pragmatic solution to the problem of induction (1973 [1955]: xxii).

Fact, Fiction and Forecast inventively recasts Hume's problem of induction and proposes a solution to it. Goodman illustrates his "new riddle of induction" by the following kind of example (1983 [1953a]: 59ff.). Suppose we define a predicate "grue": an object is grue if it is observed to be green and first examined before January 1 2029 or it is examined after January 1 2029 and it is observed to be blue. The hypothesis "all emeralds are grue" has just as much inductive support (in 2013) as does the hypothesis "all emeralds are green." For on the grue hypothesis, any emerald observed now, or in the past, which is green is also grue. Goodman asks what valid principle we could be using to select the predicate "green" to apply to emeralds, rather than the predicate "grue" or one of the infinite number of its variants. Induction rests solely on the enumeration of observed instances and hence the inductive evidence underdetermines the choice between all of these hypotheses. Why do we expect that if an emerald were to be found in 2030 it would be green, rather than blue?

Goodman's answer is essentially Peirce's: not all regularities result in the formation of a habit of expectation (1983 [1953a]: 82). We do not expect first-examined emeralds after 2029 to be blue, despite the fact that we have "confirmed" the grue hypothesis by observing thus far that all emeralds are green.

On Peirce's account, the choice between the grue and green hypotheses would not be a matter for induction, but for abduction. The conclusion "all emeralds are green" does not result from an inductive inference that all emeralds thus far have been observed to be green. Rather, had we been interested enough to inquire into the matter, "all emeralds are green" would have been inferred as the best explanation of the fact that all observed emeralds have thus far been green. It would have been an abductive inference, the conclusion of which would have then been tested (successfully thus far) by induction. That is, Peirce would have argued that the abductive origin of the green hypothesis gives it a weight that the grue hypothesis does not have. Like Goodman, he sees that regularities abound, but only some of them want explanations. Only unexpected or surprising regularities make a demand on us to explain them. If, in 2030, we start observing that all emeralds are blue, this will be a great surprise and we will cast about for a way of explaining the phenomenon. But until we are surprised, we will not conjecture that all emeralds are grue. That is why we can ignore the grue hypothesis. We have no genuine doubt of the explanatory power of the green hypothesis.

Goodman's solution is remarkably similar. It depends on the idea of "entrenchment." We have practices that we codify and rely upon to make our inductive inferences. Goodman's account of inquiry is deeply pragmatist:

A rule is amended if it yields an inference we are unwilling to accept; an inference is rejected if it violates a rule we are unwilling to amend. The process of justification is the delicate one of making mutual adjustments between rules and accepted inferences; and in the agreement achieved lies the only justification needed for either.

[1983 [1953a]: 64]

We should stop asking ourselves for guarantees that we will never obtain. We should understand that all we have is reliance on our practices and their norms and standards. These norms, in logic and in other kinds of inquiry, are human and revisable, rather than set in some kind of necessary stone.

In inductive inference, our practices turn upon projectable or entrenched or habitual predicates. Induction operates by "taking some classes to the exclusion of others as relevant kinds" (1978: 10). Hume was right. Our inductive (and causal) inferences rely upon habit. Philosophers owe Hume, as Goodman puts it, a belated apology for insisting for generations that he missed the point. Hume was right to say that rather than look for a proof for the validity of inductive inference, we must look to our practices of making inductive inferences and see what standards we find there. What we find in our practices is that not all predicates are projectable or law-like. The task we engage in is the task of confirmation theory. That theory must take on the "projection problem"—it must distinguish between when it is right to inductively generalize from a sample to a population and when it is not. It must try to codify our current inductive practices, while allowing for "leeway for progress, for the introduction of novel organizations that make, or take account of, newly important connections and distinctions" (1978: 128). It must leave room for, one might say, the breaking of bad habits and for extending our practices in ways we might not right now be able to anticipate.

It is, of course, very difficult to say what "important" and "bad" amount to. Peirce put tremendous effort into trying to set out some principles for projectability and so does Goodman. In his view, we must look to whether a hypothesis has actually been violated; to "the record of past predictions actually made and their outcome" (1983 [1953c]: 85, 93); to the idea that "variations in purpose may result in variations in relevant kinds" (1978: 128); and to whether the hypothesis is entrenched in our past practice (1983 [1953c]: 94). It should be obvious that none of these principles has the status of necessity.

This is a pragmatic solution (or as Goodman nicely puts it, a "reorientation") to the vexing problem of induction. Do not look for certainty. Look rather to the fact that we "do not come empty-headed but with some stock of knowledge, or of accepted statements, that may fairly be used in reaching a solution" (1983 [1953c]: 86). As Goodman's student Putnam notes:

What we have in Goodman's view . . . are practices, which are right or wrong depending on how they square with our standards. And our standards are right or wrong depending on how they square with our practices. This is a circle, or better a spiral, but one that Goodman, like John Dewey, regards as virtuous.

[Introduction to the 1983 4th edition of *Fact, Fiction, and Forecast*: ix][4]

Goodman's pragmatism manifests itself in his work on other topics as well. In 1975, he published a paper called "Words, Works, Worlds," in which he first put his argument that the symbol systems of the sciences, philosophy, the arts, perception, and everyday discourse constitute "ways of worldmaking," the title of his controversial 1978 book. Here is how he puts the idea which lies at the heart of his pragmatism: "We start, on any occasion, with some old version or world that we have on hand and that we are stuck with until we have the determination and skill to remake it into a new one" (1978: 97). With respect to induction, our habitual use of the predicates "green" and "blue" are part of our inherited world. If we were to abandon them for the predicate "grue," this would be "to make, and live in, a different world" (1978: 101).

Goodman proposed to admit on an equal footing a multiplicity of "world versions" such as those of art and music. There is not one underlying correct account of the way the world is. Rather, there are conflicting versions of the world. He sees himself here as following in the path of Lewis—a tradition:

that began when Kant exchanged the structure of the world for the structure of the mind, continued when C. I. Lewis exchanged the structure of the mind for the structure of concepts, and that now proceeds to exchange the structure of concepts for the structure of the several symbol systems of the sciences, philosophy, the arts, perception, and everyday discourse.

[1978: x]

Goodman's views did not sit well with many of his contemporaries. Hempel, for instance, says that he has an "uneasy feeling that we are being offered a coherence theory of knowledge, in which simplicity, scope, and coherence are the dominant requirements for acceptable theories" (1980: 196). He thinks that Goodman offers us an "exaggeration": "If adherents of different paradigms did inhabit totally separate worlds, I feel tempted to ask, how can they ever have lunch together and discuss each other's views? Surely, there is a passageway connecting their worlds; indeed it seems that their worlds overlap to a considerable extent" (1980: 197).

Goodman wants to reject Hempel's description of him. Goodman's "arch enemy" is "the anti-intellectualist, the mystic," who thinks that all our beliefs are conventional descriptions, where the world is filtered and distorted through the mind (1972 [1960]: 25). He sees that many will think that he must be friends with his arch-enemy and he does his best to rebut the accusation. While he may not have been successful in convincing his colleagues on this big point, he was very successful in making

---

[4] Another of his pragmatist students, Israel Scheffler, also was clear that Goodman's solution to the problem of induction is a pragmatist solution (1963: 311).

more local points. Part of Goodman's brilliance is in showing us how the practices of the sciences and the arts, for instance, have their own standards and norms. Those standards range from deductive validity; to determining whether a piece of cloth is a fair sample of the bolt it was cut from; to understanding the value of different styles of painting and how they give us different ways of seeing a subject; to using projectable predicates (1978: 125–34). He argues that we cannot import the standards and norms from one practice into another and keep intact all of the things that are vital to human flourishing. For another of his opponents is "the monopolistic materialist or physicist who maintains that one system, physics, is preeminent and all-inclusive, such that every other version must be reduced to it or rejected as false or meaningless."[5] This is where he breaks away from Quine's staunch materialism.

Goodman is also brilliant at showing us how what we aim at cannot be captured merely by thinking about truth in a standard way—such as the correspondence theory or the Tarskian schema. Such views of truth, he says:

cannot be the only consideration in choosing among statements or versions . . . even where there is no conflict, truth is far from sufficient. Some truths are trivial, irrelevant, unintelligible, or redundant; too broad, too narrow, too boring, too bizarre, too complicated, or taken from some other version than the one in question, as when a guard, ordered to shoot any of his captives who moved, immediately shot them all and explained that they were moving rapidly around the earth's axis and around the sun.

[1978: 120–21]

It is true that the captives were moving. But it is not true in the sense relevant to the guard's set of orders. In deciding what to do, the guard needs to go beyond what is strictly true and false and take seriously other, "pragmatic," features of the situation. At the time Goodman was writing, an argument was raging over whether or not such pragmatic considerations are relevant to truth and theory choice. The "scientific realists" argued that only the "epistemic" considerations of observation and logic were relevant to truth, as conceived as something like correspondence. Some of their opponents argued that "pragmatic" factors such as simplicity, are not relevant to truth, but are nonetheless important in theory choice. Notice that, only if truth is correspondence is it impossible to show how "pragmatic" criteria might be relevant to truth. If truth is what the pragmatist has in mind, the question is immediately answered in the affirmative.

Goodman for the most part stays in the background in this debate and lets others slug it out. But his position is interesting and leads to some problems for him. He assumes that truth is as the correspondence theorist sees it and then argues that truth is not all that it is cracked up to be. We want to say that what he is reaching for is the pragmatist account of truth: truth is not a matter of correspondence to the world, but what we human inquirers, with our interests and aims, would take to stand up to our scrutiny.

---

[5] 1978: 4. He takes himself here to be following Ernst Cassirer, the German-Polish neo-Kantian idealist. The links between pragmatism and Kantianism are strong and ever-present.

Goodman sees that his view is a "companion" to that of the pragmatists, but he, like so many philosophers at the time, takes pragmatism to identify truth with "utility" (1978: 125, 122–23). He merely flirts with the pragmatist account of truth, suggesting "that truth might be equated with permanent credibility." But he rejects (at least his understanding of) pragmatism: "We often believe what is not credible and disbelieve what is credible. Standards of credibility do not vary with individual opinion, over the worlds in the world of worlds sketched in *Ways of Worldmaking*. But neither are they absolute; they may vary from one world of worlds to another. Relativity goes all the way up." Goodman fails to see that there is a kind of pragmatism that is focused on what is *really* credible, rather than what we happen to believe.

He does see that he has *something* in common with the pragmatism of James. One angle on this proximity, I would offer, is that both Goodman and James put forward sharply expressed pragmatist views, the edges of which they then try to smooth away. The way that Goodman views the affinity is to note that the very title of James's *The Pluralistic Universe* nicely captures the complexities he is trying to get at: "The issue between monism and pluralism seems to evaporate under analysis. If there is but one world, it embraces a multiplicity of contrasting aspects; if there are many worlds, the collection of them all is one" (1978: 2). Goodman prefers to call himself a "pluralist." His way of thinking of the puzzle is to say that there are multiple versions of the world, not reducible to the version that physics presents to us. The idea of a one-and-only world is "a world well lost." What we have is our descriptions of phenomena, various as they might be. Identification of anything rests on classification and classification is shaped by our interests, goals, and habits. Descriptions of the world by the sciences and by the arts might differ but each be correct, given the purposes relevant to each. We can have an "overall organization" which embraces all of these descriptions—which embraces each of the sets of standards that are internal to each way of describing the world (1978: 5).

In a way that is consistent with his solution to the problem of induction, Goodman tries to respond to the deep pragmatist challenge. How can we distinguish between "genuine and spurious worlds" (1978: 1)? How can we decide which rules, standards, and norms are good ones and which lead us astray? And how can we even make sense of the idea of being led astray, once we see that our rules, standards, and norms are not given to us by the world, or by God, but are merely human? He argues that we can and we do assess our norms. In all domains of inquiry, we operate with standards and the concept of rightness—"standards different from yet no less exacting than those applied in science are appropriate for appraising what is conveyed" in other kinds of inquiry (1978: 5). Even in ethics, which he mostly leaves to others, Goodman thinks that "the relativity of rightness and the admissibility of conflicting, right renderings in no way precludes rigorous standards from distinguishing right from wrong" (1978: 110). We must see, though, that not all right standards are equally good for every purpose we might have:

we do not welcome molecules . . . as elements of our everyday world, or combine tomatoes and triangles and typewriters and tyrants and tornados into a single kind; the physicist will count none of these among his fundamental particles; the painter who sees the way the man-in-the-street does will have more popular than artistic success.

[1978: 21]

Instead of focusing on how to get true beliefs, we should focus on "understanding" (1978: 22). That comes in many forms and it is always shaped by prior experience and by "conceptualization" (1978: 92). Once we see that the aim of inquiry is understanding, we shall see that the arts "must be taken no less seriously than the sciences as modes of discovery, creation, and enlargement of knowledge" (1978: 102). *All* facts are theory laden, to use the expression that was in vogue amongst philosophers at the time (1978: 96).

But in every way of understanding, our theories are also, Goodman thinks, "fact-laden." The view he articulates:

plainly points to a radical relativism, but severe restraints are imposed. Willingness to accept countless alternative true or right world-versions does not mean that everything goes, that tall stories are as good as short ones, that truths are no longer distinguished from falsehoods, but only that truth must be otherwise conceived than as correspondence with a ready-made world. Though we make worlds by making versions, we no more make a world by putting symbols together at random than a carpenter makes a chair by putting pieces of wood together at random. The multiple worlds I countenance are just the actual worlds made by and answering to true or right versions.

[1978: 94]

When we start with our worlds and build from there, we do not "start from careless guesses. We follow our confidence and convictions, which are subject to strengthening or weakening or even reversal as we strive to build right versions or world . . . No starting points or ending points or points along the way are either absolute or arbitrary" (1980: 212).

Once we give up on the metaphysical ambitions of the correspondence theory and turn to the standards imbedded in our practices, we can see that there are indeed constraints on all of our inquiries. The standards internal to the scientific enterprise, for instance, require that a hypothesis "agrees with the established evidence," predicts correctly the outcome of further observations and experiments and is "simple" (1972 [1958]: 279). With respect to the standard of simplicity, Goodman argues as follows: science is not looking for a collection of truths; it is looking for a system of truths and systematization requires considerations such as simplicity. Goodman puts a tremendous amount of energy into the difficult and technical problem of how we can measure it.

Many of Goodman's contemporaries were not satisfied with these answers. Quine thought that his "sequence of worlds or versions founders in absurdity" (Quine 1981a: 98). Hempel wondered "how the empirical character of scientific claims or versions is accommodated in this conception of making versions from versions and adjudicating proposed hypotheses by their fit with the accepted system" (1980: 196). He calls for more attention to be paid to "the stubbornness of facts," which by now the reader knows is exactly what Peirce called for. What Quine, Hempel, and Peirce argue is that we must bring the force of experience to bear on our world-making. Then and only then can we make sense of it being non-arbitrary. Goodman wants to agree. There is no unconceptualized given or unstructured content, but that does not entail that "experience is a pure fiction, that it is without content, or even that there is no given element." He thinks that he can avoid "irresponsible nihilism" (1952: 162). Whether he speaks clearly and frequently enough of the given, or brute, or non-arbitrary element of experience is another question. Like James, Goodman tends, at least when he is talking about ways of world-making, to prefer punchy, revolutionary ways of expressing his point.

12.3 Wilfrid Sellars: Norms and Reasons

Wilfrid Sellars (1912–89) was the son of Roy Wood Sellars, the critical realist who, with Santayana and others, tilled the same patch of ground as the pragmatists in the early-to-mid-1900s. Sellars's educational path did not conform to the Harvard-dominated model. He took his undergraduate degree at the University of Michigan, made an excursion to the University of Munich, and then did an MA at Buffalo. He took a second BA as a Rhodes Scholar in Oxford in the mid-1930s—a rather uncongenial place and time for pragmatism—and started to work on a DPhil on Kant. After a year he went to Harvard and there was taught by Lewis and Quine. His own career unfolded at the universities of Minnesota, Yale, and Pittsburgh.

One might say that the son inherited his father's naturalism, as well as an awkward stance towards pragmatism. For the younger Sellars fits beautifully into the pragmatist tradition, yet he does not consistently align himself with the pragmatists.[6] Perhaps this was because he was wary of those pragmatists who "misconceive" their important insights about meaning and truth as *analyses* of meaning and truth (2007 [1954]: 40). Sellars, like Peirce, was alert to the possibility that the pragmatist need not *define*, for instance, truth as successful prediction in the long run (1962: 29). Indeed, Sellars perfectly exemplifies the spirit of the Peirce-Lewis brand of pragmatism. He knew much about the founder of pragmatism, making frequent use of Peirce's distinction between type and token, and Richard Bernstein talked to him in depth about Peirce.[7] His connection to Dewey is even more explicit. But his intellectual relationship

---

[6] Robert Neville was a student of Sellars' and (in correspondence) describes him as taking a dim view of John E. Smith, a scholar of pragmatism in the Yale Philosophy Department, because he thought of Smith as a mere interpreter of others, not engaged in solving philosophical problems directly. Neville says that Sellars came to Yale with the explicit intent of making it an analytic philosophy department, which set him in tension with those who operated with an ideology of pluralism. He also remarks that Sellars saw himself as trying to do exactly as his father had done in philosophy, except in an analytic mode. Richard Rorty was just finishing his graduate work as these debates heated up. Rorty left Yale, Neville says, as a Sellarsian. We shall see in the next chapter that Rorty's allegiances on this matter were complex.

[7] Private correspondence.

to Lewis is another one of those gaps in scholarship that seems to plague Lewis's reputation.

Like Lewis, the major influences on Sellars were logical empiricism and Kant. From Kant, he took the message taken by all the pragmatists: you cannot understand experience without concepts. Again like Lewis and against Quine, he is deeply interested in ethical judgments as well as scientific ones. In 1950, before the appearance of the famous essay "Empiricism and the Philosophy of Mind," Sellars contributed to Sidney Hook's ninetieth-birthday symposium on and for Dewey. His paper is titled "Language, Rules and Behavior" and in it he foreshadows the view that was to be his major contribution to philosophy—a naturalist/empiricist/pragmatist position with a coherent and deep account of the normative notions of validity or correctness.

In this paper, Sellars tells us that pragmatism has often been characterized as a crude descriptivism on which "all meaningful concepts and problems belong to the empirical or descriptive sciences." He is gesturing at Dewey when he says that the pragmatist sometimes offers those descriptivist interpretations of truth and moral obligation "with all the fervor of a Dutch boy defending the fertile lands of Naturalism against a threatening rationalistic flood" (1949: 291–2). But pragmatism can be more sophisticated than that (1949: 289–90). He wants to take the pragmatist's insights and offer something less fervent and more rationalist. He wants to come to a naturalist position that makes sense of the normative.

His aim is to explore our evaluative practices—the way we justify something we have done and the way we assess an action as right or wrong, an argument as valid or invalid, a belief as well-grounded or ill-grounded. This exploration is to be conducted, he says, by looking at "some typical contexts in which the terms 'valid' and 'correct' appear to be properly, shall I say correctly, employed" (1949: 293). We know how to apply normative terms in our language. It is a skill that one can be better or worse at, just as the one can be better or worse at applying the rules of bridge. He thus calls for "a philosophically oriented behavioristic psychology" (1949: 289) or a "pragmatic empiricism" (1949: 301) that will enlighten us about what it is to follow a rule and be justified in doing so. He calls for the teasing out of when and why we take it that something is to be done because of a rule or from a kind of necessity.

He is also gesturing at Dewey, positively this time, when he says that "science consists exactly in the attempt to develop a system of rule-governed behavior which will adjust the human organism to the environment" (1949: 312). The system of rule-governed behavior we call "science" is what we need to first explore, not just from a descriptive ("this is what we do") perspective, but also from a normative ("is this what we ought to do") perspective. In science, we are always trying to modify and revise our rules. We are also aware that there are alternative rules and hence we cannot say that we know with certainty that we have the right ones in hand. But sometimes we find "rules which even the most startling advances in science have not tempted us to abandon" rules to which we seem to have "no serious alternatives" (1949: 313–14).

We take them to be core, bedrock, or stable. The reader will note that this thought is one that every pragmatist shares.[8]

Sellars sees that he will have to make sense of the idea of *really* getting something right in the face of the fact that the rules of language, science, and logics can change. Here his pragmatist colors are very much on display:

Why one set of rules rather than another? How is the adoption of a set of rules itself to be justified? I should like to be able to say that one justifies the adoption of rules pragmatically, and, indeed, this would be at least a first approximation to the truth. The kinship of my views with the more sophisticated forms of pragmatism is obvious.

[1949: 314–15]

He ends on "a note of caution," expressing with Wittgenstein the view that we cannot really get to the very bottom of our rules. The "real connections" or the necessities are merely "shadows" of our rules and not able to be seen in a straight-on way. We operate in a framework of "living rules" and we cannot grasp them or their justification by somehow stepping outside of that framework to get a more objective view on them.

With all other sophisticated varieties of pragmatism, Sellars brings together the insights of both empiricism and rationalism by looking hard at what it is to have an experience. He is not going to take from the rationalist the idea that "must" or "ought" is explained "in terms of a non-linguistic grasp of a necessary connection between features of reality" (1949: 301). That is the mistake of the rationalist. But he is going to bring some Kant into the empiricist picture. He is well aware of the pragmatist roots of this move: "Here we must pay our respects to John Dewey, who has so clearly seen that the conception of the cognitive given-ness of sense-data is both the last stand and the entering wedge of rationalism" (1949: 304–5). Anything that is given to us by sense involves cognition. This is the insight of rationalism, appreciated most keenly by Peirce and Lewis.

Sellars is interested in the moral "ought" as well as other kinds of necessities. He tackles the issue by staying close to the practice of making evaluative judgments. In his view, the emotivist does not give us explanations that ring true of our attempts to justify our moral obligations. Emotivism is not "faithful to the phenomenology of moral thought and experience" (1949: 294). "To make the ethical 'ought' into even the second cousin of the "hurrah" of a football fan is completely to miss its significance" (1949: 294).

Sellars went on, to great acclaim, to develop the ideas in "Language, Rules and Behavior." The naturalist or empiricist account of rule-regulated behavior he outlined there gets its most famous expression in the 1956 "Empiricism and the Philosophy of Mind," a long article very much like Quine's "Two Dogmas of Empiricism" in a number of respects. It too is considered one of the century's most important articles in philosophy. It too is an attack on logical empiricism. It too had a profound impact on

---

[8] The reader will also note the similarity with Wittgenstein's bedrock and hinge propositions. See Bakhurst and Misak (forthcoming) and Howat (2011).

some of the leading lights of contemporary pragmatism. And it too, in Richard Bernstein's words, "reads like a commentary on a famous series of papers that Peirce published in 1868–69 . . . I do not think that there is an argument presented by Sellars that is not anticipated by Peirce."[9]

Bernstein is right. Sellars's arguments are very similar to those Peirce put forward in "Questions Concerning Faculties Claimed for Man," where he argued that there is no immediate awareness, as "every cognition is determined logically from previous cognitions." I will not take the reader through the comparisons, one by one, but will merely summarize the pragmatist nature of Sellars's position as it appears in "Empiricism and the Philosophy of Mind." He builds on these pragmatist themes for the rest of his career—for instance, in his Locke Lectures of 1966, published as *Science and Metaphysics*.

Sellars turns his back on the metaphor of foundations for knowledge:

Above all, the picture is misleading because of its static character. One seems forced to choose between the picture of an elephant which rests on a tortoise (What supports the tortoise?) and the picture of a great Hegelian serpent of knowledge with its tails in its mouth (Where does it begin?). Neither will do. For empirical knowledge, like its sophisticated extension, science, is rational, not because it has a *foundation* but because it is a self-correcting enterprise which can put *any* claim in jeopardy, though not *all* at once.

[1997 [1956]: 79]

This, of course, is strongly reminiscent of Peirce's idea that science is a self-correcting enterprise that revises beliefs only as they come to be thrown into doubt.

Sellars mounts a sustained and fatal attack on what he calls the "myth of the given." It is an attack on "a piece of professional—epistemological—shoptalk" (1997 [1956]: 13) and the shop is primarily that of the logical empiricists, although he takes on the Cartesian and the Humean as well. The Myth is that "observation 'strictly and properly so-called' is constituted by certain self-authenticating non-verbal episodes, the authority of which is transmitted to verbal and quasi-verbal performances" (1997 [1956]: 77). The Myth is the very strong idea, straight out of the logical empiricist's book, that "epistemic facts can be analyzed without remainder . . . into non-epistemic facts, whether phenomenal or behavioral, public or private" (1997 [1956]: 19). That is, much of Sellars's unhappiness with the idea of the given is due to the penchant of philosophers in the mid part of the twentieth century to think that "the task of the philosopher" is "analysis in the sense of definition—the task, so to speak, of 'making little ones out of big ones.'" This "atomistic philosophy," Sellars says, "is a snare and a delusion" (1997 [1956]: 80).

Sellars explodes the myth of the given. He argues that there are no basic or pure kinds of knowledge—a belief can only be justified by another belief. Moreover, all beliefs have an inescapably conceptual element. To grasp even something as simple

---

[9] Bernstein (2006: 4–5). Brandom (1997) and Rorty (1997: 5) also see the similarity between Sellars's work and these papers of Peirce's.

as a triangle requires the concept of triangle so that one can classify it as such. To become aware of something in the first place is to respond to it by applying a concept. Awareness—all of it—"is a linguistic affair" (1997 [1956]: 63). We have seen this very thought in Peirce, Lewis, and every other pragmatist. Sellars puts it in crisp, new language: one can only be said to have a belief if one is able to locate that belief within the "logical space of reasons." The very meaning of a sentence and the very act of knowing, for Sellars, is its function or role within the game of asking for and accepting reasons—of "justifying and being able to justify what one says" (1997 [1956]: 76).

Because knowledge and understanding are conceptual and inferential, they are open to error. This was a point made very clearly by Peirce in 1868 and with the same clarity by Lewis. Sellars goes on to argue that these practices are fundamentally normative: to have possession of a concept means that one is able to employ it correctly so that one can give or withhold reasons for applying it. The ability to use language lies at the heart of human life and normativity lies at the heart of using language.

While it might seem that the practices of giving and asking for reasons are entirely human, and hence radically subjective, Sellars in fact wants to defend scientific realism against an empiricism that sees human beings as being stuck within the realm of observation, never having knowledge of the external world. He says:

If I reject the framework of traditional empiricism, it is not because I want to say that empirical knowledge has *no* foundation. For to put it this way is to suggest that it is really "empirical knowledge so-called", and to put it in a box with rumours and hoaxes. There is clearly *some* point to the picture of human knowledge as resting on a level of propositions—observation reports— which do not rest on other propositions in the same way as other propositions rest on them.

[1997 [1956]: 78]

Like Lewis and Peirce, Sellars wants to take experience seriously without making it something mythical—something it cannot be. It cannot be pristine or free of our concepts.

For Sellars, truth is correct semantic assertibility. Correct semantic assertibility will look different in different kinds of inquiry—scientific, moral and mathematical. But, nonetheless, statements in all these domains can be correctly asserted. He says:

for a proposition to be true is for it to be assertible, where this means not *capable* of being asserted (which it must be to be a proposition at all) but *correctly* assertible; assertible, that is, in accordance with the relevant semantical rules, and on the basis of such additional, though unspecified, information as these rules may require . . . "True", then, means *semantically* assertible . . . and the varieties of truth correspond to the relevant varieties of semantical rule.

[1992 [1968]:101]

This, of course, is the Peircean account of truth. And like Quine, Sellars thinks that "science is the measure of all things, of what is that it is, and of what is not that it is not" (1997 [1956]: 83). For science is one of our most important and oldest discourses—"the flowering of a dimension of discourse which already exists in what historians call the 'prescientific stage'" (1997 [1956]: 81). Sellars, that is, makes the move from traditional empiricism to full pragmatism or naturalism. The strong logical empiricist does not make that move. For instance, the logical empiricist's anti-realism with respect to theoretical or unobservable entities is based on a picture of knowledge on which all knowledge must be grounded in what can be observed. So the logical empiricist will not say, with the pragmatists, that if the best science tells us that certain unobservable entities exist, then they exist.

In "Philosophy and the Scientific Image of Man," Sellars deals with the problem that science and ordinary perception often seem to be in tension. There is a confrontation between two apparently rival images. The "manifest image" is the common-sense image of ourselves in the world. We arrive at this image from observation, bolstered by age-old philosophical and other emendations. The "scientific image" has as its objects things like atoms and other imperceptible entities in the foreign-seeming worlds of theoretical physics. Sellars takes the aim of philosophy to be to find a way of seeing these two images as not being in tension. He argues that they must be seen as a single "stereoscopic" image of human beings *in the world* (1962: 40). This idea harkens back to Dewey's attempt to see our value-laden selves and our environment as one. But Sellars's account, on which our second-order reflections on our first-order practices fuse together the two perspectives into one coherent picture, does not carry with it the metaphysical baggage that Dewey could not discard.

With the best of the pragmatists, Sellars wants to stay away from the suggestion that the current theories of science are true:

the perspective of the philosopher cannot be limited to that which is methodologically wise for developing science. He must also attempt to envisage the world as pictured from that point of view—one hesitates to call it Completed Science—which is the regulative ideal of the scientific enterprise. As I see it, then, substantive correspondence rules are anticipations of definitions which it would be inappropriate to implement in developing science, but the implementation of which in an ideal state of scientific knowledge would be the achieving of a unified vision of the world in which the methodologically important dualism of observation and theoretical frameworks could be transcended and the world of theory and the world of observation would be one.

[1963: 77–78]

There can be no doubt that Sellars belongs to the pragmatist tradition.

He too, of course, must wrestle with the question of whether we can really make sense of the idea of getting something right if we are to start with our own practices of inquiry and reason-giving. It would be foolhardy to say that Sellars, or any other pragmatist, answers it perfectly. Mark Lance recounts putting a form of the query directly to his teacher in the mid-1980s. He and a fellow student:

laid out for him what we called the distinction between 'right-' and 'left-' Sellarsianism. Right-Sellarsianism took it that norms...are reducible to a pattern of behavior, reinforcement and criticism of behavior...etc. Left-Sellarsianism takes the normative to be irreducible—'norms all the way down'. Simply put, we never got a straight answer as to which view he endorsed: Sellars always insisted that this distinction was too crude and that we needed to read more.

[Lance 2008: 413]

The best kind of pragmatist, I have argued, agrees with Sellars that we can find a position in between these two extremes. We start with what we have and then, with the help of the shock of recalcitrant experience, we reinforce, criticize, and revise where appropriate, until we have a belief that really stands up to evidence and arguments—a belief that would continue to be assertible. But in the next chapter, we shall see how an extreme left–Sellarsianism became the dominant face of pragmatism for the next few decades.

13

Richard Rorty (1931–2007)

13.1 Pragmatism vs. Analytic Philosophy

Although Richard Rorty takes much of his inspiration from Dewey, it is tempting to think of him as contemporary pragmatism's William James. Paul Carus's metaphor for James is just as apt for Rorty. Carus said that James's *Pragmatism* appeared in 1907, "cometlike on our intellectual horizon" (1911: 14). Rorty's *Philosophy and the Mirror of Nature* appeared, also cometlike, in 1979, reviving the fortunes of a certain kind of pragmatism. His narratives, Rorty says, "tend to center around James's version (or, at least, certain selected versions out of the many that James casually tossed off) of the pragmatic theory of truth" (Rorty 1995c: 71). And like James, Rorty often puts forward a moderate pragmatist view, but it is his less moderate, contentious remarks that have stuck in the minds of philosophers, doing harm to pragmatism's reputation. Recall Peirce's howl of outrage that his pragmatism had fallen into "literary clutches." Peirce could see how James's provocative statements were going to damage the more carefully expressed position they shared. He would say the same about Rorty.

Rorty took his MA at the University of Chicago while it still retained the remnants of its great pragmatist tradition. He wrote his thesis on Whitehead's metaphysics, under Charles Hartshorne, one of the editors of Peirce's *Collected Papers*. He went on to do his PhD at Yale, where again his teachers—John Smith and Rulon Wells—knew a lot about pragmatism.[1] While there, he became impressed with Sellars's work. He says that he spent the rest of his career extending it (2010a: 8).

While the young Rorty worked well within the analytic mode, he would later become a great opponent of it. By 1970, his uneasiness with analytic philosophy was emerging (2010a: 18). He felt that it had become the mainstream and was flooding out other genres of philosophy, including the history of philosophy.[2] His attack on analytic philosophy was unusual in that it was launched from within—by a highly respected philosopher with manifest abilities in the methodology he was disparaging. When Rorty left his faculty position at Princeton in 1982, it was in large part because he was disillusioned with professional philosophy. He left for an interdisciplinary position as

---

[1] See Gross (2008: 140ff.) for a full account of Rorty's exposure to pragmatism as a student.
[2] See Gross (2008: 192–98).

Professor of Humanities at the University of Virginia and then went to Stanford in 1998 to be Professor of Comparative Literature.

The attack was unusual also in that his antidote to what he saw as the poison of analytic philosophy was a pragmatism that took its lead from James and Dewey. We have seen that, up until that point, the analytic pragmatism of Lewis, Goodman, White, Quine, and Sellars had become dominant. Rorty veered from the direction the pragmatist tradition was taking and returned pragmatism to the path that had been cleared by James and Dewey. Rorty thinks that pragmatism, as a movement, contains "ambiguities" that have made it "seem a very muddled movement indeed—neither hard enough for the positivist nor soft enough for the aesthetes" (1991: 64). It became "crushed" between these positions after Dewey's death, and Rorty takes his job to be to extricate it. Though he lauds the efforts of Sidney Hook to keep Deweyan philosophy alive, it is telling that he finds Hook's appeal to scientific method mistaken. In Rorty's view, Hook is too close to Quine, who argues that there is no line between science and philosophy and hence science can replace philosophy. As Rorty brings his preferred version of pragmatism into the spotlight, those who hold science in high esteem recede into the background. In his view, it is not clear "why natural science, rather than the arts, or politics, or religion, should take over the area left vacant" by philosophy (1979: 171).[3] But, while we have seen that this complaint about Quinean holism—that it leaves no room for inquiry apart from science and logic—is warranted, we have also seen that Lewis, White, Goodman, and Sellars were putting forward pragmatist positions that did not privilege science.

The very categories of analytic versus Continental philosophy, over the last decades, have been disintegrating. In Russell's day, "analysis" had a precise meaning. One term was to be reduced by another set of terms, rendered clear without residue. In Sellars's memorable words, the big are made small. That characterization of analytic philosophy had already started to dim by the time Rorty was writing. It is no longer clear just what is meant by the label, hence my weak characterization of analytic philosophy as simply a rigorous way of thinking about philosophical problems. Nonetheless, the 1960s and 1970s saw the emergence of a movement of "pluralists"—philosophers who wanted to see more diversity in the kinds of papers presented at the American Philosophical Association meetings and the kind of appointments made in top departments. In 1979, Rorty was president of the Eastern APA and had to deal with an unprecedented alternative nomination for his successor from the floor. The pluralists had packed the business meeting and nominated John Smith, a Yale scholar of American pragmatism and one of Rorty's old teachers. There were questions about the legitimacy of the maneuver and about procedural irregularities. In the end, Rorty declared the election valid and became very publically identified with the challenge to the dominance of

---

[3] Rorty (1979: 192) attempts to bring Quine into the embrace of his own view. Quine rejects the invitation (Føllesdal and Quine 2008: 149).

mainstream methods. The episode made the *New York Times*.[4] Its reverberations are still felt in some quarters of philosophy today.

To further complicate matters, Rorty was fighting not just against analytic philosophy, but against philosophy in general. In his view, philosophy cannot answer important age-old questions. What it does is dissolve philosophical problems. We have seen some version of this theme run through the work of all the pragmatists. But Rorty puts the idea in an especially sharp way. Explicitly joining forces with Wittgenstein,[5] he wants to do away with the very enterprise that he and Wittgenstein so successfully engaged in (2010a: 14f.). Philosophy is merely a kind of "therapy." It is more like poetry than science. Philosophy must replace the idea of knowledge with the idea of hope and in doing so the value of philosophy is reduced almost to a vanishing point. Notice also the similarity with logical empiricism here—especially interesting given that logical empiricism was supposed to be the height of science-obsessed analytic excess.

Rorty's Presidential Address at that contentious APA was titled "Pragmatism, Relativism and Irrationalism." In it, he calls on philosophers to revisit Dewey and James. He notes that the pragmatists are acknowledged by analytic philosophers for making "various holistic corrections of the atomistic doctrines of the early logical empiricists" (1982: 160). But he argues that what is really going on in Dewey and James is a wholesale rejection of the aims of analytic philosophy, not an attempt at making it better. Philosophy is to abandon the quest for certainty, the attempt at grounding our beliefs, and the very ideas of truth and objectivity. Rorty reconnects Dewey's linkage of pragmatism with culture and politics and tries to unhook pragmatism from epistemology.

Smith's leadership of the APA and Rorty's call for the abandonment of philosophy did not do much for the status of pragmatism in America. Many of Rorty's followers still believe that to have been his student or to work on pragmatist topics is to put oneself at risk of failure in the academic job market. In the preface to his volume in the *Library of Living Philosophers*, which Rorty saw to completion in the final days of his life, Randy Auxier says: "Rorty prudently exiled himself from professional philosophy so as not to damage the careers of those who wanted to study with him" (2010: xxix). Note, though, that Rorty nonetheless proceeded to single-handedly bring into being a renaissance for a certain kind of pragmatism and to become one of the best-known philosophers in the world. Some of his students, such as Robert Brandom and Michael Williams, have gone on to enormous philosophical success.

Rorty's brand of pragmatism acknowledges that Quine, Sellars, and Davidson ought to be seen as pragmatists (1979: 7). But he wants to extend those lines of thought away from what he takes to be analytic philosophy. He wants to take Quine's holism and Sellars's attack on the given in James's direction: "I argue that when extended in

---

[4] Dec. 30, 1979. See Gross (2008: 219–27) for a blow-by-blow account.
[5] The part of Wittgenstein that Rorty is in contact with here is the quietest Wittgenstein. See Rorty (1989), especially Ch. 1.

a certain way they let us see truth as, in James' phrase, 'what is better for us to believe,' rather than as 'the accurate representation of reality'" (1979: 10). His interpretation of Sellars, for instance, has Sellars arguing that "knowledge is inseparable from a social practice—the practice of justifying one's assertions to one's fellow-humans" (1997: 4). We shall see that where Rorty goes wrong is in not taking seriously enough what those practices in fact include.

13.2 Rorty's Revolutionary Pragmatism

Rorty says that his "philosophical heroes" are Wittgenstein, Heidegger, and Dewey. Like Dewey and Wittgenstein, at least, Rorty argues that we should not attempt to solve the traditional problems of philosophy; we should attempt, rather, to "get over them" in Dewey's words (*MW* 4: 14; 1909). One of traditional philosophy's doomed-to-fail projects is trying to provide foundations for knowledge. Here he is on the same page as all the pragmatists. But his reading of Dewey on this matter has reinforced a certain kind of Dewey scholarship and marks Rorty off from many of his other pragmatist predecessors. He takes the following to be one of Dewey's crucial insights: "In [Dewey's] ideal society, culture is no longer dominated by the ideal of objective cognition but by that of aesthetic enhancement" (1979: 13). In his "Intellectual Autobiography" for the *Library of Living Philosophers* volume, Rorty takes a final opportunity to refine that assessment of Dewey: Dewey focuses us on the ideal of "social cooperation in public life and of aesthetic enhancement in private life" (2010a: 19). The insight he takes from Dewey is the double-barreled idea that objectivity is intersubjective agreement—it is "what is needed to carry out cooperative social projects"—and aesthetic enhancement is "a matter of idiosyncratic self-creation" (2010a: 20). We shall see that the problems that haunted Dewey's position continue to haunt it as expressed by his successor. To wit: how can we speak to questions such as "what social projects are odious?" and "what kind of self created selves are better and what kind are worse?"

Rorty is also a Deweyan in his passion for democracy and in his whole meliorism. He takes our task to be to improve the situation in which we find ourselves—not simply "cognitively improve" (1991: 175–96). But he pulls away from Dewey in that he asserts that there is no link between democracy and pragmatism. One can be a good pragmatist and also a good Nazi (1990: 636–37; 1999: 15; 2000d: 130). Robert Westbrook points out that Rorty's reading of Dewey underplays the fact that Dewey thought that democracy and community were *the* path to human self-realization (Westbrook 1991: 54). Rorty detects a whiff of foundationalism in that Deweyan view and maintains that recognizing anything as "privileged foundations" for knowledge also directs us to make them "the foundations of culture," forcing a kind of homogeneity upon us (1979: 163). J. B. Schneewind puts Rorty's position as follows: any attempt to find foundations in philosophy stand "in the way of progress" (2010: 489). That includes the attempt to privilege democracy.

RICHARD RORTY (1931–2007) 229

Rorty is not a fan of Peirce's, opining that Peirce's "contribution to pragmatism was merely to have given it a name, and to have stimulated James" (1982: 61). He does not like "what Peirce called 'the opinion that is fated to be agreed to by all who investigate.'" He became convinced that "the idea of such a destined terminus—the idea that rational inquirers must necessarily converge to a common opinion—was just one more attempt to escape from time into eternity" (2010a: 3). He compares Sellars with Peirce:

That mixture of logic-worship, erudition, and romance was reminiscent of Peirce, with whose writings I had spent a lot of time, hoping to discover the nonexistent secret of his nonexistent "System" . . . Sellars and Peirce are alike in the diversity and richness of their talents, as well as in the cryptic style in which they wrote. But Sellars, unlike Peirce, preached a coherent set of doctrines.

[2010a: 8]

Peirce, Rorty thinks, was a "system builder" and Sellars "the debunking sort" (2010a: 11). Rorty is very clear that he wants to be the latter, not the former.

It is certainly true that Peirce wanted a coherent system and yet was all over the map—partly because he wrote so little in the way of finished material and experimented so much with many drafts of his ideas. But we have seen that there is a striking similarity between his position and Sellars'. We have also seen that Peirce does not think that rational inquirers must necessarily converge. He holds, rather, that for any given question we are inquiring into, we must hope or assume that there would be an answer on which we would converge.

With Rorty, the idea of pragmatism as a kind of anti-representationalism grows in strength. It can be seen as a radical following-through of the Darwinian idea that so occupied Wright and Dewey. Humans do not represent the world. They cope with it.[6] We have seen some version of this thought run through the whole of American pragmatism. The difference between Rorty and his predecessors is that Rorty thinks that his predecessors focus too much on experience. "Experience," he thinks, is a term we should give up. We should replace it with "discourse." We should "Forget, for the moment, about the external world, as well as about that dubious interface between self and world called 'perceptual experience'" (1991: 93). Rorty is more radical than James and Dewey at their most radical.

13.3 Truth and Our Practices

Like all pragmatists, Rorty argues that our concept of truth cannot outrun our practices: "there is nothing deep down inside us except what we have put there ourselves, no criterion that we have not created in the course of creating a practice, no standard of rationality that is not an appeal to such a criterion, no rigorous argumentation that is not obedience to our own conventions" (1982: xlii). We must

---

[6] See Bacon (2012) for this way of understanding pragmatism.

cease thinking of the mind as a great mirror that reflects and represents the world and turn, rather, to our practices to get leverage on our concept of truth.

When Rorty looks at the practices of first-order inquiry or our current and ongoing "conversations" in which we must form our beliefs, make our decisions, and live our lives, he finds that the notions of truth and objectivity are irrelevant. If one takes the ideas of truth and objectivity in their strongest senses, Rorty is still in line with every other pragmatist. Yearning for an "impossible, indefinable, sublime" thing comes at the price of "irrelevance to practice" (2000a: 2). Inquirers simply cannot aim at that sort of truth and objectivity.

But Rorty then takes a step beyond all his predecessors, except perhaps Schiller. Inquirers aim not at truth, but at solidarity. In his most extreme moods, he asserts that "truth" and "objectivity" are merely labels for what our peers will let us get away with saying (1979: 176). He would like to see a "post-philosophical culture" in which there are no appeals to authority of *any* kind, including appeals to truth and rationality (1982: xlii; 1995c: 71). Truth is "not the sort of thing one should expect to have an interesting philosophical theory about" (1982: xiii). He would like us to "substitute the idea of 'unforced agreement' for that of 'objectivity'" in every domain of inquiry—science as well as morals and politics (1991: 36–38). It is pretty clear that if Paul Carus were alive today, he would argue that Rorty is James's successor in the project of putting truth on trial.

If the pragmatist resists the Peircean move to identify something we can aspire to—something that goes beyond mere unforced agreement—then a set of objections come to the fore. They have been put sharply to Rorty. He really is a relativist, holding that one belief is no better than another, and that we must "treat the epistemic standards of any and every epistemic community as on a par" (Haack 1995: 136). He leaves us with no non-local way of adjudicating claims and no way of making sense of the idea that we might improve our beliefs. This is not only an unsatisfactory view, but it is incompatible with Rorty's commitment to his own set of beliefs and with his practice of arguing or giving reasons for them. One of Rorty's responses to this clutch of objections is to say that he does not have to treat the epistemic standard of every community as on a par: "I prize communities which share more background beliefs with me above those which share fewer" (1995d: 153). He thinks that there is nothing incoherent about asserting that your community has it right, for all "right" amounts to is what your community agrees upon.

I have argued (Misak 2000: 12ff.) that this kind of comeback puts Rorty in a very difficult position, giving him nothing to say against the likes of Carl Schmitt, the authoritarian philosopher of law who jumped on the Nazi bandwagon. Schmitt, like Rorty, held that there is no truth or rationality in politics. He went on to argue that the aim is to get substantive homogeneity in a population and win out over weaker groups. We know what this view's horrific practical implications are. The epistemological implication is that a democrat or liberal like Rorty has an impossible time in giving us—and himself—reasons for opting for his view rather than his fascist opponent's view. Once you abandon aiming at truth—once you abandon aiming at something that goes beyond the standards of your own community—then you give up the wherewithal to argue against the might-is-right view.[7] This is what is wrong with taking the contingency of historical circumstance to entail the contingency of standards. While all pragmatists see that standards are human standards, not all of them think that this means that there are no facts about the matter at hand, whether that matter be one of science or morals.

Rorty's second response to the charge of relativism aligns him even more closely with James and Dewey—with their claim that pragmatism is a dissolver of philosophical debates.[8] Rorty says that once we drop the vocabulary of truth, reason, and objectivity, we shall see that both relativism and its opposites (realism, absolutism, etc.) are spurious doctrines. The very idea of a claim's being relative or having only relative validity makes sense only if we have something against which to contrast it— something like absolute validity (1989: 47). Rorty is not putting forward a theory of truth, hence he is not putting forward a relativist theory of truth (1991: 24; 1989: 53).

But the dangers do not disappear so easily. Calling for a dissolution of a dualism, such as that between relativism and absolutism, does not guarantee that one succeeds in escaping the pitfalls of one or the other of the two positions. And it does not guarantee that one will not end up shuttling between the two disliked positions, depending on the particular critique to which one is responding. That is, after the call for the abandonment of a way of looking at things, one must replace the problematic mode of thinking with a new way that really does undercut the problems endemic in the old way of seeing the issue. One must replace the old dichotomy of "objective standards or no standards at all" with low-profile, non-absolutist conceptions of truth and objectivity which can guide us in our inquiries and deliberations. The pragmatist must replace the old dichotomy with distinctly pragmatist accounts of truth, objectivity, and normativity.

One way of getting at the heart of the debate between the Peirce/Lewis/Sellars position and the James/Rorty position is to ask what happens when we interrogate our practices. The fundamental pragmatist tenet is that we must illuminate our philosophical concepts by showing what their role is in our practices. We must come to our concept of truth, for instance, without engaging in spurious metaphysics—we must stay with the natural as opposed to the supernatural. This much, all pragmatists can agree upon. But we are immediately presented with a fork in the road. We have seen that the Peircean position is that when we examine our practices, we find the

---

[7] I have also argued that the pragmatist linkage of truth with inquiry justifies democratic deliberation. The right answers to our political question are not the answers given by a sovereign, or by a deity, or by some canon of Reason, but rather, the right answers are those that we (the people) would arrive at were we (the people) to debate, deliberate, and inquire in an open fashion (Misak 2000). What we have here is a kind of deliberative democracy, of the sort expressly envisioned by Dewey, implicit in Peirce, and hinted at by James. See Talisse (2007) for a contemporary expression of this position.

[8] He explicitly invokes James as a fellow traveler here: (1991: 128).

following. We want to settle belief, but we find that it is not so easy to really settle belief. If a belief is determined by "circumstances extraneous to the facts," doubt will be triggered. We will not be satisfied by beliefs that are produced by a method that does not take experience seriously. As Jeffrey Stout puts the point today: "getting something right . . . turns out to be among the human interests that need to be taken into account in an acceptably anthropocentric conception of inquiry as a social practice."[9] The norms of truth and rightness are interwoven throughout our practices of assertion, belief, and inquiry.

Rorty, on the other hand, denies that truth plays a part in our practices. Hilary Putnam has taken him to task on precisely this issue:

> Let us recognize that one of our fundamental self-conceptualizations, one of our fundamental "self-descriptions," in Rorty's phrase, is that we are *thinkers* and that *as* thinkers we are committed to their being *some* kind of truth, some kind of correctness which is substantial.
>
> [Putnam 1983b: 246]

Huw Price puts a similar objection to Rorty. He argues that if we start with the pragmatist thought that the best way to inquire about a concept is to examine its function in human discourse, we shall find that when you examine practice, truth is not just solidarity or what this or that community happens to find best to believe. When we examine practice, we in fact find that the goal of inquiry is truth as we have always thought of it—something stable and independent of what this or that person or community might think. The pragmatist is committed to keeping philosophical concepts tied to our practices. But Rorty's brand of pragmatism pulls against the commitments we actually have in dialogue, argumentation, and inquiry. Pragmatists of Rorty's sort "have often ignored the resources of their own theoretical standpoint— even, in a sense, their own principles—in seeking to equate truth with something like warranted assertibility" (Price 2011: 16).

Rorty tries to answer some of the objections to his position by saying that he does indeed have a conception of truth: truth is disquotation.[10] He thinks the "greatest of my many intellectual debts to Donald Davidson is my realization that no one should even try to specify the nature of truth" (1991: 3). The disquotational schema says it all. In turn, Rorty has influenced Brandom and Williams in the direction of the disquotational theory. Here is Williams: "[W]hen we have pointed to certain features of the truth predicate (notably its 'disquotational' feature) and explained why it is useful to have a predicate like this (e.g. as a device for asserting infinite conjunctions), we have said just about everything there is to be said about truth" (1988: 424).

---

[9] Stout (2007: 18). Frank Ramsey also held that the pragmatist need not take "*p* is true" to be identified with "*p* is useful." For the belief *p* will be useful *only if p*. See his "Facts and Propositions."

[10] Rorty develops one version of truth as disquotation in his "Pragmatism, Davidson, and Truth," and later refines that version in response to Davidson's repudiation of Rorty's interpretation of his account of truth. See Rorty (1986; 1995: 281–87).

But the questions articulated above about the role of truth in our practices can also be put to Rorty with respect to his move to disquotationalism. The fact that no speaker would deny instances of the disquotational schema does not entail that truth is merely disquotation. It is clear that there is more to our practice of using "is true" than that enabled by the disquotational schema. While it is right that no competent speaker would deny that "'p' is true if true if and only p," disquotational truth seems too thin to play a proper role in an adequate theory of the general features of assertion, commitment, and judgment. As Price puts it, pragmatists start not by asking what the analytic definition of truth is, but rather, why speakers have the notion of truth that they have (2011: 48). They should see, he thinks, that our notion of truth does not line up neatly with warranted assertibility, nor with disquotation. We need a stronger notion of truth than is provided by either of those notions (2011: 16). The concept of truth engages with our practices in many ways. One of those ways is that speakers assent to "'p is true' if and only if p." But the pragmatist had best not make heavy weather out of this fact. It is, in Peirce's terminology, a nominal definition, of limited use. It is not the most interesting or illuminating thing that we might say of truth, but say it we can. We need to mine the insight that truth is connected to assertion to find some gems about how truth is then related to evidence, reasons, and inquiry. The classical deflationist, such as Paul Horwich (1990), need not engage in the project to put some air back in the concept of truth for he may not be focused on the idea that truth is bound up with our practices. But the adoption of a thin disquotation-only account of truth is a disaster for the pragmatist, who starts out with a commitment to be true to practice.

Rorty disputes this claim. He says that it is the Peircean pragmatist who owes him an account of "how the behavior of Peircean inquirers differs from that of radical deflationists like myself" (2010b: 44). Fair enough. One behavioral difference, I suggest, would be an enhanced willingness to seek out and take seriously new evidence and argument. The Peircean inquirer aims at getting beliefs that *would* stand up to whatever evidence and argument could come their way, hence it is only rational to expose beliefs to all the available evidence and argument to see if they meet interim bar.

Price also offers an account of these behavioral differences—one that turns on a thought experiment. He asks us to imagine a community that uses language primarily for expressing preferences in restaurants—a community of speakers that obeys only the weaker norms of subjective assertibility (sincerity) and personal warranted assertibility (justification). A person who meets both of these norms may be said to have done as much as possible, by her own current lights, to ensure that her assertion is in good order. These speakers can criticize each other for being insincere or for making personally unjustified statements, but not for failing to tell the truth. They have merely opinionated assertions (MOAs). "Mo'ans" are like dedicated lunchers whose language atrophies to the bare essentials. They might criticize expressed preferences on the ground that they were not sincere or on the ground that they were not well-founded by the speaker's own lights. Mo'ans, that is, use linguistic utterances to express their beliefs, preferences, and desires. They differ from us in that they do not take disagreement to indicate that one or the other speaker is at fault or mistaken. A Mo'an cannot be criticized for, as we would put it, getting things wrong, even when he is not talking about what he would like to eat, but about whether there is E. coli in the petri dish or whether there is milk in the refrigerator.

We can now see what the norm of truth adds to our practice. As Price puts it, in the Mo'ans' practice we cannot find dialogue and argumentation as we know them. We cannot find the *engagement* of individual opinions, as opposed to the mere roll call of individual opinions. The norm of truth, that is, plays an essential role in assertion and dialogue. To do without truth is to silence our conversations—both our conversations with others and our own internal conversations. For the very essence of the norm of truth is to give disagreement its immediate normative character. It is to make disagreement matter. Without the grit provided by the concept of truth, the wheels of argument do not engage; disagreements slide past one another.

We have seen that mere warranted assertibility and mere disquotation do not do justice to our practices. But there is an additional problem with Rorty's adoption of disquotation—one that arises because he adopts a particular brand of pragmatism. We saw that Quine alludes to the correspondence thought which he takes to be implicit in the disquotational schema—to the idea that truth transcends "man's faltering approximations." Those pragmatists who want their notion of truth to reach for something or those pragmatists who employ a notion of experience that has the world impinging on our attempts to get it right can accept the disquotationalist idea. But this move is not available to Rorty, who is very clear that nothing transcends man's faltering approximations and that experience is not one of his words. The stumbling block for Rorty is that he wants to say that truth is nothing more than disquotation but he fails to see that the very idea of disquotation is connected to the idea of aiming at getting things right. John McDowell nails the point in his *Mind and World*:

Amazingly enough, Rorty seems to think it is merely routine to separate what we want to think of as norms of inquiry from the straightforward notion of getting things right that is connected with the notion of disquotability . . . [H]e says, without ceremony, that it "seems paradoxical" to suggest that "There are rocks" is implied by "At the ideal end of inquiry, we shall be justified in asserting that there are rocks," because "there seems no obvious reason why the progress of the language-game we are playing should have anything in particular to do with the way the rest of the world is." But that is an extraordinary thing to say. It is the whole point of the idea of norms of inquiry that following them ought to improve our chances of being right about "the way the rest of the world is."

[1996: 150–51]

Rorty cannot put forward a radically subjectivist epistemology and then unproblematically import the disquotationalist notion of truth. The two cannot live together in his philosophical household. If the pragmatist is going to adopt the notion of disquotation, he needs to be the kind of pragmatist who thinks that we can make sense of a right or true belief that goes beyond what this or that believer or community might think.

The disquotational schema is everywhere in truth theory these days and every pragmatist will have to take a stand on it. They can adopt it as a nominal definition that alludes to the notion of rightness and leaves room to say more about the function of truth. Or they can take the route that would have us say nothing more about truth than disquotation and then try to do what may be the impossible: to square that view with all the other things that, as pragmatists, they want to say about assertion, inquiry, and the growth of knowledge.

13.4 Rorty's Less Revolutionary Pragmatism

Another way Rorty reminds one of James is that they both tend to present to the reader their most provocative, side—as Santayana said of James, "a worst in which there is always a good side" (2009 [1920]: 60). But when under the fire of criticism, both bring their good side to light. Rorty, for instance, admits that he has sometimes made the mistake of going "from criticism of attempts to define truth as accurate representation of the intrinsic nature of reality to a denial that true statements get things right" (2000c: 374). He says, in these less revolutionary moods, that "true" does name a word–world relationship—just not one that is causal and justificatory.

Rorty also sometimes distances himself from his extreme idea that truth is linked to "whatever my community thinks is right." The relationship between truth and our community, rather, must be understood in terms of inquirers constantly trying to enlarge the community. "For pragmatists, the desire for objectivity is not to escape the limits of one's community, but simply the desire for as much intersubjective agreement as possible, the desire to extend the reference of 'us' as far as we can" (1991: 23). We need to "expand the frontiers of inquiry" (2000b: 60). The ideas of truth and objectivity are not to be replaced with the idea of solidarity or agreement in our local community. They are to be replaced with something like the idea of agreement amongst the enlarged community of inquirers, extending into the future. In these moods, Rorty asserts that we need to retain the "cautionary" use of "is true," which marks the contrast between justification and truth (2000a: 4). His "pragmatist view of the truth-justification distinction" is that we need to distinguish between "old audiences and new audiences"; we need to be able to say that "people in different circumstances—people facing future audiences—may not be able to justify the belief which we have triumphantly justified to all the audiences we have encountered" (2000a: 4). The gap between justification and truth is "the gap between the actual good and the possible better. From a pragmatist point of view, to say that what is rational for us now to believe may not be *true*, is simply to say that somebody may come up with a better idea" (1991: 23).

This is getting extraordinarily close to Peirce's view. But there are two residual differences between this better version of Rorty and Peirce. First, Rorty wants to extend the reference of "us" into the future—he wants to have truth *be agreement* not here and now but *agreement* as the conversation continues. Peirce, on the other hand, is concerned with beliefs withstanding criticism and the force of experience in the future and *hence* commanding agreement. Second, Rorty thinks that "once one has explicated the distinction between justification and truth by that between present and future justifiability, there is little more to be said" (2000a: 5). Peirce would respond that there is certainly a lot less to be said than the transcendental or representationalist truth theorist has wanted to say. But in making the justification–truth distinction, one is already saying quite a lot. One is already committing oneself to a substantial notion of truth.

The best way to see the problem with even Rorty's less revolutionary view is to notice a tension in it. He is quite clear that he thinks he can hold on to both the thought that "true" is a term that we "can apply to all the assertions we feel justified in making, or feel others are justified in making" (2000b: 57) and to the justification–truth distinction. But to hold onto "both an endorsing and a cautionary use" of "true" is to import a tension into one's concept of truth: *p* is true (I endorse it), but "of course somebody someday (maybe we ourselves, today) may come up with something (new evidence, a better explanatory hypothesis, etc.) showing that that assertion was not true" (2000b: 57). The endorsing use and the cautionary use pull against each other. They require us to think, in one thought, that *p is* true, but it might be shown to be false.

The point is that in making the justification–truth distinction, one is committed to a thought Rorty is loathe to accept. There is something at which we *aim* that goes beyond what seems right to us here and now. The Peircean pragmatist calls that the truth. The Rortyian pragmatist insists that we do not aim at truth, as we could never realize we had finally reached it (1995a: 298). The Peircean view, Rorty thinks, requires one to tacitly make an "utterly unjustified empirical prediction" every time one acquires a belief—one has to predict what "would happen in a potentially infinite number of justificatory contexts before a potentially infinitely diverse set of audiences" (2000b: 56). But that is an infelicitous way of stating the required prediction. Someone who asserts *p* needs to predict that her assertion would stand up to the evidence and argument now and to subsequent evidence and argument. If that assumption is defeated in the future, then despite all the evidence currently in its favor and despite the fact that it may have been rational for her to believe it given the evidence that was available to her, the belief in fact is false. A believer both accepts this possibility and bets that it will not come about.

If truth is as the Peircean pragmatist sees it—as something that is linked to (but does not altogether transcend) justified belief, then we can indeed make sense of aiming at the truth. The idea is to wrench our gaze from the correspondence view and see truth as indefeasible belief. We aim at getting a belief that goes beyond our local justification of it; we aim at getting a belief that always would stand up to the rigors of inquiry; we aim at a belief that would never lead to disappointment. On the Peircean pragmatist view, truth is within our reach (it is the best that *we* could do) but nonetheless, it is something that is always to be aspired to (we can never be sure we have it).

At the very end of his life, Rorty makes clear that he regrets some of his stronger pronouncements. Truth and objectivity are *not* what our peers will let us get away with saying. "That was incautious and misleading hyperbole" (2010b: 45). He states that he does not want to abandon the concept of truth, for precisely the pragmatist reasons Price and I have pressed upon him: "grasping a concept is knowing how to use a word, and . . . 'true' is a very useful word" (2010b: 44). But it is interesting and frustrating that in the same volume (the *Library of Living Philosophers* volume), we find him continuing to argue that the only project for philosophy is to "construct narratives" that have a "therapeutic function" (2010a: 4).

Also in that volume, Rorty asserts that where he would like pragmatism to go is the way of his student Robert Brandom (2010b: 45). Brandom's "semantic inferentialism" holds that words have no meaning in isolation—meaning is made by the inferential connections we make amongst beliefs. A concept is given meaning in the context of human practices and its meaning will evolve as it will. Norms arise within the practice or game of giving and asking for reasons, and in accepting reasons players bind themselves to standards that go beyond their individual commitments. Speakers, that is, take themselves to be subject to norms when they engage in reasoning. Brandom's project is the Sellarsian one of explaining what it is for us to think of ourselves, and to treat others, as normative beings capable of undertaking commitments and accepting responsibility for them.[11] There is much to recommend this position and the attentive reader will hear resonances with Peirce's view that meaning partially resides in the commitments we incur when we believe or assert. This is one of the major routes that pragmatism has taken, post-Rorty.

Rorty has made a perhaps indelible mark on the history of pragmatism. Many scholars outside of philosophy departments (and many within them) were persuaded by his revolutionary position and hence a new wave of Jamesian and Deweyan pragmatists came on to the scene. They were not well received by what they thought of as the dominant analytic hegemony in philosophy. But they made Rorty's brand of pragmatism prominent and dominant. Indeed, Menand's very characterization of pragmatism in his philosophically problematic but otherwise splendid *The Metaphysical Club* is, anachronistically, precisely Rorty's version.

Rorty's revolutionary position has also provided a sharp contrast against which a different kind of pragmatism can fruitfully set itself. Pragmatists who think that (low-profile, non-absolutist) concepts of truth and objectivity are central to inquiry have a new way of delineating the context for their view—they can set themselves against both the absolutist "mirror of nature" views of truth and objectivity and also against the Rortyian revolutionary pragmatist view. The first challenge (and opportunity) faced by this kind of pragmatist is to wrest the label "pragmatism" from Rorty.

---

[11] See Brandom (1994) and (2000).

14

Hilary Putnam (1926–)

14.1 Pragmatist Pedigree

Hilary Putnam took his undergraduate degree from the University of Pennsylvania. He tells us that he studied under "C. West Churchman, who taught a version of pragmatism informed by a substantial knowledge of and interest in the logic of statistical testing," "with Sidney Morgenbesser, who was himself still a graduate student," and Morton White, who taught "logic and American philosophy" (1994 [1991b]: 99). He then did a year of graduate study at Harvard, where he "came under the influence" of Quine, before moving in 1949 to do a PhD at UCLA with Hans Reichenbach. He taught at Harvard from 1965 and is the last member of the Harvard pragmatist dynasty.

His work is exceptionally wide-ranging and on occasion subject to position swings. In his early work, he had written important papers in philosophy of science, metaphysics, and philosophy of mathematics. There was not much in that material to signal what would by 1980 be a major shift towards pragmatism. Since then, the version of pragmatism he has put forward has moved across the landscape of Peirce, Dewey, and now James, always with Putnam's fine philosophical ability adding modern elements to the views of his predecessors.

In his 1976 Presidential address to the American Philosophical Association, Putnam drew what was to become a famous distinction between metaphysical realism and internal realism, arguing against the former and for the latter. Internal realism is a kind of Peircean pragmatism. It holds that truth is what would be ideally rational to believe. This view flourishes in Putnam's work in the 1980s. But he is always wary of identifying his position with Peirce's because he, like Quine, mistakenly takes Peirce's position to be that truth can be "defined as what inquiry would converge to in the long run" or that there will be an ideal, utopian, situation in which all truths are simultaneously known (1994b: 152; 1990: viii).

In the mid-1990s, his view takes a more Deweyan turn, in which he calls for a renewal of philosophy. He drops the idea of idealized rational assertibility and his focus shifts more intensely to ethics and on how pragmatism and democracy are connected. His account of the scientific enterprise also starts to follow Deweyan lines, with an emphasis on a community of inquirers trying to improve their cognitive position (1994b: 172). More recently, he has become interested in the Jamesian topic of how religion fits into our world-view, for instance in his 2008 *Jewish Philosophy as a Guide to Life* and in the 1997 "God and the Philosophers." He holds that we can bring religious answers into play in ethics:

> Any "existential commitment," religious or secular, that rejects or flouts [pragmatic] principles flies in the face of what I, for one, am willing to call reason. Conversely, any serious commitment that accepts these principles and lives up to them is one that should have no conflicts with autonomous moral judgment.
>
> [1997: 183]

Hence: "There is nothing wrong with the choice of the person who chooses to stay within a traditional way and to try to make it as good and as just and as fulfilling as possible—as long as he or she does not try to force that way on everyone else" (1994 [1992]: 194).

14.2 Truth and Metaphysics

As David Macarthur puts it, Putnam, once he becomes a pragmatist, rejects the foundationalist and essentialist pretensions of traditional metaphysics (2008: 41). In step with his pragmatist predecessors, he is suspicious of metaphysics, which he thinks is for the most part a "fantasy" (Putnam 1999: 6). He wants naturalized or human concepts of truth and reality—ones that retain a place for value. Putnam sees that at the heart of pragmatism lie four claims: fallibilism, anti-skepticism, the breaking down of the dichotomy of fact and value, and the idea that practice is primary in philosophy (1994b: 152). He subscribes to all four and finds in them the keys to the central problem of epistemology. How can we both acknowledge our inability to see things as they Really Are, while still maintaining that there is a right and wrong in belief and action? His steady aim, throughout all his attempts to work out what he thinks about truth and objectivity, is to keep human beings at the center, but not go so far as Rorty's "nihilism." The very titles of his papers and books make that clear—for instance, *Reason, Truth and History*, "Realism without Absolutes", and *Realism with a Human Face*. Indeed, Putnam declines Rorty's persistent invitations to enrol him into his own program. He says that he, unlike Rorty, is a "commonsense" realist. "Mountains and stars are not created by language and thought and are not parts of language and thought, and yet can be described by language and thought" (1997 [1993]: 303). He thinks that Rorty has made an illicit move "from a conclusion about the unintelligibility of metaphysical realism (we cannot have a guarantee—of a sort that doesn't even make sense!—that our words represent things outside of themselves) to a skepticism about the possibility of representation *tout court*" (1997 [1993]: 300).

Putnam's pragmatist magnum opus is his 1981 *Reason, Truth and History*. In the early chapters, he presents what he then took to be a knock-down model-theoretic argument against metaphysical realism. That kind of realism, he argues, cannot get off the ground because there are an infinite number of interpretations of any given sign that preserve truth-value. There is no way for the metaphysical realist to non-arbitrarily specify which relation is the reference relation. This challenges the correspondence theorist's claim that one and only one fact corresponds to a proposition.

He also argues, mining a more pragmatist vein, that all of our experiential inputs into knowledge are conceptually contaminated. There aren't any inputs that are not themselves shaped by our concepts. We cannot stand outside of our own perspective to look at the world in the way it "really is." Our world, he says, is a human world, and is ultimately dependent on our human judgments of likeness and difference (1981: 102). He wants to make the "radical claim that what *counts* as the real world depends on our values" for we judge the real world as that which is true and relevant—and relevance presupposes a wide set of interests and values (1981: 137). He concludes that the human world (what we count as the world) is determined partly by our values. Rationality is also value-laden, since meta-science, like science itself, evolves—at different times, different people may have different conceptions of what it is to be rational. Rationality, Putnam says, is the ability to determine relevant questions and warranted answers and hence the "theory of truth presupposes theory of rationality which in turn presupposes our theory of the good" (1981: 215).

Putnam sees the implications that some have drawn from this sort of internalist thesis as disturbing, and he wants to avoid them. If we "make the world," it may seem that that truth is then relative and there are no facts to get right or wrong. Truth would be only accuracy from a certain perspective or within a cultural paradigm. Putnam argues that such a thesis is self-refuting, for a relativist cannot claim that relativism is correct if he at the same time holds that all claims are relative—that we cannot evaluate any as being better than others. This kind of epistemological anarchy, favored by Rorty, destroys itself (1981: 113f.):

[It] is not so much a position as the illusion or mirage of a position; in this respect it resembles solipsism, which looks like a possible (if unbelievable) position from a distance, but which disappears into thin air when closely examined. Indeed, Rorty's view is just solipsism with a "we" instead of an "I".

[1990: ix]

Putnam instead opts for a pragmatist view on which "'Truth' ... is some sort of (idealized) rational acceptability—some sort of ideal coherence of our beliefs with each other and with our experience *as those experiences are themselves represented in our belief system*—and not correspondence with mind-independent or discourse-independent 'states of affairs'" (1981:49). Truth and justification are not one and the same thing, for the kinds of reasons offered by Russell and Moore: justification can be lost, while truth is timeless.[1] Nonetheless, truth and justification are internally related and cannot be rendered asunder. Truth is what "*would be* assertible, were someone sufficiently well-placed" (1997 [1991]: 275).

---

[1] See Putnam (1983a: 84).

While this account of truth is much like Peirce's, Putnam has a burden that Peirce avoids. Putnam must now tell us, in a non-question-begging way, just what "ideal" and "sufficiently well-placed" might amount to. Peirce wisely stays away from such concepts. Nonetheless, the 1980s Putnam is Peircean in spirit, offering us a gentle verificationism that allows for all sorts of inquiries other than that of physical science. He refuses "to *limit in advance* what means of verification may become available to human beings" (1990: ix). He says: "The difference between 'verificationism' in *this* sense and 'verificationism' in the positivist sense is precisely the difference between the generous and open-minded attitude that William James called 'pragmatism' and science worship" (1990: ix). We have seen that this broad-minded conception of experience is indeed a cord that runs through the tradition of pragmatism, with the glaring exception of Quine, and that it is the major contribution of very early American thinkers to the pragmatist tradition.

Putnam turns away from some of the elements of internal realism (the verification-ism, the model-theoretic argument) in the 1990s and starts to call his position "prag-matic" realism or "natural" realism. Still set against metaphysical realism, he continues to offer a "realism with a human face." He attempts to keep this human-focused view of truth responsible to the world without stepping over one line into spurious metaphysics or over another line into destructive (and self-destructive) relativism. His pragmatic realism offers "a middle way between reactionary metaphysics and irresponsible relativism. We must give up the 'God's-eye view' of world without giving up the idea that there is a world to which we respond to" (1999: 5).

14.3 Against Disquotationalism

Putnam does not jump on the disquotationalist bandwagon. He thinks there are two classes of analytic philosophers these days: those "who see truth as a substantial notion which still remains to be philosophically explicated in a satisfactory way" and those "who feel that the problem of truth, if there ever was one, has been solved" (1997 [1983]: 315). The second kind of philosopher includes the disquotationalists—those who think that to say that "snow is white" is true is "just to affirm the statement" (1990 [1989]: 222). Putnam is clear whose side he is on. Those who reject metaphysical accounts of truth, and then invoke the disquotational theory to say what truth is, are mistaken. Putnam says that Rorty and Quine are in agreement with each other "on what *I* find shocking: the idea that 'truth' is an empty notion" (1997 [1985]: 300). "The very criticism that the modern view makes of Dewey—that he loses the distinction between warranted assertibility and truth—is, in a way, valid against the modern view itself" (1990 [1989]: 222).

Putnam's paper "Does the Disquotational Theory of Truth Solve All Philosophical Problems?" delivers the resounding answer "no" to the question in its title. He argues that the "notions of assertibility and truth take in each other's wash; the notion of assertibility presupposes the notion of truth; it cannot be used to supplant it" (1994 [1991a]: 266). What makes "there is a chair in front of me" assertible is, for the logical empiricist, that I have something like chair-shaped sense data in my visual field. What makes it assertible for the realist is that it is a fact that there is a chair in front of me. The new generation of disquotationalists rejects both of these answers. But Putnam argues that what they have in mind when they talk about what is assertible is unclear, to say the least. One cannot dodge the problem of saying what truth is by replacing truth with assertibility and then not saying what assertibility is. And once one says what assertibility is, one is taken to a substantial view of truth.

Putnam's positive argument for a more substantial theory of truth (as opposed to the negative argument that disquotationalism does not adequately answer the question about truth) is one that we have seen deployed against Rorty. We need a theory of truth that fits with our practices and disquotation does not fit with our practices. Putnam puts it thus:

In my view . . . we do have a notion of truth, even if we don't have an enlightening account of 'the nature of truth' in the high metaphysical sense, and in my view truth is a property of many of the sentences we utter and write—a characteristic we want those sentences to have when we are not trying to deceive each other (or ourselves).

[1997 [1991]: 264–65]

We use the concept of truth to mark out what we aim at when we believe something. We need to have a concept of truth that makes sense of that and makes sense of the idea that some of our beliefs are better than others.

As I have suggested, disquotationalism and pragmatism share a core insight. Both hold that what it is to assert that "'p' is true" is to assert p itself. A certain kind of pragmatist says, with the classical delflationist, that we must stop there and insist that this is all truth is. Another kind of pragmatist—most explicitly, Putnam—says that stopping there does not give us the sustantial concept of truth that our practices require.

14.4 Fact and Value

Another stable element in Putnam's work is the idea that there is no pulling apart fact and value. The fact–value dichotomy, he thinks, is "the last dogma of empiricism" (2002: 145). We have seen that *Reason, Truth and History* makes the case by arguing that epistemic notions such as "coherence" and "simplicity" are not entirely descriptive and not entirely normative. But in that book, Putnam is already concerned with an issue that will absorb him later—the values imbedded in ethics, as well as the values embedded in our epistemic notions. He says:

Today we tend to be too realistic about physics and too subjectivistic about ethics, and these are connected tendencies. It is *because* we are too realistic about physics, because we see physics (or some hypothetical future physics) as the One True Theory, and not simply as a rationally acceptable description suited for certain problems and purposes, that we tend to be subjectivistic about descriptions we cannot 'reduce' to physics. Becoming less realistic about physics and becoming less subjectivistic about ethics are likewise connected.

[1981: 143, emphasis in original]

In the 1990s, in an important paper titled "Pragmatism and Moral Objectivity," Putnam adds an indispensability argument to his thoughts about how we cannot separate fact from value. Indispensibility arguments, we have seen, go hand in hand with the idea that practice is important. That is, they are arguments of special interest to the pragmatist. Putnam is no exception: "According to the pragmatists, normative discourse—talk of right and wrong, good and bad, better and worse—is indispensible in science and in social and personal life as well" (1994 [1979]: 154). He is careful not to offer us the kind of indispensability argument that on occasion tempted James— one that has it that "If we find the belief that p is 'indispensible' then that is all the justification we need for saying that p is true" (Putnam 1994:155). On Putnam's view, we must always be alert to sound reasons against p, even if we find p indispensible.

Putnam notes that there is more disagreement in morals than in science and argues that this aspect of our practice must not be ignored. But neither can we ignore the fact that we are always employing ethical concepts and could not imagine ceasing to do so. As Peirce would say, we must try to make sense of this practice, in the hope that we can. The way that Putnam makes the attempt has a venerable pragmatist history: he tries to show how ethics is a kind of inquiry. We inherit values and then we question and criticize them. We take ethical disputes as matters to be settled by intelligent argument and inquiry, not by appeals to authority (1994b: 175).

Of course, some people engage in better, more sensitive, and more careful ethical inquiry than others. Hence, Putnam's argument is not about what my and your practices in fact are, but what they ought to be. He identifies this as a more Kantian than pragmatist approach, but we have seen some of the pragmatists (Peirce and Lewis especially) make precisely the move that Putnam thinks is important:

> if there are ethical facts to be discovered, then we ought to apply to ethical inquiry just the rules we have learned to apply to inquiry in general . . . an ethical community—a community which wants to know what is right and good—should organize itself in accordance with democratic standards and ideals, not only because they are good in themselves (and they are), but because they are the prerequisites for the application of intelligence to the inquiry.
>
> [1994b: 175]

That last line is Deweyan. But we have seen that all the pragmatists, save Quine and Rorty, think that democratic standards and ideals undergird the very idea of an inquiry aimed at getting things right.

Putnam sees that this might seem to be pulling oneself up by one's bootstraps. What reason do we have to value the application of intelligence to inquiry? What criteria do we use to tell us that our inquiry has succeeded? But his point is a careful one. There are two kinds of justification. We can aim at convincing the skeptic or we can aim at convincing those who are already a part of a community in that they presuppose certain things together. We have seen that standing at the very heart of pragmatism is the thought that we can only do the latter: we cannot start by doubting everything.

We are always immersed in a context of inquiry, where the decision to be made is a decision about what we are to believe from here, not what to believe were we able to start from scratch or from certain and infallible foundations. This holds in both science and ethics. If participants in an ethical disagreement are not coercive or violent or do not refuse to discuss the matter in question, then they share a number of factual assumptions and value assumptions. They commit themselves to gather as much information as possible, encourage freedom of expression and participation in debate, and so on. They are democratic inquirers. For what is right and what is good is what would stand up to scrutiny in that kind of inquiry.

Much more work needs to be done, of course, to give us reason to maintain our hope that our ethical language and practices aim at something objective. Putnam sees the challenge clearly and undertakes much of the spadework. He knocks down some of the unsound reasons against the claim that there are moral values. For instance, the argument that says that there are no moral values because they would be "queer" ontological entities (unlike the concrete entities of science) is wrong-headed because it rests on a wrong-headed picture of metaphysics—one that has it that the only things that exist are concrete things. In any case, he does not take his indispensability argument to have ontological implications—he takes himself to have shown that there are genuine truths about values, not that abstract entities like values exist (2004). He argues also that "believing that ethical objectivity is possible is not the same thing as believing that there are no undecidable cases or no problems which, alas, cannot be solved" (1994b: 176). Hence, his picture of ethics is the sophisticated one on which disagreement and regret that we could not act on all the reasons cannot always be resolved perfectly or without residue.

He also tries to carve out some examples of standards for science and for ethics that would stand up to scrutiny. He suggests that we ought to accept scientific theories that are simple, elegant, and well-confirmed and that we ought to accept moral norms such as "maximize benefit" because they are the products of normative reflection on our practices (1994b: 168f.). We cannot know, with certainty, that these are the norms that should govern our inquiries. But when we learn from experience and reflect on the presuppositions of acting in the ways we act, we find principles such as these. We may revise them on further reflection. This ongoing task of scrutiny is the only source of evaluative thinking we have.

"Maximize benefit" is a norm held dear by the utilitarian. But most of the norms identified by Putnam come from the liberal democrat's stable. In his 1989 Gifford Lectures, Putnam urges us to reconsider Dewey's philosophy and he coins the now-popular phrase in political philosophy "epistemological justification of democracy." Inquiry, of any kind, must operate on democratic principles: it must provide opportunity and incentive to challenge accepted hypotheses, to criticize evidence and accepted norms, and to offer rival hypotheses. It must respect autonomy and reciprocity (1994b: 172f.). Democratic norms, that is, lie at the heart of inquiry and knowledge. "To reject democracy is to reject the idea of being experimental" (1994a: 64). We need to put in place the conditions—the freedom—under which inquiry can proceed in an unimpeded fashion. We must avoid "relations of hierarchy and dependence", and "insist upon experimentation where possible, and observation and close analysis of observation where experiment is not possible. By appeal to these and kindred standards, we can often tell that views are irresponsibly defended in ethics and the law as well as in science" (2002: 105).

Putnam rightly finds these thoughts in the work of Peirce and James as well as in Dewey. He locates them in Peirce's requirement that we not block the path of inquiry and in James's assertion that the practical consequence of pragmatism "is the well-known democratic respect for the sacredness of individuality . . . Religiously and philosophically, our ancient national doctrine of live and let live may prove to have a far deeper meaning than our people now seem to imagine" (1983 [1899]: 4–5). He sees that James's "The Moral Philosopher and the Moral Life" is one of his strongest pieces and follows James in arguing that, although individual demands may be irreconcilable, we can hope to work out conflicts between our ideals and come to a more inclusive vision (1990 [1989]: 224).

15

The Current Debates

15.1 Inheritors of the Classical Positions

Pragmatists are committed to the project of connecting philosophical concepts to practices. We have seen that some recurring themes arise from that commitment. These include the ideas that our beliefs and theories must be linked to experience; experience must not in principle exclude the experience of value; we must in both philosophy and other inquiries start with where we find ourselves—laden with a set of fallible beliefs on which we act; inquiry is sparked by doubt or a problem and is an attempt to improve our beliefs. From this shared set of themes, two kinds of pragmatism emerge. One kind tries to retain a place for objectivity and for our aspiration to get things right while the other is not nearly so committed to that.

Both kinds of pragmatism are flourishing in contemporary philosophy and both kinds of pragmatism attract scholars of the tradition as well as those who put forward new pragmatist accounts of truth, meaning, knowledge, and norms without paying much attention to their predecessors.[1] Indeed, it can seem that pragmatists are thick on the ground these days. Philosophers everywhere seem to be engaged in the pragmatist project of making sense of normative notions such as truth, justification, and improvement of belief while staying within our human practices of belief, assertion, and inquiry. This makes it harder to articulate just what is distinctive about the pragmatist project. That is a happy evolution for a way of thinking. The fact that pragmatists today may find it difficult to identify a position that can stand out in sharp relief against others means that we have come a long way from the days of The Metaphysical Club, where pragmatism seemed so radical an idea. It should also not be surprising that the seeds of pragmatism have been sown far and wide. Gone are the days when a theory has as its home a few local institutions such as Harvard, Chicago, and Michigan. Pragmatism is not only a well-established concern from shore to shore in America, but it has also drifted well over its borders and thrives all over the world.

In what follows, I will gesture at some of the major participants and salient issues in the current debates. The landscape is shifting as we speak and hence I shall merely

---

[1] One contemporary philosopher who has arrived at a pragmatist view in an ahistoric manner is Crispin Wright. He argues that a sentence is true if it is superassertible—if it is warranted now and would continue to be warranted, as we continue to improve our knowledge state. See Wright (1992) and see Misak (1998, 2007b) for an analysis of how his position is extremely close to Peirce's.

trace the broad contours, rather than show in any detail which philosophers are tilling and shaping what ground. For the lay of the land will look different from the way I describe it even by the time this book rolls off the press.

15.2 Naturalism, Anti-representationalism, Disquotationalism

We have seen that pragmatism and naturalism walk hand in hand. When Charles Peirce, William James, and Chauncey Wright founded pragmatism, they demanded natural, as opposed to supernatural, answers to our philosophical questions. We must start from where we find ourselves—human beings, already possessed of beliefs and practices, trying to make sense of ourselves and our world. Thus, when it comes to the concept of truth, pragmatism declines to start with the world and whether our beliefs correspond to or represent it. Pragmatism, that is, pulls against representationalism. We must not begin with the question "what are truth-makers?"—a question that carries with it a very particular set of metaphysical pictures of what it might be that makes statements or beliefs true. Pragmatists want to deflate metaphysical concepts of truth and argue, rather, for slimmed-down theories that reflect our actual practices and our use of the concept of truth.

We have seen that one debate that has emerged in the twentieth century is whether the idea of truth ought to be deflated to mere disquotation. Some pragmatists, most famously Rorty, argue that when we examine our practices, we find that the concept of truth is not bound up with those practices at all and we should abandon it. If there is a legitimate use of the concept of truth, it is merely the minimal disquotationalist use. This view has come under attack by contemporary pragmatists such as Putnam and Price. I have added my voice to theirs, intermittently in the pages of this book and in a more sustained way elsewhere.[2] The fact that no speaker would deny instances of the disquotational schema does not entitle us to conclude that that is all truth amounts to. There is more to be explained—there is more to the practical value or the function of "is true"—than is addressed by the disquotational schema.

An allied debate is whether the naturalization of truth entails that truth is mere warranted assertion or whether there is room for a more normative idea of truth. I have suggested that the best kind of pragmatist thinks that truth is out of our reach, but not in that it marks a relationship between our beliefs and the believer-independent world. Truth is out of our reach in that it marks the indefinite betterment of our beliefs and our practices of justification.[3] Sellars has shaped one modern instantiation

[2] See Misak (1998, 2007b).
[3] As Akeel Bilgrami says, the pragmatist recovers the idea of truth from those who would make it something that goes beyond our capacities. It is only a global recovery, "since *no particular* truth about the world is known to be a truth by inquirers. But recovery it is. Truth cannot any longer be described as being out of reach in the way that a strict transcendental realism would have it" (Bilgrami 2000: 247).

of this Peircean position. He has been an inspiration to a growing group of important pragmatist philosophers, such as John McDowell, Huw Price, and Robert Brandom. With all pragmatists, they reject the myth of the given and the reprentationalist idea that our epistemology should start with the thought that our beliefs or sentences aim at mirroring the world. These contemporary pragmatists follow Sellars and Peirce in holding that to assert something is to be committed to a justificatory burden in the practice of giving and asking for reasons. Fulfilling that burden is all that can be asked of asserters and inquirers.

A third persistent and allied debate is whether the pragmatist, who starts with human inquirers and their practices, ends up leaving room for the world. All pragmatists reject the picture that has experience giving us objective access to the inquirer-independent world. Some pragmatists, from the days of The Metaphysical Club to today, argue that we can nonetheless make sense of the idea that experience is what we have to go on in coming to our beliefs about the world. These pragmatists think that we have no choice but to think that experience indicates that there is a world not of our making—a world we are trying to get right, despite the fact that our ways of trying to get it right are human ways, loaded with our interests, capacities, and concepts. Other pragmatists disagree and argue that when we start with our practices, we leave the world behind. We cannot make sense of trying to get the world right.

One manifestation of this debate about the world is that Rorty, for instance, brooks no possibility of any version of what Robert Kraut has called the Bifurcation Thesis. This is the thesis that some vocabularies are about the world and some are not (1990: 158–59). We have seen that Rorty thinks that the world is "a world well lost" and that "experience" is a term best abandoned for the term "discourse" (1972). Other pragmatists argue that what counts as getting something right varies in different kinds of inquiry—the philosopher must be sensitive to the fact that we have to make sense of different kinds of deliberation. In some inquiries, such as chemistry or asking about everyday objects, the world will be brought in. In these domains we take ourselves to be agreeing or disagreeing about a world that exists and has characteristics independent of human inquirers. In other kinds of inquiry—such as the moral or the mathematical—"getting it right" will have a different feel to it. This kind of pragmatist, that is, argues that a wide variety of kinds of deliberations fall under the scope of our cognitive practices of assertion, belief, and inquiry. We must pay attention to these variations, lest we try to jam all assertion, belief, and inquiry into one ill-fitting suit.

McDowell is one contemporary pragmatist[4] who is open to the Bifurcation Thesis. He leaves the path clear for the possibility that when you look at the practice of physical science or discourse about medium-sized dry goods, you find that we do indeed try to get beliefs that track a world not of our making. If correctness is always

---

[4] For his statement on the pragmatist content in his view, see his (1996: 154–55). See Bernstein (2002) for the argument that his view is similar to Peirce's.

simply about making moves in a language game, McDowell wonders where the idea comes in that some of our assertions are meant to be about the world and must be responsive to it. Experiences, for McDowell, cannot be locked into the world of reasons—they must be both reasons and causes. If we reject the myth of the given, we have a choice between arguing that experience has no rational bearing on thought but is merely a cause of belief and a neo-Kantian (and one might say, neo-Deweyan) alternative, which is to argue that experience is always-already in the domain of the conceptual. McDowell has been a champion of the latter position. We should not think of experiences as possessing non-conceptual content that is then "conceptual-ized" by our mind. What we receive in experience is already conceptual in character. McDowell then portrays resistance to this idea to follow from scientism, from a commitment to the idea that reality is "disenchanted" (1996: 70, 182). He wants to say that his approach is a better way than Rorty's of capturing what is right in the pragmatist's insights, and that Rorty is stuck with dualisms (for example between nature and reason) that ought to be transcended.

Another way of putting this point is with Jeffrey Stout, who sets out a pragmatism that respects the human interest in aiming at the truth. In his view: "Philosophers who believe that classical pragmatism was on to something important . . . have recently renewed the effort to provide accounts of inquiry that are both recognizably pragmatic in orientation and demonstrably hospitable to the cognitive aspiration to get one's subject matter right" (Stout 2007: 7).

These debates—is truth mere warranted assertibility? can we make sense of trying to come to correct beliefs about the world and other matters not of our making?—have always been divisive. We saw that they were accompanied by verbal fisticuffs in Peirce and James's day. Sentiments continue to run high today. Nicholas Rescher, for instance, feels that Rorty and company are "pseudo-pragmatists" in that they "turn their backs on the pursuit of objectivity and impersonality" (1993: 737). He wants to return to "Peirce in seeking to validate our metaphysical commitments through their serviceability for accomplishing the cognitive and practical tasks that characterize the circumstances of our existence as best rational inquiry reveals them to us" (2005b: ix). Susan Haack (1995: 136) has called Rorty's kind of pragmatism "vulgar." She argues instead for a pragmatist account of truth that involves the correspondence idea, insofar as the scientific method of inquiry is answerable to the inquirer-independent world (Haack 1976). It will be interesting to see how Rorty's position lives on in the hands of his successors, who are less concerned than he was with making provocative statements.

15.3 One Community or Many?

Another major divide in pragmatism, with much the same cast of characters lining up on either bank is as follows. On one side, we have those who think that there are a number of worlds, each with its own standards. Those already enrolled in a way of thinking form a community, and getting it right is a matter for that community's standards. This seems, at least on occasion, to be the pragmatism of James, Schiller, Goodman, and Rorty. The problem with this view is that it leaves us bereft of the ability to talk, agree, or disagree across communities and bereft of the ability to adjudicate claims across those borders. It is also unclear how we could individuate communities and thus the position seems to be without protection from the idea that each of us constitutes our own epistemic community, with our own measures of what is right and wrong or true and false.

On the other side of the divide, we have those pragmatists who argue that there is but one, broad, community of inquirers, in effect agreeing and disagreeing with each other and trying to find across-the-board right answers to questions. Advocates of this position have to work through many issues, such as whether all matters are such that there are determinate answers or whether in some matters there is room for cultural variability and regret that not all reasons could be acted upon. Despite plenty of significant internal debates, this is the pragmatism of Peirce, Lewis, Putnam, and perhaps Quine. (I say "perhaps Quine" because his abandonment of value is a deeply unpragmatist move.) I have also tried to offer a pragmatist position along these lines (Misak 2000). It is also the pragmatism of Jürgen Habermas and Karl Otto Apel, who, in a kind of marrying of Dewey and Kant, argue that the pragmatic presuppositions of discourse give us reason to think that democratic norms are not only true, but necessarily true. It is a pragmatic presupposition of communication, for instance, that we aim at and expect consensus in our deliberations and that we treat others equally and with respect.[5] We have seen, however, that invoking the notion of necessity is also deeply unpragmatist.

It is not very clear where Dewey himself would have come down on the question of whether we should think in terms of one community of inquirers or many, but he certainly is an inspiration to those who ask it. He has also had a major impact on allied questions about community and democratic politics. It should be no surprise that his successors fall into a number of camps. Isaac Levi, for instance, has his focus on Dewey's idea that an agent's current state of knowledge stands in no need of justification unless a good reason can be given for calling some of its elements into question and trying to improve it. He has added to this Deweyan epistemology a logical rigor that has brought to the position advances in decision theory and statistical inference and has taken it to heights that his predecessor was not able to achieve. Dewey's epistemic justification of democracy has also survived, in different ways, in the work of Elizabeth Anderson, Henry Richardson, Robert Talisse, and Cornel West, among many others. His views about democracy continue to resonate throughout political theory and political philosophy and they are also present in contemporary philosophy of science. Arthur Fine's Natural Ontological Argument, for instance, has it that truths are the products of

---

[5] Apel (1990: 24), see also Habermas (1990b: 79–80). The best guide to the German variety of pragmatism is Bernstein (2000).

inquiry and the more voices, methodologies, and interests brought into the process (be it scientific or moral/political inquiry) the better the process will be and the more likely it is that we will reach the truth (2004: 121). I have suggested in this book that this may be a more Peircean than a Deweyan position. But these are interfamilial issues. Despite the debates outlined in this book, it is well worth remembering that the pragmatists have much more in common with each other than not.

Conclusion

The core pragmatist thought is about the human predicament. We must try to explain our practices and concepts, including our epistemic norms and standards, using those very practices, concepts, norms, and standards. This is the pragmatist's task and we have found that, within the pragmatist tradition, there are different ways of trying to fulfill it. One of my aims in this book has been to trace the outlines of those debates as they first appeared on the philosophical scene in 1860s America and as they subsequently unfolded. We have seen that Menand's suggestion is not borne out. The promise and the challenges encountered by pragmatism throughout its history had very little, if anything, to do with a felt need arising from anxieties about the Civil War and then the Cold War, for less anti-authoritarian and then more authoritarian world-views. They had everything to do with the philosophical merits and problems associated with different versions of pragmatism. The problems were so strenuously articulated, especially by Russell and Moore, that pragmatism has never been able to fully shake off the reputation it attracted in the early 1900s. Indeed, the objections put to James's view, so clearly seen when he first launched it, continue to press in on some of the inheritors of that position today.

Another of my aims has been to show the merits of the other strain of pragmatism, carefully carved out first by Charles Peirce and Chauncey Wright; resurrected by C. I. Lewis; and then carried forward into modern philosophy, not entirely self-consciously, by Sellars and only partially by Quine. It is interesting to note that this kind of pragmatism has relatively recently become well-entrenched in Oxford and Cambridge—those sites of hostility to pragmatism in the early to late 1900s. This is in part due to Donald Davidson. He was Quine's most famous student and we have seen that he also knew Lewis's work well. Amongst many other things, he put forward a kind of pragmatism that rejects the foundationalist account of knowledge in favor of what he sometimes called a coherence theory (1983). Davidson gave the John Locke lectures in Oxford in 1970. Those lectures were titled "On the Very Idea of a Conceptual Scheme" and they culminated in a short and influential article by the same name. Davidson argues against what he takes to be the third, and final, dogma of empiricism, which he thinks is found in Carnap, Lewis, and Quine. This is the dichotomy between conceptual scheme and content in which our conceptual frameworks are supposed to interpret or organize the raw data of experience.

One thing wrong with the distinction is that scheme cannot be pulled apart from content. As Peirce argued, the most we can say about our inputs is that they impinge upon us. As soon as we acknowledge them, we form beliefs or judgments and it is those beliefs (not the raw data itself) that stand in justificatory relationships with other beliefs. The second thing wrong with the distinction is that it can play out in "conceptual relativism"—the idea that there are a number of incommensurable conceptual schemes whose task it is to organize unconceptualized empirical input (Davidson 1974: 5–6). Davidson argues that the fact that we can translate across what we think are different conceptual schemes and understand old scientific theories even after massive conceptual change suggests that there are no incommensurable schemes. His point is similar to Hempel's point against Goodman: how might inhabitants of different conceptual schemes ever have lunch together and discuss each other's views? Davidson rejects the idea in Quine (and Goodman and Carnap) that we in some way choose a framework or a language which enables us to interpret and give sense to what James called the blooming buzzing experience, or as Davidson so nicely puts it: "its classmates like surface irritations, sensations and sense data" (1974: 15).

In place of that picture, Davidson puts forward something very similar to Peirce's pragmatist position. While what counts as real is relative to our ways of organizing and conceptualizing experience, there is only one framework. We might as well call it, I suggest, the human framework. Also like Peirce, Davidson thinks it a mistake—a "folly"—to try to define truth. This "does not mean we can say nothing revealing about it: we can, by relating it to other concepts like belief, desire, cause and action" (1996: 265). As I have put Peirce's view, there is not much point in trying to define truth. We must try to get a fix on the concept by seeing how it is related to our practices of belief, inquiry, and action. While Davidson might well have residual quarrels with Peirce,[1] I want to suggest that it is Peirce's position, more or less, that produced what philosophical lore calls the "Davidsonic Boom"—the sound made by a research program when it hits Oxford.[2] We have come full circle from the days where the views of Schiller and James were reviled across the Atlantic.

Davidson, however, has an uneasy relationship to pragmatism. Like so many philosophers, he understands the pragmatist account of truth to be the Jamesian or Rortyian idea that truth is "the merely useful or approved" (2000: 71). He is right to think this a "hopeless idea" (2000: 67). But he nonetheless sees an insight even in this kind of pragmatism: it has "the merit of relating the concept of truth to human concerns, like language, belief, thought, and intentional action, and it is these connections which make truth the key to how mind apprehends the world" (2000: 73). He expressly agrees with Rorty to this extent: "nothing counts as justification unless by reference to something we already accept, and there is no way to get outside our beliefs and our language so as to find some test other than coherence" (2006 [1983]: 228).

---

[1] Perhaps the central difference is over whether truth is a goal of inquiry. Davidson says not (2000: 67).
[2] See Dennett and Steglich-Petersen (2008).

Rorty, in "Pragmatism, Davidson and Truth," tries to bring Davidson fully into his pragmatist camp (1991: 126f.). But as far as Davidson is concerned, Rorty holds fast to the last dogma of empiricism—that there are different conceptual schemes we might choose from to organize experience.

Once we give up scheme–content distinction, Davidson says, "it is not clear that there is anything distinctive left to call empiricism" (1974: 11). What is left, I suggest, is the kind of pragmatism I have been tracing in this book: a naturalized account of truth and knowledge, in which we deal with anomalies or the surprise of experience "against a background of common beliefs and a going method of translation" (Davidson 1974: 18). We assume general agreement on a shared body of beliefs, against which disagreement can make itself manifest. We revise in light of recalcitrant experience, coming to beliefs that better stand up to the pressures of experience and argument.

On this view, the distinction between analytic and synthetic, while perhaps useful for some purposes, is not one that marks off a "certainly true" or "true in virtue of meanings" breed of statement from a breed that is shown to be true by experience or evidence. Neither is there a distinction between non-empirical value statements and statements that are responsive to experience and evidence. All beliefs are subject to the pressure of evidence. But our evidence is shaped by our theories and cannot be cleanly pulled apart from them.

Whether the position that I have identified becomes the standard-bearer of the pragmatist tradition remains to be seen. Perhaps the Jamesian branch of pragmatism, propped up by the disquotationalist theory of truth, will be the survivor of the position hammered out so many years ago in The Metaphysical Club. The more likely outcome, of course, is that the debate will continue in much the same spirit. That is because the issues are real, deep, and pressing. They speak to important disagreements and to issues that require our careful attention.

One thing, however, should be clear from my account of the fortunes of pragmatism. Those who would argue that pragmatism was bullied into the backwaters by the logical empiricists (and the new analytic philosophy they ushered into America) have their intellectual history wrong. Not only were there strong connections between pragmatism and logical empiricism, but the logical empiricists drifted closer and closer to their pragmatist cousins until the views were almost indistinguishable. That is part of the relatively unwritten history of pragmatism I have tried to uncover in this book. Only by attending to it will we be able to see how pragmatism is manifested in contemporary philosophy and how it really is part of the mainstream.

Bibliography

Addams, Jane (1907 [1902]). *Democracy and Social Ethics*. New York: Belknap Press.

——(1965 [1899]). "A Function of the Social Settlement." Repr. in *The Social Thought of Jane Addams*, ed. Christopher Lasch. Indianapolis: Bobbs-Merrill.

Adler, Jonathan (2002). *Belief's Own Ethics*. Cambridge, MA: The MIT Press.

Anderson, Douglas (2008). "Peirce and Pragmatism: American Connections." In Misak (2008a), 38–59.

Anderson, Elizabeth (1993). *Value in Ethics and Economics*. Cambridge, MA: Harvard University Press.

——(2006a). "The Epistemology of Democracy." *Episteme*, 3/1–2: 8–22.

——(2006b). "Replies to My Critics." *Symposia on Gender, Race and Philosophy* (<http://www.mit.edu.sgrp>), 2/1.

Anderson, Paul and Max Fisch (eds.) (1969 [1939]). *Philosophy in America from the Puritans to James*. New York: Appleton-Century.

Anderson, Wallace E. (1980). "Editor's Introduction." In *Works of Jonathan Edwards*. 25 vols. Vol. vi. Gen. ed. Perry Miller. New Haven, CT: Yale University Press, 1–143.

Apel, Karl-Otto (1990). "Is Ethics of the Ideal Communication Community a Utopia? On the Relationship between Ethics, Utopia, and the Critique of Utopia." In S. Benhabib and F. Dallmary (eds.), *The Communicative Ethics Controversy*. Cambridge, MA: The MIT Press.

Atkins, Richard (forthcoming). "This Proposition is not True: C.S. Peirce and the Liar Paradox." *Transactions of the Charles S. Peirce Society*.

Auxier, Randall (2010). "Preface." In Auxier and Hahn (2010).

Auxier, Randall and Lewis Hahn (eds.) (2010). *The Philosophy of Richard Rorty*. Chicago, IL: Open Court.

Ayer, A. J. (1936). *Language, Truth, and Logic*. London: Victor Gollancz.

——(1959). *Logical Positivism*. New York: Free Press.

——(1968). *The Origins of Pragmatism: Studies in the Philosophy of Charles Sanders Peirce and William James*. San Francisco: Cooper, Freeman, and Co.

——(1992). "My Mental Development." In *The Philosophy of A. J. Ayer*. Ed. Lewis Hahn. Open Court, 3–40.

Bacon, Michael (2012). *Pragmatism*. Boston, MA: Polity Press.

Bakhurst, David and Cheryl Misak (forthcoming). "Wittgenstein and Pragmatism." In Hanjo Glock and John Hyman (eds.), *The Blackwell Companion to Wittgenstein*.

Barcan Marcus, Ruth (2010). "A Philosopher's Calling." In Proceedings and Addresses of the American Philosophical Association. Newark: University of Delaware.

Behrens, P. J. (2005). "The Metaphysical Club at the Johns Hopkins University (1879–1885)." *History of Psychology*, 8/4: 331–46.

Bernstein, Richard J. (1970). "In Defense of American Philosophy." In *Contemporary American Philosophy*. Ed. J. E. Smith. London: Humanities Press.

——(2000). *The Pragmatic Turn*. Cambridge: Polity Press.

——(2002). "McDowell's Domesticated Heglianism." In *Reading McDowell: On Mind and World*. Ed. Nicholas Smith. London: Routledge.

——(2006). *The Pragmatic Century: Conversations with Richard Bernstein*. Ed. Sheila Grave Davaney and Warren G. Frisina. Albany, NY: State University of New York Press.

——(2010). *The Pragmatic Turn*. Cambridge: Polity.

Bilgrami, Akeel (2000). "Is Truth a Goal of Inquiry?: Rorty and Davidson on Truth." In Brandom (2000).

Bixler, Julius Seelye (1930). "Professor Dewey Discusses Religion." *Harvard Theological Review*, 23/1: 213–33.

Borradori, Giovanna (1994). *The American Philosopher: Conversations with Quine, Davidson, Putnam, Nozick, Danto, Rorty, Cavell, MacIntryre, and Kuhn*. Trans. R. Crocitto. Chicago, IL: University of Chicago Press.

Bourne, Randolph (1964). *War and the Intellectuals: Collected Essays 1915–1919*. Ed. Carl Resek. New York: Harper and Row, 53–64.

——(1964 [1917]). "Twilight of Idols." Repr. in Bourne (1964).

——(1997 [1913]). "Trans-National America." Repr. in *Randolph Bourne and the Politics of Cultural Radicalism*. Ed. Leslie Vaughan. Lawrence, KS: University Press of Kansas.

Bradley, F. H. (1876). *Ethical Studies*. London: Henry S. King & Co.

Brandom, Robert (1994). *Making It Explicit: Reasoning, Representing, and Discursive Commitment*. Cambridge MA: Harvard University Press.

——(ed.) (2000). *Rorty and his Critics*. Oxford: Oxford University Press.

Brent, Joseph (1998 [1993]). *Charles Sanders Peirce: A Life*. Bloomington: Indiana University Press.

Bridgman, Percy (1960 [1927]). *The Logic of Modern Physics*. New York: Macmillan.

Brownell, Baker (1951 [1940]). "Santayana, the Man and the Philosopher." In Schlipp (1951 [1940]).

Burke, Kenneth (1930). "Intelligence as a Good." *The New Republic*, 64: 77–79.

Burke, Thomas (1994). *Dewey's New Logic: A Reply to Russell*. Chicago, IL: University of Chicago Press.

Burke, F. Thomas, D. Micah Hester, Robert B. Talisse (eds.) (2002). *Dewey's Logical Theory: New Studies and Interpretations*. Nashville: Vanderbilt University Press.

Caldwell, William (1913). *Pragmatism and Idealism*. Repr. in Shook (2001a), iv.

Campbell, James (2006). *A Thoughtful Profession: The Early Years of the American Philosophical Association*. Chicago: The Open Court.

Carnap, Rudolph (1935). *Philosophy and Logical Syntax*. London: Kegan Paul.

——(1936). "Testability and Meaning." *Philosophy of Science*, 3/4: 419–71.

——(1937). *The Logical Syntax of Language*. London: Routledge and Kegan.

——(1939). *Foundations of Logic and Mathematics* in *International Encyclopedia of Unified Science*. i/3. University of Chicago Press.

——(1942). *Introduction to Semantics*. Cambridge, MA: Harvard University Press.

——(1950). "Empiricism, Semantics, and Ontology." *Revue Internationale de Philosophie*, 4: 20–40.

——(1956 [1947]). *Meaning and Necessity*. Chicago: University of Chicago Press.

——(1963). "Replies and Systematic Expositions." In Schlipp (1963).

Cartwright, Nancy *et al.* (1996). *Otto Neurath: Philosophy between Science and Politics.* New York: Cambridge University Press.

Carus, Paul (2001 [1911]). *Truth on Trial: An Exposition of the Nature of Truth.* Repr. in Shook (2001a), iii.

Clebsch, William (1973). *American Religious Thought: A History.* Chicago: University of Chicago Press.

Clendenning, John (1999). *The Life and Thought of Josiah Royce.* Rev. and expanded ed. Nashville: Vanderbilt University Press.

Clifford, William K. (1886 [1877]). "The Ethics of Belief." In L. Stephen and F. Pollack (eds.), *Lectures and Essays.* New York: Macmillan.

Cohen, Morris Raphael (1949 [1940]). "Some Difficulties in John Dewey's Anthropocentric Naturalism." In *Studies in Philosophy and Science,* New York: Henry Holt and Company.

Colden, Cadwallader (1939 [1751]). "The Principles of Action in Matter, The Gravitation of Bodies, and the Motion of the Planets Explained from those Principles." In Anderson and Fisch (1969 [1939]).

Comte, August (1875). *The Positive Philosophy.* 2 vols. Vol. i. Trans. A. Martineau. London: Trubner.

Creath, Richard (2004). "Quine on the Intelligibility and Relevance of Analyticity." In *The Cambridge Companion to Quine.* Ed. Roger F. Gibson Jr. Cambridge: Cambridge University Press, 47–64.

Dalton, Thomas Carlyle (2002). *Becoming John Dewey: Dilemmas of a Philosopher and Naturalist.* Bloomington: Indiana University Press.

Davaney, Sheila Greve and Warran G. Frisina (eds.) (2006). *The Pragmatic Century: Conversations with Richard J. Bernstein.* Albany, NY: State University of New York Press.

Davidson, Donald (1974). "On the Very Idea of a Conceptual Scheme." *Proceedings and Addresses of the American Philosophical Association,* 47: 5–20.

——(1996). "The Folly of Trying to Define Truth." *Journal of Philosophy,* 93/6: 263–78.

——(2000). "Truth Rehabilitated." In Brandom (2000), 65–73.

——(2004). "An Interview with Donald Davidson." In *Problems of Rationality,* Oxford: Clarendon Press.

——(2006 [1983]). "A Coherence Theory of Truth and Knowledge." Repr. in *The Essential Davidson.* Oxford: Clarendon Press, 225–37.

Dayton, Eric (1995). "C. I. Lewis and the Given." *Transactions of the Charles S. Peirce Society,* 31/2: 254–87.

De Caro, Mario and David Macarthur (2004). *Naturalism in Question.* Cambridge, MA: Harvard University Press.

——(2010). *Naturalism and Normativity.* New York: Columbia University Press.

Deledalle, Gérard (2001). "A la source de la semiotique triadique." *Recherches Semiotic-Semiotic Inquiry,* 21/1, 2, 3: 211–27.

Dennett, Daniel and Asbjorn Steglich-Petersen (2008). *The Philosophical Lexicon.* <http://www.philosophicallexicon.com>.

De Waal, Cornelis (2008). "A Pragmatist World View: George Herbert Mead's Philosophy of the Act." In Misak (2008a), 144–68.

Dewey, John (1939). *International Encyclopedia of Unified Science,* ii/4: *Theory of Valuation.* Chicago: University of Chicago Press.

——(1967 [1887]). *Psychology*. In *The Early Works of John Dewey 1882–1898*. Vol. ii: *Psychology*. Ed. Jo Ann Boydston. Carbondale IL: Southern Illinois University Press.

——(1969 [1891]). "Moral Theory and Moral Practice." In *The Early Works of John Dewey 1882–1898*. Vol. i: *Essays, Leibniz's New Essays Concerning the Human Understanding*. Ed. Jo Ann Boydston. Carbondale IL: Southern Illinois University Press, 93–109.

——(1981 [1886]). "The Psychological Standpoint." In *The Later Works of John Dewey 1925– 1953*. Vol. i: *Experience and Nature*. Ed. Jo Ann Boydston. Carbondale IL: Southern Illinois University Press, 122–44.

——(1981 [1939]). "Creative Democracy: The Task Before Us." In *The Later Works of John Dewey 1925–1953*. Vol. xiv: *Essays*. Ed. Jo Ann Boydston. Carbondale, IL: Southern Illinois University Press, 224–30.

——(1982 [1920]). *Reconstruction in Philosophy*. In *The Middle Works of John Dewey 1899–1924*. Vol. xii: *Essays, Reconstruction in Philosophy*. Ed. Jo Ann Boydston. Carbondale IL: Southern Illinois University Press, 77–202.

——(1982 [1948]). "Introduction: Reconstruction as seen Twenty-Five Years Later." In *The Middle Works of John Dewey 1899–1924*. Vol. xii: *Essays, Reconstruction in Philosophy*. Ed. Jo Ann Boydston. Carbondale IL: Southern Illinois University Press, 256–78.

——(1983 [1930]). "Foreword to the 1930 Modern Library Edition." In *The Middle Works of John Dewey 1899-1924*. Vol. xiv: *Human Nature and Conduct*. Ed. Jo Ann Boydston. Carbondale Illinois, 228–31.

——(1984 [1926]). *The Public and Its Problems*. In *The Later Works of John Dewey 1925–1953*. Vol. ii: *Essays, The Public and Its Problems*. Ed. Jo Ann Boydston. Carbondale IL: Southern Illinois University Press, 235–372.

——(1984 [1927]). "Half Hearted Naturalism." In *The Later Works of John Dewey 1925–1953*. Vol. ii: *Essays, The Public and Its Problems*. Ed. Jo Ann Boydston. Carbondale IL: Southern Illinois University Press, 73–82.

——(1986 [1938]). *Logic: The Theory of Inquiry*. In *The Later Works of John Dewey 1925–1953*. Vol. xii: *Logic: The Theory of Inquiry*. Ed. Jo Ann Boydston. Carbondale IL: Southern Illinois University Press.

——(1989 [1946]). "Peirce's Theory of Linguistic Signs, Thought, and Meaning." In *The Later Works of John Dewey 1925–1953*. Vol. xv: *Essays*. Ed. Jo Ann Boydston. Carbondale IL: Southern Illinois University Press, 141–53.

——(1998 [1911]). "The Problem of Truth." In Hickman and Alexander (1998). Vol. ii, 101–30.

——(1998 [1925]). "The Development of American Pragmatism." In Hickman and Alexander (1998). Vol. ii, 3–13.

——(2008). *The Correspondence of John Dewey, 1871–1952*. Vols. i–iii. Ed. Larry A. Hickman. Carbondale: Southern Illinois University.

Dewey, John and J. H. Tufts (1908). *Ethics*. In *The Middle Works of John Dewey 1899–1924*. Vol. v: *Ethics*. Ed. Jo Ann Boydston. Carbondale IL: Southern Illinois University Press.

Dickstein, Morris (1998). "Introduction: Pragmatism Then and Now." In *The Revival of Pragmatism*. Ed. Morris Dickstein. Durham: Duke University Press.

Drake, D. (1920). "The Approach to Critical Realism." In D. Drake *et al.*, *Essays in Critical Realism: A Cooperative Study of the Problem of Knowledge*, London: Macmillan, 3–34.

Drake, D. *et al.* (1920). *Essays in Critical Realism: A Cooperative Study of the Problem of Knowledge.* London, Macmillan.

Duhem, Pierre (1951 [1914]). *La théorie physique son objet et sa structure.* 2nd ed. Paris: Chevalier et Rivière. (English Translation Phillip Wiener, *The Aim and Structure of Physical Theory.* Princeton: Princeton University Press, 1954.)

——(1990 [1917]). "Logical Examination of Physical Theory." *Synthese* 83/2: 183–88.

Dykhuizen, George (1973). *The Life and Mind of John Dewey.* Ed. Jo Ann Boydston. Carbondale: Southern Illinois University Press.

Dyzenhaus, David (1997). "Holmes and Carl Schmitt: An Unlikely Pair?" *Brooklyn Law Review*, 63: 165–88.

Edwards, Jonathan (1957–2006). *Works of Jonathan Edwards.* Gen. ed. Perry Miller (vols. i–ii), John E. Smith (vols. iii–ix), and Harry S. Stout (vols. x–xxv). New Haven, CT: Yale University Press.

——(1980 [1723]). "The Mind." In *Works of Jonathan Edwards.* 25 vols. Vol. vi. Gen. ed. Perry Miller. New Haven, CT: Yale University Press, 332–95.

——(1999 [1734]). "A Divine and Supernatural Light." In *Works of Jonathan Edwards.* 25 vols. Vol. xvii. Gen. ed. Perry Miller. New Haven, CT: Yale University Press, 405–26.

Eldridge, Michael (2004). "Naturalism." In *The Blackwell Guide to American Philosophy.* Ed. A. T. Marsoobian and J. Ryder. Oxford: Blackwell.

Emerson, Ralph Waldo (1885). *Nature, Addresses and Lectures.* Philadelphia: H. Altemus.

——(1940). *The Complete Essays and Other Writings of Ralph Waldo Emerson.* Ed. B. Atkinson, New York: Modern Library.

——(1971). *The Collected Works of Ralph Waldo Emerson.* Ed. Robert E. Spiller. Cambridge MA: Belknap Press.

Emmet, Dorothy (1994). *The Role of the Unrealisable.* London: Macmillan.

Festenstein, Matthew (2008). "John Dewey: Inquiry, Ethics, and Democracy." In Misak (2008a).

Fine, Arthur (1986). "The Natural Ontological Attitude." In *The Shaky Game: Einstein, Realism and the Quantum Theory.* Chicago: University of Chicago Press, 112–35.

——(2004). "The Viewpoint of No One in Particular." In *Pragmatic Turn in Philosophy: Contemporary Engagements Between Analytic and Continental Thought.* Ed. William Egginton and Mike Sandbothe. Albany: SUNY Press, 115–30.

——(2007). "Relativism, Pragmatism, and the Practice of Science." In Misak (2007a).

Fisch, Max (1942). "Justice Holmes, the Prediction Theory of Law, and Pragmatism." *Journal of Philosophy*, 39/4: 85–97.

——(1947). "Evolution in American Philosophy." *Philosophical Review*, 56/4: 357–73.

——(1954). "Alexander Bain and the Geneaology of Pragmatism." *Journal of the History of Ideas*, 15: 413–44.

Fisch, Max H. and Jackson I. Cope (1952). "Peirce at the Johns Hopkins University." In *Studies in the Philosophy of Charles Sanders Peirce.* Ed. Philip P. Wiener and Frederic H. Young. Cambridge: Harvard University Press, 277–311.

Flewelling, R. T. (1938). "F. C. S. Schiller: An Appreciation." *Personalist*, xix.

Frank, Philipp. "Physical Theories of the Twentieth Century and School Philosophy." In *Modern Science and Its Philosophy.* Cambridge, MA: Harvard University Press, 90–121. (Trans. of "Was

bedeuten die gegenwärtigen physikalischen Theorien für die allgemeine Erkenntnislehre?"
Erkenntnis 1: 126–57.)

——(1950). *Relativity: A Richer Truth.* Boston: Beacon Press.

——(1951). "The Logical and Sociological Aspects of Science." *Contributions to the Analysis and Synthesis of Knowledge; Proceedings of the American Academy of Arts and Sciences*, 80: 16–30.

Frege, G. (1950 [1884]). *The Foundations of Arithmetic: A Logico-Mathematical Enquiry into the Concept of Number.* Trans. J. L. Austin. Oxford: Basil Blackwell.

Friedman, Michael (1999) *Reconsidering Logical Positivism.* Cambridge: Cambridge University Press.

——(2007). "Introduction." In *The Cambridge Companion to Carnap.* Ed. Michael Friedman and Richard Creath. Cambridge: Cambridge University Press.

Gale, Richard M. (2010). *John Dewey's Quest for Unity: The Journey of a Promethean Mystic.* Amhurst, NY: Prometheus Books.

Goodman, Nelson (1952). "Sense and Certainty." *The Philosophical Review*, 61: 16–167.

——(1955). *Fact, Fiction, and Forecast.* Cambridge MA: Harvard University Press.

——(1972 [1958]). "The Test of Simplicity." In *Problems and Projects*, New York: Bobbs-Merrill, 279–94.

——(1972 [1960]). "The Way the World Is." In *Problems and Projects*, New York: Bobbs-Merrill, 24–32.

——(1972 [1964]). "Snowflakes and Wastebaskets." In *Problems and Projects*. New York: Bobbs-Merrill, 416–419.

——(1978). *Ways of Worldmaking.* Indianapolis, IN: Hackett Publishing Company.

——(1980). "On Starmaking." *Synthese*, 45/2: 211–15.

——(1983 [1953a]). "The New Riddle of Induction." In *Fact, Fiction, and Forecast*, 4th ed. Cambridge MA: Harvard University Press, 59–83.

——(1983 [1953b]). "The Passing of the Possible." In *Fact, Fiction, and Forecast*. 4th ed. Cambridge MA: Harvard University Press, 31–58.

——(1983 [1953c]). "Prospects for a Theory of Projection." In *Fact, Fiction, and Forecast*. 4th ed. Cambridge MA: Harvard University Press, 84–124.

——(1983 [1973]). "Note to the Third Edition." In *Fact, Fiction, and Forecast*, 4th ed. Cambridge MA: Harvard University Press, xxi–xxiv.

Goodman, Russell (1990). *American Philosophy and the Romantic Tradition.* Cambridge: Cambridge University Press.

——(2002). *Wittgenstein and William James.* Cambridge: Cambridge University Press.

Green, C. D. (2007). "Johns Hopkins' First Professorship in Philosophy: A Critical Pivot Point in the History of American Psychology." *American Journal of Psychology*, 120/2: 303–23.

Gross, Neil (2008). *Richard Rorty: The Making of an American Philosopher.* Chicago: University of Chicago Press.

Gunter, Susan E. (2009). *Alice in Jamesland: The Story of Alice Howe Gibbens James.* Lincoln, NE: University of Nebraska Press.

Haack, Susan (1976). "The Pragmatist Theory of Truth." *The British Journal for the Philosophy of Science*, 27/3: 231–49.

——(1995). "Vulgar Pragmatism: An Unedifying Prospect." In Saakamp (1995).

Habermas, J. (1990a). "Discourse Ethics: Notes on a Program of Philosophical Justification" in S. Benhabib and F. Dallmary (eds.), *The Communicative Ethics Controversy*, Cambridge, MA: The MIT Press.

——(1990b). *Moral Consciousness and Communicative Action*. Trans. C. Lenhardt and S. Weber Nicholsen. Cambridge: MIT Press.

Hahn, Hans (1987 [1933]). *Logik, Mathematik, Naturerkennen*, Vienna: Gerold.

Hall, G. Stanley (1888). "Critical Notice of *Pscyhology*, by James McCosh, *Introduction to Psychology* by Borden P. Bowne, and *Psychology* by John Dewey." *American Psychology*, 1: 156–57.

Hempel, C. G. (1964 [1945]). "On the Nature of Mathematical Truth." *American Mathematical Monthly*, 52. Repr. in Benacerraf and Putnam (1964). *Philosophy of Mathematics: Selected Readings*, N. J., Prentice-Hall.

——(1980). "Comments on Goodman's *Ways of Worldmaking*." *Synthese*, 45/2: 193–99.

Hickman, Larry A. and Thomas M. Alexander (eds.) (1998). *The Essential Dewey*. 2 vols. Bloomington: Indiana University Press.

Holmes, Oliver Wendell (1886). *Ralph Waldo Emerson*. Boston, MA: Houghton Mifflin.

——(1882). *The Common Law*. London: MacMillan.

——(1952 [1897]). "The Path of Law." In Holmes (1952 [1920]), 167–202.

——(1952 [1920]). *Collected Legal Papers*. New York: Harcourt, Brace, and Company.

——(1995 [1870]). "Codes, and the Arrangement of Law." In *The Collected Works of Justice Holmes: Complete Public Writings and Selected Judicial Opinions of Oliver Wendell Holmes*. 3 vols. Vol i. Ed. Sheldon M. Novick. Chicago: University of Chicago Press, 212–21.

——(1995 [1872]). "Review." In *The Collected Works of Justice Holmes: Complete Public Writings and Selected Judicial Opinions of Oliver Wendell Holmes*. 3 vols. Vol. i. Ed. Sheldon M. Novick. Chicago: University of Chicago Press, 294–97.

Hook, Sidney (1949). *John Dewey, Philosopher of Science and Freedom: A Symposium*. New York: Barnes and Noble.

——(1959). "John Dewey—Philosopher of Growth." *The Journal of Philosophy*, 56/26: 1010–18.

——(1959–60). "Pragmatism and the Tragic Sense of Life." In *Proceedings and Addresses of the American Philosophical Association*, 33: 5–26.

Hookway, Christopher (1999). "Modest Transcendental Arguments and Sceptical Doubts." In *Transcendental Arguments: Problems and Prospects*. Ed. R. Stern. Oxford: Clarendon Press, 173–88.

——(2000). *Truth, Rationality, and Pragmatism: Themes from Peirce*. Oxford: Clarendon.

——(2008). "Pragmatism and the Given: C. I. Lewis, Quine, and Peirce." In Misak (2008a), 269–89.

Horwich, Paul (1990). *Truth*. Oxford: Basil Blackwell.

Houser, Nathan (1986). "Introduction." In *The Writings of Charles S. Peirce: A Chronological Edition*. 7 vols. to date. Vol. iv. Gen ed. N. Houser. Bloomington: Indiana University Press.

Howat, Andrew W. (2011). "Regulative Assumptions, Hinge Propositions and the Peircean Conception of Truth." Erkenntnis, online publication.

Howe, Mark DeWolfe (ed.) (1941). *Holmes–Pollock letters: The Correspondence of Mr. Justice Holmes and Sir Frederick Pollock, 1874–1932*. 2 vols. Cambridge MA: Harvard University Press.

Hume, David (1975 [1777]). *Enquiries Concerning the Human Understanding and Concerning the Principles of Morals*. 3rd ed. Ed. L. A. Selby-Bigge. Rev. P. H. Nidditch. Oxford: Clarendon.

——(1978 [1740]). *A Treatise of Human Nature: An Attempt to Introduce the Experimental Method of Reasoning into Moral Subjects.* 2nd ed. Ed. L. A. Selby-Bigge. Rev. P. H. Nidditch. Oxford: Clarendon.

Huxley, T. H. (1877). "A Modern Symposium." *Nineteenth Century*, 1/9: 536–39.

Isaac, Joel (2011). "Missing Links: W. V. Quine, the Making of 'Two Dogmas', and the Analytic Roots of Post-Analytic Philosophy." *History of European Ideas*, 37: 267–79.

Jackman, Henry (1999). "Prudential Arguments, Naturalized Epistemology, and the Will to Believe." *Transactions of the Charles S. Peirce Society*, 35/1: 1–37.

——(2008). "William James." In Misak (2008a), 60–86.

James, Henry (ed.) (1920). *The Letters of William James.* 2 vols. Boston: Atlantic Monthly Press.

James, William (1969 [1911]). *William James and Other Essays on the Philosophy of Life.* Freeport, NY: Books for Libraries Press.

——(1975–88). *The Works of William James.* 18 vols. Ed. F. H. Burkhard, F. Bowers, and I. K. Skrupskelis. Cambridge MA: Harvard University Press.

——(1975 [1898]). "Philosophical Conceptions and Practical Results." In *Pragmatism: A New Name for Some Old Ways of Thinking*, in *The Works of William James.* Vol i, 257–70.

——(1975 [1907]). *Pragmatism: A New Name for some Old Ways of Thinking.* In James (1975–88). Vol. i.

——(1975 [1909]). *The Meaning of Truth.* In James (1975–88). Vol. ii.

——(1976 [1904a]). "Does 'Consciousness' Exist?" In James (1975–88). Vol. iii, 3–20.

——(1976 [1904b]). "A World of Pure Experience." In James (1975–88). Vol. i, 21–44.

——(1977 [1904]). "The Chicago School." In James (1975–88). Vol. v, 102–6.

——(1977 [1909]). *A Pluralistic Universe.* In James (1975–88). Vol. iv.

——(1979 [1879]). "The Sentiment of Rationality." In James (1975–88). Vol. v: *Essays in Philosophy*, 32–64.

——(1979 [1884]). "The Dilemma of Determinism." In James (1975–88). Vol. vi: *The Will to Believe and Other Essays in Popular Philosophy*, 114–40.

——(1979 [1891]). "The Moral Philosopher and the Moral Life." In James (1975–88). Vol. vi: *The Will to Believe and Other Essays in Popular Philosophy*, 141–62.

——(1979 [1896]). "The Will to Believe." In James (1975–88). Vol. i: *The Will to Believe and Other Essays in Popular Philosophy*, 13–34.

——(1981 [1890]). *The Principles of Psychology.* In James (1975–88). Vols. xiii–x.

——(1983 [1899]). "On a Certain Blindness in Human Beings." In James (1975–88). Vol. xii: *Talks to Teachers on Psychology*, 132–49.

——(1985 [1902]). *The Varieties of Religious Experience.* In James (1975–88). Vol. xv.

——(1987 [1875]). "The Universe Unseen, by Peter Guthrie Tait and Balfour Stewart." In James (1975–88). Vol. xvii: *Essays, Comments, and Reviews*, 290–94.

——(1987 [1885]). "Review: *The Religious Aspect of Philosophy*, by Josiah Royce." In James (1975–88). Vol. xvii: *Essays, Comments, and Reviews*, 383–87.

——(1987 [1903]). "Review: *Personal Idealism* ed. by Henry Sturt." In James (1975–88). Vol. xvii, 540–45.

——(1987 [1909]). "James on Tausch." In James (1975–88). Vol. xvii: *Essays, Comments, and Reviews*, 189–90.

——(1988 [1899]). "Royce's Argument for the Absolute." In James (1975–88). Vol. xviii: *Manuscripts Essays and Notes*, 203–8.

——(1992–2004). *The Correspondence of William James*. Vols. i–xii. Ed. I. K. Skrupskelis and E. M. Berkeley. Charlottesville: University Press of Virginia.

Jewett, Andrew (2011). "Canonizing Dewey: Columbia Naturalism, Logical Empiricism, and the Idea of American Philosophy," *Modern Intellectual History*, 8/1: 91–125.

Kappy Suckiel, Ellen (1982). *The Pragmatic Philosophy of William James*. Notre Dame: Notre Dame University Press.

Kellogg, Frederic R. (2007). *Oliver Wendell Holmes, Jr.: Legal Theory, and Judicial Restraint*. Cambridge: Cambridge University Press.

Kerr-Lawson, Angus (1991). "Santayana on James: 1891." *Overheard in Seville*, 9: 36–38.

Ketner, Kenneth Laine (ed.) (1995). *Peirce and Contemporary Thought: Philosophical Inquiries*. New York: Fordham University Press.

Klein, Alexander (2008). "*Divide et Impera!* William James's Pragmatist Tradition in the Philosophy of Science." *Philosophical Topics*, 36/1: 129–66.

——(2009). "On Hume on Space: Green's Attack, James's Empirical Response." *Journal of the History of Philosophy*, 47/3: 415–49.

——(forthcoming). *The Rise of Empiricism: William James, Thomas Hill Green, and the Struggle over Psychology*.

Knox, Howard (2001 [1909]). "Pragmatism: The Evolution of Truth." *Quarterly Review*, 210/2, reprinted in Shook (2001a).

Koopman, Colin (2009). *Pragmatism as Transition: Historicity and Hope in James, Dewey, and Rorty*. New York: Columbia University Press.

Kraut, Robert (1990). "Varieties of Pragmatism." *Mind*, 99/394: 157–83.

Krikorian, Yervant (ed.) (1944). *Naturalism and the Human Spirit*. New York: Columbia University Press.

Kuklick, Bruce (1977). *The Rise of American philosophy, Cambridge, Massachusetts, 1860–1930*. New Haven, CT: Yale University Press.

——(1985). *Churchmen and Philosophers: From Jonathan Edwards to John Dewey*. New Haven, CT: Yale University Press.

——(2001). *Philosophy in America: A Cultural and Intellectual History, 1720–2000*. Oxford: Oxford University Press.

Lachs, John (2003). *A Community of Individuals*. New York: Routledge.

Ladd-Franklin, Christine (1916). "Charles S. Peirce at the Johns Hopkins." *The Journal of Philosophy, Psychology, and Scientific Methods*, 13: 716–17.

Lamont, Corliss (1959). *Dialogue on John Dewey [by] James T. Farrell [and others]*. New York: Horizon Press.

Lance, Mark (2008). "Placing in a Space of Norms: Neo-Sellarsian Philosophy in the Twenty-First Century." In Misak (2008a), 403–29.

Leuba, James A. (1903). "Professor William James's Interpretation of Religious Experience." *International Journal of Ethics*, 14: 326.

Levi, Isaac (1983). *The Enterprise of Knowledge: An Essay on Knowledge, Credal Probability and Chance*. Boston: MIT Press.

——(2012). *Pragmatism and Inquiry: Selected Essays*. Oxford: Oxford University Press.

Lewis, C. I. (1918). *A Survey of Symbolic Logic*. Berkeley: University of California Press.

——(1956 [1929]). *Mind and the World Order: An Outline of a Theory of Knowledge.* New York: Dover.

——(1968a). "Autobiography." In Schlipp (1968).

——(1968b). "Replies to my Critics." In Schlipp (1968).

——(1970). *Collected Papers.* Ed. John D. Goheen and John L. Mothershead, Jr. Stanford, CA: Stanford University Press.

——(1970 [1926]). "The Pragmatic Element in Knowledge." In Lewis (1970), 240–57.

——(1970 [1930a]). "Logic and Pragmatism." In Lewis (1970), 3–19.

——(1970 [1930b]). "Review of John Dewey's *The Quest for Certainty.*" In Lewis (1970), 66–77.

——(1970 [1930c]). "Pragmatism and Current Thought." In Lewis (1970), 78–86.

——(1970 [1934]). "Experience and Meaning." In Lewis (1970), 258–76.

——(1970 [1936]). "Verification and Types of Truth." In Lewis (1970), 277–93.

——(1970 [1941a]). "Logical Positivism and Pragmatism." In Lewis (1970), 92–112.

——(1970 [1941b]). "The Objectivity of Value Judgments." In Lewis (1970), 162–74.

——(1970 [1950]). "The Empirical Basis of Value Judgments." In Lewis (1970), 175–89.

——(1970 [1952]). "The Given Element in Empirical Knowledge." In Lewis (1970), 324–30.

——(1971 [1946]). *An Analysis of Knowledge and Evaluation.* La Salle: Open Court.

Lippmann, Walter (1922). *Public Opinion.* New York: Free Press.

——(1925). *The Phantom Public.* New York: Macmillan.

Locke, Alain (1992 [1916]). *Race Contacts and Interracial Relations.* Ed. Jeffrey C. Stewart. Washington DC: Howard University Press.

Lovejoy, Arthur (1908). "The Thirteen Pragmatisms." *The Journal of Philosophy,* 5/1: 5–12.

——(1909a). "Pragmatism and Realism." *The Journal of Philosophy, Psychology and Scientific Methods,* 6/21: 575–80.

——(1909b). "Review of Dewey and Tufts' *Ethics.*" *American Journal of Theology,* 13: 140–43.

——(1920a). "Pragmatism as Interactionism." *The Journal of Philosophy, Psychology and Scientific Methods,* 17/ 22: 589–96.

——(1920b). "Pragmatism *versus* the Pragmatist." In D. Drake *et al.* (1920), 35–84.

——(1922). "Time, Meaning and Transcendence—I. The Alleged Futurity of Yesterday." *Journal of Philosophy,* 19/19: 505–15.

——(1963). *The Thirteen Pragmatisms and Other Essays.* Baltimore: Johns Hopkins Press.

Macarthur, David (2008). "Quinean Naturalism in Question." *Philo,* 11/1.

——(2009). "Pragmatism, Metaphysical Quietism and the Problem of Normativity". In *Philosophical Topics, special issue on Pragmatism and Contemporary Philosophy.* Ed. Stephen Levine. University of Arkansas Press.

——(forthcoming). "Putnam, Pragmatism and the Fate of Metaphysics." In *The Cambridge Companion to Pragmatism.* Ed. Alan Malachowski. Cambridge: Cambridge University Press. (Repr. from *European Journal of Analytic Philosophy,* 4/2: 33–47.)

McDowell, John (1996). *Mind and World.* Cambridge MA: Harvard University Press.

McGilvary, Bradley, G. Watts Cunningham, C. I. Lewis, and Ernest Nagel (1939). "A Symposium of Reviews of John Dewey's Logic: The Theory of Inquiry." *The Journal of Philosophy,* 36/21: 561–81.

Mach, Ernst (1911 [1872]). *History and Root of the Principle of the Conservation of Energy.* Trans. P. E. B. Jourdain. Chicago: Open Court.

Madden, Edward (1963). *Chauncey Wright and the Foundations of Pragmatism*. Seattle: University of Washington Press.

——(1979). "Introduction." In *The Works of William James*. Vol. vi: *The Will to Believe and Other Essays in Popular Philosophy*. Ed. F. H. Burkhard, F. Bowers, and I. K. Skrupskelis. Cambridge MA: Harvard University Press, xi–xxxviii.

Margolis, Joseph (1998). "Peirce's Fallibilism." *Transactions of the Charles S. Peirce Society*, 34: 3.

Marsden, G. M. (2003). *Jonathan Edwards: A Life*. New Haven, CT: Yale University Press.

Mead, George Herbert (1967 [1934]). *Mind, Self and Society*. Chicago: University of Chicago Press.

——(1982). *The Individual and the Social Self: Unpublished Works of George Herbert Mead*. Ed. David Miller. Chicago, University of Chicago Press.

Menand, Louis (2001). *The Metaphysical Club: A Story of Ideas in America*. New York: Farrar, Straus, and Giroux.

Migotti, Mark (2011). "Pragmatist Theories of Truth." In *Introducing Philosophy*. Ed. Robert C. Solomon and Douglas McDermid. New York: Oxford University Press.

Mill, John Stuart (1973 [1872]). *A System of Logic Ratiocinative and Inductive, Being a Connected View of the Principles of Evidence and the Methods of Scientific Investigation*. In *The Collected Works of John Stuart Mill*. Vol. ix. Ed. J. M. Robson. Toronto: University of Toronto Press.

Miller, D. S. (1898) "The Will to Believe and The Duty to Doubt." *International Journal of Ethics*, XI: 169–95.

Misak, Cheryl (1994). "Pragmatism and the Transcendental Turn in Truth and Ethics." *Transactions of the Charles S. Peirce Society*, 30/4: 739–75.

——(1995). *Verificationism: Its History and Prospects*. London: Routledge.

——(1998). "Deflating Truth." *The Monist*, 81/3: 407–25.

——(2000). *Truth, Politics, Morality: Pragmatism and Deliberation*. London and New York: Routledge.

——(ed.) (2004a). *The Cambridge Companion to Peirce*. Cambridge: Cambridge University Press.

——(2004b). "C. S. Peirce on Vital Matters." In Misak (2004a), 150–74.

——(2004 [1991]). *Truth and the End of Inquiry: A Peircean Account of Truth*. 2nd ed. Oxford: Oxford University Press.

——(ed.) (2007a). *New Pragmatists*. Oxford: Oxford University Press.

——(2007b). "Pragmatism and Deflationism." In Misak (2007a), 68–90.

——(ed.) (2008a). *The Oxford Handbook of American Philosophy*. Oxford: Oxford University Press.

——(2008b). "Experience, Narrative, and Ethical Deliberation." *Ethics*, 118: 614–32.

——(2008c). "The Reception of Early American Pragmatism" in Misak (2008a).

——(2010). "Richard Rorty's Place in the Pragmatist Pantheon." In Auxier and Hahn (2010).

——(2011). "American Pragmatism and Indispensability Arguments." *Transactions of the Charles S. Peirce Society*, 47: 3.

——(forthcoming). *Cambridge Pragmatism*.

Montague, William Pepperell (1940). *The Ways of Things: A Philosophy of Knowledge, Nature, and Value*. New York: Prentice Hall.

Moore, Addison W. (1909). "What is Pragmatism?." *American Journal of Theology*, 13/3: 477–8. (Repr. Shook (2001a). Vol. i).

Moore, G. E. (1992 [1907]). "Professor James's "Pragmatism"." *Proceedings of the Aristotelian Society*, 8: 33–77. (Repr. in Olin (1992), 161–95.)

Morgenbesser, S. (ed.) (1977). *Dewey and his Critics*. Lancaster: Lancaster Press.

Morgenbesser, S., P. Suppes, and M. White (1969). *Philosophy, Science, and Method*. New York: St. Martin's Press.

Morris, Charles (1934). *Pragmatism and the Crisis of Democracy*. Chicago: University of Chicago Press.

——(1937a). *Logical Positivism, Pragmatism, and Scientific Empiricism*. Paris: Hermann.

——(1937b). "Peirce, Mead, and Pragmatism." *Proceedings and Addresses of the American Philosophical Association*, 11: 109–27.

——(1938a). *International Encyclopedia of Unified Science*, i/2: *Foundations of the Theory of Signs*. Ed. Otto Neurath, Rudolf Carnap, and Charles Morris. Chicago: University of Chicago Press.

——(1938b). "The Unity of Science Movement and the United States." *Synthese*, 3/12: 25–29.

——(1942). *Paths of Life: Preface to a World Religion*. New York: Harper.

——(1946a). *Signs, Language and Behaviour*. New York: Prentice Hall.

——(1946b). "The Significance of the Unity of Science Movement." *Philosophy and Phenomenological Research*, 6/14: 508–15.

——(1948). "Signs about Signs about Signs." *Philosophy and Phenomenological Research*, 9: 115–33.

——(1963) "Pragmatism and Logical Empiricism." In Schlipp (1963).

Mulvaney, R. and P. Zeltner (eds.) (1981). *Pragmatism: Its Sources and Prospects*. Columbia: University of South Carolina Press.

Munitz, Milton (1951 [1940]). "Ideals and Essences in Santayana's Philosophy." In Schlipp (1951 [1940]).

Murphey, Murray G. (2005). *C. I. Lewis: The Last Great Pragmatist*. Albany NY: SUNY Press.

Murray, David (2001 [1912]). *Pragmatism*. In Shook (2001b). Vol. iii.

Nagel, Ernest (1929). "Can Logic be Divorced from Ontology?" *The Journal of Philosophy*, 26/26: 705–12.

——(1940). "Charles S. Peirce: Pioneer of Modern Empiricism." *Philosophy of Science*, 7/1: 69–80.

——(1955). "Naturalism Reconsidered." *Proceedings and Addresses of the American Philosophical Association*, 28: 5–17.

——(1986). "Introduction." In *The Later Works of John Dewey 1925–1953*. Vol. xii: *Logic: The Theory of Inquiry*. Ed. Jo Ann Boydston. Carbondale Il: Southern Illinois University Press, pp. ix–xxviii.

Neurath, Otto (1938), "Unified Science as Encyclopedic Integration." In Neurath *et al.* (1938), 1–27.

——(1983 [1932–33]). "Sociology in the Framework of Physicalism." Repr. in *Philosophical Papers 1913–1946*. Ed. R. S. Cohen and M. Neurath. Dordrecht: Reidel.

Neurath, Otto *et al.* (1938). *International Encyclopedia of Unified Science*, i/1: *Encyclopedia and Unified Science*. Chicago: University of Chicago Press.

Norton, Charles Eliot (1971 [1877]). "Biographical Sketch of Chauncey Wright." In Wright (1971 [1877]).

Olin, Doris (1992). *William James: Pragmatism in Focus*. London: Routledge.

Pearce, Trevor (forthcoming). *Pragmatism's Evolution: Organism and Environment in Early American Philosophy*.

Peirce, Charles Sanders (1900–). *The Writings of Charles S. Peirce: A Chronological Edition*. Gen. ed. E. Moore. Bloomington: Indiana University Press.

——(1931–58). *Collected Papers of Charles Sanders Peirce*. Ed. C. Hartshorne and P. Weiss (vols. i–vi), A. Burks (vols. vii and viii). Cambridge MA: Belknap Press.

——(1953). "Charles S. Peirce's letters to Lady Welby." Ed. Irwin C. Lieb. New Haven: Whitlock's Inc.

——(1976). *The New Elements of Mathematics*. Vols. i–iv. Ed. Carolyn Eisele. The Hague: Mouton Publishers.

——(1979 [1903]). "Review of *Personal Idealism*." In *Charles Sanders Peirce: Contributions to "The Nation"*. Vol. 3. Ed. Kenneth Laine Ketner and James Edward Cook. Lubbock, TX: Texas Technological University Press.

——Charles S. Peirce Papers, Houghton Library, Harvard University.

Perry, Ralph Barton (1907a). "A Review of Pragmatism as a Theory of Knowledge." *The Journal of Philosophy, Psychology, and Scientific Methods*, 4/14: 365–74.

——(1907b). "A Review of Pragmatism as a Philosophical Generalization." *The Journal of Philosophy, Psychology, and Scientific Methods*, 4/16: 421–28.

——(1910). "The Cardinal Principle of Idealism." *Mind*, New Series, 19/75: 322–36.

——(1976 [1935]). *The Thought and Character of William James*. 2 vols. Originally published by Harvard University Press. Repr. Vanderbilt University Press.

——(1977 [1917]). "Dewey and Urban on Value Judgments." *The Journal of Philosophy, Psychology, and Scientific Methods*, 14/7: 169–81. (Repr. in Morgenbesser (1977).)

Popper, Karl (1963). *Conjectures and Refutations: The Growth of Scientific Knowledge*. New York: Harper and Row.

Poulos, Kathleen (1986) "Textual Commentary." In *The Later Works of John Dewey 1925–1953*. Vol. xii: *Logic: The Theory of Inquiry*. Ed. Jo Ann Boydston. Carbondale IL: Southern Illinois University Press, 533–49.

Pratt, James B. (2001 [1909]). *What is Pragmatism?* Repr. in Shook (2001a). Vol i.

Pratt, Scott L. (2004). "Knowledge and Action: American Epistemology." In *The Blackwell Guide to American Philosophy*. Ed. A. T. Marsoobian and J. Ryder. Oxford: Blackwell, 306–24.

Pratt, Scott L. and John Ryder (eds.) (2002). *The Philosophical Writings of Cadwallader Colden*. Amherst, NY: Humanity Books.

Price, Huw (2011). *Naturalism without Mirrors*. Oxford: Oxford University Press.

Putnam, Hilary (1981). *Reason, Truth, and History*. New York: Cambridge University Press.

——(1983a). "Reference and Truth." In *Realism and Reason: Philosophical Papers*. Vol. iii. Cambridge MA: Harvard University Press, 69–86.

——(1983b). "Why Reason Can't be Naturalized." In *Realism and Reason: Philosophical Papers*. Vol. iii. Cambridge MA: Harvard University Press, 229–47.

——(1988). "After Metaphysics, What?" In *Metaphysik nach Kant?* Ed. Dieter Henrich and R. P. Horstmann. Stuttgart: Klett-Cotta, 457–66.

——(1990). *Realism with a Human Face*. Cambridge, MA: Harvard University Press.

——(1990 [1989]). "William James' Ideas." In Putnam (1990).

——(1992). *Renewing Philosophy*. Cambridge, MA: Harvard University Press.

——(1994a). "Between the New Left and Judaism." In *The American Philosopher: Conversations with Quine, Davidson, Putnam, Nozick, Rorty, Cavell, MacIntyre, and Kuhn*. Ed. G. Borradori. Chicago: University of Chicago Press, 55–69.

——(1994b). "Pragmatism and Moral Objectivity." In *Words and Life*. Ed. James Conant. Cambridge, MA: Harvard University Press, 151–81.

——(1994c). *Words and Life*. Cambridge, MA: Harvard University Press.

——(1994 [1979]). "The Place of Facts in a World of Values." In *Realism With a Human Face*, 142–62.

——(1994 [1983]). "On Truth." In *Words and Life*. Ed. James Conant. Cambridge, MA: Harvard University Press, 313–29.

——(1994 [1985]). "A Comparison of Something with Something Else." In *Words and Life*. Ed. James Conant. Cambridge, MA: Harvard University Press, 330–50.

——(1994 [1991a]). "Does the Disquotational Theory of Truth Solve All Philosophical Problems?" In *Words and Life*. Ed. James Conant. Cambridge, MA: Harvard University Press, 264–78.

——(1994 [1991b]). "Reichenbach's Metaphysical Picture." In *Words and Life*. Ed. James Conant. Cambridge, MA: Harvard University Press, 99–114.

——(1994 [1992]). "Pragmatism and Relativism: Universal Values and Traditional Ways of Life." In *Words and Life*. Ed. James Conant. Cambridge, MA: Harvard University Press.

——(1994 [1993]). "The Question of Realism." In *Words and Life*. Ed. James Conant. Cambridge, MA: Harvard University Press, 295–314.

——(1995a). *Pragmatism: An Open Question*. Oxford: Blackwell.

——(1995b). "Peirce's Continuum." In Ketner (1995), 1–22.

——(1997). "God and the Philosophers." *Midwest Studies in Philosophy*, 21: 175–87.

——(1998). "A Politics of Hope." *Times Literary Supplement* (22 May 1998).

——(1999). *The Threefold Cord*. New York: Columbia University Press.

——(2002). *The Collapse of the Fact/Value Dichotomy*. Cambridge, MA: Harvard University Press.

——(2004). *Ethics without Ontology*. Cambridge, MA: Harvard University Press.

——(2008). *Jewish Philosophy as a Guide to Life*. Bloomington, IN: Indiana University Press.

Quine, Willard van Orman (1961 [1950]). "Identity, Ostension, and Hypostasis." In *From a Logical Point of View*, 2nd ed. Cambridge MA: Harvard University Press, 65–79.

——(1969). *Ontological Relativity and Other Essays*. New York: Columbia University Press.

——(1980). "Preface." In *From a Logical Point of View*. 2nd ed. Cambridge MA: Harvard University Press.

——(1980 [1951]). "Two Dogmas of Empiricism." Repr. in *From a Logical Point of View*. 2nd ed. Cambridge MA: Harvard University Press, 20–46.

——(1981a). *Theories and Things*. Cambridge, MA: Belknap Press.

——(1981b). "Empirical Content." In Quine (1981a), 24–30.

——(1981c). "On the Very Idea of a Third Dogma." In Quine (1981a), 38–42.

——(1981d). "The Pragmatist's Place in Empiricism." In Mulvaney and Zeltner (1981), 21–39.

——(1981 [1979]). "On the Nature of Moral Values." In Quine (1981a), 55–66.

——(1984). "Relativism and Absolutism." *Monist*, 67: 293–96.

——(1986). "Reply to Morton White." In *The Philosophy of W. V. Quine*. Ed. Lewis Hahn and Paul Arthur Schlipp. La Salle: Open Court, 663–65.

——(1987). *Quiddities: An Intermittently Philosophical Dictionary*. Cambridge, MA: Belknap Press.

——(1987 [1978]). "On the Nature of Moral Values." Repr. in Quine (1981a), 55–66.

——(1990). "Comments on Parsons." In *Perspectives on Quine*. Ed. R. Gibson and R. Barrett. Oxford: Blackwell.

——(1992 [1990]). *Pursuit of Truth*. Rev. ed. Cambridge, MA: Harvard University Press.

——(2008). *Confessions of a Confirmed Extensionalist and Other Essays*. Cambridge, MA: Harvard University Press.

——(2008 [1975]). "On Empirically Equivalent Systems of the World." Repr. in Quine (2008), 228–43.

——(2008 [1992]). "Replies to Professor Riska's Eight Questions." In *Quine in Dialogue*. Ed. Dagfinn Føllesdal and Douglas B. Quine. Cambridge, MA : Harvard University Press, 2008, 213–15.

——(2008 [1999]). "Where Do We Disagree?" In *Quine in Dialogue*. Ed. Dagfinn Føllesdal and Douglas B. Quine. Cambridge, MA: Harvard University Press, 159–68.

Ramsey, F. P. (1990 [1927]). "Facts and Propositions." In *F. P. Ramsey: Philosophical Papers*. Ed. D. H. Mellor, 34–51.

Randall, John Herman (1953). "John Dewey, 1859-1952." *The Journal of Philosophy*, 50/1: 5–13.

Rawls, John (1971). *A Theory of Justice*. Cambridge MA: Belknap Press.

Reichenbach, Hans (1938). *Experience and Predication: An Analysis of the Foundations and the Structure of Knowledge*. Chicago: University of Chicago Press.

——(1939). "Dewey's Theory of Science." In Schlipp (1939), 157–92.

Reisch, George (1995). "A History of the *International Encyclopedia of Unified Science*." PhD Dissertation. University of Chicago.

——(2005). *How the Cold War Transformed Philosophy of Science: To the Icy Slopes of Logic*. Cambridge: Cambridge University Press.

Rescher, Nicholas (1993). "American Philosophy Today." *The Review of Metaphysics*, 46/4: 717–45.

——(2005). *Reason and Reality: Realism and Idealism in Pragmatic Perspective*. Lanham, MD: Rowman & Littlefield Publishers.

Reynolds, Andrew (2002). *Peirce's Scientific Metaphysics*. Nashville, TN: Vanderbilt University Press.

Richardson, Alan (1998). *Carnap's Construction of the World: The Aufbau and the Emergence of Logical Empiricism*. Cambridge, MA: Cambridge University Press.

——(2007). "Carnapian Pragmatism." In *The Cambridge Companion to Carnap*. Ed. Michael Friedman and Richard Creath. Cambridge: Cambridge University Press, 295–315.

——(2008). "Philosophy of Science in America." In Misak (2008a), 339–74.

Richardson, Henry (1995). "Beyond Good and Right: Toward a Constructive Ethical Pragmatism." *Philosophy and Public Affairs*, 24/2: 108–41.

——(1999). "Truth and Ends in Dewey's Pragmatism." In Misak (ed.), *Pragmatism*. Alberta: University of Calgary Press.

Richardson, Robert (2006). *William James: In the Maelstrom of American Modernism*. Boston: Houghton Mifflin.

Robin, Richard (1967). *Annotated Catalogue of the Papers of Charles S. Peirce*. Worcester: University of Massachusetts Press.

Rorty, Richard (1961). "Pragmatism, Categories, and Language." *The Philosophical Review*, 70/2: 197–223.

——(1962). "Review of *American Pragmatism: Peirce, James and Dewey*, Edward C. Moore." *Ethics*, 72/2: 146–47.

——(1964). "Review of *Chauncey Wright and the Foundations of Pragmatism*, Edward Madden." *Philosophical Review*, 73/2: 287–89.

——(1972). "The World Well Lost." *The Journal of Philosophy*, 69/16: 649–65.

——(1979). *Philosophy and the Mirror of Nature*. Princeton: Princeton University Press.

——(1980). "Pragmatism, Relativism, and Irrationalism." *Proceedings and Addresses of the American Philosophical Association*, 53: 719–38.

——(1982). *Consequences of Pragmatism (Essays 1972–80).* Minneapolis: University of Minnesota Press.

——(1986). "Pragmatism, Davidson and Truth." In *Truth and Interpretation: Perpsectives on the Philosophy of Donald Davidson.* Ed. Ernest LePore. Oxford: Blackwell, 333–55.

——(1989). *Contingency, Irony, and Solidarity.* New York: Cambridge University Press.

——(1990). "Truth and Freedom: A Reply to Thomas McCarthy." *Critical Inquiry*, 16/3: 633–43.

——(1991). *Objectivity, Relativism, and Truth: Philosophical Papers.* 4 vols. Vol. i. Cambridge: Cambridge University Press.

——(1995a). "Is Truth a Goal of Enquiry?" *Philosophical Quarterly*, 45: 281–300.

——(1995b). "Response to Charles Hartshorne." In Saatkamp (1995), 29–36.

——(1995c). "Response to Richard Bernstein." In Saatkamp (1995), 68–71.

——(1995d). "Reponse to Haack." In Saatkamp (1995), 148–53.

——(1997). "Introduction." In Sellars (1997 [1956]), 1–12.

——(1998 [1993]). "Hilary Putnam and the Relativistic Menace." *The Journal of Philosophy*, 90: 443–61. (Repr. in Putnam, *Truth and Progress.* Cambridge: Cambridge University Press.)

——(1999). *Philosophy and Social Hope.* New York: Penguin.

——(2000a). "Universality and Truth." In Brandom (2000), 1–30.

——(2000b). "Response to Jurgen Habermas." In Brandom (2000), 56–64.

——(2000c). "Response to Bjorn Ramberg." In Brandom (2000), 370–77.

——(2000d). "The Overphilosophication of Politics." *Constellations*, 7: 128–32.

——(2003). "A Pragmatist View of Contemporary Analytic Philosophy." In *The Pragmatist Turn in Philosophy.* Ed. William Egginton and Mike Sandbothe. New York: SUNY Press, 131–44.

——(2010a). "Intellectual Autobiography." In Auxier and Hahn (2010), 1–24.

——(2010b). "Reply to Misak." In Auxier and Hahn (2010), 44–45.

Roth, Robert (1993). *British Empiricism and American Pragmatism: New Directions and Neglected Arguments.* New York: Fordham University Press.

Royce, Josiah (1885). *The Religious Aspect of Philosophy.* New York: Houghton, Mifflin and Company.

——(1891). "Review of *Outlines of a Critical Theory of Ethics,* John Dewey." *International Journal of Ethics*, 1: 503–5.

——(1899). *The World and the Individual.* Vol. i. New York: MacMillan.

——(1901). *The World and the Individual.* Vol. ii. New York: MacMillan.

——(1904). "The Eternal and the Practical." *The Philosophical Review*, XIII: 113–42.

——(1915 [1898]). *Studies of Good and Evil: A Series of Essays upon Problems of Philosophy and of Life.* New York: Appleton.

——(1951 [1908]). "The Problem of Truth in the Light of Recent Discussion." In *Royce's Logical Essays: Collected Logical Essays of Josiah Royce.* Ed. Daniel S. Robinson. Dubuque, Iowa: W. C. Brown Co., 63–97.

——(1951 [1913]). "Hypotheses and Leading Ideas." In *Royce's Logical Essays: Collected Logical Essays of Josiah Royce.* Ed. Daniel S. Robinson. Dubuque, Iowa: W. C. Brown Co., 260–67.

——(1967 [1892]). *The Spirit of Modern Philosophy.* New York: W. W. Norton and Company.

——(1968 [1880]). "On Purpose in Thought." In Royce (1968 [1920], 219–60).

——(1968 [1913]). *The Hope of the Great Community*. New York: Macmillan.

——(1968 [1918]). *The Problem of Christianity*. Chicago: University of Chicago Press.

——(1968 [1920]). *Fugitive Essays*. Freeport, New York: Books for Libraries Press.

——(1995 [1908]). *The Philosophy of Loyalty*. Nashville: Vanderbilt University Press.

Royce, Josiah *et al.* (1909 [1987]). *The Conception of God: A Philosophical Discussion concerning the Nature of the Divine Idea as a Demonstrable Reality*. New York: Macmillan.

Russell, Bertrand (1959). *Wisdom of the West: A Historical Survey of Western Philosophy in its Social and Political Setting*. London: MacDonald.

——(1983 [1919]). "Professor Dewey's *Essays in Experimental Logic*." In *The Collected Papers of Bertrand Russell*. Vol. viii: *The Philosophy of Logical Atomism and Other Essays, 1914–19*. London: Routledge, 132–56. (Repr. from *The Journal of Philosophy, Psychology, and Scientific Method*.)

——(1992 [1908]). "William James's Conception of Truth." In *Philosophical Essays*. London: Allen and Unwin. (Repr. in Olin (1992), 196–211.)

——(1992 [1909]). "Pragmatism." In *Logical and Philosophical Papers, 1909–13*. London: Routledge, 257–84.

——(1997 [1945]). "Logical Positivism 1945." In *Collected Papers of Bertrand Russell*. Vol. xi: *Last Philosophical Testament 1947–1968*. London: Routledge, 148–55.

Ryan, Alan (1995). *John Dewey and the High Tide of American Liberalism*. New York: W. W. Norton.

Ryder, John (2004). "Early American Philosophy." In *The Blackwell Guide to American Philosophy*. Ed. A. T. Marsoobian and J. Ryder. Oxford: Blackwell, 3–21.

Saatkamp, H. J. (ed.) (1995). *Rorty and Pragmatism: The Philosopher Responds to his Critics*. Nashville: Vanderbilt University Press.

Santayana, George (1910). *Three Philosophical Poets: Lucretius, Dante, and Goethe*. Cambridge MA: Harvard University Press.

——(1920). "Three Proofs of Realism." In D. Drake *et al.* (1920), 163–86.

——(1923). *Scepticism and Animal Faith: Introduction to a System of Philosophy*. London: Constable.

——(1925). "Dewey's Naturalistic Metaphysics." *The Journal of Philosophy*, 22: 673–88.

——(1942 [1938]). *The Realm of Truth*. In *The Realms of Being*. Single-volume edition. New York: Scribner's, 401–548.

——(1944). *Persons and Places*. New York: Scribner and Sons.

——(1951 [1940]). "Apologia Pro Mente Sua." In Schlipp (1951 [1940]).

——(1957 [1900]). *Interpretations of Poetry and Religion*. New York: Harper.

——(1962 [1905]). *The Life of Reason, or the Phases of Human Progress*. 5 vols. New York: Charles Scribner. New York: Collier Books.

——(1967 [1900–31]). *The Genteel Tradition: Nine Essays by George Santayana*. Ed. D. Wilson. Cambridge MA: Harvard University Press.

——(2000 [1922]). *Soliloquies in England and Later Soliloquies*. London: Constable.

——(2001). *The Letters of George Santayana*. 6 vols. Ed. William G. Holzberger. Cambridge MA: MIT Press.

——(2009 [1911]). "The Genteel Tradition in American Philosophy." In *The Genteel Tradition in American Philosophy and Character and Opinion in the United States*. Ed. James Seaton. New Haven: Yale University Press, 3–20.

——(2009 [1920]). "Character and Opinion in the United States." In *The Genteel Tradition in American Philosophy and Character and Opinion in the United States*. Ed. James Seaton. New Haven: Yale University Press, 21–122.

Savery, William (1951 [1939]). "The Significance of Dewey's Philosophy." In *The Philosophy of John Dewey*. Ed. Paul Schlipp. The Library of Living Philosophers. LaSalle: Open Court.

Scharp, Kevin and Robert Brandom (eds.) (2007). *In the Space of Reasons: Selected Essays of Wilfrid Sellars*. Cambridge, MA: Harvard University Press.

Scheffler, Israel (1963). *The Anatomy of Inquiry: Philosophical Studies in the Theory of Science*. New York: Alfred A. Knopf.

Schiller, F. C. S. (1902). "Axioms and Postulates." In *Personal Idealism*. Ed. H. Sturt. London: MacMillan.

——(1903). *Humanism: Philosophical Essays*. London: MacMillan.

——(1909–10). "Are Secondary Qualities Independent of Perception? A Discussion Opened by T. Percy Nunn and F. C. S. Schiller." *Proceedings of the Aristotelian Society*, New Series, 10: 191–231.

——(1910 [1891]). *Riddles of the Sphinx*. London: Swan.

——(1934 [1927]). "William James and the Making of Pragmatism." In *Must Philosophers Disagree?: And Other Essays in Popular Philosophy*. London: Macmillan, 93–105.

——(1939). *Our Human Truths*. New York: Columbia University Press.

——(1939 [1936]). "Must Pragmatists Disagree?" In Schiller (1939), 57–64.

——(1969 [1907]). *Studies in Humanism*. Freeport, New York: Books for Libraries Press.

Schinz, Albert (1909). *Anti-Pragmatism: An Examination into the Respective Rights of Intellectual Aristocracy and Social Democracy*. Boston: Small, Maynard and Company. (Repr. in Shook (2001a). Vol. ii.)

Schlick, Moritz (1936). "Meaning and Verification." *The Philosophical Review*, 45/4: 339–69.

——(1962 [1939]). *Problems of ethics*. Trans. David Rynin. New York: Dover.

Schlipp, Paul Arthur (ed.) (1939). *The Philosophy of John Dewey*. Evanston: Northwestern University.

——(ed.) (1951 [1940]). *The Philosophy of George Santayana*. New York: Tudor.

——(ed.) (1963). *The Philosophy of Rudolph Carnap*. LaSalle: Open Court.

——(ed.) (1968). *The Philosophy of C. I. Lewis*. La Salle: Open Court.

Schneewind, J. B. (2010). "Rorty on Utopia and Moral Philosophy." In Auxier and Hahn (2010), 479–505.

Schneider, Herbert (1963 [1946]). *A History of American Philosophy*. 2nd ed. New York: Columbia University Press.

Schwartz, Robert (2012). *Rethinking Pragmatism*. Wiley Blackwell.

Scott, Frederick J. Down (1973). "Peirce and Schiller and Their Correspondence." *Journal of the History of Philosophy*, 11/3: 363–86.

Sellars, Roy Wood (1907). "Professor Dewey's View of Agreement." *The Journal of Philosophy, Psychology and Scientific Methods*, 4/16: 432–35.

——(1920). "Knowledge and its Categories." In D. Drake *et al.* (1920), 187–222.

Sellars, Wilfrid (1949). "Language, Rules and Behavior." In Hook (1949), 289–315.

——(1962). "Truth as Correspondence." *The Journal of Philosophy*, 59/2: 29–56.

——(1963). "Theoretical Explanation." In *Philosophy of Science: The Delaware Seminar*. Ed. Bernard Baumrin. 2 vols. Vol. ii. New York: Interscience Publishers, 61–78.

——(1963 [1956]). "Empiricism and the Philosophy of Mind." In *Science, Perception, Reality*. New York, Humanities Press.

——(1992 [1968]). *Science and Metaphysics: Variations on Kantian Themes*. London: Routledge & Kegan Paul.

——(1997 [1956]). *Empiricism and the Philosophy of Mind*. Cambridge, MA: Harvard University Press.

——(2007 [1954]). "Some Reflections on Language Games" in Scharp and Brandom (2007).

Shaw, Bernard (1921). *Androcles and the Lion*. London: Constable and Company Ltd.

Shook, John (ed.) (2001a). *Early Critics of Pragmatism*. 5 vols. Bristol: Thoemmes Press.

——(ed.) (2001b). *Early Defenders of Pragmatism*. 5 vols. Bristol: Thoemmes Press.

——(2006). "F. C. S. Schiller and European Pragmatism." In *A Companion to Pragmatism*. Ed. J. Shook and J. Margolis. Oxford: Basil Blackwell, 44–53.

Short, T. L. (2007). *Peirce's Theory of Signs*. Cambridge: Cambridge University Press.

Sinclair, Robert (2011). "Morton White's Moral Pragmatism." *Cognitio: Revista de Filosofia*, 12: 143–55.

——(forthcoming). "Quine and Conceptual Pragmatism." *Transactions of the Charles S Peirce Society*.

Smith, John E. (2001 [1968]). "Introduction." In Royce (1968 [1918]), 1–36.

Sprigge, T. L. S. (1969). "Santayana and Verification." *Inquiry*, 12: 265–86.

——(1997). "James, Aboutness and his British Critics." In *The Cambridge Companion to William James*. Ed. Ruth Anna Putnam. Cambridge: Cambridge University Press, 125–33.

——(2006). *The God of Metaphysics: Being a Study of the Metaphysics and Religious Doctrines of Spinoza, Hegel, Kierkegaard, T. H. Green, Bernard Bosanquet, Josiah Royce, A.N. Whitehead, and Charles Hartshorne*. Oxford: Clarendon Press.

Stern, Robert (2007). "Peirce, Hegel, and the Category of Secondness." *Inquiry*, 50/2: 123–55.

Stout, Jeffery (2007). "On Our Interest in Getting Things Right: Pragmatism without Narcissism." In Misak (2007a), 7–31.

Strawson, Peter (1962). *Freedom and Resentment*. London: Oxford University Press.

Sturt, Henry (1902). "Preface." In *Personal Idealism*. Ed. Henry Sturt. London: Macmillan, v–viii.

Szahaj, Andrzej (2006). "Biography and Philosophy." In *Take Care of Freedom and Truth Will Take Care of Itself: Interviews with Richard Rorty*. Ed. Eduardo Mendieta. Stanford: Stanford University Press, ch. 12.

Talisse, Robert (2002). "Two Concepts of Inquiry." *Philosophical Writings*, 20: 69–81.

——(2005). *Democracy after Liberalism*. London: Routledge.

——(2007). *A Pragmatist Philosophy of Democracy*. London: Routledge.

Tarski, Alfred (1941). "On the Calculus of Relations." *The Journal of Symbolic Logic*, 6/3: 73–89.

——(1983 [1956]). "The Concept of Truth in Formalized Languages." In *Logic, Semantics, Metamathematics: Papers from 1923 to 1938*. Trans. J. H. Woodger. 2nd ed. edited and introduced by John Corcoran. Indianapolis: Hackett, 152–268.

Taylor, Eugene (1996). *William James on Consciousness Beyond the Margin*. Princeton, NJ: Princeton University Press.

Thayer, James Bradley (1971 [1878]). *Letters of Chauncey Wright: With Some Account of his Life*. New York: Lennox Hill.

Tiller, Glenn (2002). "Peirce and Santayana: Pragmatism and the Belief in Substance." *Transactions of the Charles S. Peirce Society*, 38/3.

——(2008). "George Santayana: Ordinary Reflection Systematized." In Misak (2008a), 125–43.

Uebel, Thomas (2004). "Carnap, the Left Vienna Circle and Neopositivist Critique of Metaphysics." In *Rudolph Carnap: from Jena to LA*. Ed. S. Awodey and C. Klein. Open Court: Chicago, 247–78.

Van Leer, David (1986). *Emerson's Epistemology*. Cambridge: Cambridge University Press.

Venn, John (1883). "Review of Studies in Logic." *Mind*, 8: 594–603.

Wald, Alan M. (1987). *The New York Intellectuals: The Rise and Decline of the Anti-Stalinist Left from the 1930s to the 1980s*. Chapel Hill: University of North Carolina Press.

Watson, John (1914). "Review of Caldwell, *Pragmatism and Idealism*." *Queen's Quarterly*, 21/4: 465–72. (Repr. in Shook (2001b). Vol. iv.)

Weiner, Philip (1945). "Chauncey Wright, Darwin and Scientific Neutrality." *The Journal of the History of Ideas*, 6: 19–45.

Welchman, Jennifer (1995). *Dewey's Ethical Theory*. Ithaca: Cornell University Press.

Westbrook, Robert (2005). *Democratic Hope: Pragmatism and the Politics of Truth*. London: Cornell University Press.

White, Morton (1956). *Toward Reunion in Philosophy*. Cambridge, MA: Harvard University Press.

——(1957). *Social Thought in America: The Revolt against Formalism*. Rev. ed. Boston: Beacon Press.

——(1972). *Science and Sentiment: Philosophical Thought from Jonathan Edwards to John Dewey*. New York: Oxford University Press.

——(1981). *What Is and What Ought to Be Done*. Oxford: Oxford University Press.

——(1999). *A Philosopher's Story*. University Park, PA: University of Pennsylvania Press.

——(2002). *A Philosophy of Culture: The Scope of Holistic Pragmatism*. Princeton, NJ: Princeton University Press.

——(2005). *From a Philosophical Point of View: Selected Studies*. Princeton: Princeton University Press.

——(2005 [1949]). "Value and Obligation in Dewey and Lewis." Repr. in White (2005), 160–66.

——(2005 [1950]). "The Analytic and the Synthetic: An Untenable Dualism." Repr. in White (2005), 97–106.

——(2005 [1957]). "Harvard's Philosophical Heritage." Repr. in White (2005), 143–48.

White, Morton and Lucia White (1962). *The Intellectual versus the City, from Thomas Jefferson to Frank Lloyd Wright*. Cambridge, MA: Harvard University Press.

Wiggins, David (2002). "Marks of Truth: An Indefinibilist cum Normative View." In *What is Truth?* Ed. R. Shantz. Berlin: DeGruyter.

——(2004). "Reflections on Inquiry and Truth arising from Peirce's Method for the Fixation of Belief." In Misak (2004a).

Wilde, Norman (1908). "Review of Dewy and Tufts, *Ethics*." *Journal of Philosophy, Psychology, and Scientific Methods*, 5/23: 636–39.

Williams, Michael (1988). "Epistemological Realism and the Basis of Scepticism." *Mind* 97/387: 415–39.

Wilson, Daniel (1990). *Science, Community, and the Transformation of American Philosophy, 1860–1930*. Chicago: University of Chicago Press.

Winetrout, Kenneth (1967). *F. C. S. Schiller and the Dimensions of Pragmatism*. Columbus: Ohio State University Press.

Winkler, Kenneth (forthcoming). *A New World: Philosophical Idealism in America*.

Wittgenstein, Ludwig (1938) *Lectures and Conversations on Aesthetics, Psychology, and Religion*. Ed. Cyril Barrett. Berkeley: University of California Press.

——(1975 [1969]). *On Certainty*. Oxford: Basil Blackwell.

——(1980). *Remarks on the Philosophy of Pscyhology*. 2 vols. Vol. i. Ed. G. E. M. Anscombe and G. H. von Wright. Trans. G. E. M. Anscombe. Chicago: University of Chicago Press.

Woodbridge, Frederick (1930 [1977]). "Experience and Dialectic." In Morgenbesser (1977).

Woolley, Helen Thompson (1909). "Review of Pratt: *What is Pragmatism?*" *Journal of Philosophy*, 6/11: 300–2.

Wright, Chauncey (1865a). "Natural Theology as a Positive Science." In Wright (1971 [1877]).

——(1865b). "The Philosophy of Herbert Spencer." In Wright (1971 [1877]).

——(1865c). "McCosh on Intuitions." In Wright (1971 [1877]).

——(1866). "Mason's Recent British Philosophy." In Wright (1971 [1877]).

——(1867). "Mansel's Reply to Mill." In Wright (1971 [1877]).

——(1870). "Limits of Natural Selection." In Wright (1971 [1877]).

——(1871). "The Genesis of Species." In Wright (1971 [1877]).

——(1872). "Evolution by Natural Selection." In Wright (1971 [1877]).

——(1873a). "Evolution of Self-Consciousness." In Wright (1971 [1877]).

——(1873b). "John Stuart Mill: A Commemorative Notice." In Wright (1971 [1877]).

——(1875a). "McCosh on Tyndall." In Wright (1971 [1877]).

——(1875b). "Speculative Dynamics." In Wright (1971 [1877]).

——(1875c). "Books Relating to the Theory of Evolution." In Wright (1971 [1877]).

——(1971 [1877]). *Philosophical Discussions*. Ed. Charles Eliot Norton. New York: Burt Franklin.

Wright, Crispin (1992). *Truth and Objectivity*. Cambridge, MA: Harvard University Press.

Name Index

Taylor, Eugene 55 n.
Thompson, Helen Bradford 139
Thompson, Manley 143
Thrasymachus 84–6
Tiller, Glenn 144 n., 146, 149 n.

Uebel, Thomas 161 n.
University of Chicago 106, 109, 115, 129,
    139, 143, 169, 225, 246

Van Leer, David 7, 11–12
Venn, John 47

Welby, Lady Victoria 49
Welchman, Jennifer 120 n., 131, 135 n.
Wells, Rulon 225
West, Cornell 250
Westbrook, Robert 3–4, 228
Whewell, William 47

White, Morton 131, 136, 164, 175, 187,
    195, 197, 200 n., 207, 208 n., 209–11,
    226, 238
Whitehead, Alfred North 225
Wiggins, David 31, 36
Williams, Michael 227, 232
Winetrout, Kenneth 95
Winkler, Kenneth 11 n.
Witherspoon, John 9
Wittgenstein, Ludwig xvi, 61, 102, 220,
    227, 228
Woodbridge, Frederick 150
Wright, Chauncey ix–x, xii, 1, 3, 7, 9, 11,
    14–25, 26, 27, 28, 37, 43, 44,
    48, 53 n., 54, 57, 61 n., 62–3, 65,
    70, 77, 82, 128, 163, 202–3, 229,
    247, 252
Wright, Crispin 246 n.
Wundt, Wilhelm 55

Subject Index